Desire in the *Iliad*

Desire in the *Iliad*

The Force That Moves the Epic and Its Audience

RACHEL H. LESSER

OXFORD
UNIVERSITY PRESS

OXFORD
UNIVERSITY PRESS

Great Clarendon Street, Oxford, OX2 6DP,
United Kingdom

Oxford University Press is a department of the University of Oxford.
It furthers the University's objective of excellence in research, scholarship,
and education by publishing worldwide. Oxford is a registered trade mark of
Oxford University Press in the UK and in certain other countries

First Edition published in 2022
Impression: 1

Published in the United States of America by Oxford University Press
198 Madison Avenue, New York, NY 10016, United States of America

British Library Cataloguing in Publication Data
Data available

Library of Congress Control Number: 2022935646

ISBN 978–0–19–286651–6

DOI: 10.1093/oso/9780192866516.001.0001

Printed and bound in the UK by
TJ Books Limited

For Elana

Acknowledgments

Many people have helped to make this book possible and I am profoundly grateful to all of them. My undergraduate teachers, Helene Foley and Oliver Taplin, first inspired and shaped my appreciation for the *Iliad*. Mark Griffith, my dissertation supervisor at the University of California, Berkeley, shepherded this project from its inception and then provided crucial feedback and support as I developed it into a book. The other members of my dissertation committee, Leslie Kurke, Richard Martin, Andrew Stewart, and James Turner, also nurtured this project in its initial stages, and Andrew Stewart has continued to be an invaluable mentor. I am likewise indebted to Seth Schein for his mentorship, and this book has benefited from his careful commentary on several chapters. Ruby Blondell, Joanne Myers, and my mother, Priscilla Hunt, also provided important feedback on individual chapters, while the Provost's Office at Gettysburg College financially supported my research, and the anonymous readers for Oxford University Press guided me to improve this book in countless ways.

For their encouragement and advice, I am thankful to my Women's Classical Caucus mentor Lillian Doherty and my Gettysburg College colleagues Christopher D'Addario, Nathalie Lebon, Benjamin Luley, Joanne Myers, GailAnn Rickert, and Kerry Wallach. I have also relied on the wisdom and moral support of many other friends, including Lidia Anchisi, Alice Broadway, Andy Celestia, Jessica Chen, Rachel Denison, Christen Lambert, Richard Lambert, Serena Le, Virginia Lewis, Antony Millner, Christopher Oechler, Jacqueline Oechler, Sarah Olsen, Douglas Page, Lauren Steyn, Victoria Suchodolski, Mercedes Valmisa, Carolyn Walker, Naomi Weiss, and Janelle Wertzberger. My fellow members of the Berkeley Greek Reading Group buoyed me throughout this project, and among them Rodney Merrill and the late Gary Holland and Thomas Walsh particularly enriched my understanding of Homer.

Finally, I have cherished and relied on the support of my family throughout this project. For their sustaining love, humor, and counsel, I give thanks to all my uncles and aunts, and in particular my late aunt Jennifer Hunt, to my cousins Nancy Fudem and Jonathan Fudem, to my in-laws Avis Freedman, Nick Evanson, and Skye Nashelsky, to my cousin and dear friend Christine Hunt, to my brother Daniel Lesser and sister-in-law Rebecca Herst, and especially to my beloved parents Victor Lesser and Priscilla Hunt, who have taught me so much and always been there for me. My utmost gratitude goes to my wife Elana Nashelsky, who nourished me and cheered me on every step of the way, and our son Isaac Nashelsky, who brightens my days.

Acknowledgments

Table of Contents

Introduction

Ilias ipsa quid est aliud, nisi adultera, de qua
inter amatorem pugna virumque fuit?
quid prius est illic flamma Briseidos, utque
fecerit iratos rapta puella duces?

What else is the *Iliad* itself, if not an adulteress, over whom
a war erupted between lover and husband?
What in it is prior to flaming passion for Briseis, and how
the stolen girl made the leaders enraged?[1]

Ovid, *Tristia* 2.371–74

"Narratives both tell of desire—typically present some story of desire—and arouse and make use of desire as a dynamic of signification."

Peter Brooks, *Reading for the Plot: Design and Intention in Narrative* (1984), p. 37

What if the *Iliad* were not only a story of wrath and "the poem of force"[2] but also an epic of desire? Ovid made that proposition roughly two thousand years ago when, in defense of his own amorous literary works, he invoked the *Iliad* as erotic poetry, together with numerous other Greek and Latin classics, including the *Odyssey*. Along similar lines, the literary critic Peter Brooks has asserted that all, or nearly all, fictional narratives—starting with the *Iliad*—are driven by desire, in some form or another, and aim to provoke too the desires of their listeners or readers.

Indeed, as Ovid recognized, at the root of both the quarrel and the war that tend to define our view of the *Iliad* are triangles of desire—passionate competition between Achilleus and Agamemnon over Briseis, and between Menelaos and Paris over Helen—which Homer explores in depth, especially in Books 1 and 3 of the epic. Moreover, within and beyond these and other triangles, the poet describes and thematizes throughout the poem the multiform desires of his characters with an extensive, flexible, and ubiquitous vocabulary of fervent urges, longings, and wishes. These various desires are not only romantic and sexual but also mournful and aggressive, and much more. This book examines comprehensively for the first

[1] Latin text of Ovid is from the revised Loeb edition. All translations are my own.
[2] Weil 1956 [1939].

Desire in the Iliad: *The Force That Moves the Epic and Its Audience.* Rachel H. Lesser, Oxford University Press.
 DOI: 10.1093/oso/9780192866516.003.0001

time how desire, broadly conceived, manifests itself in the *Iliad*, and how it motivates the epic's plot.

In this book I am also concerned with the audience's or reader's corresponding desire to engage with the *Iliad*. Brooks' contention that narratives are designed to stimulate desire is supported, in the case of the *Iliad*, by the *Odyssey*'s portrayal of Iliadic poetry's powerful allure through Odysseus' encounter with the Sirens (*Od.* 12.166–200). In their call to Odysseus to heed their song, the Sirens present themselves as Iliadic Muses, who "know all the things which the Argives and the Trojans suffered in wide Troy by the gods' will"; located in an eroticized flowery meadow, they describe their voice as "honeyed" (*μελίγηρυν*), figuring their song as a sweet temptation that arouses the appetite. Indeed, Odysseus recounts how "my heart wished to listen" (*ἐμὸν κῆρ/ ἤθελ' ἀκουέμεναι*), causing him to beg his sailors to unloose the bonds keeping him from the Sirens.[3] I theorize the nature of the desire for epic that overwhelms Odysseus and other Iliadic audiences, and show how that external desire is aroused, shaped, and satisfied by the *Iliad*'s plot and its internal motivating desires.

In its investigation of Iliadic desire in relation to epic plot and audience reception, this book brings together two previously distinct areas of inquiry. Since the 1990s, influenced by the burgeoning field of gender and sexuality studies, scholars have begun to explore desire in the *Iliad*, but in reference to specific characters, incidents, or kinds of desire, rather than as a major, integrated force organizing the epic as a whole.[4] Meanwhile, there has been a renewal of interest in the *Iliad*'s narrative structure, with multiple important studies that consider the poem's narrative in a detailed and sustained way, involving fresh narratological perspectives, attention to significant formal patterns and repetitions, and appreciation for Homer's complex artistry and his text's relation to an intended audience.[5] I build on and combine these two spheres of scholarship, offering new insight into the motivation, form, and appeal of the *Iliad* in its entirety. My approach to the poem is also informed by studies of desire in ancient and modern

[3] On the Iliadic nature of the Sirens and their song, see further Pucci 1998 [1979]: 1–4 and Peponi 2012: 76–80. Peponi 2012: 70–94 and Liebert 2017: 40–43 explore how the Sirens and their song are presented as erotic objects and particularly objects of Odysseus' desire. Later in the *Odyssey*, the poet is even more explicit about audiences' desire for song, though this time it is not particularly Iliadic; after the suitors' slaughter, the palace bard "roused a yearning for sweet singing and blameless dancing" (*ἵμερον ὦρσε/μολπῆς τε γλυκερῆς καὶ ἀμύμονος ὀρχηθμοῖο*, 23.144–45). On this and other passages in archaic Greek poetry where song is eroticized, see Liebert 2017: 48–62. Throughout this book, Greek text of the *Odyssey* and *Iliad* is taken from Monro and Allen's Oxford Classical Texts, and English translations are based on these editions.

[4] Pavlock 1990, Luca 2001, Pironti 2007, Fantuzzi 2012, Blondell 2013, Holmberg 2014, Austin 2021. Holmberg 2014: 322 has observed that scholarly interest in homosexuality has left the "predominant heterosexuality" of the *Iliad* "under-theorized."

[5] De Jong 1987a, Lynn-George 1988, Richardson 1990, Morrison 1992, Taplin 1992, Lowenstam 1993, Stanley 1993, Rabel 1997, Scodel 2002, Wilson 2002, Grethlein 2006, Heiden 2008.

literature more broadly, psychoanalytic theories of desire, loss, and mourning, queer theory, and cognitive approaches to literature.

This book clarifies how the *Iliad* is fundamentally an epic about human feelings and human relationships rather than spectacular violence. The poem's capacious language of desire and interpersonal triangles demonstrate an acute sensitivity to the diverse wants, impulses, and attachments that drive people—and their social origins and consequences. With this study, I hope to put to rest evolutionary notions of literary history that view Homeric epic as primitive and unrealistic, lacking interior depth and a recognizable concept of intellect.[6] On the contrary, though the *Iliad* represents human thoughts and emotions differently than the nineteenth-century novel, for example, and espouses a theory of mind that departs from our own,[7] I join those who find its portrayal of human psychology realistic, profound, and illuminating.

Therein, I argue, lies the epic's primary attraction. Homer's depiction of the characters' desires and the plot they motivate are key factors that draw audiences and readers to the *Iliad*, eliciting their own desires. This book shows how a poem of such extraordinary length and complexity has for eons kept diverse audiences enthralled all the way to its end and beyond.

The Characters' Triangular Desires

One of my central arguments in this book is that triangles of desire are basic and pervasive structures within the *Iliad*'s narrative. Indeed, the triangle of desire may be understood as another traditional epic theme or pattern that reflects early Greek understandings of human psychological and social organization.[8] Scholars have long recognized this structure in its initial instantiation as a "pattern of bride-stealing and rescue" or "dual theme of the seizure/return of a woman."[9] First, the priest Chryses attempts to ransom his captured daughter Chryseis from the Greek leader Agamemnon, who has claimed her as his concubine; then, a dispute arises between Achilleus and Agamemnon over sexual possession of the enslaved woman Briseis; finally, we witness a duel between Menelaos and Paris over who will have Helen as his wife. In each of these cases, a man has taken away a woman from another man, to whom she "rightfully" belongs, causing the two men to compete for control over her.

[6] Thus, Auerbach 2003 [1953] and Snell 1953.

[7] On the multi-part and externalized Homeric mind, see especially Dodds 1951: 1–27 and Snell 1953: 1–22. For recent support of a Homeric theory of mind, see Russo 2012 and Scodel 2012.

[8] Thus, the triangle of desire is also a fundamental structure of the *Odyssey*, appearing most obviously in Odysseus' competition with the suitors for sexual possession of Penelope and in Demodokos' song about Hephaistos' parallel dispute with Ares over Aphrodite (*Od.* 8.266–366).

[9] Lord 2000 [1960]: 190 and Stanley 1993: 39.

These are not, however, the *Iliad*'s only similar narrative triangles. I show how the quarrel between the divine couple Hera and Zeus over the fate of the Greeks and Trojans, as well as Helen's dispute with Aphrodite over Paris, mirror the contests between mortal men over women. Likewise, Achilleus' deadly conflict with Hektor over the killing of his beloved companion Patroklos parallels and replaces his previous clash with Agamemnon over Briseis. A final narrative triangle is constituted in Priam's supplication of Achilleus for the ransom of Hektor's body. Though some of these latter triangles do not exhibit the explicitly sexual element that is present in the "pattern of bride-stealing and rescue," I argue that all of the epic's triangular conflicts and confrontations are rooted in desire of various kinds, and I examine how these dynamics of desire operate in each triangle, often in repeated ways.

The epic's simplest form of desire occurs in two of these triangles, but is not in itself truly triangular: direct, unmediated sexual passion for another person. The Greek terms *erōs* ("lust") and *himeros* ("yearning") and their cognates most obviously denote this desire. Sexual *erōs* is inspired by visual perception of the desired person,[10] and requires the desiring subject and desired object to be in close proximity. It is presented as an outside force that "veils" (*ἀμφεκάλυψεν*) or "dominates" (*ἐδάμασσεν*) the desiring subject's mind or heart (3.442 ~ 14.294; 14.316). Similarly, sexual *himeros* "seizes" (*αἱρεῖ*) the subject (3.446 = 14.328) and it is associated with the external power of Aphrodite and her magical embroidered strap, the *kestos himas* (14.198, 14.216).[11] Indeed, the coercive presence of the goddess Aphrodite can also imply this kind of overwhelming desire, as can the verb *lilaiomai* ("to desire") and the noun *thumos* ("passion" or "heart"). This desire demands and usually achieves instant gratification and keeps the subject focused nearly exclusively on the desired object until it is satisfied. It motivates not only Paris but also Helen, as I argue, to join in adulterous union, and distracts Zeus from his will to make the Trojans temporarily triumphant on the battlefield.

A second kind of desire that I distinguish in the *Iliad*'s triangles is longing for a beloved person who has been abducted or killed. Unlike sexual passion, this desire is provoked by the malign intervention of a third person or group of people responsible for removing or eliminating the object of desire. Whereas *erōs* and *himeros* are aroused through immediate sensory or mental stimulation and are of relatively short duration, this desire is predicated upon loss and absence, sustained through memory of the beloved, and does not necessarily come with the

[10] Plato, in his treatment of *erōs*, asserts repeatedly that it flows in through the desirer's eyes (*Cra.* 420b1; *Phdr.* 250d4–252b3, 253e6–254c3, 255b3–256a7).

[11] Weiss 1998: 50–53 etymologizes both *himeros* and *himas* from an Indo-European root meaning "to bind," and suggests that *himeros* originally indicated a "magical binding." The externality of *himeros* (in its appearance as an urge to lament) is indicated by its ability to independently leave the subject's heart and limbs (*καί οἱ ἀπὸ πραπίδων ἦλθ' ἵμερος ἠδ' ἀπὸ γυίων*, 24.514). On sexual *erōs* and *himeros* in early Greek epic, see further *Lexikon des frühgriechischen Epos* (*LfgrE*) s.v. and Müller 1980: 11–21.

expectation of attaining the desired object. It is sometimes explicitly denoted by the Greek word *pothē* ("longing") and its cognates,[12] but it is also implied by its accompanying emotion of grief (*achos*, *penthos*) as well as by grief's manifestation in tears and, in the case of the desired object's death, lamentation.[13] Thus, I also associate the more urgent and satisfiable impulse to lament, expressed as a *himeros* or *erōs* for lamentation (*goos*), with the most intense variety of this longing for a lost beloved.[14] Achilleus experiences both *pothē* and mournful *himeros* when Patroklos is killed, and, as I argue, he feels a less extreme form of this same type of desire when he loses Briseis, as does Chryses when he is first unable to ransom Chryseis, and Agamemnon when he is ultimately forced to give her up. The Trojan royal family too experiences this longing and its attendant desire for lamentation after their loss of Hektor to Achilleus.

The third and most complex sort of desire that I identify in these triangles is the aggressive desire that articulates the relationship between the subject who has lost a beloved object and the rival responsible for that loss. The subject wishes to dominate or destroy the rival, and the rival often reciprocates this desire. On the one hand, the Homeric verbs of wishing and wanting (*ethelō*, *boulomai*, *eeldomai*) and their cognate nouns (*boulē*, *eeldōr*) can express the general will to best and undo the other. On the other hand, a wide array of terms designate acute urges to do violence against one's antagonist: the noun *menos* ("force, drive, rage") and cognate verbs *meneainō*, *menoinaō*, and *memona* ("to desire eagerly, to rage"), the last usually as the participle *memaōs* ("eager");[15] *erōs* and its cognate *eramai* when their object is war or fighting; and other verbs of desire that appear regularly in the epic's battle narrative (*lilaiomai*, *hiemai*). Like sexual passion, this kind of aggressive drive is not entirely controlled by the subject; for example, another person can rouse a subject's *menos*, a god can inspire *menos* or "stop" (παύσουσα, 1.207) it, and *menos* can also independently seize one, although a desiring subject too is thought to be capable of stopping his own *menos* (1.282). Aggressive

[12] In the *Iliad*, *pothē* is used to designate longing for a particular man or the attributes of a man (not a woman), except for the one case where it describes Achilleus' desire for battle-cry and war when he has withdrawn from the fighting (1.492). It appears most commonly in male homosocial contexts to designate an army's or hero's longing for an absent leader (1.240, 2.703, 2.709, 2.726, 2.778, 6.362, 11.471, 14.368, 15.219) or comrade (7.690, 17.704, 19.321, 23.16, 24.6). Thrice it is used analogously of horses' longing for their absent charioteers (5.234, 11.61, 17.439 [in this last case it appears uniquely in the variant form *pothos*]). Once it predicts a wife's longing for her husband if he should die in battle (5.414). Weiss 1998: 33–34 explains that *pothē*/*pothos* derives from a verb meaning "to pray" and originally meant "the act of praying," which implies "a desire for that which is not easily obtained by the subject's actions alone," that is, "desire for that which is not at hand." On the meaning of *pothē* in the *Iliad*, see further *LfgrE* s.v. and, especially, Austin 2021: 17–49.

[13] Gorgias describes *pothos*, a variant of *pothē*, as "intimate with grief" (φιλοπενθής) in his *Encomium of Helen* (ch. 9).

[14] Cf. Plato, *Cra.* 420a4–8, where Sokrates argues that *pothos* and *himeros* describe the same experience, except that the object of *pothos* is absent while the object of *himeros* is present. See also Vernant 1989: 140–41.

[15] Snell 1953: 21 defines *menos* as "the force in the limbs of a man who is burning to tackle a project." See also Dodds 1951: 8–10 and *LfgrE* s.v.

impulses are the dominant type of desire within the *Iliad*, and are experienced by most of the epic's characters, notably Achilleus, Menelaos, and Hera.

This brings us to Achilleus' wrath, which is announced in the *Iliad*'s first line as the theme of the epic. I interpret anger (*mēnis* and *cholos*) as an accompanying signifier of aggressive desire, which connotes this impetus together with or in the absence of explicit language of desire. Indeed, like the grief that attends longing, the anger that attends aggressive desire is itself represented as a pressing appetite akin to the desire for sex or food.[16]

While aggressive desire manifests itself consistently in these ways, I argue that Homer actually represents two different, and sometimes overlapping, aggressive mechanisms at work in his triangles of desire. In the first, aggressive desire represents a transmutation of the subject's longing for the lost love object in accordance with psychoanalytic theories of mourning. Sigmund Freud, Melanie Klein, and others posit that when a person loses someone beloved, the bereaved person begins a complex psychological process of coming to terms with this loss.[17] The subject has invested "libido," a psychic energy or drive (sometimes sexual) emanating from their unconscious,[18] in the lost object, and must find a way of dealing with this libidinal attachment, which is always, to a greater or lesser degree, ambivalent.[19] One strategy is the mourning subject's preservation of the simultaneously loved and hated lost object through identification with and internalization of that object. This can manifest in "melancholia," a psychic self-abuse caused by introjection of the negative libidinal energy associated with the lost object, who has now become a part of the self.[20] But another response to loss is the external redirection of that aggressive libido onto a substitute "bad" object.

In his perceptive book chapter on the *Iliad*, Henry Staten (1995) has recognized this kind of psychological mechanism in the epic's repeated narrative triangles. He writes:

[16] Liebert 2017: 82–102, 109. She cites and builds on Aristotle's definition of anger (*orgē*) as "a desire, accompanied by pain, for apparent revenge" (ὄρεξις μετὰ λύπης τιμωρίας φαινομένης, *Rh.* 1378a). On *mēnis* in the *Iliad*, see Muellner 1996; on *cholos*, see Walsh 2005.

[17] Freud 1957 [1916] and 1960 [1923]; Lagache 1993 [1938]; Klein 1994 [1940]; Eng 2000; Butler 2004.

[18] See Freud 1960 [1923]: 67–71.

[19] Lagache 1993 [1938]: 19–20. Freud 1957 [1916]: 256 writes that "The ambivalence is either constitutional, i.e. is an element of every love-relation formed by this particular ego, or else it precedes precisely from those experiences that involved the threat of losing the object." Lagache 1993 [1938]: 25 describes three main sources of the aggressive component that appears in mourning: "the aggression inherent in every inter-human relationship, the resentment provoked by the departure of the dead person, and the aggression inherent in the work of mourning, which is to destroy the love object and eliminate the affective cathexes of him." Eng 2000: 1278 argues that ambivalence can also come from attachment to socially "disparaged" or "devalued" objects.

[20] With the terms "melancholia" or "melancholic," I refer exclusively to the psychoanalytic understanding of this emotional state. For a broader view of "melancholia" and a comprehensive history of its meaning, see Bell 2014.

> We may reconstruct the underlying logic of this series in terms of a libidinal situation involving possession of an object, one that is libidinally cathected (a woman or friend); followed by the loss of this object, against the will of the possessor and without compensation; after which reparation is required, either through vengeful aggression against a substitute object that comes into one's possession (the living or dead body of the enemy), or through the option that is so hard to come by in the *Iliad*, acceptance of *apoina* [ransom] as conciliating reparation.[21]

In this reading, aggressive desire derives from a subject's emotional investment in the lost object and represents a transferal of libidinal energy toward a "substitute object," the rival who has perpetrated the loss.[22] Building upon Staten, I show how Achilleus' aggressive desire for revenge, first against Agamemnon and then against Hektor, is generated in this way, and I trace this dynamic in other narrative triangles as well, starting with Chryses' conflict with Agamemnon over Chryseis. In addition, I demonstrate how Achilleus and other characters also react to loss by identifying with the lost object and redirecting their aggressive libido toward themselves, which results in "melancholia" and physical self-harm that appear in conjunction or alternation with external aggression.

In the other aggressive mechanism in the *Iliad*'s triangles, the desire to dominate is primary, rather than secondary, and not dependent on longing for a lost object. In his study of triangular desire in the modern novel, René Girard (1965) first identified and explained this kind of aggressive desire as "mimetic" or "imitative" in character. The subject, who appears to desire the object, more truly desires to emulate the third person in the triangle, who already possesses or desires the object; thus, "Imitative desire is always desire to be Another."[23] Girard terms this third person the "mediator," since they mediate the subject's (derivative) desire for the object. When the mediator is the subject's direct rival for the object, mimetic desire can take the hostile form of a will to overcome that rival and take their place.

In her study of bonds between men in English literature, Eve K. Sedgwick (1992) has linked this competitive form of mimetic desire specifically to men within patriarchal societies. Recognizing that Girard's literary triangles generally feature male subjects in rivalry over a female object, she argues that this structure represents the negotiation of male relationships and masculine identity in terms of

[21] Staten 1995: 29–30. Wilson 2002 has expanded Staten's work from an anthropological and narratological perspective in a book-length study examining the *Iliad*'s "compensation theme" and offering detailed explanation of the mutually exclusive paths of ransom (*apoina*) and revenge (*poinē*) in response to loss. Her analysis of the *Iliad*'s narrative structure is largely congruent with my own.

[22] Cf. Austin 2021: 75–96, who agrees that Achilleus' anger derives from his grievous longing (*pothē*) for Patroklos, but analyzes that anger as fundamentally "aimless."

[23] Girard 1965: 83.

sexual ownership of women,[24] with aggressive "male homosocial desire" driving and shaping the interaction more than heterosexual desire for the contested woman. Likewise, the psychoanalyst Nancy Chodorow (2015) has recently posited that "repudiation of subordinate masculinity," that is, the desire to be domineering instead of humiliated in relation to other men, is "bedrock" to male psychology. She suggests that this competitive desire may be more central for understanding male development than other models emphasizing the importance of the mother, such as the Oedipus Complex. She finds in the *Iliad*, and specifically in the conflict between Achilleus and Agamemnon, "the great psychomythic story of male-male humiliation."[25]

As Chodorow recognizes, this kind of primary aggressive desire between men appears to be fundamental to the *Iliad*'s narrative triangles and its patriarchal social world more generally. Hans van Wees (1992) has called the Homeric heroes "status warriors" because of their acute interest in increasing and maintaining their status. As he has shown, status is dependent upon honor (*timē*), which is accumulated in various ways, almost always in competition against others, and acknowledged by respectful deference or the bestowal of favors, gifts, and prizes, such as a female slave.[26] Building on previous scholarship,[27] I track how Agamemnon's and Achilleus' aggressive desires to sustain prestige motivate their conflict over Briseis in whole and part respectively, and how Menelaos' desire to best his rival Paris drives his war of revenge more than libidinal attachment to Helen. This competitive, aggressive desire for honor—and for its extension in fame (*kleos*)[28]—also animates the Greek and Trojan soldiers who are implicated in the epic's central triangles of desire tangentially as proxies, especially the heroes Diomedes, Patroklos, and Hektor. Finally, the divine world replicates this mortal status competition, yet without the gender asymmetry. I show how

[24] Here she draws upon Gayle Rubin's landmark 1975 essay, which works from the anthropological theory of Claude Lévi-Strauss to identify "traffic in women" as the foundation of patriarchy and heterosexuality (Rubin 2011: 33–65 and Lévi-Strauss 1969).

[25] Chodorow 2015: 267.

[26] Van Wees 1992: 69–75; similarly Scodel 2008 (where status is measured in terms of "face").

[27] MacCary 1982: 135 asserts that in the *Iliad* "men define themselves in terms of other men, and women are only a means of strengthening and formalizing men's relations with each other"; similarly, Wöhrle 2002: 233–36. Felson and Slatkin 2004: 93–100 and Lyons 2012: 53–63 discuss how the Trojan War fought over Helen and the parallel conflict between Achilleus and Agamemnon over Briseis represent the violent, dysfunctional face of a patriarchal society constituted through the exchange of women.

[28] Honor (*timē*) is conferred by one's own community and represents a hero's status in that community while he is alive, whereas fame (*kleos*) is conferred by anyone who speaks of the hero, and particularly epic bards, and represents a hero's status everywhere and forever, during his lifetime and after death. On *timē* and *kleos* as motivation for Iliadic heroes to fight in the front lines and so risk a premature death, see Sarpedon's speech to Glaukos (12.310–28) and also Redfield 1994: 100–1. Two Homeric terms often associated with *kleos* are *kudos* and *euchos*. Benveniste 1973: 346–56 and Muellner 1976: 108–12, however, show that *kudos* and *euchos* express the hero's experience or declaration of triumph rather than the social or poetic effects of that victory, although the first category can lead to the second.

Hera and Zeus too direct aggressive desire at one another, mostly of this primary, competitive type, negotiating their relationship in terms of control not over individual women but over armies of mortal men.

The Plot(s) of the *Iliad* and This Book

Literary plots are both the sequential expressions of story (what happened) in narrative discourse (the telling) and, as Peter Brooks recognized, "intentional structures." He explains (1984: 12): "the organizing line of plot is more often than not some scheme or machination, a concerted plan for the accomplishment of some purpose which goes against the ostensible and dominant legalities of the fictional world, the realization of a blocked and resisted desire." That is, the meanings of "plot" in terms of literature and criminal enterprise tend to coincide, and character desire is identified as the structuring principle of literary plot.

Along with direction, this desire also provides plot with its motivating energy. As Brooks (1984: 38) observes, "Desire is always there at the start of a narrative," disturbing stasis, forcing a change, and initiating the momentum of plot; he offers as an example the quarrel between Achilleus and Agamemnon over Briseis at the beginning of the *Iliad*. Tony Tanner (1979) likewise recognizes the importance of desire in propelling plot in his study of adultery in the novel, and pinpoints the triangle of desire as particularly conducive for plot's commencement: "it is the unstable triangularity of adultery, rather than the static symmetry of marriage, that is the generative form of Western literature as we know it." Tanner cites as example the adulterous union of Paris and Helen, which disrupts both a marriage and a guest-friendship, and thus starts the war that forms the basis of the *Iliad*'s story.[29]

In this book, expanding on the insight of Brooks and Tanner, I show how the triangular desires of the *Iliad*'s characters work in complex ways to drive and shape two related plots. First, I define the epic's "main plot" as the realization—with complication by the gods—of Achilleus' intention to make Agamemnon and his fellow Greeks regret the demeaning removal of Briseis, and then to take revenge on Hektor and the Trojans for the killing of Patroklos. It is thus bipartite, containing what Joachim Latacz (2015: 158) has described as two overlapping "arcs of suspense," the first grounded in Achilleus' quarrel with Agamemnon, which is initiated in Book 1 and resolved in Book 19, and the second consisting of Achilleus' grievance with Hektor and his people, which begins once he discovers the death of Patroklos in Book 18 and is finally resolved with the funeral of Hektor at the end of Book 24. Aristotle appears to anticipate this analysis of the *Iliad*'s

[29] Tanner 1979: 12; 24–26.

main plot, which coheres around the character of Achilleus and his two parallel conflicts, when he comments that "only one tragedy can be made out the *Iliad* or the *Odyssey*, or *at most two*" (*Poetics* 59b, my emphasis).

The *Iliad*'s other plot is the story of the Trojan War—Menelaos' successful war to recover Helen from Paris—as related in the epic's discourse. I call this the "superplot" since it expresses the overarching myth within which Achilleus' main plot is but one episode. While the main plot is paused in Books 3–7 of the epic, the superplot comes to the fore in scenes that replay the war's origin, explore the nature of battle at Troy and anticipate the city's fall. When Patroklos and then Achilleus enter battle in the last third of the *Iliad*, turning the tide in the Greeks' favor and moving the narrative ever closer to Troy's defeat, the main plot and the superplot converge. However, the *Iliad* ends with the superplot still unresolved, with fighting about to resume.

The first two chapters of this book trace the genesis of the *Iliad*'s main plot in the three imbricated triangles of desire of Book 1. What begins with Chryses' longing to reclaim his daughter Chryseis from the Greeks results in Agamemnon's seizure of Briseis and the arousal of Achilleus' own longing and accompanying aggressive desires for revenge and honor. These desires lead the hero to plot the worsting of the Greeks in battle through the divine power of Zeus. At this juncture, Homer marks Achilleus' authorial function by having him retell the epic's opening to his goddess mother Thetis and direct her solicitation of the divine king's cooperation. Zeus's agreement to join his will with that of Achilleus incites Hera's opposing desires to preserve the Greek army and challenge her husband's supremacy. Therefore, while Achilleus' triangular desires appear to formulate and initiate the epic's main plot, it has multiple motivations, both human and divine, and its direction is contested.[30]

Chapters 3 and 4 show how Homer similarly situates the triangular desires of first mortals and then gods as the engines of the Trojan War superplot, while also exploring perspectives in opposition to this plot. In *Iliad* 2, a renewed attack on Troy is shown to be contingent upon Nestor provoking the Greek soldiers' entwined desires to rape Trojan women and dominate their men. Book 3 dramatizes the motivating desires of Menelaos, Paris, and also Helen herself through a duel and sexual encounter that replay the original illicit coming together of the Trojan prince and Spartan queen under the sign of Aphrodite. Here Homer positions Helen as a key generator of the superplot by depicting her as a poet-figure weaving a representation of the war and as a desiring subject and speaker who recalls Achilleus. In Books 4 and 5, the poet thematizes the mirroring aggressive desires of Hera and the Greek fighters as drivers of continued warfare, despite the disinclination of Zeus to prolong the conflict. Discontent with the war

[30] The plot's complex motivation reflects the very nature of Iliadic desire as imagined to be afflicting one from the outside (often through a divine actor) rather than originating spontaneously from the self.

is foregrounded in *Iliad* 6 through the presentation of the anguished desiring subjectivities of Andromache and the other Trojan women, who want safety, rather than glory, for their husbands, their children, and themselves.

In Chapters 5 and 6, I return with the epic narrative to the main plot and demonstrate how it progresses and develops through the machinations of competing subjects of desire in *Iliad* 8–16. After Zeus begins to accomplish Achilleus' plot for Greek devastation on the battlefield, Agamemnon sends a conciliatory embassy to the hero in Book 9 that ultimately reignites, instead of quells, his motivating aggressive desires. This re-energizes the main plot and results in the "Great Day of Battle" that features the gradual advance of the Trojans on the Greek camp. In Book 14 Hera temporarily subverts this plot and reintroduces the superplot of Greek dominance by seductively inspiring Zeus's erotic desire for herself and thereby refocusing his prevailing will away from the war. When Zeus reasserts control, he integrates Hera's desire with his own, merging the trajectories of main plot and superplot. He accomplishes this through Patroklos' death in Book 16, which is also directly motivated by Patroklos' own desire to defeat the Trojans in opposition to Achilleus' continuing desire to force deference from the Greeks.

The last two chapters of this book track how Achilleus' consequent longing for Patroklos and desire for revenge against Hektor power and determine the second arc of the main plot until they are remediated at the *Iliad*'s end. This second set of triangular desires, working in concert with divine desire for Troy's destruction, motivates Achilleus' glorious re-entrance into battle, killing of Hektor, and subsequent mutilation of his corpse. The loss of Hektor in turn arouses a Trojan longing for their champion, which remains unresolved due to Achilleus' aggressive fixation on Hektor's body, in a concluding triangle of desire. Longing and accompanying desire for lamentation impel Priam, with the gods' support, to seek the recovery of his son's corpse in a successful supplication that resolves Achilleus' driving desires as well as the Trojans' longing, and thus brings the *Iliad*'s main plot and its narrative to a close.

Throughout the book, I also argue that Homer characterizes three of his most important narrative agents, Achilleus, Paris, and Helen, as queer subjects, thereby explaining and underscoring their capacity to rend the social fabric and generate martial epic. Whereas "queer" is popularly associated with gay, lesbian, bisexual, or transgender subjects, I follow other queer theorists in using the term more widely to denote deviance from established norms of gender and sexuality.[31] I show how Achilleus transgresses masculine norms in his withdrawal from battle,

[31] e.g. Cohen 1997 has argued that poor people of color in the United States, who have been demonized for "nonnormative sexual behavior and family structures" (458), such as having sex and children out of wedlock, should be considered "queer" and included in queer politics. For introduction to queerness and queer theory, see further Halperin 1995: 62–66, Sullivan 2003: 37–56, and Acadia 2021.

quasi-conjugal intimacy with Patroklos, and mourning over his death, and how Paris does so in his clandestine abduction of Helen and preference for sex over fighting. Meanwhile, Helen departs from feminine norms in her adulterous desire and aggressive, status-conscious confrontation with Aphrodite. Through their gender and sexual difference, queer individuals challenge normative social structures and undermine existing systems of power.[32] Yet, as David Halperin (1995: 66) observes, "Resistance to normativity is not purely negative or reactive or destructive . . . it is also positive and dynamic and creative."[33] With their queer behaviors, Achilleus, Paris, and Helen cause devastating conflict, but in so doing they also produce the *Iliad*.

Narrative Desire

Although this book's primary focus is elucidating desire and its relation to plot within the *Iliad*, its secondary project is mapping, as I make my way through the epic, how these internal features elicit and structure audiences'—or readers'—engagement with the poem. More exactly, I identify and discuss three kinds of desire that motivate audiences to listen: narrative desire, sympathetic desire, and empathetic desire. While each of these desires has a different genesis and nature, they augment one another and together invest audiences in the epic narrative until—and even beyond—its close. In this section, I will explain what narrative desire is and how it works for the *Iliad*'s audience.

I borrow the term "narrative desire" from Brooks, and develop its concept from his reading of Roland Barthes, though I use it in a more restricted and specific sense than he to describe a reader's or audience's desire to comprehend a narrative in all its meaning.[34] This desire takes the form of a drive to find out what will happen, and how and when it will happen, a drive that is rooted in one's limited knowledge about the content and shape of plot. As Brooks observes, a narrative's complete meaning can only be grasped at its end; to access this meaning, the reader (or audience member) must follow plot from start to finish over a period of time, gradually making sense of "the logic of actions" and "the questions and answers that structure a story," what Barthes (1974) called the "proairetic" and

[32] The idea of the incompatibility of queerness with the normative social, political, and temporal order has been termed "the antisocial thesis" and derives especially from the work of Bersani 1995 and Edelman 2004, who argue for an embrace of this positionality. For discussion and debate of this thesis, see Caserio et al. 2006.

[33] See also Muñoz 2019 [2009] on "queer futurity"—the association of queerness with hope and new horizons of sociality.

[34] Brooks 1984 coins "narrative desire" as a general, catch-all term for the powering desire within a narrative and the external desire for a narrative: "the notion of desire as that which is initiatory of narrative, motivates and energizes its reading, and animates the combinatory play of sense-making" (48).

"hermeneutic" codes of narrative. The "enigmas" of the hermeneutic code in particular produce a "space of suspense" that we have to traverse in order to achieve revelation. According to Barthes (1966: 27), the fervor that animates readers is therefore "the passion for meaning" (*la passion du sens*), explained by Brooks (1984: 19) as "the active quest of the reader for those shaping ends that, terminating the dynamic process of reading, promise to bestow meaning and significance on the beginning and the middle." Narrative desire, then, is our compulsion to decode an enigmatic, suspenseful plot, to know and understand the full story.

Psychologists W. F. Brewer and E. H. Lichtenstein's empirical research on readers' enjoyment of stories supports the conclusion that a discourse structure that withholds key aspects of story—and then finally provides this information—is compelling to readers. Brewer and Lichtenstein (1982: 480–83) identified three different discourse structures that induce, respectively, surprise, curiosity, or suspense through delayed dissemination of important information; they found that readers preferred narratives that produced these affects followed by an emotional resolution when the missing information was ultimately revealed.

Though the *Iliad* recounts the traditional story of the Trojan War, its new and authoritative retelling of myth leaves room for narrative desire. The epic implies an audience with basic knowledge of the Olympian gods and the Trojan War, including its major actors (Agamemnon, Menelaos, Helen, Paris, and Priam), but other salient information for interpreting the plot is presented within the narrative itself.[35] The *Iliad* constitutes, at the very least, an original version of a time-honored story, and it may include entirely new myths or characters invented by the poet to suit his purpose.[36] In Book 2, the narrator calls upon the Muses to share accurate and detailed information about the ships and leaders who went to Troy "because you are goddesses and you are present and you know everything, whereas we hear a report only and know nothing at all" (*ὑμεῖς γὰρ θεαί ἐστε,*

[35] Scodel 2002: 64; 99–112. On the knowledge of the *Iliad*'s audience, see also Mueller 1984: 28 and de Jong 1987a: 60–64, 93–96. Scodel (2002: 62) differentiates between two kinds of implied audiences in the Homeric poems, the "narrative audience" and the "authorial audience." The "narrative audience" exists entirely in the fictional world and does not realize it is fictional. The "authorial audience," on the other hand, is external to the world of the poem and understands that the narrative is an artistic creation (Scully 1986: 139–40 makes a similar distinction between the "narrator's audience" and "authorial audience"). As Scodel argues, the *Iliad*'s poet implies a "narrative audience" with a higher level of knowledge than its "authorial audience." For example, the narrator refers to many characters without immediately explaining who they are, which implies a "narrative audience" that is already familiar with these characters. However, the poet then goes on to reveal the necessary attributes and background of these same characters, which suggests an "authorial audience" that is not expected to have prior knowledge of this information. The implication of a knowledgeable "narrative audience" has the rhetorical effect of making the *Iliad* seem completely traditional, and constructs an intimacy of shared culture between narrator and audience, which Scodel (2002: 92) calls the "rhetoric of inclusion."

[36] See Lang 1983 on Homer's adaptation of traditional myth. Willcock 1964 argues that Homer composes new myths as paradigms for his main story. On the possibility that Homer invented the character of Patroklos, see Janko 1992: 313–14 and Burgess 2001: 71–73. On the Homeric poems' aspiration to be "new songs," see Currie 2016: 72–73.

πάρεστέ τε, ἴστέ τε πάντα,/ ἡμεῖς δὲ κλέος οἶον ἀκούομεν οὐδέ τι ἴδμεν, 2.485–86). Here Homer claims special, divinely inspired insight into what happened at Troy, and suggests that his narrative can provide enlightenment to an ignorant audience.[37] Thus, fluency in the mythical tradition does not enable the audience to understand the *Iliad*'s entire plot in advance.

Nor are the epic's many internal predictions complete giveaways for the plot. Even when the narrator or other characters (such as a god) foretell a particular story event, the audience does not know precisely how and when it will appear within the epic narrative. Furthermore, as James Morrison (1992: 19) has explained, "All predictions are partial or incomplete in some way, for the narrative's fullest presentation of an event naturally comes at the moment of enactment."[38] Predictions can also be false: Morrison has shown how Homer, at various moments, disappoints audience expectations shaped by traditional myth or narrative predictions by gesturing toward one outcome but making the plot unfold in an unanticipated way.[39] His work demonstrates that the *Iliad* is meant to be surprising. Once again, the obscurity of the epic's plot creates the conditions for its audience to experience narrative desire.

At the same time, the very features that provide clues to the *Iliad*'s story—its embeddedness in tradition and frequent predictions—appear to be key to the arousal of narrative desire. In his pioneering book on epic foreshadowing and suspense, George Duckworth (1933) observed that foreknowledge creates a "suspense of anticipation." The listener, because he knows (to a limited degree) what to expect, "remains in a state of emotional tension and is on the lookout for something which he either wishes or dreads to see happen."[40] Essentially, the *Iliad*'s traditionality and internal forecasts give us a taste of what is to come that makes us hungry for more. As I track throughout the epic, these elements invite us to pursue all the way to its revelatory end this unique rendering of a familiar myth.[41]

[37] See further Myers 2019: 22–23 on the opposition in this scene between the "you" of the divine Muses, endowed with vision and knowledge, and the "we" of the epic's narrator and audience, defined by their "mortality, distance, and ignorance/hearsay."

[38] See also Owen 1946: 13, who writes that the poet "does not reveal [his main design] fully but gives just enough to face the expectation in the right direction."

[39] Morrison 1992 *passim*. See also Duckworth 1933: 5–26 for a detailed catalogue of the many varieties of predictions found in the *Iliad* and other ancient epics, from direct forecasts to ambiguous foreshadowing, and especially 21–24 on "false foreshadowing."

[40] Duckworth 1933: 37. See also Richardson 1990: 136, who, in agreement with Duckworth, remarks that "Suspense is heightened by full disclosure of the facts," and Kozak 2017: 147, who argues that "knowing an ending builds *more* intense engagement and curiosity than not knowing" (her italics). See further Thornton 1984: 59–63 for one account of how the *Iliad* creates and resolves the "suspense of anticipation" throughout its narrative.

[41] Owen 1946: 13 expresses the same basic observation about how prediction helps the audience to plot the *Iliad*: "The shape which the poet is imposing on his diverse material he thus makes us progressively impose for ourselves; we place the incidents as they occur in relation to a known end,

Psychologists Jonathan Leavitt and Nicholas Christenfeld (2011) have provided empirical evidence that foreknowledge actually increases a reader's appreciation of a story. Inspired by the observation that people enjoy re-reading stories although they know the outcome, and by other psychological studies that link "perceptual fluency" with "aesthetic pleasure, positive affect, and story engagement," the authors' aim was to find out whether spoilers really spoil stories. They discovered that research subjects at the University of California, San Diego, rated their enjoyment of stories more highly when they were provided with initial summary paragraphs that exposed the stories' denouements. The authors concluded that "spoilers may allow readers to organize developments, anticipate the implications of events, and resolve ambiguities that occur in the course of reading." That is, spoilers encourage and help readers to follow plot, working in the same way as mythical tradition and prediction in the context of the *Iliad*.

As the epic's first, programmatic prediction, the *Iliad*'s proem plays an important part in initiating the audience's narrative desire by presenting limited but provocative pieces of information. In the proem, the narrator says that Achilleus' wrath "laid myriad pains on the Achaians," "sent many powerful souls of heroes to Hades," and "made them a prey for dogs and for all the birds" (1.2–5). Line 5 ends with the statement that "the will of Zeus was being accomplished," thereby introducing another character, Zeus, and presenting his design as an apparent source and determinant for the events of the story. In the last two lines of the proem, the narrator announces Agamemnon as a third named character and identifies his quarrel with Achilleus as the temporal beginning of the realization of Zeus's will.[42] This account of the poem's story is extremely minimalist, acknowledging only three out of the *Iliad*'s many characters and sketching out the events and their causality in the vaguest form. Second, even its bare outlines are incomplete, since it ignores many episodes that do not advance the main plot, like the duel of Paris and Menelaos, and Hektor's brief return to Troy, and it gives almost no hint of the death of Hektor—a key event—or the consequent suffering of the Trojan royal family and people.[43] In addition, the proem provides no

and follow the poet's plan by knowing in advance what it is." Cf. Kozak 2017: 8 on the narrative device of the "mission," which provides "an end point that the audience can anticipate and look forward to, and obstacles for characters to overcome along the way."

[42] Following Redfield 1979: 96–97, I read *ἐξ οὗ* of line 6 as "from the time when," referring back to the will of Zeus in the preceding line, *contra* Kullmann 1955: 167 and Kirk 1985: 53 *inter alios*, who prefer "from the point at which," referring back to the first line imperative for the Muse to sing Achilleus' wrath. Besides Redfield's linguistic argument, I offer the following justifications for this choice: (1) the syntactic juxtaposition of Zeus's will and *ἐξ οὗ* suggest, especially to a listening audience, that they are meant to be understood together; (2) the narrative proper actually begins with Chryses' embassy, not with the quarrel; (3) if, following Kullmann 1955, we accept the *Διὸς βουλή* as the diminishment of humankind through fighting in the Trojan War, that plan within the *Iliad*'s narrative only comes to fruition after the quarrel. Cf. Lynn-George 1988: 38–39, who sees *ἐξ οὗ* as deliberately ambiguous.

[43] Duckworth 1933: 6. Cf. Bassett 1938: 179, Morrison 1992: 51–71, and Rutherford 2001: 128.

guidance on how the narrative will lead us from point A (the quarrel) to point B (the deaths of heroes), nor does it explain how or when we will learn more about the enigmatic "will of Zeus."[44] This tantalizing but incomplete prevision of the epic plot is a key mechanism for eliciting the audience's narrative desire. By posing unanswered questions, the proem arouses our appetite to know the *Iliad*'s full story and grasp its meaning.

The proem, along with other narrative predictions, also *structures* the audience's narrative desire by providing a frame of reference for interpreting the reappearance of forecasted story material in the rest of the narrative. The proem summarizes in seven lines some of the main events of the epic's story, and then the narrative continues with a few more lines that summarize in reverse order the very beginning of the story (Chryses' embassy and Apollo's anger).[45] After these introductory overviews, the narrator begins to tell the story again, but this time in greater detail and in correct temporal order, as part of the *Iliad*'s main narrative. We are thus hearing the story for the second time and this repetition invites us to compare the second account to the first. When in its repetition the story is expanded, familiar elements function as signposts that keep us engaged along the way and assist us, like Leavitt and Christensen's spoilers, in plotting the complete story successfully.

Any repeated element can shape and guide the audience's narrative desire in this way. In the first two chapters of this book, I show how *Iliad* 1 presents three successive and interrelated conflicts rooted in triangular desires that are homologous variations of each other, manifesting repetitions on the levels of structure, theme, and diction. The first and last conflicts are told from beginning to end in Book 1, while the central conflict—the quarrel between Achilleus and Agamemnon—remains unresolved. I suggest that the two other conflicts function like predictions to provide a template for the *Iliad*'s main plot of Achilleus' withdrawal and return. They create audience expectation that Achilleus' conflict will be resolved in a similar way, and deviations from their pattern delay the audience's gratification until Book 24. Thus, the *Iliad*'s repeated triangles of desire serve the external purpose of focusing our narrative desire and helping us to make sense of plot as it develops.

Repetition is a vital and omnipresent aspect of the *Iliad*'s narrative on both macrocosmic and microcosmic levels. Since the discovery of the *Iliad*'s oral-formulaic style, scholars have struggled to differentiate between significant repetition and repetition that is merely a requirement of meter or an accident of the oral style, with its limited repertoire of expression. In the spirit of more recent

[44] See Duckworth 1933: 54–55 on the gradual exposition of Zeus's plan.

[45] This retrospective narrative was termed "epic regression" by Krischer 1971: 136–40 and also analyzed by Genette 1980: 36–37. The opening narrative does not, however, take a straight line backward, but oscillates in forward and backward movement within a larger path of retrospection.

scholarship, I regard the *Iliad*'s poet as a master craftsman who knew how to use traditional scenes and language in the service of his narrative.[46] Therefore, I will tend to search for meaning in repetitions of all types, analyzing the ways that they, together with predictions, encourage and steer us in our passionate endeavor to understand the epic's narrative.[47]

Sympathetic and Empathetic Desires

Brooks, influenced by Aristotle's and the Formalists' elevation of story above character as the fundamental feature of narrative, primarily considered how plot—in its withholding of information—evokes the desire of readers. More recent literary theorists, however, drawing on insights from cognitive science, have recognized the importance of characters in engaging readers and audiences. In everyday social relations, neurotypical people are constantly imagining what is going on in other people's minds on the basis of their speech and actions; Lisa Zunshine (2006) has contended that we perform this same "mind reading" when confronted with literary characters, and that we consume fiction because we relish the cognitive challenge of interpreting what they are thinking and feeling. Blakey Vermeule (2010) has further proposed that reading the minds of fictional characters is compelling because it offers a risk-free opportunity to learn how to assess others' intentions, putting us in a better position to navigate the complex social world of real life.

The *Iliad*, in its thematization of its characters' desires, focuses attention on their thoughts and feelings and invites audiences to exercise their mind-reading capability.[48] I suggest that reading characters' minds can further arouse the desire

[46] See Segal 1971c, Martin 1989: 171–79, Stanley 1993, Lowenstam 1993, Louden 2006, and Bakker 2013 as models for treating the repetition of diction and narrative patterns as significant to the interpretation of Homeric poetry. For further explanation of this approach's methodology, see Segal 1971c: 1–8, Lowenstam 1993: 13–57, 59–60, and Louden 2006: 1–5. For theoretical discussions of intratextual and intertextual Homeric allusion, see Bakker 2013: 157–69 and Currie 2016: 1–36.

[47] Flatt 2017 also recognizes audiences' narrative desire for the *Iliad* but in relation to characters' mourning rather than prediction and repetition. He connects narrative desire with yearning for lamentation (*himeros gooio*) on the basis of the link between lamentation and epic poetry, which both grant heroes fame (*kleos*), and argues that Homer promotes narrative desire in both the *Iliad* and the *Odyssey* by deferring satisfaction of *himeros gooio* through "pivotal contrafactuals of mourning" until the epics' culminating ritual closures. Cf. Felson-Rubin 1994: 11–19 and *passim*, who contends that the *Odyssey* both inspires narrative desire and denies complete gratification through the enigmatic character of Penelope; Christensen 2019, who discusses the audience's desire to know how the *Odyssey*'s story ends and to understand its nature; and Elmer 2020, who argues that the *Odyssey* provokes narrative desire and then satisfies it through dynamics of expansion and compression, amnesia and recollection, disguise and recognition, and fragmentation and integration.

[48] While Zunshine and Vermeule argue that convoluted, unreliable, and sophisticated representations of characters' minds—such as those found in epistolary and detective novels—especially invite us to read literary minds, Caracciolo 2016 contends that we engage with characters as if they were real people (entering what he calls a "character-centered illusion") whenever we "come to value a fictional representation of mind because of its interest, effectiveness, or plausibility" (8). Shay 1994 certainly

of Iliadic audiences by activating their sympathy and empathy. *Sympathy* is feeling *for* a person—caring about them without actually sharing their mental experience.[49] When we sympathize with a character, we conceive a corresponding wish for that character to come to a good end, which I term "sympathetic desire." *Empathy* (sometimes called "identification") is partially adopting another's emotions, thoughts, and perspective. In the case of literary empathy, we temporarily think and feel *with* a character, placing ourselves in the character's shoes, even as we remain aware that we are not that character and also hold separately our own thoughts, emotions, and (superior) knowledge.[50] When we empathize with desiring characters, we share their urges, wishes, and longings, thus experiencing what I term "empathetic desire."

In this book, then, along with demonstrating how the *Iliad*'s plot arouses and structures the audience's narrative desire, I also show how the epic characters—and particularly, their psychologies—may inspire in audience members these sympathetic and empathetic desires, which further invest them in the evolving narrative.[51] I argue that the *Iliad* invites the audience to sympathize and empathize with multiple characters, including those with opposing desires.[52] Therefore, the epic's conclusion, by resolving the grievous desires of both Achilleus and the Trojans, offers a high degree of gratification for the audience.

My discussion of the Iliadic audience's possible sympathetic and empathetic responses is based in scholarly theory and research on particular narrative modes

views Achilleus' psychology in this way when he makes the argument that Achilleus' portrayal in the *Iliad* parallels the experience of American GIs who suffered moral injury and Post Traumatic Stress Disorder in Vietnam. Given the significant differences between Homer's conception of mind and our contemporary understandings, we can only guess how much more resonant Homeric characters were to the Greeks of Homer's time and afterwards, who either shared the poet's theory of mind, or whose communal, collective way of living was at least reflected in that conception (Russo and Simon 1968: 496–97). Cf. Felson-Rubin 1994: 126–28 on listeners' and especially her own "psychologizing" of Penelope in the *Odyssey*, and Minchin 2019 on how the *Odyssey* exercises its audience's mind-reading ability through its depiction of Odysseus telling lies.

[49] Coplan 2004: 145–46 and Keen 2007: 5.

[50] Coplan 2004: 143–44, 148–49. See also Caracciolo 2016: 39–40, who identifies five different potential aspects of empathetic response to literary characters: somatic, perceptual, emotional, epistemic, and axiological.

[51] In its attention to the audience's engagement with the *Iliad*'s characters, this book overlaps to some degree with Kozak 2017, although there are some key differences in our approach. Kozak concentrates primarily on the audience's response to Hektor, while I focus on the audience's reaction to the epic's main hero, Achilleus. Moreover, Kozak analyzes the audience's engagement within the framework of Smith's (1995: 81–86) "structure of sympathy," tracking the audience's "recognition" of characters, and "alignment" and "allegiance" with them, whereas I draw on various theories and empirical studies in my account of audience response, and consider audience empathy as well as sympathy.

[52] At the same time, I acknowledge that audience members may respond to the *Iliad*'s characters in many different and unpredictable ways, depending upon who they are, when and where they are living, and the conditions of their reception of the narrative, including the nature of the bard's performance. As Keen 2007: 75 observes, "empathy for a fictional character need not correspond with what the author appears to set up or invite." On the contingency of reader response, see also Caracciolo 2016: 15–17.

and character traits that are likely to elicit the sympathy and/or empathy of readers and audiences. First, these reactions may be especially evoked when a narrative brings to the fore the perspective of a character—often the protagonist—for a sustained period. According to Marco Caracciolo (2016: 8), this kind of narrative attention gives readers a sense of "getting to know" the character as they would a real person. In Murray Smith's (1995: 83–84) model for audience engagement with films, this focus places the audience in "alignment" with the character, opening the way for sympathy and empathy. Indeed, scientific studies show how readers more successfully process narrative details that accord with the protagonist's point of view, suggesting that they empathize with the protagonist as they move through a narrative.[53]

Second, in their empirical research on young readers, psychologists Paul E. Jose and William F. Brewer (1984: 918–19) found that perceived similarity with a character and the goodness of a character independently engendered both the sympathy and empathy of readers, and that sympathy also led to empathy and vice versa. The first factor they identify—the reader's perceived similarity with a character—is also recognized by other researchers as a determinant of empathetic response.[54] The reader's (or listener's) identity obviously plays a large part in perceived similarity and—as a variable external to the text—suggests the unpredictability and contingency of audience response.

However, there is some experimental evidence that a narrative providing implicit, rather than explicit information about a character's mind encourages readers to imaginatively construct a character along the lines of their own identity and experience—leading to the impression of similarity.[55] That is, the experience of reading the mind of an "underdetermined" character as much as a character that is clearly similar to oneself may generate empathy—and sympathy, too, by the same process.[56] In the context of the *Iliad*, this means that full exposition of character is not necessary to induce these audience responses and may in fact work against them, depending on the listener's identity; instead, evocative clues about a character's psychology may better provoke an audience's empathy and/or sympathy.[57]

While Jose and Brewer find that "good" characters elicit readers' sympathy and empathy,[58] "bad" characters may also be able to activate these responses. Terry

[53] Coplan 2004: 141–42.

[54] See Bortolussi and Dixon 2003: 86–87; Keen 2007: 94; Caracciolo 2016: 40.

[55] Bortolussi and Dixon 2003: 90–94.

[56] See also Smith 1995: 98 on the power of "underdetermined narrative representation" to elicit empathy, and further Keen 2007: 94–96.

[57] Cf. Keen 2007: 69, who theorizes that "*empathy for fictional characters may require only minimal elements of identity, situation, and feeling, not necessarily complex or realistic characterization*" (her italics).

[58] Smith 1995: 84–86 similarly connects the moral evaluation of character with audience sympathy or antipathy. Our judgments of character are based on our interpretation of the textual evidence but

Eagleton (2003: 155) asserts that "we can, in fact, feel for those whom we find disagreeable," and offers Flaubert's Emma Bovary as an example; he suggests that being human is the only characteristic necessary for the evocation of pity. Suzanne Keen (2007: 74–76) describes how some readers report empathizing with "unsavory" or "demonized" characters, including those who are minor rather than central characters.[59] Similarly, Smith (1995: 103–4) theorizes that Hitchcock's film *Saboteur* provokes viewers' empathy with the "repugnant" eponymous character by showing close-ups of his terrified face as he falls to his death from the Statue of Liberty.

Caracciolo (2016: 42) has argued that readers feel free to empathize with many different kinds of characters because empathy with fictional persons is low-stakes. He writes, "fiction provides a safe haven for entertaining—and experimenting with—experiences, beliefs, and values that we tend to discard or regard as unacceptable in real life." With this conclusion, Caracciolo builds on Keen's contention that textual cues about a narrative's fictionality unleashes readers' empathy because it allows them to abandon the self-protective skepticism or suspicion that they might feel if the characters were real people.[60] All this suggests that Iliadic audiences may feel both sympathy for and empathy with a wide range of characters, even those who act badly. Moreover, empathy may be activated by aspects of the narrative that signal its fictionality, such as the formal naming of characters with epithets or the conspicuous presence of divinities.

Keen (2007: 71) identifies one more narrative feature relevant to the *Iliad* that appears to prompt empathy: characters' negative emotions. Based on college students' reports about their reading experiences, she writes that "a character's negative affective states, such as those provoked by undergoing persecution, suffering, grieving, and experiencing painful obstacles, make a reader's empathizing more likely." Since the *Iliad*'s thematic emotions are wrath and grief—both expressions, as I argue, of unfulfilled desire—the epic seems to be ripe for inducing its audience's empathy, and particularly its empathetic desire.

Plato provides testimony that Homeric epic could indeed inspire both the empathy and sympathy of ancient Greek audiences. In *Ion*, the eponymous Homeric rhapsode recounts what appears to be his own and his audience's empathetic identification with Homer's characters. He describes how his eyes are filled with tears when he performs something "piteous" (ἐλεεινόν) and how his hair stands on end and his heart thumps when he recites something "dreadful

also determined by the definitions of "good" and "bad" that we choose to apply. Kozak 2017: 18 observes that we can judge characters within our own moral framework and/or within the characters' moral framework—potentially with different results.

[59] Keen also observes that the practice of writing new novels or fan fiction from the perspective of a marginalized or "misunderstood" character finds its basis in empathy with such a character.

[60] Keen 2007: 34, 88, 98, 168. Plato anticipates this argument when he asserts that beholding the sufferings of others in poetry causes us to release the mournful part of our nature (*Rep.* 606a–b). See Peponi 2012: 58–59 and Liebert 2017: 160–61, 168 for analysis of the Platonic passage.

or fearful" (φοβερὸν ἢ δεινόν, 535c), and also reports seeing his audience "crying, and looking fearfully, and amazed at my words" (κλαίοντάς τε καὶ δεινὸν ἐμβλέποντας καὶ συνθαμβοῦντας τοῖς λεγομένοις, 535e).[61]

In his famous critique of poetry in Book 10 of the *Republic*, Plato's Sokrates similarly asserts that we experience empathy—and what seems to be narrative desire too—in reaction to suffering characters in Homeric epic or in tragedy: "surrendering ourselves, we follow along, empathizing and being eager" (ἐνδόντες ἡμᾶς αὐτοὺς ἑπόμεθα συμπάσχοντες καὶ σπουδάζοντες, 605d). Later in this passage, Sokrates also claims that we respond sympathetically, with admiration and compassion, to such representations of grief: "[the best part of our nature] is not ashamed in itself, if another man who purports to be good is grieving inappropriately, to praise and pity him" (ἑαυτῷ οὐδὲν αἰσχρὸν ὂν εἰ ἄλλος ἀνὴρ ἀγαθὸς φάσκων εἶναι ἀκαίρως πενθεῖ, τοῦτον ἐπαινεῖν καὶ ἐλεεῖν, 606b).

Sympathetic desire for characters' wellbeing and empathetic desire in identification with characters not only engage the audience with the epic on their own terms but also amplify the audience's narrative desire. Jose and Brewer, in the same study discussed above, found that when their subjects read a suspenseful story, liking of the story's character (i.e. sympathy) and a sense of becoming the character (i.e. empathy) increased feelings of suspense and, ultimately, liking of the story. They explain this result on the general basis that the more a reader is invested in a character, the more that reader cares about what will happen to that character[62]—that is, the more powerful the reader's narrative desire will be to follow the plot to its denouement.

In my analysis of Iliadic audience response, I identify and discuss two specific ways in which sympathetic and empathetic desires augment and inform narrative desire. If we sympathize and empathize with a character whose desires produce plot and control its direction, our resulting sympathetic and empathetic desires reinforce and amplify our narrative desire, as they all move in alignment toward the same goal—the realization of plot. In these circumstances, we not only are more engaged in the ongoing narrative but also experience greater satisfaction upon the resolution of plot. This dynamic is operative when the *Iliad* provokes our sympathy for or empathy with the epic's central desiring hero and main generator of plot, Achilleus.

[61] See also Liebert 2017: 110–11, who argues that Plato represents Ion's response as "a form of emotional contagion," and Blondell 2018: 115–16, who discusses how rhapsodes "imitated each character... much like a theatrical actor" with the goal of "arousing the audience's emotional engagement with the story and characters." Greek text of Plato is from the online Loeb editions.

[62] Jose and Brewer 1984: 912 and 917. See also Gerrig 1993: 81, who suggests, in his discussion of this study, that identification with characters "encourages the reader to work more actively to imagine how the characters might be able to extricate themselves from the threatening situation." This relationship between engagement with characters and with plot can also go the other way: Keen 2007: 79–80 explains how suspenseful plot can generate a reader's "situational empathy" with a character, that is, empathy related to an unresolved problem that a character encounters in a narrative.

However, if we sympathetically and empathetically engage with a character whose wellbeing and desires are at odds with the direction of the plot, our sympathetic and empathetic desires will oppose our narrative desire. As I show, the appearance of Andromache in Book 6 may generate our sympathetic desire for her safety and happiness, and empathetic desire for Hektor's preservation, both of which conflict with our narrative desire—shaped by tradition and internal prophecies—to find out exactly how and when Hektor will die and Troy will fall. I suggest that this cognitive dissonance gives the audience pause, disrupting the flow of narrative reception and encouraging reflection on the meaning of the *Iliad*'s plot, including its morality.[63] In addition, sympathizing with a doomed character will inflect our narrative desire with pity and fear for that person, transforming it into what Duckworth calls "dreadful anticipation."[64] Again, I understand this complex form of narrative desire to be more intense, keeping us transfixed until we find satisfaction in the revelation and resolution of the *Iliad*'s plot.

Pain, Pleasure, and Satisfaction

Iliadic desire has a complicated relation to pain and pleasure. On the one hand, as we have seen, longing for a lost love object, yearning for lamentation, and aggressive desire are linked with the largely unpleasant emotions of grief and anger. Moreover, the epic associates sexual *erōs* and the goddess Aphrodite with madness, sleep, death, and violence, and depicts these feelings subduing and undoing the desiring subject.[65] On the other hand, sexual yearning (*himeros*) is repeatedly characterized as "sweet" (γλυκύς, 3.139, 3.446, 14.328), and Achilleus calls anger (*cholos*) "sweeter than honey" (γλυκίων μέλιτος, 18.109);[66] Rana Liebert (2017: 60) suggests that there is a "self-destructive pleasure" in desire's "deferral" of satisfaction.[67] Additionally, the fulfillment of desire is represented as an enjoyable experience through use of the verb *terpomai* ("take pleasure") in its alpha-stem form (*tarp-*) to describe hitherto desiring subjects "taking satisfaction" of

[63] Cf. Caracciolo 2016: 44–50, who theorizes that a reader's empathy with a character who holds a very different worldview from the reader causes "cognitive dissonance," which in turn "fuels interpretation."

[64] Duckworth 1933: 37 and *passim*.

[65] Pironti 2007: 209–31. For these associations in early Greek epic and lyric more generally, see Liebert 2017: 52–60.

[66] Similarly, Plato's Sokrates includes desire (*pothos* and *erōs*), and also anger (*orgē*) and lament (*thrēnos*), in a list of psychic pains that have "unmanageable pleasures" (ἡδονῶν . . . ἀμηχάνων) mixed in with them (*Prt.* 47d–48e).

[67] Cf. Telò 2020: 26–27 on the *jouissance* of the death drive, which finds satisfaction in endless repetition rather than in self-mastery and self-preservation (the goal of the life instinct and source of its pleasure).

sexual intercourse, nourishment, lamentation, or sleep.[68] Elsewhere, however, the poem is more neutral about the resolution of desire, describing satiation (*korennumi, aō*) of food, lamentation, and violent conflict, "putting away *erōs*" for food and drink and for lamentation, and, once, *himeros* for lamentation leaving the body (24.514).

Given the painfulness, or at best, ambivalence of desire within the *Iliad*, how do desiring audience members—and particularly those desiring empathetically—endure listening to the poem? In the passage from Plato's *Republic* cited previously, where Sokrates asserts our empathetic, sympathetic, and desirous responses to Homeric and tragic representations of grieving characters, he also maintains that "we enjoy" (χαίρομεν) the experience and that "we praise as a good poet the one who especially disposes us in this way" (605d). That is, Plato conceives of audiences taking pleasure in the painful desires and emotions generated by their affective and cognitive engagement with epic and tragic characters. Liebert proposes that this variety of "tragic pleasure" derives from the way these intense empathetic and sympathetic feelings increase the vividness of our experience and expand our consciousness.[69]

Even if we share a character's pain, our ability to differentiate between ourselves and the anguished character may help us cope with empathetic desire. This recognition of separateness—key to empathy—allows for a degree of aesthetic distance that may keep empathetic suffering from overwhelming us.[70] We know that the empathetic desire we feel is not truly our own, and that it properly belongs in a narrative sphere that is apart from our reality. All the same, when a character's

[68] On this use of *terpomai*, see further Latacz 1966: 176–91. Weiss 1998: 35–47 argues that *erōs* and its cognates derive from an Indo-European root meaning "to divide (for oneself)"—still preserved in Greek through ἔρανος, the term for a feast to which everyone contributed a share—which came to mean "enjoy," and then "seek to enjoy," i.e. "desire." If he is right, this establishes a fundamental association between *erōs* and pleasure, and also explains the wide usage of *erōs* beyond sexual lust. Sissa 2008: 37–38 contends that one needs to desire first in order to feel pleasure later, but that craving and enjoying are represented as separate, sequential experiences: "Pleasure marks the end of desire... Desire is the past of pleasure. Desire is unpleasant."

[69] Liebert 2017: 112–19, drawing on Altieri 2003. Liebert does not differentiate between the "tragic pleasure" that is provided by epic and tragedy, but I suggest that epic's expansiveness and multiplicity of characters create a more extensive, if less intense and more diffuse, pleasure than the distilled "catharsis" of tragedy. For other explanations of tragic pleasure, particularly in relation to audience pity and fear, see Eagleton 2003: 153–76.

[70] Without acknowledgment of differentness, the sharing of another's feelings may result in "personal distress" rather than empathy. As Keen 2007: 4–5 explains, "*Personal distress*, an aversive emotional response also characterized by apprehension of another's emotion, differs from empathy in that it focuses on the self and leads not to sympathy but to avoidance." In the *Odyssey*, Penelope seems to be experiencing "personal distress" when she asks the Ithakan narrator Phemios to stop singing about the homecomings of the Achaians because it "always wears down the heart in my breast, since unforgettable sorrow has overtaken me especially. For, always remembering my husband, I long for such a man as him, whose wide glory stretches throughout Greece and the middle of Argos" (1.341–44). See further Peponi 2012: 33–63 for nuanced and insightful discussion of aesthetic distance and the lack thereof represented in the *Odyssey*.

desire is finally satisfied or, at least, resolved, the empathetically desiring audience will be privy to a corresponding pleasure or release.

While empathetic desire may provide, then, an amalgamation of pain and pleasure for the *Iliad*'s audience, narrative desire seems linked to a purer experience of enjoyment. In the Odyssean episode of Odysseus' encounter with the Sirens, which was discussed at the beginning of this Introduction, the Sirens assert that anyone who listens to their desirable Iliadic song "will depart having taken pleasure and knowing more" (*ὅ γε τερψάμενος νεῖται καὶ πλείονα εἰδώς*, *Od.* 12.188). Here the *Odyssey* not only depicts the Sirens' song as a source of pleasure but also specifically connects this pleasure with the acquisition of knowledge—that is, the realization of narrative desire.[71] This pleasure may be identified as the cognitive gratification of gaining full narrative understanding (resolving interpretive puzzles, unlocking meaning) or more simply as the joy of enlarging one's knowledge of the world through stories.

Differently, Brewer and Lichtenstein (1982: 480–82) explain their experimental finding that readers enjoy suspenseful stories on the basis of the psychologist Berlyne's theory of pleasure, which proposes that enjoyment is produced by the elevation of arousal followed by its reduction. According to the authors, this pleasurable "arousal-boost-jag" is what readers experience when they feel narrative suspense and then have it resolved.[72] In this interpretation, narrative desire and its subsequent fulfillment together produce a pleasure that is affective—rather than intellectual—in nature.

Brewer and Lichtenstein seem to imagine narratives offering a single and discrete sequence of suspense and resolution, yet narrative desire and its satisfaction may be better conceived of as an arc—or, in the case of the *Iliad*, multiple arcs. Unlike other desires, which aim toward a single instance of fulfillment (sexual union, consumption of food, killing of the enemy), narrative desire begins to be satisfied almost as soon as it has been aroused as the audience incrementally gains knowledge of the unfolding plot. Moreover, in a complex narrative such as the *Iliad*, even as the desire for one part of the story is realized, desires for further parts of the story are stimulated or ignited anew. This repeated arousal of narrative desire and its progressive satisfaction through the revelation of the

[71] Therefore, I think that Redfield 1994: 220 makes a false distinction when he writes, "poetry offers not *gratification* but *intelligibility*. In tragic art, the pains and terrors of life are transformed from experiences to objects of knowledge" (my italics). The *Odyssey* repeatedly links together gratification and knowledge as the rewards of epic poetry. Cf. Liebert 2017: 41–43, who observes that the Sirens' promise of knowledge may be false since we have no way of determining the reality of the knowledge they claim to confer.

[72] Cf. Meyer 1956, who theorizes that in music, "Affect or emotion-felt is aroused when an expectation—a tendency to respond—activated by the musical stimulus situation, is temporarily inhibited or permanently blocked" (31). He further argues that one has a pleasant emotional experience when one believes that one's emotion will be resolved (18–20).

epic's plot may bring continuous pleasure—both cognitive and emotional—to the *Iliad*'s audience.[73]

Yet our sympathy for doomed characters, like our empathetic suffering, finally complicates that pleasure. When our sympathetic desire for a character's well-being is partially or fully disappointed as the plot reaches its denouement, a sense of pain and frustration inflects our narrative satisfaction. This feeling, I submit, rather than detracting from our narrative experience, adds to it gravity and value. An entirely happy ending, while eminently pleasurable, is also facile and fantastical. As Achilleus reminds Priam during their culminating encounter, suffering is an ineluctable part of the human condition, and the best we can hope for is to receive a mix of good and evil from Zeus's two urns (24.525–33). Thus the epic's refusal to satisfy the audience's sympathetic desires contributes to its realism and gives it greater seriousness and human meaning.[74]

Narrative desire is, ultimately, the desire for the end of the story and thus for the end of desire itself.[75] Reaching those twin ends furnishes the maximum but also final pleasure offered by a narrative. The *Iliad*'s mythical counterpart, the Sirens' song, apparently denies those terminations, holding audiences so enthralled that they stay on the singers' island until they reach instead the ends of their lives, giving the lie to the Sirens' promise of departure (*Od.* 12.39–54).[76] Such indefinite prolongation of audience desire and its ongoing satisfaction, with the attendant pains and pleasures, is what makes the Sirens' song a true reflection of the *Iliad*. The epic withholds the end of its story, not only through its monumental 15,693 lines of narrative but even, as I will show, in its conclusion, eternally captivating and enchanting audiences.

[73] See also Liebert 2017: 61, who writes, "Poetic pleasure on this account consists of prolonged desire only intensified through its continual fulfillment—more of the story (or of the music and dance) only strengthens its psychic and physical hold on the audience. The poet arouses a longing to hear his poetry even as he satisfies it." Cf. Christensen 2019: 143, who argues with reference to the *Odyssey* that a story must have an ending to make it pleasurable.

[74] Cf. Eagleton 2003: 26–27 on tragedy's capacity to illuminate the value of human life.

[75] Brooks 1984: 52, 58. See also Flatt 2017: 389.

[76] On the danger of the Sirens' song, see also Pucci 1987: 210–14 and Doherty 1995: 60–62. On the ambivalence of erotic and poetic enchantment in archaic Greek literature more generally, see further Liebert 2017: 52–59.

1

Triangles of Desire at the *Iliad*'s Opening

After a brief proem, the *Iliad*'s main narrative begins in Book 1 with two successive and interlocking triangular conflicts between men over the possession of a woman. Scholars have long recognized the opening dispute between Chryses and Agamemnon over Chryseis as a miniature paradigm for the subsequent quarrel between Achilleus and Agamemnon over Briseis, which is the epic's main subject.[1] In this chapter, I show how similar longings and aggressive desires, which are expressed primarily through the emotions of grief and anger, underlie these parallel devastating conflicts, and how the first initiates the second. In this way, *Iliad* 1 introduces desiring subjects as generators of an epic plot defined by discord, suffering, and death—and more desire, as Achilleus vows to inspire the Greeks' longing (*pothē*) for himself. I also demonstrate how the poet encourages our sympathy for and empathy with the aggrieved Chryses and Achilleus, and arouses our narrative desire to find out how their wrongs will be righted.

The First Triangle: Chryses, Chryseis, and Agamemnon

The priest Chryses appears on the Iliadic stage, at the Achaian camp, already in a state of desire. According to the narrator,[2] he comes to the Greek ships in order to ransom his enslaved daughter (1.12–13). Chryses, therefore, is implicitly motivated by a longing for his captured child (Chryseis) and by a corresponding desire to oblige the Achaians to return her.

These two interconnected desires are manifest in the priest's actions and words. He brings "boundless ransom" that encourages the release of his daughter by providing compensation for her value. When he "entreats" (*λίσσετο*)[3] the whole army, and particularly its leaders, the two sons of Atreus,[4] to accept his ransom

[1] Schadewaldt 1966 [1938]: 144–48; Lord 2000 [1960]: 188–89; Segal 1971b: 102–3; Scully 1986: 142–48; Stanley 1993: 39–50; Rabel 1997: 38–42; Wilson 2002: 43, 64–67.

[2] In this chapter, and throughout the book, I distinguish between the external "narrator" who recounts the action and "the poet" or "Homer," that is, the creative author(s) who crafted the narrative.

[3] As Alden 2000: 191–99 has shown, *λίσσομαι* ("to entreat") does not independently indicate the ritual gesture of supplication; she argues convincingly that Chryses does not perform a supplication here since there is no account of the ritual gestures of the suppliant (207), *contra* Thornton 1984: 113.

[4] Chryses' specific address to Agamemnon and Menelaos together points to the roles of both brothers in creating the circumstance for his entreaty. While Agamemnon is the one with Chryseis in his possession, as we soon discover, Menelaos' attempt to reclaim his stolen wife from Paris has

Desire in the Iliad: *The Force That Moves the Epic and Its Audience*. Rachel H. Lesser, Oxford University Press.
 DOI: 10.1093/oso/9780192866516.003.0002

and free his daughter (15–21), he begins with a polite wish that the gods might give them victory over the Trojans and a safe homecoming, which is meant to make them more well-disposed toward him and his plea. In this speech, Chryses also asserts his rightful intimacy with his daughter by referring to her with the kinship term "child" (παῖδα) coupled with the adjective *philos*, "close" or "dear" (φίλην).[5] Moreover, he strengthens his entreaty and invokes the Greeks' piety by carrying the fillets and scepter of his patron god Apollo (14–15), and by ending his speech with a call for his addressees to "respect the son of Zeus, the far-shooter Apollo" (21). These last words also constitute a veiled threat of Apollo's retribution should his petition be refused, in a hint of the aggressive quality of the "homosocial" desire that he directs at the Achaians. In this opening scene, then, Homer introduces a triangle of desire with Chryses as the desiring subject, Chryseis as the desired object, and the Greek army as the rival responsible for Chryses' loss.

Yet it immediately becomes clear that Chryses' rival is more properly Agamemnon than the Greek army as a whole. The Achaian troops express their approval of the ransom agreement, but Agamemnon is not pleased with Chryses' offer (1.22–23). Agamemnon's following speech reveals that Chryseis is his slave and concubine, and that he has the authority to accept or decline Chryses' ransom.[6] The priest's powerful plea, however, positions Chryses as an obstacle to Agamemnon's continued enjoyment of his concubine. Chryses' connection to Apollo, as well as the army's support for his mission, strengthens his standing vis-à-vis the Achaian leader.[7]

Agamemnon's response to Chryses' appeal shows that the pressure to give up Chryseis has activated his own desire for her and a consequent aggressive impulse

brought the Achaians to the Troad and thus led to Chryseis' captivity. Menelaos' desire functions as a first cause of this opening conflict, as well as of the *Iliad*'s narrative as a whole, although he does not emerge as an important character until Book 3.

[5] The terms *philos*, *phileō*, and *philotēs* are used in early Greek poetry to describe a range of interpersonal relations: kinship by blood or marriage, sexual intercourse, military fellowship, alliance, guest-friendship, the concord guaranteed by a peace treaty. Their common factor is the closeness or connectedness of the parties involved; I understand this intimacy to be the primary meaning of the *phil-* root in the *Iliad*, from which emotional implications of friendliness and love have been derived as secondary meanings. While many have argued that *philos* refers to a specific social connection (such as guest-friendship), with attendant duties and benefits (Glotz 1904: 139; Adkins 1963: 30–37; Benveniste 1973: 273–82; Sinos 1980: 41–42; Taillardat 1982), I see the core meaning of *philos* as more relational than social, i.e. defining a relation between people, and between people and things, but tied neither to a particular cultural institution nor to certain interpersonal acts or obligations. My definition is congruent with the etymology proposed by Schwartz 1982: 194–95, and overlaps with the entries in the *LfgrE*, deriving from the same methodology; cf. Aristotle for a similar meaning of *philia* (*Nic. Eth.* 1161b11–1166a30). The fact that *philotēs* can represent non-consensual sexual intercourse in epic diction (Pironti 2007: 46–53) seems to discount arguments for the priority, or even exclusivity of the *phil*-root's affective meaning (Hooker 1987; Robinson 1990; Konstan 1997: 28–31).

[6] Elmer 2013: 63–74 argues that the army's collective will is prescriptive, and that Agamemnon violates the political norm in subsequently asserting his personal will.

[7] See also Scodel 2008: 127–28, who interprets Chryses' invocation of Apollo and the army's attempt to dictate Agamemnon's response as a face-threat to Agamemnon.

to master Chryses as his rival. Agamemnon threatens to injure Chryses if he does not leave the camp, and he refuses to release the priest's daughter (1.25–29). Furthermore, in an aggressive boast of his power over Chryseis, directed at Chryses,[8] the Greek leader asserts that she will spend her life in captivity in Argos, "going back and forth at the loom and visiting my bed" (ἱστὸν ἐποιχομένην καὶ ἐμὸν λέχος ἀντιόωσαν, 31). With these words, he negates Chryses' association with his daughter, referring to Chryseis with middle and active participles that position her responding to his own needs rather than as the priest's child or by the proper name that links her with her father.[9] At the same time, this description indicates her economic and sexual worth to him, and by refusing to exchange Chryseis for material wealth, Agamemnon rejects her commodification and signals that he wants *her*.[10] Agamemnon's concluding line ordering Chryses to go away "or else" (32) repeats his opening warning to the priest, creating a ring around his image of Chryseis as his concubine in Argos. This narrative shape locates desire for Chryseis at the core of this dispute between men, signifying how Agamemnon's aggression toward the father derives from libidinal investment in the daughter.

The relation between Chryses and Agamemnon exhibits the dynamic that René Girard calls "internal double mediation." "Internal mediation" describes a situation in which the desiring subject and rival—whom Girard terms the "mediator" since he "mediates" the subject's desire for the object—occupy the same social universe, as do Chryses and Agamemnon. This allows the subject and rival to be in direct competition for possession of the object in their triangle of desire. "Double mediation" occurs when subject and rival become indistinguishable, both directing desire at one another as they vie for the same object; this is clearly the case with Chryses and Agamemnon. Their reciprocal triangle is distinct from the simpler scenario of desire emanating from only one party, which was the initial situation when Chryses approached the Achaian camp as a desiring subject attempting to reclaim Chryseis from the Greek army.[11]

The voice and subjectivity missing from this triangle of desire is Chryseis'. As Irene de Jong (1987b: 110) has noted, Chryseis is one of the *Iliad*'s silent characters, and this reflects her lowly social position as a foreign female captive, even if she comes originally from a relatively high-status priestly family. We never get any direct insight into her psychology. In its beginning, the *Iliad* establishes the

[8] Wöhrle 2002: 232 and 236.

[9] As Reinhardt 1961: 50–51 explains, her name means either "daughter of Chryses" or "girl from Chryse," the hometown of both father and daughter.

[10] Cf. Wilson 2002: 26, who argues that by offering ransom (*apoina*), family members are trying to preserve the "person" status of a female captive, keeping her from becoming prestige wealth equivalent to cattle or luxury goods. Conversely, if the captor accepts their offer, he also accepts the equivalency of the captive with those prestige goods, which Agamemnon declines to do here. See also Scodel 2008: 80 and 128.

[11] Girard 1965: *passim*, esp. 9 for "internal mediation"; 99–102 for "double mediation."

woman as a desired object, and the normative female as disempowered, her interiority irrelevant. Men alone are agents and desiring subjects.

In this capacity, they are also producers of plot, as becomes evident in the aftermath of Agamemnon's dismissal of Chryses. The priest withdraws in fear, but the rebuff only seems to heighten his longing for his daughter and to make definitively hostile the desire he directs toward Agamemnon and the Achaians, which is expressed in a speech-act aimed at revenge. Alone on the beach, he prays to Apollo, "accomplish this wish for me: may the Danaans pay back my tears through your arrows" (*τόδε μοι κρήηνον ἐέλδωρ·/ τείσειαν Δαναοὶ ἐμὰ δάκρυα σοῖσι βέλεσσιν*, 1.41–42). Chryses' tears appear to be manifestations of the intense grief and desire occasioned by his continued separation from his daughter;[12] with his prayer, Chryses takes this libidinal energy and redirects its aggressive component toward the Greek army as a substitute object. Despite Agamemnon's refusal of his offer, he does not differentiate between the leader and his army. Since he is personally weak, Chryses asks Apollo, his divine patron, to act as his champion against the Achaians,[13] and he specifically frames Apollo's violence—his arrows—as equivalent to his own tears of longing.

When Apollo heeds the priest's prayer and sends a plague on the Achaian camp (1.43–53), he accepts the role of Chryses' vengeful surrogate and confirms him as a generator of narrative. As the god is initiating the plague, the narrator twice describes him as "angry" (*χωόμενος, χωομένοιο*, 44; 46); Apollo here assumes the anger that attends aggressive desire, taking on this emotion, like the revenge itself, on behalf of his priest. Chryses' desires therefore cause, through the heart and hand of Apollo, a plot of death and suffering for the Greeks.

The priest's desires in this opening sequence also further activate the audience's desire for knowledge of the *Iliad*'s story after the titillation of the epic's proem. The proem had briefly introduced Achilleus' wrath and Zeus's will as motivating forces and promised a story of devastation, starting from a quarrel between Achilleus and Agamemnon. But instead of immediately recounting that quarrel, the narrator had gone on to report that Apollo first brought the Greek kings into conflict through his plague, and then begun Chryses' story. The desiring priest's unexpected introduction piques our narrative desire both by delaying the revelation of Achilleus' main plot and by initiating a subplot—Chryses' plot of revenge with Apollo against the Achaians. We now want to know how Chryses' story will end and how it will bring about the predicted strife between Achilleus and Agamemnon.

At the same time, we begin to react to—and possibly with—Chryses and his antagonist Agamemnon as we read their minds and evaluate their words and actions. In his attachment to his daughter, Chryses is sympathetic, and his fear

[12] Cf. Stanley 1993: 45 on Chryses' tears.

[13] See also Wilson 2002: 43–45 on Apollo as champion of Chryses.

and tearful distress after Agamemnon's harsh refusal invite our pity. Sympathy encourages empathy with the priest, along with several other factors: the negativity of Chryses' emotions, which has been associated with empathetic response; the briefness of Chryses' characterization, which allows space for the audience to construct him as similar to themselves; and the poet's choice to begin the narrative proper with Chryses' approach to the Greek camp, entreaty, and prayer to Apollo, which aligns the audience with the priest. At the same time, Agamemnon's cruelty toward Chryses and Chryseis, and impiety toward Apollo—in contradiction to the will of the other Achaians—make him unsympathetic and further invite allegiance with Chryses. If we sympathize and empathize with Chryses, we will wish for his reunification with his daughter and share his desire for revenge; these sympathetic and empathetic desires will intensify our parallel narrative desire to follow the course of Chryses' plot.

Kalchas' Inflammatory Mediation

Chryses' revenge plot is relatively short lived, since the seer Kalchas reveals the cause of and solution to the Greeks' suffering during an assembly on the tenth day after the start of the plague. Keith Dickson (1990) has identified Kalchas' role as that of the typical mediator, who offers counsel or insight at a moment of crisis, and whose intervention marks a juncture in the story. Kalchas announces that Apollo sent the plague, "on account of his priest, whom Agamemnon dishonored (ἠτίμησ'), and he did not release his daughter and he did not accept the ransom" (1.94–95). His words constitute a repetition of the narrator's preceding account of the plague and its motivation in lines 33–52,[14] and provide a neat summary of the triangle of desire behind the affliction: two men locked in a contest for dominance over possession of a female object. This narrative mirroring has the function of guaranteeing the authenticity of Kalchas' vision and his subsequent prescription for reversing the plague, and also situates Kalchas as a counterpart to the narrator, with the power to change the direction of plot.[15]

In the prophecy with which he concludes his speech, the seer does just that. He foretells that Apollo will not "ward off shameful destruction from the Danaans" (*Δαναοῖσιν ἀεικέα λοιγὸν ἀπώσει*) until Chryseis is returned to Chryses unransomed, along with a hecatomb to propitiate the angry god (1.97–100). Agamemnon's indication that he plans to return Chryseis (116–17) leads the audience to expect resolution to this opening conflict along the lines of Kalchas' prescription, and begins to satisfy our narrative desire for the ending of Chryses' story.

[14] Dickson 1992: 331–33. [15] Dickson 1992: 329–38.

While Kalchas' intervention likewise promises to satisfy Chryses' longing for his daughter, which has been driving the plot, it reignites, on the contrary, Agamemnon's answering desire for Chryseis and his aggressive desire toward whomever would take her away. The narrator's characterization of Agamemnon as "grieving" (ἀχνύμενος, 1.103) in response to Kalchas' words signifies the longing that the prospective loss of Chryseis arouses. But along with pain, this loss also stimulates an aggressive impulse: Agamemnon's mind is filled with "rage" (μένεος) and his eyes glitter like fire (103–4).[16] The victim of Agamemnon's aggressive desire becomes obvious when he verbally abuses Kalchas during the assembly (106–8); Agamemnon's wrath is directed at the seer because Kalchas has advocated the fulfillment of Chryses' desire and his own consequent capitulation.

After insulting Kalchas, Agamemnon publicly reasserts his attachment to Chryseis, confirming the fact that his homosocial aggression is implicated with desire for a female object. Here Agamemnon finally introduces Chryseis' proper name (1.111), validating her individual personhood and thereby elevating her as his particular erotic object.[17] He then goes on to articulate more clearly his reasons for not initially releasing Chryseis, using the verbs of desire *ethelō* and *boulomai* ("to will," "to want"). He says, "I was not willing (ἔθελον) to take [the ransom], since I very much want (βούλομαι) to have her in my house" (112–13). He explains that he "prefers" (προβέβουλα) Chryseis to his "wedded wife" (κουριδίης ἀλόχου) Klytaimnestra, "since she is no worse than her, either in form or stature or wits or skill at all" (113–15). This appraisal of Chryseis as equal to or better than Klytaimnestra is a strong statement of the worth that Agamemnon imputes to his concubine.[18] It points to the magnitude of his loss, should he give up Chryseis, and the force of his desire. At the same time, Agamemnon's public disrespect of his wife in favor of his concubine annuls the audience sympathy that the leader might have elicited with his grief in the face of pressure to give up a beloved sexual partner.

Ruth Scodel (2008: 130–31) has argued that Agamemnon's high praise of Chryseis—and especially the comparison of her to his wife—is a rhetorical tactic by which he saves face in front of the army. In Scodel's formation, Agamemnon acknowledges that his actions have caused the plague but mitigates his face-loss by

[16] See also Segal 1971b: 100, who remarks on Agamemnon's anger, and compares this image to "the nightlike darkness of Apollo's deadly approach and the burning of the pyres in the night," thus lending Agamemnon's rage an ominous significance.

[17] Naming Chryseis also constitutes an acknowledgment of the woman's relation to her father (see above, n. 9). In this way, Agamemnon admits Chryses' claim to his daughter and prepares the way for his own submission to the priest.

[18] Muellner 1996: 98–99 observes that "a hero's wife in the Homeric hierarchy of value is the most costly and valuable of all exchangeable goods" and argues that Agamemnon's words make Chryseis' value "incommensurable." Wilson 2002: 50 explains that by comparing Chryseis to his wife, Agamemnon transfers her to the "sphere of persons": he now makes clear that when he rejected Chryses' ransom, "he did not reject goods for goods, but goods for a person."

arguing that he was motivated by true desire rather than by selfishness or status-concerns.[19] However, Agamemnon's description of Chryseis' appeal here cannot be interpreted as purely opportunistic since it is a repetition with elaboration in chiastic order of his previous image of Chryseis working at the loom and serving his bed (1.31). Agamemnon first conjured this image in his refusal of Chryses' ransom, and its reappearance here provides evidence of the consistency of his desire.[20]

Nevertheless, since Kalchas has confronted Agamemnon with the necessity of relinquishing Chryseis, the Greek leader reluctantly shifts his libido away from his concubine and toward the other Achaians. Using the very same verbs with which he described his desire for Chryseis, he asserts that his desire to preserve the army is greater still: "but even so I am willing (ἐθέλω) to give her back, if this is better; I want (βούλομ') the men to be safe rather than to perish" (1.116–17). But by going on to demand recompense for giving up Chryseis, Agamemnon makes very clear the competitive nature of his relation with his fellow soldiers. That is, Agamemnon accepts (albeit grudgingly) Kalchas' mediation and the loss of his cherished concubine,[21] but not without a price; his personal sacrifice is predicated upon recognition of his status. He orders the Achaians to furnish him with a substitute prize of honor (*geras*) and he emphasizes the forcefulness of his position by repeating *geras* in three successive lines (γέρας, ἀγέραστος, γέρας, 118–20).

A *geras* is a material form of acknowledgment that brings a hero more honor (*timē*),[22] and this is the first description of Chryseis as a *geras* in the narrative. With this sudden change in language, Agamemnon removes the personhood of Chryseis and thus her status as his erotic object, and instead commodifies her as a war prize that can be exchanged for any other of equal value.[23] By disavowing his desire for Chryseis as an individual, he saves face. In eliding Chryseis' identity, he also dismisses his triangle with Chryses and thereby lessens Chryses' triumph.

Significantly, this dehumanization of Chryseis goes along with a redirection of Agamemnon's homosocial aggression from the foreign priest toward his own people, the Achaian army, who had previously aligned themselves on the side of Chryses in the ransom dispute. Agamemnon sets aside his losing conflict with Chryses over a specific woman whom he must give up, and creates a new negotiation with the Achaians over a generic *geras*—a status competition where

[19] Cf. Wilson 2002: 50–51, who argues that Agamemnon presents himself as the injured party when he compares Chryseis—whom he must give up—with his own wife.

[20] See also Muellner 1996: 98–99, who reads Agamemnon's desire as very real and the basis for his destructive lapse of leadership and the betrayal of his obligations to the army.

[21] *Contra* Dickson 1990: 62, who suggests that Kalchas' mediation is a failure, focusing on Agamemnon's abusive response to the seer.

[22] Van Wees 1992: 69–70.

[23] As Lyons 2012: 55 recognizes, Agamemnon's earlier comparison of Chryseis to his wife Klytaimnestra already suggests Chryseis' exchangeablity, even as it affirms her worth. *Pace* Muellner 1996: 98–99.

he believes he can emerge preeminent. Thus, while this speech of Agamemnon anticipates the resolution of the *Iliad*'s opening conflict, it also introduces the second and central conflict of Book 1, and of the first two-thirds of the epic, as the Greek leader's frustrated desire for Chryseis, now transmuted into an aggressive desire for honor, gives rise to a new development of plot.

The Second Triangle: Achilleus, Briseis, and Agamemnon

The Greek hero Achilleus, by answering Agamemnon's speech on the Achaians' behalf, makes himself, rather than the army as a whole, the main target of Agamemnon's aggressive libido, the leader's rival in a second triangle of desire. Before we turn to Achilleus' reply itself, it is important to observe that Homer has already laid the ground for this positioning and hinted at a competition between the two kings. It is Achilleus who, inspired by Hera, calls the assembly to address the plague and advises consulting a seer about what will make Apollo willing "to ward off destruction from us" (1.54–67). Kalchas then seeks Achilleus' protection in order to speak the truth freely, expressing fear of the Greek leader's anger (74–84). Achilleus promises to shield Kalchas from Agamemnon, and while this is not a direct challenge, Achilleus situates himself in a potentially antagonistic position vis-à-vis the Achaian commander. Moreover, he describes Agamemnon as the one "who now boasts that he is much the best of the Achaians" (ὃς νῦν πολλὸν ἄριστος Ἀχαιῶν εὔχεται εἶναι, 91), avoiding acknowledgment of Agamemnon's real-world status, and suggesting the possibility that Agamemnon's claim to preeminence may be no more than a "dubious boast."[24]

When Kalchas reveals that Agamemnon's dishonoring of Chryses is behind the plague, Achilleus becomes associated with the renewed pressure on Agamemnon to return the priest's daughter and make amends—in a role analogous to Chryses' own.[25] This makes nearly inevitable a future conflict with Agamemnon.[26] And by positioning Achilleus on the side of Kalchas and Chryses, Homer signals to the audience that they should interpret the subsequent escalation between Achilleus and Agamemnon as a variation on the preceding confrontation.

In his response to Agamemnon's demand for a substitute *geras*, Achilleus definitively situates himself in opposition to Agamemnon and as a surrogate for

[24] Kirk 1985: 62. Cf. Griffin 1980: 52–53 on how "Achilles believes, and will very soon say, that *he* is the best man among them." Indeed, traditional epic diction primarily named Achilleus, or perhaps Odysseus, but certainly not Agamemnon, "the best of the Achaians," as Nagy 1979: 26–58 has shown.

[25] Alden 2000: 212.

[26] Scodel 2008: 129 interprets Kalchas' and Achilleus' interchange as an ill-advised and inappropriate face-threat to Agamemnon. *Contra* Taplin 1990: 79–81, who argues that Achilleus' stance toward Agamemnon is justified, since Agamemnon acts improperly toward both Chryses (refusing the ransom and disrespecting him) and the Achaians (not taking responsibility for the harm inflicted and demanding a new prize).

both Chryses and the Achaian army. First, he dismisses the legitimacy of Agamemnon's desire for recompense when he insultingly addresses him as "most acquisitive of all" (1.122),[27] and then he refuses Agamemnon on the grounds that there are no available undistributed prizes, while commanding him to return Chryseis and promising three- or four-fold future compensation should the army sack Troy (121–29). As Achilleus understands, Agamemnon's aggressive desire for status recognition from the army, rather than from an outside player, is socially problematic, because some other Achaian will have to give up his *geras*—and its attendant honor—in order for the Greek leader to receive another *geras*, in a zero-sum scenario.[28]

Achilleus' denial only heightens Agamemnon's desire for dominance and causes him to reject Achilleus' solution, just as he had rejected Chryses' offer of ransom. As Scodel (2008: 132) notes, he wants "face" not wealth, and so Achilleus' promise of future compensation misses the point.[29] Agamemnon warns Achilleus that if the Achaians do not give him an appropriate *geras*, he will go ahead and take his (as yet unspecified) *geras*, or Ajax's or Odysseus', causing anger to whomever he chooses (1.135–39). With this threat, Agamemnon explicitly posits the situation as one in which his own honor depends on another's dishonor, and in which his own resentment is displaced upon another, and he targets Achilleus as a particular victim of his status-rivalry.[30]

Achilleus' response reveals that, though he is fully implicated in male status competition, he has not yet been drawn into a new triangle of desire. Rather, he is driven by a primary desire for honor that is untargeted and, at best, weakly triangulated. As he explains, his libidinal investment in this particular war is tangential: he fights at Troy only in solidarity with the Atreidai, winning honor for them from the Trojans, with whom he has no independent conflict (1.152–60). At the same time, Achilleus makes clear his wish to augment his own status with spoils of war when he insults Agamemnon as "clothed in shamelessness" and "greedy-minded" (149) for threatening to abscond with his (unnamed and seemingly inanimate) *geras* and for always taking the larger prize despite his own greater contribution to the war effort—"I never have a *geras* equal (ἶσον) to you" (163–68). Nevertheless, the hero's final declaration that he will go home to Phthia rather than remain at Troy "dishonored" (ἄτιμος) as Agamemnon profits (169–71) demonstrates that he is ready to look elsewhere to satisfy his competitive desire.

[27] Kirk 1985: 66 calls it "gratuitous" but perhaps "less insulting in an acquisitive heroic society than we should profess to find it." For the view that this is indeed a serious insult, see Pomeroy et al. 1999: 57.

[28] Staten 1995: 23 and 31. See also Elmer 2013: 70, who describes Achilleus here as "a spokesman for Achaean social norms" opposing Agamemnon's "suspension of the order determined by collective will in favor of the privilege asserted by the king."

[29] Similarly, Agamemnon's embassy to Achilleus in Book 9 will offer wealth, but not honor.

[30] Scodel 2008: 133–34.

All of this changes after Agamemnon's next speech, which combines an explicit diminution of Achilleus' honor with a clear declaration that he will take away the hero's concubine, in a reanimation of the triangular mechanism of desire. He begins by telling Achilleus to go home, that he does not need him—he has others, and especially Zeus, to "honor" (*τιμήσουσι*) him (1.173–75). Moreover, he says that he hates Achilleus and his interest in warfare, that if Achilleus is "strong" (*καρτερός*), a god (rather than the hero himself) deserves the credit, and that he does not care if Achilleus feels offended (176–81). With these statements Agamemnon belittles Achilleus and his martial accomplishments, thus denying his claim to prestige. He is now directly attacking the warrior.

But then Agamemnon goes a step further by asserting that he will follow through on his earlier threat to take away Achilleus' *geras*, and this time he specifies that *geras* as a particular woman, Briseis (1.182–87):

> *ὡς ἔμ' ἀφαιρεῖται Χρυσηΐδα Φοῖβος Ἀπόλλων,*
> *τὴν μὲν ἐγὼ σὺν νηΐ τ' ἐμῇ καὶ ἐμοῖς ἑτάροισι*
> *πέμψω, ἐγὼ δέ κ' ἄγω Βρισηΐδα καλλιπάρῃον*
> *αὐτὸς ἰὼν κλισίηνδε, τὸ σὸν γέρας, ὄφρ' ἐῢ εἰδῇς*
> *ὅσσον φέρτερός εἰμι σέθεν, στυγέῃ δὲ καὶ ἄλλος*
> *ἶσον ἐμοὶ φάσθαι καὶ ὁμοιωθήμεναι ἄντην.*
>
> Since Phoibos Apollo is taking Chryseis away from me,
> her I shall send with my ship and my companions,
> but I shall lead away Briseis the fair-cheeked,
> myself going to your tent, your prize of honor, so that you may know well
> how much more powerful I am than you, and also so that another may shun
> to speak on equal footing with me and assert that we have the same status.

When he mentions Chryseis by name and his forced separation from her, Agamemnon re-acknowledges his desire for her. But the momentary admission of his loss of face in his conflict with Chryses has a greater utility. For Agamemnon invokes the earlier triangle only to lay claim to a different position in a new triangle of desire with Achilleus, which he is now initiating. The Greek leader places himself in the spot that, from his perspective, is occupied by Chryses and Apollo: the role of rival, the one who separates the subject from the beloved object, provoking longing. His choice to invoke Apollo rather than Chryses constitutes a statement of his power to inflict pain as well as an assertion of his significantly higher status relative to Achilleus.[31]

[31] Pulleyn 2000: 173; Scodel 2008: 137. Pulleyn 2000: 173 also notes that by mentioning Apollo, rather than Chryses, Agamemnon mitigates his disgrace; in his account he was defeated by a god, not "worsted by an old man."

Agamemnon's diction focuses on the likeness of Chryseis and Briseis, thereby emphasizing the way that Achilleus' longing will replace his own. He uses a parallel μὲν . . . δέ construction to cite Apollo's appropriation of Chryseis as a paradigm for his own confiscation of Briseis. He speaks Chryseis' and Briseis' names, which are derived similarly and share an ending, only two lines apart and in the same accusative case and line position (1.182 and 184), creating a neat rhyme. He also pairs Briseis' name with the adjective "beautiful-cheeked" (Βρισηΐδα καλλιπάρηον), a noun-epithet grouping that almost exactly reproduces, in the same line-end metrical position, his mention of "Chryseis the beautiful-cheeked" (Χρυσηΐδα καλλιπάρηον) in an earlier speech (143). Agamemnon's words show how he intends his seizure of Briseis to hurt Achilleus just as much as the removal of Chryseis has hurt him.[32]

The end of Agamemnon's speech also confirms that his competitive desire drives the creation of this new triangle and development of plot. He says he will take Briseis away so that Achilleus realizes his superiority, and as an example to others who consider claiming equality with him (1.185–87). Up to this point, the argument has been about each hero receiving his due honor (*timē*), without the explicit avowal that *timē* itself—as opposed to the *gera* that can bestow it—is a zero-sum commodity.[33] Agamemnon's use of the comparative "more powerful" (φέρτερος) denies the possibility that both men could be similarly honored, and frames Achilleus' and his own desires for *timē* as a contest in which one will emerge with definitively higher status at the expense of the other. To that end, Agamemnon takes Achilleus' language about *gera* and applies it to *timē*, warning that others do not have status, in the form of speaking rights, "equal" (ἶσον) to himself. This changes the terms of the debate and establishes the quarrel as a hierarchical struggle for symbolic supremacy within a newly scarce economy of honor.[34] And, as Georg Wöhrle (2002: 233) has observed, Agamemnon's seizure of Briseis—as opposed to some other, material *geras*—is meant "to injure not only Achilles' honor as a war hero, but also his honor as a man" (*nicht nur Achills Ehre als Kriegsheld, sondern auch seine Ehre als Mann verletzt*).

Agamemnon's aim to cut Achilleus deeply is successful. Whereas the previous back-and-forth about a generic *geras* had been symbolic and abstract, the naming of Briseis makes the situation personal. If Achilleus had remained relatively sanguine and detached before, now "grief" (ἄχος, 1.188) afflicts the hero. Achilleus' feeling mirrors that of Agamemnon, who was himself "grieving" (ἀχνύμενος, 103) after Kalchas told him that he had to return Chryseis in order

[32] *Pace* Pulleyn 2000: 157, who contends that the two concubines' "parallelism neatly points up how alike and, in a sense, interchangeable the two girls are. Agamemnon will take Briseis if he loses Chryseis because one foreign concubine is much like another." Cf. Dué 2002: 42–44, 49–57 on the links between the histories and situations of Chryseis and Briseis.

[33] See Cairns 2001: 215–16 on how *timē* is not always zero-sum. Cf. Scodel 2008: 16–22.

[34] See also Scodel 2008: 19.

to end the plague. In both cases, this grief appears to mark the kings' powerful longings for favored concubines who are soon to be relinquished. Agamemnon has made Achilleus feel a mirroring desire for a lost female love-object, but the Greek leader does not seem fully to anticipate how he will also inspire in his adversary the same aggressive desires to replicate his pain in others and to redeem his honor.

Indeed, along with grief, Achilleus feels anger toward Agamemnon, who has now become his rival for Briseis and the specific target of his aggression.[35] It would seem that Agamemnon's prospective removal of Briseis unleashes the libido that Achilleus had invested in her, and causes it to be redirected at the Greek commander himself, overlaying and amplifying Achilleus' preexisting competitive desire. He wavers between drawing his sword and killing Agamemnon immediately, or restraining his "anger" (χόλον, 1.192). Only the intervention of the goddess Athene, who—sent by a concerned Hera—pulls him back by the hair and commands him not to commit violence (194–210), convinces him to follow the latter course, "though very angry in my heart" (μάλα περ θυμῷ κεχολωμένον, 217). Achilleus' response actualizes Agamemnon's promise that the king whose prize he takes "will be angry" (κεχολώσεται, 139). It shows that Achilleus is now truly libidinally invested, locked in a second triangle of desire with Agamemnon.

Achilleus' emotion also contributes to the satisfaction of the audience's narrative desire and guides us in our perception of the evolving plot. Now finally we are in the midst of the predicted quarrel between Achilleus and Agamemnon; after almost two hundred lines of verse we are at last treated to our first glimpse of the "wrath" (μῆνιν) of Achilleus that is introduced in the proem as the defining element of the epic's story. The only other character in the narrative up to this point to whom "anger" or "wrath" has been ascribed is Apollo (χολωθείς, 9; χωόμενος, 44; ἐχώσατο, 64; μῆνιν, 75). Achilleus is therefore positioned in analogy to the god, despite Agamemnon's efforts to align himself with Apollo and put Achilleus in the same weak position in which he had found himself as a result of the plague. Achilleus' anger thus helps the audience to continue plotting the hero as the new Chryses who commands the rage and might of Apollo, and to anticipate that he will similarly damage Agamemnon's standing and cause loss of life for the Achaian army, as was foretold in the proem.[36]

Athene's mediation in this second conflict is parallel in certain ways to the seer Kalchas' mediation in the first conflict. Both do successfully prevent (for the time being, at least) further death and derive their authority from connection to the divine world. Athene's mediation, however, is only a partial solution; she forestalls homicide but does not actually resolve the quarrel. On the contrary, she

[35] See also Nagy 1979: 80, who observes how Achilleus' *achos* leads to his *mēnis* and then to the *achos* of the Achaians (on which, see "*Pothē* for Achilleus" below).

[36] Cf. Muellner 1996: 96–102, 128–29; Rabel 1997: 39–53; Wilson 2002: 64.

encourages it. She confirms the legitimacy of Achilleus' grievance by echoing his own description of Agamemnon's action as an "outrage" (ὕβριν, 1.203; ὕβριος, 214) and by promising that he will receive three-times the gifts in recompense (213).[37] Moreover, she tells Achilleus to continue attacking Agamemnon with words (211). Athene's instigation signals to the audience that this second conflict—in contrast to the first—is only beginning. At the same time, her divine authority guarantees her promise to Achilleus of future compensation, and positions her similarly to Kalchas as an authorial figure determining the story.[38] The audience now knows the endpoint of Achilleus' quarrel with Agamemnon, but little else. Athene's promise-cum-prophecy therefore provokes our narrative desire to find out how and when Achilleus will receive satisfaction.

Athene's intervention also helps encourage the audience to feel for Achilleus. If we initially sympathized and empathized with the aggrieved Chryses in his longing for his daughter and aggressive desire for revenge, the suffering of the Achaian army during the plague promoted a competing sympathy for the Greeks. That conflict of sympathy is resolved when Kalchas reveals that returning Chryseis will also end the plague. And when Achilleus emerges as a representative of both Chryses and the army vis-à-vis Agamemnon, our sympathy naturally gravitates to this hero. Agamemnon's targeting of Achilleus and consequent arousal of his grief and anger directly encourage our care and pity for him. Finally, Athene's agreement that Agamemnon's appropriation of Briseis constitutes an "outrage" confirms the Greek leader as unjust, even as Achilleus' pious obedience to the goddess's directives continue to establish him as a righteous character deserving of sympathy.

With this sympathetic portrayal, and by bringing his thoughts and feelings to the fore, the poet also invites the audience to empathize with Achilleus. The hero's powerful and discursive rejoinders to Agamemnon—and then Athene—focus our attention on him and offer a first glimpse into his psychology, inciting us to read his mind. Indeed, Achilleus' extended quarrel with Agamemnon, which greatly expands upon Chryses' paradigmatic confrontation with the Greek leader, allows us get to know the hero in a way we never did Chryses. As we engage with Achilleus, his intense negative emotions, reported by the narrator and described by Achilleus himself, particularly beckon our empathy. As Achilleus follows Athene's instructions to continue his conflict with Agamemnon verbally, we may begin to identify with the hero, sharing his nascent desires.

[37] Alden 2000: 213.

[38] Cf. Purves 2019: 103–9 on how Athene here wrests control of the plot from Achilleus, keeping him from ending the *Iliad* prematurely by killing Agamemnon.

Pothē for Achilleus

Now Achilleus directs his aggressive desire toward both Agamemnon and the men that follow him. First, building upon his previous allegations, Achilleus launches an outright assault on Agamemnon's honor, calling him both greedy and cowardly—a leader who satisfies his acquisitiveness not through martial heroism but by taking what belongs to others (1.225–30). Yet he also faults the Achaian soldiers for letting their commander get away with this behavior when he calls Agamemnon "a community-devouring king, since you rule among nobodies" (δημοβόρος βασιλεύς, ἐπεὶ οὐτιδανοῖσιν ἀνάσσεις, 231). In this way, he indicates that he holds the whole army accountable for Agamemnon's conduct since they have failed to assert their individual or collective authority in opposition to an unjust exercise of power.[39]

Then Achilleus swears a "great oath" that he will indeed wreak havoc like Chryses and Apollo, but in a slightly different way, in a variation on the earlier conflict. He promises Agamemnon (1.240–44),

> *ἦ ποτ' Ἀχιλλῆος ποθὴ ἵξεται υἷας Ἀχαιῶν*
> *σύμπαντας· τότε δ' οὔ τι δυνήσεαι ἀχνύμενός περ*
> *χραισμεῖν, εὖτ' ἂν πολλοὶ ὑφ' Ἕκτορος ἀνδροφόνοιο*
> *θνήσκοντες πίπτωσι· σὺ δ' ἔνδοθι θυμὸν ἀμύξεις*
> *χωόμενος ὅ τ' ἄριστον Ἀχαιῶν οὐδὲν ἔτεισας.*
>
> Surely at some point longing (*pothē*) for Achilleus will come to the
> Achaians' sons,
> all of them; and then you will not be able in any way, although grieving,
> to help, when many men by the hands of man-slaying Hektor
> fall dying; and you will lacerate your heart within
> because, being angry, you honored not at all the best of the Achaians.

With this oath, Achilleus asserts that he will make everyone else share in his own feelings of desire and accompanying pain. He vows to initiate a homosocial longing for himself as object—"*pothē* for Achilleus"—by, implicitly, leaving the Greek army to carry on the war without his crucial support, in a reaffirmation of his earlier declaration that he would no longer fight for Agamemnon's gain. Achilleus is aligning the other Achaians with Agamemnon and distancing himself from the army together with its leader since the Achaians have refused to stand up

[39] See Allan and Cairns 2011 on Agamemnon's injustice here and on the community's role in the distribution of prizes. Bassett 1938: 198 finds the army at fault for not speaking up against Agamemnon and considers Achilleus' anger toward the Achaians to be justified.

to Agamemnon's unilateral appropriation of Briseis.[40] Achilleus swears his oath on a ritual scepter used, as he says, by judges when they uphold Zeus's laws (234–39), and after he speaks he hurls that scepter to the ground (245–46), in a gesture that gives closing emphasis to his vow and seems to represent his sense that Agamemnon and his army have perverted the justice that the scepter symbolizes.[41]

The longing (*pothē*) that Achilleus seeks to arouse is the first marked word for desire to appear in the *Iliad*, and in this capacity it draws attention to the theme of desire at a key moment in the narrative. *Pothē* almost always indicates a longing for a person who is absent (or dead) and therefore it describes a feeling very similar to the (unnamed) desires of Agamemnon for Chryseis or Achilleus for Briseis, although in the *Iliad* only men—never women—appear as personal objects of *pothē*. After Agamemnon has aroused Achilleus' longing for a woman as a weapon against him, Achilleus responds in kind, but in an unconventional way. Since Achilleus is not in the position to deprive all the Achaians of their concubines, he replaces the female object with a male object and so withholds himself in order to inspire *pothē*.

With this tactic, Achilleus plans to accomplish his retribution through another's hand, as Chryses had done. By withdrawing, Achilleus hopes to enable Hektor, an enemy combatant, to injure the army on his behalf and cause the grief associated with the Achaians' loss of and thus desire for him. Achilleus predicts that without him the Achaians will die in battle, causing Agamemnon to be "grieving" (ἀχνύμενος) just as he himself is now, and leaving the survivors with a doubled longing for their dead comrades and for Achilleus as their protector.[42] Achilleus, therefore, seeks to combine against his adversaries the aggressive strategies of the epic's previous desiring subjects: Agamemnon, who aroused desire in his rival, and Chryses, who brought death to his antagonists through a surrogate actor. With this repetition, he attempts to further a vicious spiral of desire and suffering and to initiate a new direction for the epic's plot.

Yet despite the familiarity of Achilleus' tactics, there is also something unusual about his vow of withdrawal. Leonard Muellner (1996: 123) has remarked on the extraordinary manifestation of Achilleus wrath (*mēnis*), in that it is passive and

[40] Muellner 1996: 114–16 notes that while Achilleus "divorces himself" from the Achaian (mortal) community, he brings himself closer to the immortal community of the gods by obeying Athene's edict. This prepares for Achilleus' supplication of Zeus through his mother Thetis.

[41] Allan and Cairns 2011: 117.

[42] See Nagy 1979: 69–83 on how Achilleus takes power (*kratos*) away from the Achaians, gives it instead to the Trojans, and replaces that *kratos* with *achos*. Kozak 2017: 26 observes that Achilleus here introduces Hektor for the first time to the audience, and argues that he "constructs Hektor as the epic's *real* antagonist, beyond this quarrel between Achilles and Agamemnon" (her italics), arousing the audience's desire to meet the Trojan hero. While this reference to Hektor does put the present internecine conflict in the context of a larger war with Trojan enemies, Achilleus' invocation of Hektor seems designed rather to draw attention to his own indispensability.

marked by negation rather than actively realized through force (*biē*).[43] Achilleus promises *not* to fight, rejecting this primary performance of heroic masculinity, which had previously provided the basis for his claim to status, and with it the masculine world of the battlefield and the society of his heroic male peers. The gender deviance of Achilleus' plan is manifested in his voluntary adoption of a position that had previously been held by enslaved female concubines: he gives up membership in the army to make himself instead the object of that army's desire. In this way, Homer begins to characterize Achilleus as queer, and therefore signals to the audience that Achilleus will be a force of social disruption undermining the Achaian status quo.

The last part of Achilleus' oath makes clear that his paradoxically passive aggression reflects not only a newfound desire for revenge but also an intensification of his previously held desire for status. Achilleus vows that the Greek leader will suffer for not honoring "the best of the Achaians," countering Agamemnon's earlier contention of self-sufficiency and superiority with his own hierarchical language. Achilleus' use of the superlative "best" (ἄριστον, 1.244) leaves no space for Agamemnon to possess the highest *timē*; Achilleus wants to be recognized as the *most* valuable member of the Greek army after suffering injury to his prestige. By promising to take away Briseis, Agamemnon has dramatically escalated Achilleus' competitive desire and definitively focused it toward himself and his army. The quarrel between the two men, like the previous one between Chryses and Agamemnon, has acquired the dynamic of "internal double mediation." Achilleus swears to cause the Greek leader pain and claims the title of "best of the Achaians" while the narrator describes Agamemnon as "waxing wroth" (ἐμήνιε, 247), in symmetrical resonance with the thematic "wrath" (μῆνιν) of Achilleus, which appears as the first word of the epic.

Nestor's Ineffective Intervention

This is the point at which the old king Nestor intervenes as a mortal counterpart to the previous divine intercessor, Athene, sharing with her a position structurally parallel to Kalchas' in the earlier dispute. The poet indicates the narrative analogy of Nestor and Kalchas by introducing both men's speech with the identical formulaic line: "with kind intentions he spoke out and addressed them" (ὅ σφιν ἐϋφρονέων ἀγορήσατο καὶ μετέειπεν, 1.73 = 253).[44] Nestor's introductory characterization as a honeyed speaker (249) and his ability to recite heroic narratives

[43] Muellner 1996: 123–32 focuses on the role of Zeus (who empowers Hektor against the Achaians) as the true actor on Achilleus' behalf. Cf. Wilson 2002: 60–61 on Achilleus' choosing *mētis* instead of *biē* as a tactic to defeat Agamemnon.

[44] Dickson 1990 identifies this formula as one associated with the figure of the mediator in Homer.

figure him as a quasi-epic singer, and, similarly to Kalchas, suggest his affinity with the *Iliad*'s narrator.[45] Like Kalchas, Nestor communicates to Agamemnon that he ought to give up the desired female object in order to resolve the conflict. Nestor, however, lacks the divine clout of the seer and ultimately echoes Agamemnon's own language and values, situating himself closer to his quarreling social peers than to the authoritative and generative role of the narrator. These variations on Kalchas' intervention encourage the audience to expect a different outcome and help us track Nestor's failure to resolve the conflict and redirect the plot.

Nestor's approach to re-establishing harmony is to disrupt the "internal double mediation" of Achilleus' and Agamemnon's symmetrical competitive desires by introducing a wider context to their conflict. First he reminds the two kings that their quarrel will be a delight to their real enemies, the Trojans, thereby attempting to redirect their aggressive impulses toward the goal of the expedition (1.255–57).[46] Then he tries to counteract their "internal mediation" by offering alternative "external mediators" instead. Girard defines "external mediation" as the circumstance in which the "mediator"—the third party at whom, in his model, the subject focuses mimetic desire—is in fact outside of the subject's immediate universe and thus can never be construed as a direct rival for the desired object.[47] An "external mediator" can be an historical person, an object of legend, or even a fictional character.

In this episode, Nestor invokes Greek heroes from an earlier generation as other and better models for Agamemnon and Achilleus to emulate than each other. In order to do so effectively, Nestor coopts and one-ups Agamemnon's own competitive diction, but changes its referent away from Achilleus. He introduces Perithoos, Dryas, Kaineus, and Theseus as his former peers, and, in a punchy line-opening anaphora, twice asserts that they were "the strongest" (κάρτιστοι, 266 and 267), even adding for good measure that they also fought against "the strongest" (καρτίστοις, 267), the monstrous centaurs; these human and bestial mythical characters are the only ones to whom Nestor awards superlatives in his speech.[48] He also twice claims that the mortal heroes were superior to the men of the present generation (262–65; 271–72), which implicitly includes both Achilleus and Agamemnon. Nestor asserts that these paradigmatic substitute "mediators" acted deferentially to Nestor himself and took his advice (260–61; 273). This behavioral model of reverence for his own judgment is what Nestor hopes to

[45] Dickson 1992: 339–49. See also Martin 1989: 101–9 on Nestor's superlative speaking skill, command of multiple speech genres, and resemblance to the epic poet.

[46] Segal 1971b: 92 argues that Nestor's following heroic *exemplum* is also meant to serve this purpose by recalling "the image of a unified heroic society undividedly directing its energies against an external aggressor."

[47] Girard 1965: 9–10 and *passim*.

[48] Segal 1971b: 92 notes Nestor's variation here on the adjective used to describe Achilleus, but interprets it as a reminder of Achilleus' greatness rather than a diminution of that greatness in comparison to heroes of old.

instill in the minds of the two Achaian kings.[49] Just as the heroes of old "obeyed" (πείθοντο, 273) Nestor's speech, Agamemnon and Achilleus should also "obey" (πίθεσθ', 259; πίθεσθε, 274) his injunctions, since it is better "to obey" (πείθεσθαι, 274). Nestor's two imperatives for obedience are in the same metrical position in the first colon of the line and frame his mythical *exemplum*.

After promoting his authority, Nestor tries to arrange a resolution to the conflict, yet he fails to be independent and objective. He tells Agamemnon to refrain from taking Briseis, since the army has given her to Achilleus as his *geras*, and he orders Achilleus to give up his status-rivalry with Agamemnon, "since not ever does a scepter-bearing king, to whom Zeus has granted triumph, have as his portion the same honor" (ὁμοίης ἔμμορε τιμῆς, 1.275–79). Although Nestor here repeats Kalchas' admonition for Agamemnon to give up a woman, he does it within the linguistic and social framework already established by Agamemnon.[50] When he mentions Zeus's favoring of supreme kings, he seems to confirm Agamemnon's earlier assertion that Zeus will honor him (175). He even more clearly echoes Agamemnon's previous words in his subsequent affirmation that Achilleus is "strong" (καρτερός) because of his divine heritage, but that Agamemnon is "more powerful" (φέρτερος) by virtue of ruling over more people (280–81).[51] Nestor seems intent on acknowledging Agamemnon's claim to higher status in order to compensate for the commander's face-loss in surrendering one prize and not receiving another. This undermines his impartiality and subverts his attempt to change the direction of the plot.

Indeed, Agamemnon refuses to admit the difference between his own desires and Nestor's. Ignoring Nestor's admonition to halt his anger and appropriation of Briseis, Agamemnon praises the old king's speech as "proportionate" (κατὰ μοῖραν, 1.286) and picks up on his statement that Achilleus should not compete with him for status, immediately claiming that Achilleus' desire for honor is actually a desire to seize control over the army. He asserts (287–89),

> ἀλλ' ὅδ' ἀνὴρ ἐθέλει περὶ πάντων ἔμμεναι ἄλλων,
> πάντων μὲν κρατέειν ἐθέλει, πάντεσσι δ' ἀνάσσειν,
> πᾶσι δὲ σημαίνειν, ἅ τιν' οὐ πείσεσθαι ὀΐω.

[49] See also Alden 2000: 76–80.

[50] See also Segal 1971b: 93–98, who argues that Nestor's deference to Agamemnon's authority makes him an ineffectual advocate for Achilleus, and Wilson 2002: 63, who recognizes that "Nestor speaks from the same model of leadership and distribution of goods as Agamemnon does." Cf. Alden 2000: 80–82, who contends that Nestor's paradigm of the Lapiths' battle with Centaurs, which—according to mythological tradition—was provoked by a drunken centaur's rape of Perithoos' bride, is meant at its deepest level as a "veiled" rebuke toward Agamemnon for stealing Achilleus' concubine. This may be true, but it appears to be too veiled to penetrate effectively the consciousness of the enraged Greek leader.

[51] Cairns 2001: 211 writes that Nestor "urges each to consider the legitimate claim to *timē* of the other." See also Lowenstam 1993: 61–65, who includes a bibliography of earlier scholarship on the issue of the two leaders' different sources of *timai* (62 n. 4). For more recent perspectives, see Wilson 2002: 63; Scodel 2008: 139; Allan and Cairns 2011: 118.

But this man wants (*ethelei*) to be supreme over everyone else,
he wants (*ethelei*) to have power over everyone, and to rule over everyone,
and to dictate to everyone, which I think that one of us will not obey.

Using language of desire and emphatic polyptoton, Agamemnon justifies his own aggression on the basis that Achilleus is threatening his power as leader of the army.[52] Moreover, Agamemnon picks up on the key idea of Nestor's speech—his own obedience—and explicitly negates it, while also redirecting his lack of obedience back in the direction of his antagonist, Achilleus. This verbal play marks the seamless imbrication of Nestor's and Agamemnon's speech, and Agamemnon's mastery of their shared discourse. In contrast to Kalchas, who spoke with the visionary and productive voice of the narrator, Nestor's intervention has failed since it is trapped within the terms established by Agamemnon.

Achilleus, in turn, confirms that he will not lower his prestige further through submission to Agamemnon, although he evinces no ambition to rule. Interrupting the Greek commander, he says that he would be called "a coward and a nobody" (δειλός τε καὶ οὐτιδανός) if he yielded to the king in everything (1.293–94). And he turns Agamemnon's words back on him, declaring, "do not dictate to me, at least; for I think that I, certainly, will no longer obey you" (μὴ γὰρ ἔμοιγε/ σήμαιν'· οὐ γὰρ ἔγωγ' ἔτι σοὶ πείσεσθαι ὀΐω, 295–96). Nestor has been proved irrelevant, as Achilleus' desire for honor, like Agamemnon's, rages unabated.

But even if Achilleus will not obey Agamemnon, he will accept the authority of the army to distribute—and redistribute—war booty, although this comes at the price of his own participation in the group. Elsewhere during the assembly, Achilleus addresses Agamemnon specifically, but at this moment he switches to the second person plural and addresses the army as a whole. He says that he will not fight the confiscation of his concubine "since you men, after giving her to me, have taken her away" (ἐπεί μ' ἀφέλεσθέ γε δόντες, 1.299). Here Achilleus definitively implicates the other Achaians in Agamemnon's plan to take Briseis,[53] making clear that his aggressive desire is directed not only at Agamemnon but also at the rest of the army. Whereas Achilleus had entered this conflict as an advocate for the army against Agamemnon, now he has come to view the army as another adversary.

Agamemnon's actual seizure of Briseis cements Achilleus' loss and confirms the hero's aggressive desires to take revenge and recoup his honor by withdrawing

[52] Agamemnon seems to manufacture this idea that Achilleus is trying to usurp his political authority and establish himself as the leader of the campaign, which is nowhere confirmed by Achilleus (Lowenstam 1993: 61 and Scodel 2008: 139–40; *pace* Muellner 1996: 106, 112–13; Wilson 2002: 54–64; Allan and Cairns 2011: 116–20). The two men's competing claim to be the "best of the Achaians" is about prestige, and what Achilleus wants from Agamemnon is the deference that affirms his *timē*.

[53] Wilson 2002: 64.

from battle. The assembly breaks up, and Agamemnon finally makes good on his interconnected promises to return Chryseis to Chryses and take away Briseis from Achilleus, repairing his own brief loss of status. First, he sends off Odysseus in a ship with Chryseis and a hecatomb, and supervises the absolution of the army from defilement (1.308–17). Then, he orders heralds to collect Briseis from Achilleus' tent, and he expresses the aggressive desire motivating this action by threatening violence if Achilleus does not comply: he himself will come to the tent "with more men," and "this will be even more miserable for him" (*τό οἱ καὶ ῥίγιον ἔσσεται*, 325). Achilleus receives the heralds and does not obstruct their mission, but calls upon them as witnesses, "if ever again, indeed, there is need of me to ward off shameful destruction from the others" (*εἴ ποτε δὴ αὖτε/ χρειὼ ἐμεῖο γένηται ἀεικέα λοιγὸν ἀμῦναι/ τοῖς ἄλλοις*, 340–42). In this way, he verifies that Briseis' appropriation means he will no longer fight on the Achaians' behalf in his desire to become properly esteemed as vital to the army's safety and success.

Even as the narrative has been focused during the preceding lines on the competitive desires between men, in this scene capping the conflict of Achilleus and Agamemnon, Homer reminds the audience of desire's triangulation and Briseis' crucial importance. At the moment of Briseis' departure, the narrator gestures toward a mutual attachment between Achilleus and Briseis when he describes her going away with the heralds "unwillingly" (*ἀέκουσ'*, 1.348) and then pictures Achilleus "shedding tears" (*δακρύσας*, 349). This is the first indication in the narrative that the female object can also be subject of her own desires, and draws attention to Briseis' personhood and her relationship with Achilleus. The bT scholia interpret this description of Briseis as a concise revelation of her "husband-loving" (*φίλανδρος*) character, although at this point we receive no further insight into why she wishes to remain in Achilleus' tent. While Achilleus' tears could represent distress over Agamemnon's injury to his honor, I take them to indicate grief over Briseis' loss and authentic longing for her.[54] As when Agamemnon's promise to take Briseis away first sparked Achilleus' grief, then anger, Briseis' actual removal not only causes Achilleus to cry but also marks the definitive rupture of his solidarity with the Achaians: he figuratively and literally separates from everyone else, sitting "apart from his companions" on the seashore (349–50).

Besides emphasizing Briseis' crucial role in Achilleus' quarrel with Agamemnon and the Achaians, this scene helps the audience to comprehend that quarrel as a repetition of Chryses' conflict with the same parties over Chryseis. Here Achilleus, after being deprived of Briseis, echoes the emotions and actions of Chryses after

[54] Homer encourages this interpretation not only by reminding us that Briseis is a real live person, rather than merely a symbolic object, but also through the example of Chryses, who similarly cries after he fails to ransom his daughter (see below). The bT scholia offer both interpretations, on which see Fantuzzi 2012: 102–4. *Iliad* scholia are quoted from Erbse 1969–1988.

Agamemnon refused his ransom offer for Chryseis.[55] Both Chryses and Achilleus shed "tears" (*δάκρυα*, 1.42; *δακρύσας*, 1.349), isolate themselves from other people (35; 349), and retreat to the "shore" of the sea (*θῖνα*, 34; *θῖν'*, 350). Achilleus will go on to successfully seek the help of his mother Thetis in a variation on Chryses' efficacious invocation of Apollo's aid: both "pray a lot" to a god (*πολλὰ . . . ἠρᾶθ'/ ἠρήσατο*, 35; 351) and the same formula marks the divinity's attentiveness in both cases: "thus he spoke . . . and [the god] heard him" (*ὣς ἔφατ'/φάτο . . . τοῦ δ' ἔκλυε*, 43; 357). These structural and verbal similarities confirm for the audience the parallelism of these two triangles of desire, eliciting our narrative desire to see how Achilleus' quarrel with Agamemnon evolves along the lines of the previous conflict, in which Chryses and Apollo inflicted suffering and death on the Achaians.

Finally, this pivotal sequence may deepen the audience's sympathy for and empathy with Achilleus. First, Agamemnon's choice to ignore Nestor's advice along with his actual seizure of Briseis—which is accompanied by a gratuitous threat of force—further alienates us from the Greek leader. Then, Briseis' grief over her separation from Achilleus, whether from care for him or fear of Agamemnon, helps to construct Achilleus as "good" and Agamemnon as "bad."[56] Lastly, Achilleus' tearful reaction to Briseis' removal elicits our pity for the hero, making us wish sympathetically for an end to his suffering. It may also summon our empathetic desires for Briseis' reclamation, for retribution against those responsible for her loss, and for reparation of Achilleus' status. All these desires aim at the same goal as our coexisting narrative desire to discover how the hero will triumph over Agamemnon and the Greeks and gain triple compensation, in a repetition of Chryses' paradigm. If, then, we identify with Achilleus, we experience a concurrence of desire that increases our emotional and cognitive stakes in the narrative and securely invests us in the *Iliad*'s unfolding plot.

[55] Kirk 1985: 88; Rabel 1997: 48–49; Pulleyn 2000: 213–14; Wilson 2002: 65.

[56] Briseis' unwillingness may also generate empathy with her, particularly among female audiences or readers. Emily Hauser's *For the Most Beautiful* (2017) and Pat Barker's *The Silence of the Girls* (2018), which are focalized in part or whole through the perspective of Briseis, represent empathetic responses to the Homeric character.

2
Achilleus' Plot and Divine Determination

This chapter explores how Homer establishes the desiring Achilleus and his divine ally Zeus as the dual authors of the epic's main plot in the second half of *Iliad* 1 despite Hera's resistance. Taking on a bardic role, Achilleus plans the worsting of the Greeks in battle, and secures Zeus's promise of assistance, in a variation on Chryses' aggression. Meanwhile, the resolution of Chryses' conflict with Agamemnon provides a template for the satisfaction of Achilleus'—and the audience's—driving desires. Hera's conflict with Zeus over the fate of the Achaian army at the end of Book 1 represents a third, similar triangle of desire, confirming the narrative pattern established by Chryses' paradigm and positioning Zeus's supreme will (*boulē*) as a crucial divine determinant of plot, even as it introduces Hera's desire as a competing force.

Achilleus' Narrative Agency

Achilleus repeats Chryses' example when he goes alone to the beach and tearfully asks a divinity for help after a beloved woman has been taken away,[1] yet Achilleus, as son of a goddess, is shown to be a privileged character who will have a far greater impact on the epic's plot. On the one hand, Chryses addresses Apollo formally, with epithets and cult titles, and appeals to him on a *quid pro quo* basis; Apollo's reception of the prayer and his pestilential retribution against the Greeks follow at once, with no personal interaction between priest and god (1.37–52). On the other hand, when Achilleus prays to Thetis for honor from Zeus and complains of Agamemnon's affront, he emphasizes their kinship relation, calling her "mother" and mentioning the fact that she bore him (352–56). Thetis acknowledges Achilleus' special claim to her intimacy and attention by "swiftly"

[1] Rabel 1988 and 1997: 48–49 and Robbins 1990: 30 argue that Achilleus deliberately imitates Chryses because he regards Chryses as a model of how to deal successfully with Agamemnon. But we have no evidence that Achilleus knows exactly what Chryses did after Agamemnon's rebuff; in his later narrative of the event, Achilleus says only that Chryses "went back" (πάλιν ᾤχετο, 1.380). Robbins 1990: 7 claims that Achilleus makes the "logical inference" that Chryses prayed to Apollo. Whatever Achilleus may guess, I see the repetitive diction as a poetic device to key the epic's audience into the large-scale repetition that Homer utilizes to structure the development of plot.

Desire in the Iliad: *The Force That Moves the Epic and Its Audience.* Rachel H. Lesser, Oxford University Press.
 DOI: 10.1093/oso/9780192866516.003.0003

(καρπαλίμως) arriving at Achilleus' side, stroking him with her hand, addressing him as "child" (τέκνον), and sympathetically asking him what is wrong (359–63). Achilleus has a closer relation to divinity than even the favored priest and is privy to direct epiphany, as Athene's intervention has already demonstrated.[2] Therefore, a scene of dialogue between Achilleus and the goddess ensues, in an expansion on Chryses' paradigm that confirms the amplified significance of Achilleus and his desires.

This scene features a long speech of Achilleus (1.365–412) that situates him as a narrative agent. In response to Thetis' query regarding his distress, Achilleus begins with what Irene de Jong (1985) has called a "mirror story," (mainly) repeating in summary the narrator's extended account of the epic's story up to that moment (12–348), which was first briefly narrated in the proem (1–7) and following introductory lines (8–12). At points, Achilleus repeats the earlier narrative verbatim (372–79 = 12–16 + 22–25) and other bits of his narration echo or carefully adapt the narrator's version, reflecting Achilleus' own perspective, all the while omitting direct speeches.[3] This third telling of the triangular conflicts over Chryseis and Briseis emphasizes for the audience their central importance, since greater frequency lends more gravity to a given story event in a narrative.[4] At the same time, Achilleus' narration and focalization of this recap foreground his voice and point of view, which were already introduced vividly during the preceding quarrel with Agamemnon, encouraging us further to empathize with him.[5]

Moreover, Achilleus' epic recitation indicates how he shares in the narrator's work of articulating the *Iliad*'s plot. As de Jong (1985: 15–17) has noted, Achilleus takes on an "authorial" position when he repeats the narrator's exact words and insight about characters' motives.[6] This affinity between external and internal narrator is underlined by the fact that their narratives are basically consistent, although Achilleus elides his incendiary support for Kalchas and abusive language toward Agamemnon, along with both Athene's and Nestor's interventions, thus presenting Agamemnon as the unilateral offender.[7] By putting the narrator's

[2] See Segal 1971b: 98–99 for discussion of Achilleus' special connection to the gods.

[3] See the analyses of de Jong 1985: 13–16 and Kirk 1985: 91–92.

[4] Richardson 1990: 85. See also Genette 1980: 113–17. Kozak 2017: 26 observes that this recap "brings the audience up to speed (including late-comers to the performance)" and suggests that before this episode the epic performer may take a break.

[5] Achilleus' obvious closeness to the divine in this episode may also entice the audience's empathy insofar as it brings our attention to his fictionality—or at least his "larger than life" status—and thus gives us permission to identify with him without qualms.

[6] Cf. the confusion of Kirk 1985: 92–93 regarding another repetition of the epic's story after the narrator has just told it at length. De Jong 1985: 11–12 summarizes the earlier scholarly approaches to this speech. For more recent treatments, see Robbins 1990; Rabel 1997: 45–54; Wilson 2002: 68–69.

[7] Scully 1986: 145 n. 14 and Pulleyn 2000: 219. Rabel 1997: 45–57 argues that Achilleus' version is substantially different, particularly in his focus on Chryses' subjectivity rather than on Apollo's agency. According to Rabel, the poet makes Achilleus' point of view "work against" the narrator's, destabilizing the authority of both characters. I do not believe that the narrator's authority is undermined here.

words into Achilleus' mouth,[8] the poet indicates how Achilleus' desires are shaping his epic conflict with Agamemnon and the Achaians.

In fact, Achilleus' speech goes even further to position him as a competitor to the narrator, and endowed with greater narrative agency. The speech's first half does not just mirror the preceding narrative; it also contains a flashback to events before the beginning of the narrator's account. When he relates what happened to Thetis, Achilleus starts with the true origin of Chryses' conflict with Agamemnon and the Greeks, narrating the sack of Thebe, the acquisition of Chryseis, and her allocation to Agamemnon (1.366–69). With this extra backstory, Achilleus demonstrates that he can create a fuller narrative of events than the narrator himself. In addition, we learn that Achilleus was part of the campaign to Thebe—he narrates it in the first-person plural (ᾠχόμεθ', διεπράθομεν, ἤγομεν)—which makes the hero at least partially responsible for the enslavement of Chryseis. Therefore, Achilleus himself not only narrates but also internally generates the story. Achilleus and the sack of Thebe are located at the root of a spiraling *mise en abyme* of conflict, loss, and desire.[9] Later, the *Iliad*'s most explicit image of Achilleus as an epic narrator (9.186–89) depicts him playing a phorminx that he took from Thebe, again connecting Achilleus' production of epic poetry with this originary raid.

In the second part of his speech to Thetis, Achilleus attempts to assert creative control over the future direction—in addition to the past—of the *Iliad*'s plot. The hero asks Thetis to supplicate Zeus on his behalf,[10] and to claim the divine king's assistance in return for the time when she freed him from bonds imposed by Hera, Poseidon, and Athene, and brought the hundred-handed Titan to protect him (1.394–407). This story of conflict among the gods constitutes another flashback external and supplementary to the narrator's main narrative. It testifies to the range of Achilleus' narrational capacity—his knowledge not just of heroic epic material but also of divine mythology, to which he has access through his goddess mother, who "often" boasted of this incident (396–97). Moreover, this narrative demonstrates the power and authority of Achilleus' discourse, as it represents a

Rather, the differences in Achilleus' account serve to emphasize the limits of his mortal perspective, as well as his lack of objectivity, in contrast to the divine inspiration of the narrator. This does not, however, take away from Achilleus' presentation as a powerful producer of narrative, who is perhaps even more effective than the narrator (see the following discussion). Cf. Bakker 2009: 128–36 on the competitive, yet codependent relationship between the external narrator and Odysseus (as internal narrator) in the *Odyssey*.

[8] On the similarity of Achilleus' discourse to that of the narrator or poet, see generally Friedrich and Redfield 1978: 270–78; Griffin 1986: 50–55; Martin 1989: 219–30.

[9] See also Muellner 1996: 118, who argues that Achilleus' new beginning of the story "rebuilds the causality between episodes in preparation for a new episode." Cf. Rabel 1997: 33–34, who understands this starting point as Achilleus' perception of his wrath's origin, thus distinguishing the hero's point of view from the narrator's.

[10] Supplication is a ritual plea that exerts special force on those addressed through its appeal to their pity, shame, and sense of justice. On supplication, see further Gould 1973; Crotty 1994; Alden 2000: 185–99; Naiden 2006.

means for the hero to demand the aid of the king of the gods. It will prove to be at once effective and predictive, as Thetis' role quelling a previous divine revolt does indeed convince Zeus to accept her supplication—sparking yet another conflict between Hera and Zeus.

The end of Achilleus' speech is a straightforward prescription for the course of the plot, in a directive-cum-prophecy.[11] He tells Thetis to request that Zeus empower the Trojans in battle until they hem in and kill the Achaians at their ships so that the Greeks "may enjoy their king" and so that Agamemnon may recognize his delusion in not honoring "the best of the Achaians" (1.407–12). Through this command to his mother, we see how Achilleus, motivated by his aggressive desires, is actively composing and forwarding a plot of death and suffering for the Greeks, in a variation on Chryses' revenge. Achilleus' prospective plot represents a more realized repetition of his earlier oaths in the assembly (240–44) and to the heralds when they removed Briseis (338–42).[12] More significantly, it also repeats and expands upon the story outline presented by the narrator in the *Iliad*'s proem—how Achilleus' wrath brought myriad pains to the Achaians and caused the deaths of many heroes in an accomplishment of Zeus's will, starting from his quarrel with Agamemnon. Once again, Achilleus rivals the narrator, providing the audience with a better sense of what is to come and thus exposing the complicity of the internal character (the desiring hero) and the external narrator in creating the epic.[13] The *Iliad*'s plot is Achilleus' plot.

Thetis' acquiescence completes this episode's echo of the *Iliad*'s proem. She promises to visit Zeus when he returns from a sojourn with the Ethiopians, but orders Achilleus in the meantime to "wax wroth" (μήνι') at the Achaians and cease from fighting (1.419–22). Her injunction employs a verb that has the same root as the first word of the *Iliad*, "wrath" (μῆνιν). In fact, the imperative she uses is almost identical with the poem's first word, and shares the same metrical position at the beginning of the line. The goddess Thetis here appears in the role of the divine Muse, whom the narrator invokes to sing Achilleus' "wrath" in the proem; like the Muse to the narrator, she is Achilleus' divine counterpart and inspiration. Her reply anticipates her important function in forwarding Achilleus' plot through supplication of Zeus.

[11] See also Duckworth 1933: 87–89 on Achilleus' predictive utterances.

[12] See also Kozak 2017: 27 on how this speech "gives the audience access to his character through his motivations and goals."

[13] Connecting the hero with the narrator also helps to emphasize how the hero is integral to narrative coherence. As Barthes 1966: 15 has noted, distinct narrative sequences are linked together not only by their interlocking structure but also by the consistent presence of key characters; he recognizes this kind of structural unity as characteristic of epic. Tomashevsky (cited in Lemon and Reis 1965: 90) has pinpointed the protagonist especially as "the means of stringing the motifs together… he embodies the motivation that connects the motifs." Achilleus' narration of what has come and what will come illustrates how he and his desires tie together not only all three conflicts of Book 1 but also the entire narrative of the *Iliad*.

Homer closes this scene between the hero and his mother with a reminder of Achilleus' motivation for calling out to Thetis and composing his plot for retribution. Thetis leaves Achilleus "angered (χωόμενον) in his heart on account of the well-girdled woman, whom they took away by force against his will" (1.429–30). This psycho-narration once again draws the audience's attention to Achilleus' longing for Briseis and concomitant aggressive desire, emphasizing how these desires drive his plot against the Greeks, and inviting us anew to sympathize and empathize with the wronged and angry hero.

Chryses' Paradigmatic Resolution

Achilleus' conversation with Thetis leaves the *Iliad*'s audience eager to find out whether Zeus will agree to promote the Trojan cause during the hero's absence from battle.[14] Homer, however, delays satisfaction of our narrative desire and intensifies our suspense regarding Achilleus' plot by returning instead to the unfinished narrative of the resolution to Chryses' opening conflict with Agamemnon and the Greek army. This transition results in Chryses' story literally surrounding the genesis of Achilleus' wrath, underscoring their causal connection and drawing attention to the contrast between the first conflict's resolution and the second's development. This sequence also opposes Chryses' story at the margins—as a relatively minor incident in the larger course of the poem—to Achilleus' central story, which is fundamental to the *Iliad* and distinctly unresolved in the epic's first book.

Yet Chryses' resolution not only contrasts with Achilleus' still developing plot—it is also a model for it. As we have seen, Achilleus' conflict has evolved in parallel to that of Chryses, and the interlocking of their narratives also emphasizes their structural similarity. The account of Chryseis' return and the Greeks' sacrifice to Apollo, which gratify Chryses and the god respectively, thus establishes a pattern for resolution to Achilleus' story. As a paradigmatic ending, it creates the terms for fulfillment of Achilleus' desires and satisfaction of the audience's narrative, sympathetic, and empathetic desires as they relate to the epic's hero. The conclusion of Chryses' story thus motivates and guides our continued engagement with the *Iliad* until Achilleus' own story is similarly resolved.

The poet trains us to look forward to this ending by forecasting resolution to Chryses' story early in Book 1, but then repeatedly delaying full narrative satisfaction. Kalchas first introduces this resolution through his oracular instruction for Agamemnon to return Chryseis and sacrifice a hecatomb to Apollo in order to end the plague (1.97–100). Then, Agamemnon's promise to give up Chryseis (116)

[14] See also Kozak 2017: 27, who observes that Achilleus' speech "builds anticipation for Thetis's mission to Zeus."

and have an Achaian leader convey her to Chryse with a hecatomb (141–47) makes us anticipate this eventuality. Our suspense increases when Agamemnon prepares the expedition, designates Odysseus as its leader, and sends off the ship at the conclusion of the contentious assembly (308–12). Now, finally, Homer gratifies his audience together with his characters through an extended narrative of the fulfillment of Chryses' longing for his daughter and the appeasement of Apollo's aggressive desire to punish the Greeks (430–87).

The length, detail, and rhetorical and dramatic features of this episode establish its programmatic importance. The narrator begins with a meticulous and technical account of the Achaian crew bringing the ship into the harbor at Chryse (1.432–35), which creates a vivid picture for the audience and gives this arrival narrative emphasis. Then he employs a storytelling flourish of a quadruple line-opening anaphora (ἐκ δ'[ἐ]) to recount the disembarkation. In a rising crescendo, the anchor-stones are thrown out, the men get out, they drive out the hecatomb, and finally Chryseis herself steps out of the ship (436–39).[15] In this way, the poet presents Chryseis as the figure most consequential to the resolution, underlining the significance of the beloved object in the epic's triangular plots.

The audience's desire is then satisfied by the long-awaited reunion of the priest Chryses and his daughter in a scene that emphasizes their restored intimacy. The narrator describes how Odysseus "put [Chryseis] into the hands of her dear (*philos*) father" (πατρὶ φίλῳ ἐν χερσὶ τίθει, 1.441) before the king goes on to announce his mission to return Chryseis and "propitiate" (ἱλασόμεθα) Apollo with a hecatomb in order to end the Greeks' suffering (442–45). After this brief speech, the narrator repeats with slight variation Odysseus' reunification of Chryseis with her father: "having spoken thus, he put [her] into his hands, and he [Chryses] received his dear (*philos*) child, rejoicing" (ὣς εἰπὼν ἐν χερσὶ τίθει, ὁ δὲ δέξατο χαίρων/ παῖδα φίλην, 446–47). This repetition is made more forceful by the fact that the phrase ἐν χερσὶ τίθει occupies the same metrical position in both instances, as does the adjective *philos*. In the first case, *philos* modifies the father and reflects Chryseis' focalization, while the second time it modifies the daughter, reflecting Chryses' perspective, and the symmetrical reiteration of this adjective highlights their mutual closeness and reciprocal affection.[16]

Chryses' feelings, however, are the major focus of this passage, as he experiences joy (χαίρων, 1.446) in his recovery of his daughter in a reversal of his grievous loss. The narrator's description of Chryseis as *philos* echoes Chryses' own earlier characterization of his daughter when he first came to Agamemnon to offer him compensation (20), and this reverberation serves to contextualize and contrast this

[15] Kirk 1985: 100 observes that the last line "provides a certain contrast and climax through its heavily spondaic rhythm." After the speed evoked by the anaphoric line-beginnings (Kirk 1985: 100; Pulleyn 2000: 233–34), we are meant to pause and feel the weight of Chryseis' climactic arrival.

[16] Pulleyn 2000: 234–35.

moment of reunion with Agamemnon's earlier refusal to give up Chryseis. Here Chryses' delight replaces the tears of longing that he had shed (42) as his separation from his daughter finally comes to an end.

In this scene, the fulfillment of Chryses' longing for Chryseis is firmly tied to the conclusion of Apollo's anger against the Achaians, which had represented the aggressive external displacement of Chryses' desire. When Odysseus leads Chryseis up to the altar in order to deliver her to her father (1.440–41), she is figured as an offering to Apollo meant to avert his wrath. Indeed, Odysseus links the return of Chryseis to the sacrifice of the hecatomb by enunciating them in parallel clauses in the same line (443).[17] The second time the narrator recounts Chryseis' return, he again juxtaposes Chryses' reception of his daughter with the presentation of the hecatomb at the altar (446–48), confirming their semantic equivalence. Indeed, line 447 begins with the word "child," representing Chryseis, and ends with the word "hecatomb."

After receiving his daughter, the priest immediately asks Apollo to end the suffering that he is inflicting upon the Greeks: "again now accomplish this wish for me: at once now ward off shameful destruction from the Danaans" (*καὶ νῦν μοι τόδ' επικρήηνον ἐέλδωρ·/ ἤδη νῦν Δαναοῖσιν ἀεικέα λοιγὸν ἄμυνον*, 1.455–56). Chryses' speech-act is a reversal of his earlier prayer for Apollo's aid, and his repetition of his opening invocation of Apollo (37–38 = 451–52) and injunction that Apollo "accomplish this wish for me" (41 ~ 455) marks this negation.[18] The narrator indicates the success of the Achaian mission by reporting that Apollo again heard Chryses' prayer (43 = 457). With this insistent syntagmatic relationship between Chyseis' return and the ritual appeasement of Apollo, Homer inextricably connects the release of longing for a beloved person with dissolution of the corresponding aggressive desire, achieved through formal deference that affirms the angered party's honor and authority.

The narrator indicates that the sacrifice itself and subsequent feast are key to this final resolution by describing their ritual stages in minute detail.[19] Indeed, Homer utilizes here eighteen of the twenty-one possible elements available in the traditional type-scene; in the Homeric *opera*, only the description of Nestor's sacrifice at Pylos in *Odyssey* 3 is more complete.[20] After the group shares in the

[17] The identification of Chryseis with the Achaians' sacrifice to Apollo is further underlined by the annular symmetry observed by Stanley 1993: 45 between Odysseus' address to Chryses and presentation of Chryseis, and the following narrative of the Greeks' sacrifice, which surround the central event of Chryses' prayer to Apollo to stop the plague.

[18] Kirk 1985: 101–2. Chryses' prayer also echoes and begins fulfilling Kalchas' prophecy that Chryseis' return and the gift of a hecatomb would be the conditions for Apollo to "ward off shameful destruction from the Danaans" (*Δαναοῖσιν ἀεικέα λοιγὸν ἀπώσει*, 1.97).

[19] See Seaford 1994: 42–43 for the structural importance of sacrifice in Homeric epic as a ritual to open, conclude, or "frame" a significant period of time. Here the sacrifice concludes Chryses' conflict, as Seaford notes.

[20] Edwards 1980: 20–21. The twenty-one elements are catalogued by Arend 1933: 64–78. On the typical Homeric feast, see also Reece 1993: 23–25.

sacrificial meal, the narrator reports their satiation twice in contiguous lines: "in no way was the heart lacking in equal feast" (οὐδέ τι θυμὸς ἐδεύετο δαιτὸς ἐΐσης, 1.468) and "they put away their lust (*eron*) for food and drink" (πόσιος καὶ ἐδητύος ἐξ ἔρον ἕντο, 469). These formulaic expressions of satiety draw attention to the way that this ritual enactment effects an end to the desires driving Chryses' plot. This resolution is also marked by celebration and enjoyment: the Achaian young men pour wine (470–71), then conciliate Apollo all day with dance and song, including a paean (472–74); the narrator recounts that the god "took pleasure (τέρπετ') in his heart while listening" (474).[21] Thus the narrative of the sacrifice and festival is framed by twin accounts of Apollo's aural attendance, the last attesting to the pleasure that replaces his wrath. The scene concludes with the men contentedly going to sleep with the setting of the sun (475–76).

Back to Achilleus—and Zeus

After Homer has resolved Chryses' triangular conflict, the epic returns to Achilleus' still developing parallel plot in yet another contrasting juxtaposition. At sunrise, we accompany the Achaian ship back to the encampment at Troy (1.477–87) and find Achilleus "waxing wroth" (μήνιε, 488) and avoiding the assembly and war (490–91), following his mother's earlier imperative (421–22). His aggressive desires for retribution and honor rage on just as Apollo's anger comes to an end. In fact, Chryses' prayer that Apollo "ward off shameful destruction from the Danaans" (456) is directly opposite to Achilleus' earlier warning to the heralds that he himself would *not* be available to "ward off shameful destruction" from the Greeks (341). Although Chryses' story first appeared to encircle Achilleus' conflict with Agamemnon, now we are shown how Achilleus' wrath spills out beyond the delimited arc of Chryses' grievance, engendering a much greater disaster.[22]

This scene also explores the hero's melancholic reaction to loss, as he suffers internally, experiencing his own painful longing (*pothē*). "Melancholia" occurs when a desiring subject identifies with the lost love object and turns against his- or herself the negative libidinal energy associated with that object.[23] The narrator pictures Achilleus in his withdrawal "withering away in his own heart" (φθινύθεσκε φίλον κῆρ, 1.491), in an apt representation of melancholic internalization of aggressive libido. Achilleus is also described "longing (*potheeske*) for the battle-cry and war" (ποθέεσκε δ' ἀϋτήν τε πτόλεμόν τε, 492): Achilleus pines for the

[21] Cf. Apollo's delight when the Ionians celebrate him on Delos in the *Homeric Hymn to Apollo* 146–50.

[22] Cf. Edwards 1980: 24, who writes "The effect of this scene is to enclose the whole Chryse episode between two passages describing Achilles' desolation."

[23] See the discussion of "melancholia" in "The Characters' Triangular Desires" in the Introduction.

fighting that had defined him as an outstanding warrior. Leonard Muellner (1996: 137–38) has called Achilleus' withdrawal an "alienation from self" and Emily Austin (2015: 149) recognizes Achilleus' *pothē* as a longing for that now-missing part of himself, the expression of a "ruptured wholeness." When we understand Achilleus' *pothē* in this way, we can see how the hero is redirecting his longing for Briseis toward and against his self. Although his absence from battle is conceived as an externally oriented act of aggression in response to loss, meant to hurt the Achaian army and arouse their *pothē* for him (240–43), first of all it hurts Achilleus himself and inspires his own unhappy *pothē* for the aspect of his identity that he has renounced.

Achilleus' longing for war draws attention to his separation from the masculine world of the battlefield and community of Greek soldiers. As when he constructed himself as an object of the Achaians' desire, putting himself in a position otherwise occupied by female concubines, here again Achilleus deviates from normative masculinity. While sitting out the battle, he inhabits the same space as female non-combatants, thus becoming identified—physically as well as psychologically—with Briseis and the other slave women in the Greek camp. Homer emphasizes this gender deviance by thematizing the internal conflict that Achilleus' withdrawal provokes. At the same time, this snapshot of Achilleus' angry and painful queer isolation re-energizes our narrative desire to discover how Zeus will respond to Thetis' appeal, and may also reaffirm our parallel sympathetic and empathetic desires for the rehabilitation of the hero's honor.

The audience's narrative desire is immediately satisfied with the following account of Thetis' audience with Zeus (1.493–530), during which Thetis acts as Achilleus' representative and accordingly takes from her son the role that Chryses had played in the epic's first triangular conflict. Complying with Achilleus' imperative to "grasp [Zeus's] knees" in a posture of supplication (*καὶ λαβὲ γούνων*, 407 = 500), she makes a familiar plea: "if indeed I ever profited you among the immortals, either in word or deed, accomplish this wish for me" (*εἴ ποτε δή σε μετ' ἀθανάτοισιν ὄνησα/ ἢ ἔπει ἢ ἔργῳ, τόδε μοι κρήηνον ἐέλδωρ*, 503–4). Here the goddess invokes a *quid pro quo* relationship with Zeus, as Chryses had done with Apollo, and her appeal "accomplish this wish for me," is a repetition, in the same metrical position, of Chryses' earlier entreaty to Apollo (41).[24] She also echoes Achilleus' own words when he had directed her to supplicate the divine king on his behalf, "if indeed you ever profited Zeus's heart in some way, either in word or even deed" (*εἴ ποτε δή τι/ ἢ ἔπει ὤνησας κραδίην Διὸς ἠὲ καὶ ἔργῳ*, 394–95). In this scene, therefore, Thetis expands Achilleus' variation on Chryses' paradigmatic petition of the divine.

[24] Pulleyn 2000: 250.

As she articulates her request to Zeus, Thetis continues to function as Achilleus' mouthpiece, thematizing his aggressive desire for honor (*timē*) as the central motivation for her appeal. In his initial outcry to his mother, Achilleus had wished for "honor" (τιμήν) from Zeus, complained that Zeus now "honored" (ἔτεισεν) him little, and lamented how Agamemnon "dishonored" (ἠτίμησεν) him through the seizure of his *geras* (1.353–56). Likewise, in his final words to Thetis, Achilleus had indicated his vengeful desire for Agamemnon to regret that he "not at all honored" (οὐδὲν ἔτεισεν) Achilleus (411–12). These are the words with which Achilleus ends his speech, making "not at all honored" the last thing he says in the *Iliad* until his reception of Agamemnon's embassy in Book 9. When Thetis begs Zeus to give the Trojans strength in battle, she similarly speaks of her son's honor five times in six lines (τίμησον, ἠτίμησεν, τεῖσον, τείσωσιν, τιμῇ, 505–10): twice she entreats Zeus himself to honor Achilleus, twice she asks him to make the Achaians honor Achilleus, and once she briefly recounts Agamemnon's dishonoring of Achilleus. This last is yet another narrative reiteration of Agamemnon's insulting removal of Briseis (here also only called a *geras*), which stresses again its pivotal function in escalating and focusing Achilleus' aggression, and repeats nearly verbatim Achilleus' own opening lament to his mother (355–56 ~ 506–7). *Timē* is the key term in Achilleus' and Thetis' discourse alike, as Achilleus endeavors with his mother's assistance to redeem his status—and take revenge on the perpetrators of his loss—through Zeus's power.

Up until this point, Thetis has been a spokesperson for Achilleus, but when Zeus hesitates to respond to her supplication, she invokes her own status in order to secure Zeus's cooperation. She demands that Zeus reply, "in order that I may know to what extent I am the most dishonored (ἀτιμοτάτη) god among all" (1.516). With these words, Thetis connects her son's honor among mortals with her own honor in the divine community, and indicates that Zeus's refusal would impugn her standing. Achilleus has already recounted how Zeus owes her honor for saving him from a divine uprising, and here the poet may also allude, as Laura Slatkin (1991: 100–22) has suggested, to Thetis' other service of maintaining Zeus's hegemony by marrying the mortal Peleus and bearing a mortal son who will never challenge Zeus's rule. The favors that Thetis has done for Zeus allow her to claim for herself and Achilleus the alliance of the highest authority in the universe. Zeus wields far more power than his son Apollo, to whom Chryses had appealed directly and on the basis of his own services to the god. Thetis' involvement, therefore, helps make Achilleus' story an amplification, rather than merely a repetition, of Chryses' paradigm, and signals to the audience that Achilleus' aggressive desires are taking on inimitable cosmic force.

This force is confirmed when Zeus agrees to accomplish Achilleus' wish for honor and verifies that promise with his consequential and highly dramatic nod (1.523–30). Wolfgang Schadewaldt (1966: 146) calls this scene "the biggest moment of the book" (*der größte Augenblick des Gesanges*) and understands

Zeus's promise and nod to be divine parallels to Achilleus' oath and subsequent throwing down of the scepter during the assembly (239–45). The nod validates the efficacy of Achilleus' vows both there and in his tent, and proves the prescriptive nature of his later elaboration to Thetis of his plot for revenge and honor. Now that we know that Zeus is collaborating with Achilleus, we conceive a fresh narrative desire to learn how and when the god will bring that plot to fruition.

As Schadewaldt (ibid.) likewise recognizes, this passage also actualizes in a powerfully graphic and symbolic way the proem's account of how "the will of Zeus was being accomplished" (Διὸς δ' ἐτελείετο βουλή, 5) in Achilleus' destructive wrath.[25] That is, this scene fulfills the proem's prediction of Zeus's involvement in Achilleus' conflict with Agamemnon and further delineates the divine king's role, encouraging us to apprehend Zeus's desire—the will of Zeus (*Dios boulē*)—as an extension of Achilleus' motivating desires.

A Third, Divine Triangle of Desire

The last section of Book 1 continues exploring divine desires and their part in producing plot through a third triangular conflict, this time between Hera and Zeus over the latter's promise to devastate the Greeks on Achilleus' behalf. The hero's quarrel with Agamemnon therefore generates this divine discord, just as Chryses' conflict with Agamemnon had led to Achilleus' conflict, in a further spiral of desire and strife that now reaches up to the heavens and acquires cosmic significance. As I will show, Hera's quarrel with Zeus is not only causally connected but also structurally similar to Chryses' and Achilleus' previous conflicts with Agamemnon, featuring multiple correspondences with the earlier episodes.[26]

This third repetition helps to confirm the audience's recognition of the triangle of desire as a key narrative structure. As Peter Brooks (1984: 99) explains, "If we think of the trebling characteristic of the folktale, and of all formulaic literature, we may consider that the repetition by three constitutes the minimal repetition to the perception of series, which would make it the minimal intentional structure of action, the minimum plot." With this quarrel between Hera and Zeus, then, the poet enables the audience to see that the triangular conflicts of *Iliad* 1 represent a significant pattern, and one, moreover, that transcends the human male homosocial world of the Greek camp and competitive desire "between men" negotiated over ownership of a woman. In the divine example, a goddess contends with a god over the fate of mortal men, situating a female divinity as desiring subject and

[25] This is true even if, as Kullmann 1955: 167–70 argues, Zeus's promise to Thetis represents only a step in the fulfillment of the Διὸς βουλή rather than the will itself in its entirety (cf. Kullmann 1955: 189).

[26] On similarities between this episode and earlier parts of Book 1, see also Wilamowitz 1916: 257–58; Sheppard 1922: 22–23; Owen 1946: 15; Lang 1983: 162; Stanley 1993: 46–50; Lowenstam 1993: 69–70; Wilson 2002: 67–68.

showing that gender in the gods' society plays a lesser role in determining status than in mortal society.[27] The presentation of the Achaian army as the desired object also confirms the cosmic hierarchy of gods over mortals, in analogy to the human social hierarchy of male over female evident in the previous triangles of desire. Despite these variations, the establishment of this pattern asks the audience to consider Achilleus' conflict in the context of the other conflicts that come before and after it, and also positions the gods' desires in relation to mortal desires as both parallel and competing sources of plot.

The poet prepares the audience for strife between Hera and Zeus and links this divine conflict with the preceding mortal ones through Zeus's concern that granting Thetis' request will cause friction with his wife. When Thetis petitions him, Zeus is "greatly troubled" (*μέγ' ὀχθήσας*, 1.517),[28] and before acquiescing, he explains his distress (518–19):

> *ἦ δὴ λοίγια ἔργ' ὅ τέ μ' ἐχθοδοπῆσαι ἐφήσεις*
> *Ἥρῃ ὅτ' ἄν μ' ἐρέθῃσιν ὀνειδείοις ἐπέεσσιν·*
>
> Surely indeed these are destructive (*loigia*) deeds, since you will drive me into hostility with Hera when she provokes me with words of reproach...

With the adjective *loigia*, Zeus connects the consequences of aiding Thetis and her son with the destruction (*loigos*) inflicted upon the Achaians by Apollo's plague as a result of Chryses' conflict with Agamemnon (67, 97, 456), and with the *loigos* promised by Achilleus during his absence from battle because of his quarrel with Agamemnon (341).[29] It also recalls Achilleus' own narrative of how Thetis "warded off shameful *loigos*" from Zeus when Hera, Poseidon, and Athene attempted to bind him (397–406). In that case, Thetis came to Zeus's rescue against Hera and the other divine rebels, earning honor from him. Now, however, Zeus foresees that acknowledging Thetis' claim and once again joining her in alliance will renew his enmity with his wife, in a pernicious pattern of discord that features Hera pitted against Zeus and Thetis.

Zeus's next words position the mortal warriors at Troy as the object of his ongoing conflict with Hera. He complains, "even as it is, she always quarrels with

[27] Pucci 2018: 18, however, argues that Hera's role as Zeus's political antagonist assimilates this challenge against Zeus's authority to a domestic, private dispute between wife and husband, making it less serious and problematic than a quarrel between Zeus and one of his co-equal brothers, such as Poseidon.

[28] Scully 1984: 21 observes that when the participle *ὀχθήσας* is applied to Zeus in the *Iliad*, he "either makes a decision which will cause a major change in the course of events or outlines the fate of man-made creations." On the appearances and meaning of *ὀχθήσας* in early Greek epic more generally, see Scully 1984: 14 n. 8.

[29] See also Stanley 1993: 46. On the connection between the *loigos* of the plague and the *loigos* suffered during Achilleus' absence, see further Nagy 1979: 74–76.

me among the immortal gods and says that I help the Trojans in battle" (1.520–21). Zeus' characterization of Hera as concerned with what happens at Troy, and antagonistic toward divine partisans of the Trojans, is congruent with her previous brief appearances in the *Iliad*'s narrative, where she is zealous for the welfare of the Greeks. It is Hera who inspires Achilleus to call the assembly in response to the plague, "for she cared (κήδετο) for the Danaans, because she saw them dying" (56). Then again, Hera is responsible for sending Athene to keep Achilleus from killing Agamemnon, "since she was close with and cared for (φιλέουσά τε κηδομένη τε) both equally in her heart" (196). Therefore, when Zeus agrees to align his will with Achilleus' desire and empower the Trojans against the Achaians, he prepares to take from Hera the Greek army that she loves and safeguards, and anticipates accordingly that this will escalate her aggression. We are presented with a familiar triangular dynamic, now featuring Hera as desiring subject, the Achaians as object, and Zeus as rival together with Thetis, who has convinced the divine king to work against the Greeks.

The predicted triangular conflict between Hera and Zeus materializes directly after Zeus returns home from his audience with Thetis. Building on the preceding account of Zeus's authoritative nod, the narrator emphasizes at the outset Zeus's divine supremacy by focusing on the other gods' deference, as they all rise respectfully on his arrival (1.533–35). Hera is then singled out from this group as "not unaware of him, having seen that silver-footed Thetis devised plots (βουλάς) with him" (536–38), and at once she addresses Zeus "sarcastically" (κερτομίοισι, 539). This introduction makes clear that Zeus's agreement with Thetis is what elicits Hera's speech, and that her following words are meant as a subtle attack, fulfilling Zeus's expectation of her hostility.[30] In this passage, the narrator also establishes a structure for the encounter between Hera and Zeus that is recognizable to the astute listener. A person of implicitly lower status approaches a kingly superior, just as Chryses and Achilleus—a foreign priest and a warrior king—had both initiated their interaction with Agamemnon, the leader of the Achaian expedition against Troy.

Hera's opening speech already testifies to her competitive desire to emulate Zeus in his authoritative *boulē* (1.540–43):

> *τίς δὴ αὖ τοι, δολομῆτα, θεῶν συμφράσσατο βουλάς;*
> *αἰεί τοι φίλον ἐστὶν ἐμεῦ ἀπονόσφιν ἐόντα*
> *κρυπτάδια φρονέοντα δικαζέμεν· οὐδέ τί πώ μοι*
> *πρόφρων τέτληκας εἰπεῖν ἔπος ὅττι νοήσῃς.*

[30] Lloyd 2004 has convincingly explained that the term *kertomia* and its cognates indicate "off-record criticism," that is, aggressive speech that is recognizable as such but also not explicit, thus leaving the speaker the option of disavowing any critique and the interlocuter the possibility of ignoring the provocation. He suggests translating it as "sarcasm" or "ironic politeness." On this passage, see Lloyd 2004: 83–84.

> Crafter of tricks, what god has again devised plots (*boulas*) with you?
> Always it is your way, being apart from me,
> to make your decisions with secret deliberations; not ever to me
> willingly have you dared to speak out what you conceive.

Hera here focuses on her distance from Zeus and his decision-making process, thematizing the lack that informs her desire to control mortal affairs. She pictures this dynamic as a constant reality with her use of the adverbs "again" and "always"; the latter echoes Zeus's previous assertion that Hera is "always" quarreling with him (520) and confirms the ongoing nature of their power struggle.[31] Hera also recognizes that, in her exclusion from Zeus's hegemonic exertion of will, a (disingenuously unnamed) third divinity has influenced the divine king.

Zeus's aggressive response to Hera shows that his own desires have also been activated, in a variation on the paradigmatic conflict between Chryses and Agamemnon. He affirms his prerogative to keep secrets from her even though she is his wife, warning her "whatever I want (ἐθέλωμι) to conceive apart from the gods, do not inquire about or question any of these matters" (1.549–50). Zeus's self-assertive vocabulary of desire here—"I want"—indicates that Hera's challenge has strengthened his own will to determine the Greeks' fate and elicited a reciprocal aggressive desire for dominance over his rebellious spouse. He utilizes the same verb *ethelō* that Agamemnon had employed to describe how he was "not willing" (οὐκ ἔθελον, 112) to accept the ransom for Chryseis. Indeed, Zeus's rebuff of Hera generally recalls Agamemnon's refusal to return Chryseis and following command for Chryses to go away, and helps to establish Zeus's parallelism to Agamemnon in this third triangle of desire.[32] As in both previous mortal conflicts, Hera and Zeus are now exhibiting Girard's dynamic of "internal double mediation," where subject and rival become indistinguishable as they direct aggressive desire toward one another in their competition for the object.

Just as Agamemnon's rejection prolongs Chryses' longing for his daughter and provokes his aggressive prayer to Apollo, Zeus's admonishment confirms Hera's longing to protect the Greek army and evokes her most explicit complaints regarding her exclusion from her husband's decision-making. She incredulously asks what Zeus has spoken, and then insists on her own previous lack of interference—and power—in Zeus's determinations, echoing his assertion of his

[31] Hera's complaint also calls to mind Achilleus' claim during the assembly that whenever there is a division of spoils, Agamemnon takes the "greater prize" while he receives something small (1.166–67).

[32] See also Elmer 2013: 147, who observes how "Zeus' plan to fulfill Thetis' request parallels Agamemnon's decision to keep Chryseis for himself, while his dismissal of Hera's concerns includes verbal echoes of Agamemnon's treatment of Chryses." Zeus, however, unlike Agamemnon, tries initially to mollify his interlocuter: in an acknowledgment of Hera's special status, he asserts she will be his first confidant if he does choose to share his mind (1.547–48).

will: "before I neither probed nor questioned you excessively, but very much at ease you would contrive whatever you might want" (θέλῃσθα, 1.553–54). She goes on to specify how she "fears terribly" that Thetis has persuaded Zeus to honor Achilleus and destroy many Achaians (555–59). With these words, Hera makes clear that she views Zeus and Thetis as her rivals, who are keeping her from her beloved Greeks and inspiring her frustrated longing for them.[33] The critique implicit in her words expresses her aggressive desire to usurp the divine king's authority and impose her own will in contradiction to his.

Zeus responds with a more forceful and aggressive assertion of his absolute hegemony, in an escalation of the conflict that repeats Agamemnon's violent threat toward Achilleus. He warns Hera that she is powerless to stop him and that her attempt to do so will only increase her distance "away from my heart" (1.562–63). Then he adds that "this will be even more miserable for you" (τὸ δέ τοι καὶ ῥίγιον ἔσται, 563), in an almost exact repetition of Agamemnon's words menacing Achilleus should he refuse to give up Briseis: "this will be even more miserable for him" (τό οἱ καὶ ῥίγιον ἔσται, 325). Zeus's threat securely identifies him with Agamemnon[34] as a leader who feels the need to defend his status and authority, although Zeus is confident enough to threaten Hera to her face, while Agamemnon only threatens Achilleus behind his back.

This repetition also situates Hera as a divine analogue to Achilleus: both challenge the leaders of their communities and encounter aggressive responses, although Achilleus desires merely his concubine and the honor that he believes he deserves—despite Agamemnon's claims that he wants to rule (287–89)—whereas Hera desires full control of the Achaians' fate, and therefore concrete power to determine the course of human affairs. Despite these differences in the stakes of the two conflicts, their parallelism suggests that Hera's quarrel with Zeus will develop along the same lines as Achilleus' conflict with Agamemnon, in which he complied with the seizure of his beloved object, even as he did not give up his aggressive desire toward his adversaries.

Zeus rounds off his speech with an order for Hera to submit to his authority and with another, more specific threat of physical harm, this time echoing not only the conflict between Achilleus and Agamemnon but also between Chryses and Agamemnon. Zeus says (1.565–67),

[33] The narrative perhaps alludes here to the extra-Iliadic myth of Zeus's courtship of Thetis (see Slatkin 1991: 70–76; Redfield 1994: 241), and suggests, for a moment, Hera's familiar mythological persona of the jealous wife who resents her husband's frequent marital infidelities. Yet, as Pucci 2018: 18 recognizes, the *Iliad* rejects this tradition, "never attribut[ing] Hera's hostility against Zeus to her [sexual] jealousy" but rather presenting her as a political actor "fighting against Zeus' support of the Trojans." The poet thus refuses to trivialize Hera and further affirms the parallelism between Hera and her mortal analogues Chryses and Achilleus.

[34] See also Stanley 1993: 50, Lowenstam 1993: 70, and Wilson 2002: 67 on the analogy of Zeus and Agamemnon.

> *ἀλλ' ἀκέουσα κάθησο, ἐμῷ δ' ἐπιπείθεο μύθῳ,*
> *μή νύ τοι οὐ χραίσμωσιν ὅσοι θεοί εἰσ' ἐν Ὀλύμπῳ*
> *ἆσσον ἰόνθ', ὅτε κέν τοι ἀάπτους χεῖρας ἐφείω.*
>
> But sit down silently, and obey my command,
> lest now the gods who are on Olympos not help you
> as I come near, when I lay my untouchable hands upon you.

Zeus's injunction for Hera to "obey my command" recalls Nestor's earlier orders for Achilleus and Agamemnon to imitate previous generations who had "obeyed [his] command" (*πείθοντό τε μύθῳ*) and to "obey" (*πίθεσθε*), "since it is better to obey" (*πείθεσθαι*, 273–74). Then, when Zeus warns Hera that the Olympian gods will not protect her from his physical attack, his words are strongly reminiscent of Agamemnon's admonition for Chryses to leave the Greek camp immediately "lest now the scepter and fillet of the god not help you" (*μή νύ τοι οὐ χραίσμῃ σκῆπτρον καὶ στέμμα θεοῖο*, 28). Both Zeus and Agamemnon employ the same line-opening formulas in their threats, and both dismiss their antagonists' divine allies as ineffectual hindrances to their threatened violence. Zeus's words furthermore evoke a scenario of internecine warfare between himself and the other gods, indicating the seriousness with which he regards Hera's challenge to his supremacy. In this way, Homer suggests the continuity of this present conflict with the previous attempt of Hera, Poseidon, and Athene to bind Zeus.

The narrator describes Hera's acquiescence to Zeus's command in terms that strongly recall both Chryses' and Achilleus' initial submissions to Agamemnon's aggression. The narrator uses the same formula to express how Chryses and Hera react with fear to their interlocutor's words (*ὣς ἔφατ', ἔδεισεν*, 1.33 = 568). Both priest and goddess directly comply with the injunctions of their superior: after Zeus orders Hera to "sit down silently" (*ἀκέουσα κάθησο*), "she sat down silently" (*καί ῥ' ἀκέουσα καθῆστο*, 569),[35] and after Agamemnon tells Chryses, "go, do not provoke me" (*ἴθι, μή μ' ἐρέθιζε*, 32), "he went away silently" (*βῆ δ' ἀκέων*, 34). Moreover, Hera, in her capitulation, "restrained her own heart" (*ἐπιγνάμψασα φίλον κῆρ*, 569), echoing how Achilleus himself, after his loss of Briseis, "was withering away in his own heart" (*φθινύθεσκε φίλον κῆρ*, 491); both line-ending phrases seem to represent their subjects' internalization of aggressive libido. With these multiple resonances, the poet continues to construct Hera as a desiring subject analogous to Chryses or Achilleus. This parallelism suggests that her desires will persist in generating a plot of divine discord until she gets what she wants, and elicits the audience's narrative desire to know if or how Zeus will maintain peace with his spouse while devastating the Achaian army on Achilleus' behalf.

[35] The narrator uses the same line-opening formula to describe Hera's silent sitting here and Zeus's silent sitting about sixty lines earlier (*ἀλλ' ἀκέων δὴν ἧστο*, 512) after Thetis asks him the first time to honor Achilleus. In both cases it seems to signify a moment when a god is at a loss for how to proceed.

Hephaistos as Mediator

The quarrel between queen and king of the gods is not confined, however, to their relationship but has ramifications for the entire divine community. After recounting Hera's submission, the narrator records that the "heavenly gods throughout the house of Zeus were troubled" (ὄχθησαν, 1.570). The contagious nature of this Olympian social disruption is indicated by how the gods' unease (ὄχθησαν) echoes Zeus's own initial unease (ὀχθήσας, 517) when he contemplated Hera's certain opposition to his granting of Thetis' petition. This larger divine agitation parallels the suffering of the whole Greek army caused or predicted as a result of the mortal conflicts, and once again underscores the cosmic stakes of Hera's strife with Zeus.

This disquiet also provides a motivation for Hephaistos' intervention in the divine conflict (1.571–94), which represents a combination of and variation on the previous intercessions of Kalchas and Nestor in the mortal conflicts.[36] Like both human mediators, Hephaistos speaks publicly to defuse the conflict, which is identified as damaging to the community. Just as Nestor had begun by describing the quarrel between Achilleus and Agamemnon as "a great grief" to the Achaian land (254), Hephaistos starts by asserting that it would constitute "destructive deeds (λοίγια ἔργ') and be no longer tolerable" if Zeus and Hera should be at odds "for the sake of mortals," thus causing disturbance among the gods and disrupting divine feasting (573–76). Hephaistos' portrayal of this quarrel as "destructive deeds" also repeats Zeus's own previous prediction that his acquiescence to Thetis would result in "destructive deeds" (λοίγια ἔργ', 518). By having Hephaistos cite Zeus's prescriptive discourse, the poet suggests from the outset that he is reinforcing Zeus's hegemony, just as Nestor had shored up Agamemnon's claim to higher status than Achilleus by repeating the Greek leader's self-aggrandizing speech.

In addition, Hephaistos' assertion that Hera and Zeus are fighting "for the sake of mortals" (ἕνεκα θνητῶν) definitively clarifies for the audience the nature of their triangular conflict and its parallelism with the preceding human conflicts. His statement firmly establishes the Greek army as the desired object in analogy to Chryseis and Briseis, echoing previous language recounting how the men contended "for the sake of a girl." Agamemnon says that Apollo sent the plague, "because I was not willing to receive the splendid ransom in exchange for the girl Chryseis" (οὕνεκ'... κούρης Χρυσηΐδος, 1.111–12). Achilleus, in turn, asserts that he will not physically fight with Agamemnon "for the sake of a girl" (εἵνεκα κούρης, 298), and later he remarks that Agamemnon sent the heralds "for the sake of the girl Briseis" (Βρισηΐδος εἵνεκα κούρης, 336).[37]

[36] See also Segal 1971b: 91 for comparison of Nestor's and Hephaistos' mediations.

[37] Cf. Aias' speech during the embassy of Book 9, when he complains of how Achilleus' heart is implacable "for the sake of a girl" (εἵνεκα κούρης, 9.637) and Apollo's objection during the second theomachy to fighting with Poseidon "for the sake of mortals" (βροτῶν ἕνεκα, 21.463).

After echoing the beginning of Nestor's intervention, Hephaistos diverges from Nestor's example to focus on Hera alone as the target of his persuasion in the face of Zeus's power. Nestor had admonished both Achilleus and Agamemnon to obey him and give way, but Hephaistos entreats only his mother Hera "to be well-disposed to dear father Zeus" to keep him from quarreling with her further and upsetting the divine feast (1.577–79). As his next words show, his approach to mediation is a practical one based on his understanding that Zeus is simply mightier than anyone else. Affirming Zeus's supreme authority, he uses *ethelō*, the verb of desire that Zeus and Hera had already employed in reference to the divine king's dominant will: "if the lightning-hurling Olympian ever should want (ἐθέλῃσιν), he could smite [us] from [our] seats, for he is by far the most powerful" (φέρτατος, 580–81). With this last phrase, the poet once again connects Zeus with Agamemnon, even as he affirms their difference. While Nestor repeats Agamemnon's own characterization of himself as "more powerful" (φέρτερος, 186 and 281), using the comparative adjective, Hephaistos designates Zeus with the superlative.[38] He thus underlines the impossibility of Hera, in contrast with Chryses or Achilleus, realizing her desires in opposition to the will of her divine adversary.

Instead, therefore, Hephaistos advises Hera to appease Zeus with language that now recalls Kalchas' prophetic intervention in Chryses' conflict with Agamemnon. Hephaistos tells Hera to address Zeus "with soft words" and asserts that "then at once the Olympian will be propitious (ἵλαος) to us" (1.582–83). His use of the word "propitious" echoes Kalchas' declaration that the Greeks may persuade Apollo to end the destructive plague once they have "propitiated" (ἱλασσάμενοι) him with a hecatomb (97–100, see also 147 and 386), a prediction that is fulfilled when the Achaians do in fact "propitiate" (ἱλασσόμεθα, 444; ἱλάσκοντο, 472) Apollo during the successful mission to Chryse.[39] In Hephaistos' speech, Zeus is figured as the angry god who needs to be propitiated in order for the conflict to end. In this way, Homer constructs a potential resolution between Hera and Zeus as an inverse of the resolution between Chryses/Apollo and Agamemnon. Instead of Hera's longing for Greek welfare being fulfilled and her aggression dissolved, Zeus is the one who must be made "propitious" again.

Yet even as Hephaistos recommends the appeasement of Zeus, he himself attempts to conciliate Hera, and the poet signals the coming success of his intervention through another echo of the resolution to Chryses' story. After speaking, Hephaistos takes up a cup and "put[s] it in the hand of his dear mother"

[38] Stanley 1993: 47. See also Lowenstam 1993: 70 on the power differential between Zeus and Agamemnon suggested in this scene.

[39] Cf. Muellner 1996: 126–27 on how the repetition of this vocabulary links together the wrath (*mēnis*) of Zeus, Apollo, and Achilleus.

(μητρὶ φίλῃ ἐν χειρὶ τίθει, 1.585), inviting Hera to forget her desires and participate instead in the divine merry-making. The narrator here deploys the same formulaic phrase used to relate Odysseus' formal return of Chryseis to Chryses—"he put her in the hands of her dear father" (πατρὶ φίλῳ ἐν χερσὶ τίθει, 441). Now Hera is being treated like Chryses, and Hephaistos seems to be taking the part of Odysseus, in this case as a self-appointed surrogate for Zeus. By associating Hephaistos, then, with both Kalchas and Odysseus, the poet suggests that he is managing a divine reconciliation in the model of Agamemnon and his army's reconciliation with Chryses and Apollo, except that Zeus does not give way in the slightest or offer Hera any recompense.

Before a resolution to the divine conflict is realized, however, Hephaistos returns to the mediation paradigm of Nestor and shares an autobiographical story in order to convince Hera to submit to Zeus. Whereas Nestor offered an heroic narrative of the Lapiths' obedience to his counsel as a positive *exemplum* (1.260–73), Hephaistos tells a theomachic narrative of the pejorative consequences of challenging Zeus as a negative *exemplum*. He prefaces the story by cautioning his mother that if she runs afoul of Zeus, he will not be able to "help" (χραισμεῖν, 589), affirming the divine king's own earlier warning that if he should lay hands upon his wife, none of the gods would come to "help" (χραίσμωσιν, 566). Hephaistos' repetition again validates Zeus's power along with his discourse, emphasizing the divine king's might in comparison to Hera's and his own. To prove his point, he recounts how Zeus hurled him by the foot off Mt. Olympos when he tried to aid his mother against the divine king; after descending for an entire day, Hephaistos landed on the earth sorely injured (590–94).[40] This narrative calls to mind Achilleus' story of how Thetis freed Zeus from an insurrection of Hera, Poseidon, and Athene, and may refer to the same episode of divine history. It again connects the present conflict with a larger struggle for divine hegemony and reminds Hera that Zeus has always come out on top.

Hephaistos' mediation is immediately successful. Hera's mood changes: instead of "restraining her heart," she "smiles" (μείδησεν, 1.595; μειδήσασα, 596). At the same time, the divine queen accepts the cup that her son has offered to her (596), showing how she likewise accepts his conciliation; rather than disrupting the gods' tranquility, she will participate in their happy celebration, which Hephaistos reinitiates by drawing nectar in turn for all the gods and arousing their laughter with his limp (597–600). Hera's quarrel with Zeus is left aside for the time being.

The poet signifies this resolution with a final scene of divine feasting and song that clearly echoes the celebration that had marked the end of Apollo's wrath and

[40] See Purves 2019: 55–59 on how Hephaistos' fall is a symbolic death that associates him with mortal rather than divine temporality. Zeus subjects Hephaistos and other gods to the experience or danger of falling, but "will always escape this form of 'gravity' himself" (Purves 2019: 62).

concluded the opening conflict between Chryses and Agamemnon.[41] The divine episode varies the earlier model to fit changed circumstances yet retains many of its basic features. There is no animal sacrifice or sacrificial meal to begin the divine revel, since the gods neither eat mortal food nor sacrifice to themselves, but both scenes include the ritualized pouring of a celebratory drink (wine, 470–71; nectar, 597–98). In both cases, the participants feast for the whole day until the setting of the sun (472, 475; 601–2), and the same formula describes and thematizes the satiety of men and gods (*οὐδέ τι θυμὸς ἐδεύετο δαιτὸς ἐΐσης*, 468 = 602). The Achaian youths "sing" (*ἀείδοντες*) a paean to Apollo, who listens with pleasure (473–74), and on Mt. Olympos, Apollo is also an important presence, playing the phorminx himself (603) while the Muses do the singing (*ἄειδον*, 604).[42] When the sun finally goes down, both mortals and gods take their rest (476; 606–11). Zeus and Hera's retirement to bed together marks their reconciliation.

Evaluating the Divine Resolution

This closing scene of Book 1 confirms for the audience the narrative pattern of resolution previously introduced through Chryses' story. Since the poet has presented the three triangular conflicts in *Iliad* 1 as analogous, the audience now firmly anticipates a similar scene concluding Achilleus' quarrel with Agamemnon and marking the resolution of his driving desires. That is, we desire this same ending to Achilleus' plot, and it alone offers the conditions for our full satisfaction.

This same parallelism between the three stories, however, also calls into question the very resolution that this divine celebration purports. Despite cessation of conflict, Hera's desire to preserve the Achaians has not been satisfied by her rival Zeus, in contrast to the way that Chryses' desire to liberate Chryseis was fulfilled by Agamemnon's delegation. Given the fact that Hera's grievance remains unresolved, it is tempting to interpret her smile—doubly emphasized by the narrator—as more than a simple expression of good humor. Simon Pulleyn (2000: 272) calls Hera's smile "enigmatic" and argues that it indicates how Hera is "dissimulating her true feelings."[43] This smile, along with the fact that Hera does not follow Hephaistos' recommendation to address Zeus "with soft words," hints to the audience that she has not abandoned the object of her desire—the Achaians—or

[41] Sheppard 1922: 23.

[42] Cf. the similar description of Apollo playing the kithara while the Muses sing on Mt. Olympos in the *Homeric Hymn to Apollo* 186–206.

[43] Pulleyn offers as evidence for this interpretation the episode in 14.222–23, where Hera is also described as smiling (with the same formulas) after she deceives Aphrodite (on which, see further Chapter 6). Cf. Hades' deceitful smile to Persephone in the *Homeric Hymn to Demeter* 357 and Lateiner 1995: 42, 194–95 on the deceitfulness and bitterness of Odysseus' smiles in the *Odyssey*.

her attempt to master Zeus's will. Hera gives way for the moment, but her conflict with Zeus does *not* seem to be *definitively* resolved.

Indeed, Hera's decision to take a step back after Hephaistos' mediation resembles Achilleus' choice not to kill Agamemnon after Athene's intervention.[44] In both cases, the intercessions of Olympian gods are at once effective in diffusing the intensity of conflict. Yet, as we saw in the previous chapter, the responsive restraint of Achilleus does not mean that he is placated; with Athene's encouragement, the hero continues to quarrel with Agamemnon verbally, and plots future retribution in response to his loss of Briseis. The consistent narrative analogy between Hera and Achilleus suggests that the divine queen similarly retains her driving desires, even after Hephaistos' apparent conciliation. Hephaistos' divinity supports his parallelism to Athene, the only goddess to intervene in a mortal conflict. And Hephaistos' structural similarity to Nestor, the second and ineffective mediator in Achilleus' conflict, also reinforces the conclusion that Hera's reconciliation with Zeus is only temporary.

Zeus's strong association with Agamemnon as he appears in both mortal triangular conflicts also belies the sense that we have witnessed a real resolution of divine strife at the end of Book 1. The poet does not present Agamemnon as an exemplary or particularly effective leader—just the opposite.[45] Zeus's structural parallelism with Agamemnon and his deployment against Hera of the same threats that Agamemnon had recklessly directed toward his best warrior suggest that Zeus is similarly disrespecting his wife. Thus Homer insinuates that Zeus is asserting his supremacy too forcefully in a miscarriage of just and effective divine leadership.[46] Zeus's apparent callousness and ineptitude is the final factor that keeps the audience from accepting the ostensible reconciliation between king and queen of the gods and that activates our narrative desire to find out how the next divine skirmish will develop.

Zeus's harsh treatment of Hera and the thematization of her frustrated desire and fear may also encourage our sympathy for and empathy with the divine queen. Hera's consistent championing of the Greek army makes her an especially appealing divinity for a Greek audience. Empathy with Hera, however, might put the audience in the position of identifying with two characters, Achilleus and Hera, who have opposing desires, even if they are structurally analogous in their respective triangles of desire. This dual identification would make our emotional investment in Achilleus' evolving plot more complex, as we share both the hero's anger against Agamemnon and Hera's pity for the targeted Achaians. It may make

[44] Lang 1983: 162.

[45] See Taplin 1990 for the negative portrayal of Agamemnon in Book 1 and the *Iliad* more generally.

[46] See also Pucci 2018: 25, who observes that "In the eyes of the audiences and readers of the poem, Zeus' brutal threats constitute a complex and troubling scene." He also notes that "Zeus has no established pact or recognized credentials that legitimize his power save for his greater physical force."

us question the justice of Achilleus' indiscriminate rage—and of the divine king who promotes it.

Hera's confrontation with Zeus not only escalates our involvement in the narrative but also introduces us to a major divine story in the *Iliad* that complicates the question of the epic's theme and motivation. As we have seen, this divine story explores Zeus's maintenance of his cosmic regime against desirous contenders—especially Hera. Starting here, this story appears repeatedly as part of the *Iliad*'s plot, and it is also explored through flashbacks to past events, such as in Achilleus' and Hephaistos' narratives of previous rebellions against Zeus's authority.[47] Laura Slatkin's (1991) and Leonard Muellner's (1996) analyses of the epic bring this divine story to the fore. They read the *Iliad* as an exploration of Zeus's strategies for stabilizing his power after the cycles of intergenerational divine violence that led to his ascendancy; the poem would thus represent a sequel to Hesiod's *Theogony*. To preserve his hegemony, Zeus not only controls the unrest of his peers but also ensures that humankind represents no threat by enforcing and accelerating men's mortality—including, ultimately, Achilleus'—through the Trojan War.

In this understanding of the epic, the will of Zeus (*Dios boulē*) announced in the *Iliad*'s proem is prior to and independent of Achilleus' desires. Wolfgang Kullmann (1955: 170–87) has identified the Iliadic *Dios boulē* with the *Dios boulē* to reduce the human race through mass death in the Trojan War that appears in Fragment 1 of the *Cypria* (West 2003: 80–83), another early Greek epic about the expedition to Troy. According to Kullmann, Zeus's promise to fulfill Achilleus' aggressive desire is in the service of his own will insofar as it prolongs the war and therefore increases human mortality. Similarly, Sheila Murnaghan (1997) reads Achilleus as a pawn in Zeus's larger plan, and Achilleus' plot as engineered by Zeus, though this reality does not emerge until later in the *Iliad*'s narrative.

Although Homer does present the conflict between Hera and Zeus as the capstone to Book 1, thematizing and affirming the determining power of Zeus's will, the *Iliad*'s narrative progression and logic locate Achilleus' desires at the origin of that "divine plot" rather than vice versa. For the audience experiencing the epic diachronically, in a forward-moving development, Achilleus' desires direct the *Dios boulē* and generate the divine conflict,[48] even if the narrative somewhat undermines this causality by positioning Hera's challenge to Zeus as

[47] Lang 1983: 147–63 catalogues the tales of earlier divine conflict alluded to in the *Iliad* and shows how they make up a coherent story that is also interconnected with heroic stories of the earlier generation, namely Herakles' mythology and the first sack of Troy. See also Nimis 1987: 74–84 on how Zeus's battle with Typhoeus (Typhonomachy) as well as with the other Titans functions as an "intertext" here and elsewhere in the *Iliad*.

[48] See also Scodel 2017: 76–80, who interprets the *Dios boulē* in the proem as, primarily, Zeus's plan for the *Iliad*, beginning with his promise to Thetis, and who sees Zeus's will as less essential than Achilleus' wrath for the generation of the epic's plot. Cf. Elmer 2013: 156–59 on the ambiguity of Zeus's will and how it reflects "competing visions for the poem" in its relation to the Trojan War tradition.

part of an ongoing opposition to the divine king's hegemony. And though the proem presents both Achilleus' wrath and Zeus's will as sources for the epic's plot, the narrator anticipates the sequence of the main narrative by beginning with the "wrath" and reaching the "will of Zeus" only near the proem's end in line 5. Moreover, the poet gives Achilleus' quarrel with Agamemnon the privileged central location in the *Iliad*'s first book. In these ways, Homer initially foregrounds Achilleus' desires and plot and subordinates (or, perhaps, "superordinates") divine desires and the divine plot, as is appropriate for an heroic rather than theogonic epic.[49]

Yet this episode of divine conflict already sows doubt regarding Achilleus' ability to maintain control of the epic's plot. On the one hand, Hera's competing desires promise to be a continuing impediment to the implementation of Zeus's and Achilleus' will. On the other hand, Hera's analogy to Achilleus in her antagonism with Zeus undermines the alignment of Achilleus' and Zeus's desires. To a perceptive listener, it suggests a potential opposition between the hero and the god, while presenting Zeus as the ultimate decision-maker who has the power to exercise his authority unilaterally, despite others' objections. This link between Achilleus and Hera supports Bruce Heiden's (2008: 29–35) argument that throughout the *Iliad* Achilleus and Zeus are in a subtle "polemical configuration," with the two characters posing successive problems for one another that keep taking the plot in new directions; Zeus emerges as "the most influential agent" in the epic. While the *Iliad*'s audience now knows no more than that Zeus has definitively promised to accomplish Achilleus' plot, this final scene in Book 1 gestures toward the complexity of the *Iliad*'s plotting through a possible divergence between the desires of Zeus and Achilleus, even as it reinforces Zeus's will as a key determinant of the epic's narrative direction.

[49] Cf. Lynn-George 1988: 39–40: "Across the opening book the epic narrative has staged two conflicting sources of determination for the action. The ultimately irreducible indeterminacy in this overdetermination is fundamental to the epic."

3

The Superplot's Beginning

Although Zeus sets Achilleus' plot in motion in Book 2, Homer suspends that plot from Books 3–7 in a narrative expansion that explores the larger myth of the Trojan War and provides context for Achilleus' story. This chapter shows how the poet introduces new desiring subjects in *Iliad* 2 and 3 and situates their desires as the motivation for this Trojan War "superplot." Key to this narrative causality is the erotic triangle of Menelaos, Paris, and Helen, which resembles the triangles of desire in *Iliad* 1. First, the poet presents Menelaos' aggressive desire to take revenge on Paris for Helen's abduction as the immediate cause of war, and then he explores the complex desires of Helen and the sexual lust (*erōs*) and yearning (*himeros*) of Paris as the original roots of the conflict, staging a re-enactment of their transgressive union facilitated by Aphrodite. These desiring subjects draw the audience away from Achilleus and his plot, and invest us in the superplot.

From the Main Plot to the Superplot

In Book 2 of the *Iliad*, Zeus moves toward fulfilling Achilleus' desires to redeem his honor and take revenge on his fellow Greeks for the removal of his concubine Briseis. After pondering how best to "honor Achilleus and destroy many beside the ships of the Achaians," Zeus decides to send Agamemnon a "baneful" dream falsely promising Greek victory that day should they attack Troy (2.3–6); Zeus's true intention is to cause suffering for Trojans and Greeks alike in battle (39–40). As the Greek troops are marshalled for the engagement, the poet repeatedly reminds the audience of Achilleus' withdrawal and his motivating desires,[1] and portrays the idle Myrmidons "longing (ποθέοντες) for their war-loving leader" (778). The Myrmidons' longing (*pothē*) emphasizes Achilleus' isolation from even

[1] First, Thersites recapitulates and even amplifies Achilleus' grievances against Agamemnon (2.225–42), and in that respect appears as a parodic surrogate for Achilleus (Willcock 1978: 200, cf. Kirk 1985: 139–41 and Lowenstam 1993: 78–80). Later, Agamemnon himself refers to his quarrel with Achilleus in regretful tones, speculating on the damage to the Trojans should they be reconciled (2.375–80). But Achilleus is conspicuously *not* one of the elders that Agamemnon invites to his tent to share in a sacrifice to Zeus (2.404–8). The narrator names Achilleus several times in the catalogues that occupy the second half of Book 2 (674, 685, 688, 769, 770) and specifically characterizes him as "angry" (χωόμενος) and "grieving" (ἀχέων) over Briseis (2.689–94), and "wrathful" (μήνιεν; ἀπομηνίσας) at Agamemnon (2.769–73). On Achilleus in Book 2, see also Schein 1984: 101–2.

Desire in the Iliad: *The Force That Moves the Epic and Its Audience.* Rachel H. Lesser, Oxford University Press.
© Rachel H. Lesser 2022. DOI: 10.1093/oso/9780192866516.003.0004

his own men,[2] and anticipates the realization of Achilleus' aggressive vow that all the Achaians would come to feel *pothē* for him (1.240). Together, these references intensify the audience's narrative desire to discover how the hero's plot will unfold. Moreover, in the Catalogue of Ships, the narrator predicts that Achilleus will soon rise up (τάχα δ' ἀνστήσεσθαι ἔμελλεν, 2.694),[3] leading us to expect the imminent satisfaction of his desires.

Yet in Books 3–7 Zeus does not act upon his promise to empower the Trojans against the Greeks during Achilleus' withdrawal from battle. Rather, this narrative sequence presents two inconclusive duels between Greek and Trojan champions framing a central episode during which the Greek hero Diomedes wreaks havoc on the Trojans on the battlefield, obviating any potential need for Achilleus. In this way, Homer interrupts Achilleus' plot until Book 8, when Zeus finally tips the scales in favor of the Trojans (8.69–74). At first, this postponement creates suspense,[4] increasing our narrative desire for the progression of Achilleus' plot. But during this extended sequence, Achilleus himself, absent from the Greek army, nearly disappears from the narrative,[5] and as this delay continues, the audience almost forgets Achilleus and his quarrel with Agamemnon and becomes captivated by new characters enmeshed in a broader conflict.

As Cedric Whitman (1958: 264–70) has shown, Books 3–7 contextualize Achilleus' wrath within the larger story of the Trojan War.[6] These books present episodes that properly belong to the war's origin and beginning, all the while recasting these events as if they were part of epic's main story, which is set in the war's ninth year (2.295).[7] This section of the *Iliad* also predicts and previews the eventual fall of Troy, especially through the meeting of Hektor and Andromache in Book 6. As Whitman (1958: 268) explains, "Homer has created a montage of a motivating crime under the guise of continuous narrative, and opposed to it a

[2] The Myrmidons' *pothē* echoes the desires of Protesilaos' and Philoktetes' men respectively for their absent leaders (πόθεόν γε μὲν ἀρχόν, 2.703 = 2.726). It suggests an equivalence between Achilleus' disengagement from battle and the other two men's more definitive absences due to death (Protesilaos) or marooning (Philoktetes). See Stanley 1993: 20–24 for discussion of the theme of the absent leader in the Catalogues and their structure as a whole.

[3] As Kirk 1985: 233 observes, the narrator uses the same formulaic diction to predict that the Achaians will soon remember Philoktetes (τάχα δὲ μνήσεσθαι ἔμελλον, 2.724). This suggests again the correspondence of Achilleus and Philoktetes (see n. 2 above), and invites the audience to perceive a functional similarity between Philoktetes' famous re-entry into the Trojan War (which initiates its final stage) and Achilleus' re-entry into battle (which will indeed cause, through the killing of Hektor, a turning point in the war).

[4] Duckworth 1933: 66–67. Cf. Morrison 1992: 35–43, 51–62, who differentiates between "false anticipation," securely expecting something that does not immediately come to be, and "epic suspense," uncertainty when faced with unexpected plot developments that are not guided by authoritative predictions, and discusses how both "misdirections" are at play in Books 2–4.

[5] Achilleus is mentioned only four times (5.788, 6.414, 6.423, 7.228). See Schein 1984: 102–4 for discussion of these references.

[6] See also Owen 1946: 27–31; Reckford 1964: 5–13; Mueller 1984: 66.

[7] Bowie 2019: 9–12 calls this technique "double narration" and also identifies Chryses' and Achilleus' stories in Book 1 as instances of this narrative strategy insofar as they evoke the war's "seminal initial event" of Helen's seizure.

foreshadowing of its ultimate results." Robert Rabel (1997: 72–112) calls this part of the epic (with the addition of Books 2 and 8) the "subplot."

I, however, designate the action of Books 3–7 and of other portions of the *Iliad* focusing on the greater Trojan War as the "superplot," because these events are really external and fundamental to Achilleus' main plot, rather than internal and subordinate to it.[8] The superplot provides the basis for Achilleus' plot and points to the ultimate consequences of that plot. Most significantly for this study, the superplot's narrative dynamics also mirror the main plot's: Homer locates triangular desires at the origin of the superplot's Trojan War story, thus confirming and deepening the link between desire and plot in the *Iliad*.

Why the Greek Army Fights

Agamemnon's testing of the troops in Book 2 is the poet's first means of exploring the motivating desires of the superplot. Before arming his men for the victory prophesied in his dream from Zeus, Agamemnon decides to assess their bravery and resolve with a speech exhorting the army to abandon the war and return to Greece (2.110–41),[9] in which he describes how "our wives and young children sit waiting in the halls" (136–37). The narrator reports that his words "roused the passion (*thumon*) in their chests" (τοῖσι δὲ θυμὸν ἐνὶ στήθεσσιν ὄρινε, 142), and, contrary to Agamemnon's apparent intention, his men charge *en masse* to the ships, "eager for home" (οἴκαδε ἱεμένων, 154). In this scene, Agamemnon unwittingly ignites the Achaians' desire for their families in Greece, which immediately drives them away from Troy and threatens to derail his planned attack.

What, then, motivated the Greek army's participation in the war for nine long years? Hera's subsequent complaint to Athene about the Achaians' putative departure presents "Argive Helen" as the reason for fighting (2.160–62):

κὰδ δέ κεν εὐχωλὴν Πριάμῳ καὶ Τρωσὶ λίποιεν
Ἀργείην Ἑλένην, ἧς εἵνεκα πολλοὶ Ἀχαιῶν
ἐν Τροίῃ ἀπόλοντο, φίλης ἀπὸ πατρίδος αἴης·

and they might leave behind as a boast for Priam and the Trojans
Argive Helen, for whose sake many of the Achaians
have perished in Troy, away from their dear fatherland...

[8] Thus, these books, as Rabel 1997: 75–79 notes, threaten to short-circuit the *Iliad*'s entire narrative with premature endings to the Trojan War (e.g. the duel between Paris and Menelaos). See also Morrison 1992: 37–43, 51–54.

[9] On this testing strategy, see Knox and Russo 1989.

Helen is here introduced in the *Iliad* for the first time with her name prominently enjambed in line-opening position, and her status as the war's objective is grammatically articulated through her placement first as direct object of the verb *λίποιεν* and then as prepositional object of *εἵνεκα*. Furthermore, Hera expresses Helen's disputed position by worrying that she might remain in the possession of "Priam and the Trojans," but then identifying her as "Argive" and the cause of the "Achaian" casualties at Troy. In her explanation of the Trojan War, Hera conjures up for the audience a familiar triangular scenario of conflict between mortal men over possession of a woman. Indeed, Hera's phrase "for whose sake" (*ἧς εἵνεκα*) echoes previous accounts of the two disputes between men in Book 1 "for the sake of" Chryseis and Briseis (1.111–12, 1.298, 1.336), and of the quarrel between Hera and Zeus "for the sake of mortals" (1.574).

In order for the Greeks to renew their attack on Troy, the Achaians' desires must be redirected from their own wives back toward Helen. Through Athene, Hera shares with Odysseus her concerns about Helen's abandonment (2.176–78 = 160–62), and instructs him to prevent the men from disembarking. Although Odysseus successfully gathers the army for another assembly and deals with Thersites' verbal disparagement of Agamemnon, his subsequent speech (284–332), even if met with approbation, is not enough to convince the men to remain at Troy. He recognizes the Greeks' grievous longing for their wives, acknowledging that fighting "is a burden for the man who desires to return" (*πόνος ἐστὶν ἀνιηθέντα νέεσθαι*), and that one "is distressed" (*ἀσχαλάᾳ; ἀσχαλάαν*) while separated from his wife (291–97). But he provides only the shame of returning empty-handed and Kalchas' prophecy of victory in the war's tenth year as motivations for staying at Troy.

It is Nestor who seals the deal by manipulating the soldiers' desires. At the center of his following speech, he exhorts the men (2.354–56),

> *τῶ μή τις πρὶν ἐπειγέσθω οἶκόνδε νέεσθαι,*
> *πρίν τινα πὰρ Τρώων ἀλόχῳ κατακοιμηθῆναι,*
> *τείσασθαι δ' Ἑλένης ὁρμήματά τε στοναχάς τε.*
>
> Therefore let no one make haste to sail home,
> before he sleeps beside some Trojan's wife,
> and exacts retribution for Helen's struggles and groans.

Here, first of all, Nestor offers to each Achaian a Trojan woman as a new object of desire and sexual substitute for his own wife. Moreover, by describing this female object as "some Trojan's wife," he seeks to activate a triangular dynamic that links access to the woman with domination of the rival enemy man who possesses her. In this way, Nestor attempts to arouse both the sexual and competitive desires of the Greek men and direct them toward the Trojans.

Then, in the third line of this passage, Nestor reminds the army of its original reason for fighting and prime object of desire, Helen.[10] She embodies at once the categories of Achaian and Trojan wife, and thus metaphorically elides for the army the distinction between the two, suggesting that there is no contradiction between desiring one's own wife and continuing to fight against the Trojans, although this is actually true for only one of the Greeks, as we shall see. Nestor's description of "Helen's struggles and groans" vividly imagines her removal to Troy as a violent rape,[11] and frames Achaian rape of "some Trojan's wife" as an equivalent "retribution."[12] Georg Wöhrle (2002: 236) observes that Helen's putative rape seems to be conceived as an injury to the honor of her Greek countrymen as much as to the woman herself; thus, Nestor's exhortation to reciprocal rape is aimed at redeeming Achaian honor through a retaliatory assault on the honor of the Trojan men[13]—and one that is predicated on their defeat in battle. Therefore, in his rhetorical treatment of Helen, Nestor again evokes at once the army's sexual desires and aggressive desires for status. After this speech, Agamemnon orders the men to prepare for war (2.381–90), and they readily comply, now willing to fight.

Through the efficacy of Nestor's words, Homer depicts the Trojan War as yet another conflict between men over women that is motivated by triangular desires. The Greeks, who wish to possess Helen and the other Trojan wives, and to dominate the Trojan men responsible for Helen's abduction, are desiring subjects structurally analogous to Chryses and Achilleus in Book 1. Helen, as the main desired object, occupies the same structural position as Chryseis and Briseis, who were also forcibly seized, while the Trojans are the rivals, in analogy to Agamemnon. The poet includes this episode in Book 2 prior to the renewal of battle in order to clarify and reinstate the desires driving the war.

The Desires of Menelaos and Paris

After introducing the Trojan War in general terms as a triangular conflict between Greek and Trojan armies over women, Homer specifies the personal triangle of

[10] Cf. Collins 1988: 41, who writes, "the contest for this particular woman and wealth has been and will be, in a sense, repeated in the acquisition of other women and wealth as booty, to be distributed among warriors."

[11] Accordingly, I read Ἑλένης as a subjective genitive, and I understand Nestor's invocation of Helen's rape as a construction that both serves his rhetorical purposes of the moment and supports more generally the Greeks' ideology of their siege of Troy as a just war of retribution waged over a worthy female object (Blondell 2010: 5–6). As Collins 1988: 57 recognizes, blaming Helen for a willing elopement with Paris would invalidate the war by making her "an unworthy object of struggle." For a thorough survey of the interpretive difficulties and possibilities of this passage, see Reichel 2002, who discusses a version of my reading (169–70) and ultimately supports a similar solution.

[12] Reichel 2002: 170 and Kirk 1985: 153.

[13] Beye 1974: 90 observes that the ultimate expression of conquest in the *Iliad* is a victor's sexual use of a captive woman.

Menelaos, Helen, and Paris as the war's nucleus, and their desires as its first cause. Immediately following the assembly that arouses anew the Achaians' desire to fight, the narrator introduces Menelaos by name for the first time since Book 1 (2.408). When Menelaos appears a second time as the leader of the Lakedaimonians during the Catalogue of Ships, he is singled out as a desiring subject (588–90):

ἐν δ' αὐτὸς κίεν ᾗσι προθυμίῃσι πεποιθώς,
ὀτρύνων πόλεμόνδε· μάλιστα δὲ ἵετο θυμῷ
τείσασθαι Ἑλένης ὁρμήματά τε στοναχάς τε.

And he came himself among them, won over by his own eagerness,
rousing them for war; and he especially desired in his heart
to exact retribution for Helen's struggles and groans.

Here the narrator, repeating exactly Nestor's earlier formulation about taking revenge for Helen's rape (590 = 356), identifies Menelaos as the man who has a special stake in the war, implicitly reminding the audience how Helen was Menelaos' wife. The Spartan king is so particularly desirous of retribution that he is personally involved in galvanizing his troops.

The poet makes clear the exact target of Menelaos' aggressive desire—his individual rival—at the start of Book 3. As the Greek and Trojan armies approach each other on the battlefield for the first time in the *Iliad*'s narrative, in a replay of the war's beginning, the narrator introduces "godlike Alexandros" at the forefront of the Trojans, shaking his spears and challenging the Achaians (3.15–20). The narrator then ignores the other Greeks and recounts Menelaos' greedy delight at the sight of Paris (Alexandros). In an epic simile, Menelaos is compared to a hungry lion who has joyfully discovered the corpse of an animal and devours it despite dogs and hunters trying to chase him away (23–28). This animal simile emphasizes Menelaos' aggressive eagerness, which is assimilated to an appetite to consume flesh. The narrator clarifies Menelaos' psychology in his following clause, "for he thought that he would exact retribution on the culprit" (*φάτο γὰρ τείσεσθαι ἀλείτην*, 28). "Exact retribution" (*τείσεσθαι*) is the same verb that was used to describe Menelaos' desire to avenge Helen's rape in Book 2, but here it has a specified object—Paris, identified as the perpetrator of Menelaos' loss. The two opposing armies have receded from view, and Menelaos and Paris have emerged as their representatives in a personal confrontation that the narrator emphasizes by juxtaposing their names around the main caesura (*ὣς ἐχάρη Μενέλαος| Ἀλέξανδρον θεοειδέα*, 27, cf. 37, 281).

After this initial focus on Menelaos' feelings, we are given the opportunity to get to know Paris. Despite his bravura, Paris shrinks in fear from fighting with Menelaos, retreating back into the Trojan ranks (3.30–37); unlike his adversary, he is not motivated by an aggressive desire to do battle. He earns a rebuke for this behavior from his brother and the Trojan commander Hektor, who addresses him as "bad-Paris, best in appearance, woman-crazy, beguiler" (*Δύσπαρι, εἶδος ἄριστε, γυναιμανές, ἠπεροπευτά*), wishes that he had never been born or had died unmarried rather than being thus an "outrage" (*λώβην*) and "object of scorn" (*ὑπόψιον*), and suggests that the Greeks are laughing at him for being foremost in beauty but lacking in strength and bravery (39–45). With these words, Hektor describes Paris as a lover of women and not a fighter of men, and presents this conduct as queer by making it an object of his own critique and others' putative mockery. Martial valor is constructed as the celebrated masculine norm, while Paris' heteroeroticism and cowardice is framed as embarrassing deviance.[14]

Moreover, Hektor goes on to authenticate Menelaos' identification of Paris as the abductor of Helen and cause of the ongoing Trojan War. He asserts, "surely being of such character (*ἦ τοιόσδε ἐών*)... you led away a gorgeous woman from a foreign land, the daughter-in-law of spearmen, a great pain to father and city and all the people, an amusement for our enemies, and a humiliation for yourself" (3.46–51).[15] Here Hektor not only lays responsibility for the war at Paris' feet but also suggests that Paris' current failure to engage directly with Menelaos is characteristic, recalling the way he shamefully stole away with Helen; Paris consistently avoids open conflict in favor of deception.[16] Hektor's words hint that the current narrative episode should be understood as a re-enactment of the series of events that led to the war.

Hektor underscores the gender deviance of Paris' behavior with the end of his reproach. He warns his brother that his kithara, "gifts of Aphrodite" (*δῶρ' Ἀφροδίτης*), and good looks would not help him were he to meet Menelaos on the battlefield (3.52–55). Hektor now associates Paris with music-making and the female divinity Aphrodite, the goddess of desire and sex—mentioned here for the first time but familiar to the implied audience[17]—and intimates that playing a stringed instrument and cultivating his erotic appeal during wartime keep him

[14] See also Ransom 2011: 42 and Warwick 2019a: 7.

[15] I take the use of the Greek particle *ἦ* here as affirmative rather than interrogative (*contra* Kirk 1985: 272 and Bowie 2019: 103). As Scodel 2012: 321 explains, *ἦ* "points to external realities that justify the speaker's perception or judgment"; here Hektor employs the particle as he gives evidence of what he regards as Paris' treacherous eroticism.

[16] As Collins 1988: 38 explains, "while martial encounters proceed by *βίη* [force], erotic encounters do so by trickery." Thus, Hektor calls Paris "beguiler" (*ἠπεροπευτά*) at the beginning of his blame speech. See further Mackie 1996: 50–53 on Paris' evasive bowmanship, and Bassi 1997: 329 on how the *Iliad* "distinguishes the idealized Greek male who fights and speaks the truth man-to-man from the woman or feminized male who fights and speaks lies or half-truths from a distance."

[17] On the audience's assumed familiarity with the Olympian gods, see Scodel 2002: 96–99. In early Greek hexameter poetry, Aphrodite is everywhere associated with desire and sex: the *Homeric Hymn to Aphrodite* describes how she imbues beasts, mortals, and immortals with desire and causes them to have sex (*H.Aphr.* 1–6, 45–46, 72–74) and Hesiod names *Eros* and *Himeros* as her attendants, and identifies sex (*philotēs*) as part of her portion (*Theog.* 201–6). Boedeker 1974: 50 catalogues the associations of *himeros* with Aphrodite.

from being prepared for the masculine duty to fight.[18] He concludes by suggesting that only fear has prevented the Trojan people from stoning Paris to death for the "evils" that he has committed (56–57), representing Paris as a problematic and despised "other."

Paris acknowledges the fairness of his brother's critique but nevertheless expresses no shame for his conduct, in a further indication of his queer fracturing of the social order. He tells Hektor that he has rebuked him "proportionally" (*κατ' αἶσαν*, 3.59), but warns his brother not to bring forward against him "the desirable gifts of golden Aphrodite" (*δῶρ' ἐρατὰ... χρυσέης Ἀφροδίτης*) since "not to be rejected are the glorious gifts of the gods" (64–65). Paris here seems to recognize that he has acted wrongly according to the norms of the *Iliad*'s epic world, but he refuses to disavow Aphrodite's gifts—his desirability and consequent sexual success. That is, Paris feels no remorse; he freely owns and defends a special association with Aphrodite. James Redfield (1994: 115) calls Paris "unsocialized," writing that "Paris is insensitive to *nemesis*, the moral disapproval of others, and has no sense of *aischos*, shame."[19] I would suggest, rather, that Paris is *antisocial*—that he knows the *Iliad*'s social codes but nevertheless rejects them, choosing instead to embrace a different way of being.[20] And both Menelaos and Hektor agree that this disregard of the norms of masculine behavior has caused Paris to be a prime mover of the Trojan War and therefore of the *Iliad*'s superplot.

The poet explores the dynamics of desire behind the war's origin by staging a duel between Menelaos and Paris. Despite his own disinclination, Paris bows to Hektor's desire that he do battle (3.67–74):

νῦν αὖτ' εἴ μ' ἐθέλεις πολεμίζειν ἠδὲ μάχεσθαι,
ἄλλους μὲν κάθισον Τρῶας καὶ πάντας Ἀχαιούς,
αὐτὰρ ἔμ' ἐν μέσσῳ καὶ ἀρηΐφιλον Μενέλαον
συμβάλετ' ἀμφ' Ἑλένῃ καὶ κτήμασι πᾶσι μάχεσθαι·
ὁππότερος δέ κε νικήσῃ κρείσσων τε γένηται,
κτήμαθ' ἑλὼν εὖ πάντα γυναῖκά τε οἴκαδ' ἀγέσθω·
οἱ δ' ἄλλοι φιλότητα καὶ ὅρκια πιστὰ ταμόντες
ναίοιτε Τροίην ἐριβώλακα, τοὶ δὲ νεέσθων...

Now then, if you want (*etheleis*) me to wage war and fight,
make the other Trojans and all the Achaians sit down,
but cast me and war-loving Menelaos together in the middle
to fight for Helen and all the possessions;

[18] Arthur 1981: 24 concludes that "Paris' primary identification is with the world of Aphrodite, the antipathetic sphere to the battlefield." See further Ransom 2011: 41–44 on the "negative masculine beauty" of Paris.

[19] See also Tanner 1979: 30; MacCary 1982: 179; Collins 1988: 29–38; van Wees 1992: 127.

[20] As Ransom 2011: 56 remarks, "If gender is a performance, Paris is simply not playing his part."

> whoever conquers and proves the stronger,
> let him take all the possessions and lead the woman home.
> And may you others, having made peace (*philotēta*) with trustworthy oaths,
> dwell in fertile Troy, but let them return...

The proposed duel completes the narrative reduction of the Trojan War into a personal conflict between Menelaos and Paris over Helen. In fact, the duel replaces the war: the two men will fight, but the two armies will come to terms and go their separate ways. Insofar as this private quarrel is at the basis of the war, its resolution must end the war.

Hektor and Menelaos confirm the centrality of this personal dispute in their subsequent discussion of the duel. Hektor publicly introduces Paris' proposal as the "speech of Alexandros, for whose sake (τοῦ εἵνεκα) the conflict arose" (3.87), again identifying Paris as the cause of war, and this time echoing Hera's previous account of Helen in that role (ἧς εἵνεκα, 2.161; 2.177); thus the poet links together the two as the reason for the fighting. Menelaos clarifies this causality further when he tells the armies he accepts the challenge since "you all have suffered many evils for the sake of my strife and Alexandros' instigation" (κακὰ πολλὰ πέπασθε/εἵνεκ' ἐμῆς ἔριδος καὶ Ἀλεξάνδρου ἕνεκ' ἀρχῆς, 3.99–100).[21] By acknowledging "my strife," Menelaos takes responsibility for attacking Troy and brings attention to his desire to dominate his rival, but he also blames Paris for the original "instigation." In so doing, he articulates the triangular dynamic that has been constructed throughout the opening of Book 3: Paris carried off Helen and aroused Menelaos' desire for retribution, as Agamemnon seized Briseis and inspired Achilleus' vengeful desire.

There are, however, some differences between these two triangles. On the one hand, Homer provides no evidence of Menelaos' passionate longing for his lost wife, in contrast to Achilleus' tears over Briseis. Menelaos seems to be almost exclusively concerned with Paris, not Helen; when he agrees to the duel he never mentions Helen and his specification that it will be a fight to the death underlines his aggressive desire to take revenge on Paris (3.101–2).[22] Either he cares more about his status among men and Paris' injury to his honor than the loss of his wife herself, or, following that loss, his libido has been entirely redirected from Helen to Paris.

On the other hand, Paris, unlike Agamemnon in his quarrel with Achilleus, does not seem to focus much aggression back toward his adversary Menelaos. As David Bouvier (2017: 192) has observed, Paris' proposal that the duel's winner "lead the woman home" (γυναῖκά τε οἴκαδ' ἀγέσθω) resembles the language of a marriage contract; Paris imagines the duel as a bride-contest for the hand of

[21] Zenodotus records the alternative reading of ἄτης ("delusion") for ἀρχῆς ("instigation"). In both readings, Menelaos points to Paris' culpability: *atē* describes a clouded state of mind, a "temporary insanity" that often results in bad behavior, yet does not excuse one from responsibility for that behavior (Dodds 1951: 3–6).

[22] On Menelaos' alteration of the duel's terms, see Bouvier 2017: 193–94.

Helen, from which both competitors can walk away alive and with the resulting marriage sealing a peace pact (*philotēs*) between Trojans and Greeks. Thus, Paris' desire appears to be aimed almost exclusively at Helen, whom he mentions by name (3.70). In René Girard's (1965: 140) terms, Paris' lust is unmediated: he is the "passionate man" who "moves directly to the object of his desire without being concerned with Others."[23]

This triangle of desire at the beginning of Book 3 once again confirms for the audience the narrative causality of desiring male subjects, while at the same time drawing our interest to the evolving superplot. As the greater and temporally prior conflict of Menelaos and Paris replaces the quarrel between Achilleus and Agamemnon in our minds, the poet induces a temporary amnesia regarding Zeus's promise to Thetis, a promise that requires the two armies to engage in battle. According to the terms of the duel, as we have seen, the war will end no matter who wins, and both Greek and Trojan soldiers "rejoice" at its agreement, "expecting to cease from miserable war" (3.111–12). The proposition of the duel concluding the Trojan War inspires our narrative desire to discover what exactly will transpire. As James Morrison (1992: 59) explains, though the implied audience, familiar with the Trojan War mythical tradition, knows that the war ends with the sack of Troy, "the duel's outcome remains a mystery" until the last part of Book 3.[24]

Helen as Subject of Desire

From the epic's opening through the beginning of Book 3, Homer situates—at the mortal level—only men's desires as engines of the plot, but after the duel has been agreed upon, he introduces Helen's desire as key to the *Iliad*'s superplot. While previously Helen had been merely referred to as a powerless object of male desire, echoing the representations of Chryseis and Briseis in Book 1, now she herself appears in the narrative as an agent of plot whose desiring subjectivity is gradually revealed. As preparations for the duel begin, the divine messenger Iris, disguised as one of Priam's daughters, comes to Helen in the hall of her palace (3.121–25), leading the audience swiftly away from the battlefield and into Troy.[25] This spatial shift of the narrative from outside to inside the city, from the opposing armies to

[23] See also Tanner 1979: 30, who describes Paris as occupying "a realm of pure desire."

[24] See also Postlethwaite 1985: 2; Morrison 1992: 41–43, 51–63; Rabel 1997: 75–79; Kozak 2017: 35–36. An astute listener might also realize that the resolution paradigm in Book 1 does not offer one-on-one combat as a narrative possibility, much less as a solution to conflict. Such a listener would thus be suspicious about the efficacy of this tactic for ending the war.

[25] Kennedy 1986: 7 calls Iris "the agent of the narrator," because her appearance to Helen is unmotivated by anything internal to the narrative. Cf. Purves 2006: 193–95 on the "almost instantaneous" movement of the gods, which is compared in an Iliadic simile to the movement of the human mind (15.80–83).

Helen in Troy, already hints at how Helen's problematic presence there is at the heart of the superplot.[26]

Iris finds Helen weaving, and the narrator's description of this weaving immediately characterizes Helen as an author of the Trojan War superplot (3.125–28):

> ἡ δὲ μέγαν ἱστὸν ὕφαινε,
> δίπλακα πορφυρέην, πολέας δ' ἐνέπασσεν ἀέθλους
> Τρώων θ' ἱπποδάμων καὶ Ἀχαιῶν χαλκοχιτώνων,
> οὓς ἕθεν εἵνεκ' ἔπασχον ὑπ' Ἄρηος παλαμάων.
>
> And she was weaving a great textile,
> double-folded, purple, and she was sprinkling in many trials
> of horse-taming Trojans and bronze-cuirassed Achaians,
> which for her sake they were suffering by the hands of Ares.

For the first time in the epic, a mortal woman actually *does* something in narrative time, functioning as an agent. Significantly, Helen is creating a representation of the ongoing Trojan War, the subject of the *Iliad*'s superplot, which has just been introduced in Books 2 and 3. The narrator's use of the imperfect verb "were suffering" (ἔπασχον) indicates that her depiction is of current events.[27] Moreover, the narrator's description of the armies on her textile suffering "for her sake" (ἕθεν εἵνεκ') linguistically links the woven image with the main narrative, in which Hera asserted that the Achaians were perishing for Helen's sake (ἧς εἵνεκα, 2.161). The textile's familiar portrayal of the war and its causality connects Helen's weaving—like Achilleus' speech—to the poet's own epic production.[28]

The difference between Achilleus' and Helen's creations represents the difference between the *Iliad*'s main plot and superplot. Achilleus' predictive speech generates future events, which constitute the linear, forward-moving main plot. Helen's weaving, however, depicts a timeless and iterative conflict between Greeks and Trojans, which constitutes a superplot that functions as a static background to the dynamic main plot. The Trojan War is *not* decided within the bounds of the *Iliad*'s narrative; the superplot is an incessant back-and-forth between Trojans and Achaians, like the putative back-and-forth of Helen's shuttle, with no final resolution. As Ann Bergren (2008) has argued, Helen's web represents this temporal suspension.[29]

While Helen clearly appears as a poet-figure in these lines, she neither speaks nor sings epic, which mitigates her identification with the narrator[30] and further differentiates her from Achilleus. Unlike the male hero, she is voiceless, silently

[26] See Purves 2010: 14–62 for a spatial conception of the *Iliad*'s plot.

[27] Kennedy 1986: 5.

[28] Clader 1976: 6–9; Kennedy 1986: 5; Lynn-George 1988: 29; Taplin 1992: 97–98; Austin 1994: 28–41; Blondell 2013: 68.

[29] See also Kennedy 1986: 12–13, who observes how Helen's visionary capacity is limited.

[30] Kennedy 1986 *passim* and Roisman 2006: 11.

weaving,[31] and her visual representation of the war seems to confirm her earlier positioning as object of male desires. Helen's entrance into the poem *in propria persona* is thus ambivalent: she is somewhere between subject and object, and her own interiority remains opaque, even as her poetic weaving indicates her active role as a generator of the *Iliad*'s superplot.

In her speech to Helen, Iris confirms that the heroine's weaving mirrors the action of the epic's superplot. The messenger goddess tells the heroine to come to Troy's walls in order to see the unexpected behavior "of horse-taming Trojans and bronze-cuirassed Achaians" (*Τρώων θ' ἱπποδάμων καὶ Ἀχαιῶν χαλκοχιτώνων*) who were before "desirous of baneful war" (*ὀλοοῖο λιλαιόμενοι πολέμοιο*), but now sit in silence with shields and spears idle (3.130–35). Iris' description of the two sides exactly repeats the narrator's account of the combatants on Helen's textile (131 = 127), connecting the opposing armies on the battlefield with the woven image.[32] Moreover, these men's previous desire for war recalls the fighting on the textile and reminds the audience of the Greek army's motivating desires, which were first presented in Book 2.

Iris also offers a new acknowledgment of Helen's subjectivity, explaining that Paris and Menelaos "will fight over you: whoever is victorious, you will be called his wife" (*μαχήσονται περὶ σεῖο·/ τῷ δέ κε νικήσαντι φίλη κεκλήσῃ ἄκοιτις*, 3.137–38). The goddess's words are a quick summary of the narrative crystallization of the Trojan War into a duel between two men over Helen. Yet now, instead of referring to Helen in the third person and grouping her together with "all the possessions" as the duel's stake, Iris addresses her in the second person. Helen is not merely an object but a subject whose affiliation as wife will be decided in the contest. Indeed, by summoning her to the walls, Iris has encouraged Helen to embody the prominent subject position of viewer of the battlefield, the same perspective that Helen assumes imaginatively as she weaves the textile of the war in her home.

Iris' encounter with Helen begins the narrative revelation of the heroine's desires: "by speaking, the goddess cast into her heart sweet yearning (*himeron*) for her former husband and city and parents" (*εἰποῦσα θεὰ γλυκὺν ἵμερον ἔμβαλε θυμῷ/ ἀνδρός τε προτέρου καὶ ἄστεος ἠδὲ τοκήων*, 3.139–40). Iris' account of Paris' forthcoming duel with Menelaos and its consequences for Helen seems to have reminded the heroine of her past life and inspired her yearning (*himeros*). She immediately leaves her chamber and makes her way to the Skaian Gates while shedding a tear (141–45); this weeping marks Helen's *himeros* as painful as well as "sweet," and recalls the tears of the desiring Achilleus in Book 1, who cried over the loss of Briseis. As Lynn Kozak (2017: 36) has observed, Helen's emotion invites the audience into her mind and "creates character alignment with her" as we

[31] In this capacity, she recalls the Fates, who spin out what will happen but do not speak it.
[32] Kirk 1985: 281.

follow her to the city's walls. Helen's suffering may also begin to activate our sympathy for and empathy with the heroine.

At the same time, this episode already figures Helen's desire as a destabilizing, generative force. Insofar as Helen's sudden *himeros* impels her from her residence deep within Troy to its liminal gates, it is physically disruptive. Similarly, on a social level the eruption of this yearning for a former spouse, home, and family threatens the integrity of Helen's current relationships in Troy. From its narrative introduction, Homer presents Helen's desire as a powerful impetus that sets the heroine—and her story—in motion.

As Helen approaches the battlements, the elders of Troy react to her in a scene that guides the audience's own response and confirms her significance for the superplot. The collective of elders are internal spectators roughly parallel to the external audience, who similarly apprehend Helen moving toward the walls, and they model for the audience the activity of interpreting her. Speaking among themselves, they agree that it is not a matter of indignation (*nemesis*) for Trojans and Achaians to suffer a long time on behalf of such a divinely beautiful woman,[33] but nevertheless wish her to sail away to avoid future pain for their children (3.156–60). That is, the elders admire Helen and concede that she is a worthy object of war, but at the same time they reject her, believing that the grievous war will end if she leaves Troy. In this way, they construct Helen as a fascinating, ambivalent subject, and admit her power to determine the continuance of the Trojan War. Their commentary encourages us to focus on this mysterious character and engage in a similar process of evaluation.

Like the elders, the Trojan king Priam directs his attention to Helen, but in opposition to them, he both claims her and attempts to elide her power. Summoning Helen to view the battlefield with him, Priam kindly addresses her as "my (φίλον) child," invites her to look at her "former spouse and in-laws and intimates (φίλους)," and declares that he considers the gods, not her, "responsible" for the grievous war (3.161–65). When he describes Helen with the adjective *philos*, Priam identifies her as a member of his family who belongs in Troy; likewise, he distances her from the Achaians below the wall by designating them her "former" family and *philoi*. Furthermore, by attributing responsibility to the divine sphere, he deflects blame from Helen and his son Paris, a move that self-servingly asserts the righteousness of the Trojans' defense of the couple[34]—but also reduces their personal agency. Yet Priam's speech still keeps Helen's desiring subjectivity in the audience's ken, since his admonition for Helen to behold her "former spouse" (πρότερόν τε πόσιν, 163) echoes the narrator's account of Helen's

[33] See Redfield 1994: 115–19 on the meaning of *nemesis* in Homeric epic. See Schönberger 1960: 200–1 and Worman 1997: 157–58 on the power of Helen's beauty.

[34] Blondell 2010: 6.

sudden yearning for her "former husband" (ἀνδρός τε προτέρου, 3.140), and provides a visual opportunity for the intensification of that desire.

When Helen finally speaks in reply, her opening words reaffirm her agency and present her as the problematic subject of conflicting desires, past and present (3.172–76):

> *αἰδοῖός τέ μοί ἐσσι, φίλε ἑκυρέ, δεινός τε·*
> *ὡς ὄφελεν θάνατός μοι ἁδεῖν κακὸς ὁππότε δεῦρο*
> *υἱέϊ σῷ ἑπόμην, θάλαμον γνωτούς τε λιποῦσα*
> *παῖδά τε τηλυγέτην καὶ ὁμηλικίην ἐρατεινήν.*
> *ἀλλὰ τά γ᾽ οὐκ ἐγένοντο· τὸ καὶ κλαίουσα τέτηκα.*
>
> To me you are venerable, my (*phile*) father-in-law, and a source of awe;
> would that evil death had pleased me, when here
> I followed your son, having left behind my marriage chamber and relatives
> and late-born daughter and desirable (*erateinēn*) group of agemates.
> But these things were not to be; therefore, truly I have melted weeping.

With this marked speech—the first time we hear a mortal woman's voice in this epic—Helen articulates her adulterous agency by asserting, as the first-person subject of a middle verb and active participle, that she "followed" Paris to Troy and "left behind" her life in Sparta. While it is theoretically possible to do both of these actions under duress,[35] they carry a connotation of intentionality and suggest an active desire, in clear contrast to the narrator's earlier third person account of how Briseis "unwillingly... went" (ἀέκουσ᾽... κίεν) with Agamemnon's heralds (1.348). Moreover, as Ruby Blondell (2010: 15) has pointed out, Helen's retrospective wish that death had pleased her implies that leaving was what pleased her instead.[36] Helen's words thus indicate agency and motivating desire—here a desire for Paris—and her opening address to Priam as her *philos* father-in-law acknowledges the consummation of that desire and her resulting affiliation with the Trojan royal family as Paris' wife.

Yet this same speech also repudiates this desire and her consequent action. Her wish that she had ended her life instead of abandoning Sparta suggests that her desire for Paris is a thing of the past. A few lines later she abuses herself as "dog-faced" (κυνώπιδος, 3.180),[37] and, near the end of the scene, worries that her brothers "fear the many disgraces and reproaches that are mine" (αἴσχεα

[35] Blondell 2010:15, who nevertheless notes that "the context makes it clear that she was impelled by her own desire."

[36] See also Blondell 2013: 62 on Helen's assertion of subjectivity in this scene.

[37] Graver 1995 interprets this insult as indicating an uncontrolled and excessive (sexual) appetite, while Franco 2014 argues more specifically that Helen evokes the "dog as traitor," enticed from its master by another who offers treats (153–56), and also the fawning dog that conceals a dangerous bite, insofar as she seduces men with her charm to destruction (204–5).

δειδιότες καὶ ὀνείδεα πόλλ' ἅ μοί ἐστιν, 242). Helen clearly regrets her decision to come to Troy.

In turn, her nostalgic evocation of her marriage chamber, family, and "desirable" peers confirms her current yearning for those in Sparta, including Menelaos, for whom the marriage chamber seems to function as a metonym.[38] Her assertion that she "[has] melted weeping" recalls and may refer to the tears that she shed on her way to the walls of Troy after being stricken with *himeros*, and again points to a painful desire for those she left behind.[39] Helen's first speech, therefore, reveals a woman who consistently desires what she does not have: when a Spartan queen, she wanted the Trojan prince Paris, and now, as a Trojan princess, she desires her Spartan family.

This current desire seems to shape and motivate the descriptions Helen provides of the Achaians on the battlefield below after Priam asks her to identify her erstwhile compatriots. When she names Agamemnon, she recalls that he was "my brother-in-law" (*δαὴρ αὖτ' ἐμός*, 3.180), recognizing him as a former kinsman. She spontaneously identifies Idomeneus and launches into a brief, unsolicited anecdote about how "war-loving (*ἀρηΐφιλος*) Menelaos often hosted him in our house" (232–33); here she introduces her former husband by name and recalls their life together in a time of peace, even as his epithet is a grim reminder of the conflict in which they are now enmeshed. Finally, Helen wonders, again without prompting, where her two brothers, Kastor and Polydeukes, are and speculates whether they came with the fleet "from desirable (*ἐρατεινῆς*) Lakedaimon" (236–42). Helen's words thematize her preoccupation with her Spartan family and her desire for them and for her home, which she describes with an adjective related to *erōs* ("lust").

Thus, this whole scene, known as the Teichoskopia ("Viewing from the Wall"), which has been rejected by some as anachronistic and superfluous,[40] functions importantly to further elucidate Helen's desiring subjectivity[41]—and it also positions her firmly as a generator of narrative. Helen's words recall the catalogues in Book 2, confirming her identification with the *Iliad*'s poet, which her woven

[38] Kirk 1985: 290. Krieter-Spiro 2015: 76 alternatively calls the "marriage chamber" (*θάλαμον*) a "metaphor for marriage and thus Menelaos."

[39] Cf. Lesser 2019: 218–19 on the possibility that Helen's representation here is modeled on that of the Odyssean Penelope, who weeps and longs for her lost husband.

[40] Analyst critics have objected to the idea that Priam would still be ignorant of the Achaian heroes in the ninth year of the war, and they also view this passage as a redundant repetition of the catalogues of leaders recently delivered in Book 2 (for bibliography, see West 2011: 132). For the idea that the display of the female prize to contestants in a bride-contest is the mythic prototype of the Teichoskopia, see Kakridis 1971: 33–37; Clader 1976: 9–10; Postlethwaite 1985: 4–6; Austin 1994: 30–47. Jamison 1994 argues that the Teichoskopia reflects the ceremonial steps of a ritual counterabduction in the Indo-European poetic tradition, as evidenced in Book 3 of the Indic epic the *Mahabharata*.

[41] On the Teichoskopia as a vehicle to further introduce Helen's character, see also Schönberger 1960: 197–99; Parry 1966: 198–201; Lendle 1968: 68–69; Kakridis 1971: 32, 35–36; Kirk 1985: 286; Postlethwaite 1985: 6.

representation of the war had already suggested.[42] The Teichoskopia illustrates how Helen's desire, like Achilleus', produces epic speech. And Helen does not only repeat the narrator; she tells a slightly new and different story that refocuses the narrative around her desires and actions. For the first time she asserts her agency in her journey to Troy, and, as Nancy Worman (2002: 48) has observed, she describes the Achaian leaders mostly in their relation to her own identity and experiences, "giving herself the central role."

In her entrance into the *Iliad*, then, Helen is presented as a powerful narrative agent, first through her silent weaving of the ongoing war and then through her speech during the Teichoskopia. The poet depicts the heroine's sequential and opposing desires for Paris and Menelaos as the respective roots of these two narrative productions. Helen's appearance therefore revises the narrative causality that had been introduced in Books 1 and 2 of the epic, in which men were the desiring subjects and narrative agents, and women only desired objects in triangular conflicts between men. While Helen seems like the archetype for this conception of women when she is first mentioned in Book 2, her gradual shift in narrative representation from third, to second, and finally to first person forces a progressive re-evaluation of this androcentric model as she is shown to be a desiring subject and the active, rather than passive, cause of war and heroic epic.

The poet further indicates how Helen introduces a new mode of female subjectivity with Priam's mention of the Amazons in response to his daughter-in-law's first words. After Helen finishes speaking, Priam compares the immensity of the Achaian hosts to the massive Phrygian army with whom he had fought "on that day when the man-like Amazons came" (*ἤματι τῷ ὅτε τ' ἦλθον Ἀμαζόνες ἀντιάνειραι*, 3.189). Amazons subvert the normative expectations for female behavior that have been presented up to this point in the poem: instead of being fought over, they fight, and Priam explicitly calls them "man-like."[43] Helen's appearance and voice seem to provoke Priam's memory of the Amazons—unusually assertive and masculine women. Indeed, he connects the advent of the Amazons with Helen's arrival by using the same aorist verb to describe how they both "came" (*ἐλθοῦσα*, 162; *ἦλθον*, 189) into his presence.

If the Amazons are "man-like" in their fighting ability, Helen is similar to the *Iliad*'s men in the disruptive power of her desire. With her consistently adulterous

[42] On Helen as a poet-figure in her echo of the catalogues in Book 2, see Clader 1976: 9 and Suzuki 1989: 40. Cf. Elmer 2005: 22–28, who subtly differentiates Helen from the poet. Martin 2003: 124–25 identifies in Helen's first words a traditional discourse of lament. He argues that she is consistently associated with lament in Greek epic, and that lament, "this antiphonal, foundational speech-act, can be represented as the original, authorizing act which lies behind *all* poetry of commemoration" (Martin 2003: 128). If we accept this, Helen, as a representative practitioner of the genre, is in yet another way associated with the production of heroic epic.

[43] DuBois 1982 (esp. 34–42) has shown how the Amazons in ancient Greek literature and art are figures of difference. Particularly, they are anti-marriage and anti-culture in their refusal to be exchanged between men. On the Amazons, see also Mayer 2014 and Penrose 2016. On the meaning of the adjective *ἀντιάνειραι*, see Silk 2007: 191–92 and Krieter-Spiro 2015: 81–82.

yearnings, she represents the threat that the desiring woman poses for the patriarchy and patriliny.[44] When a man takes a woman in marriage, he brings an outsider into his home upon whom he must depend to manage the household and produce legitimate heirs.[45] Yet the wife's original loyalty is to her natal family; one may note how Helen, unbidden, ends her speech with discussion of her brothers and even emphasizes their blood relationship (3.238).[46] In addition to the question of whether the woman will prioritize her marital family, the danger persists that she might betray her husband because of sexual desire for another man, and thus compromise the integrity of his household and the legitimacy of his offspring—and also besmirch his honor.[47]

This is exactly what Helen does when she abandons her marriage to Menelaos, along with their daughter, and "follows" Paris to Troy.[48] Yet Helen's loyalty to her second husband is also dubious, as her feelings of regret and her renewed desire for her Spartan community indicate. Helen is a sign for the instability of female allegiance, an instability that undermines male control and has the potential to wreak havoc, as it does for Menelaos and the Achaians as well as for Paris and the Trojans.[49] Like the Amazons on the battlefield, Helen is dangerous. And like them, she may be termed "queer" on the basis of her violation of the epic's norms of female passivity and fidelity, which were established in Book 1 through the characters of Chryseis and Briseis.[50]

Yet, as we have seen, Helen's queer desires, like the desires of the *Iliad*'s male heroes, are shown to generate narrative—in her case the superplot. Tony Tanner (1979: 26) has recognized the narrative productivity of female adultery, asserting that "the failure to transform, tame, familiarize, or domesticate the ambiguous

[44] Tanner 1979: 30 and *passim*; Worman 2001: 19; Felson and Slatkin 2004: 96. Cf. Blondell 2013: 15–22 on Pandora.

[45] See Tanner 1979: 26, who calls the wife "the stranger in the house," and Collins 1988: 45–67 for discussion of Helen as the paradigmatic woman who is both *philē* and *echthrē*.

[46] As Blondell 2013: 31–33 observes, Helen does not actually relocate away from her natal family when she marries Menelaos: he comes to her. This means that Helen's yearning for Sparta encompasses desires for both her original families, natal as well as marital.

[47] See Tanner 1979: 60–64.

[48] Blondell 2013: 33 notes that in both the *Iliad* and the larger mythological tradition, Helen does not have any other children with Paris (or another husband), and never gives Menelaos a male heir. Tanner 1979: 98 explains: "the negative or reverse aspect of an inclination to adultery would seem to be a disinclination to maternity... It is all part of the decomposition of that unstable, supposedly unitary trinity—the wife-mother-lover."

[49] The mythological tradition presents Helen as the ultimately mobile woman, several times abducted or married (Theseus, Menelaos, Paris, Deiphobos, Achilleus; cf. West 1975). As Blondell 2013: 29 explains, "the number—and inadequacy—of Helen's various male partners suggest that the forces of female beauty and desire are in their essence uncontrollable." Worman 2001: 19 concludes, "Simultaneously the archetypal bride and the most illustrious flouter of the marriage bond, Helen embodies the dangerous potential of all women to be unfaithful to their men."

[50] Chryseis is shuttled between her captor and father, and we receive no information at all about her subjectivity. As we have seen, Briseis is presented as "unwilling" to leave her captor Achilleus' tent (1.348), thus establishing a norm of female fidelity to the man who sexually possesses her, even as she passively accedes to her removal.

presence from 'the outside' is one of the permanently generative themes of Western literature." Female desire for someone external to her marriage breaks up both the marriage-contract[51] and the narrative stasis that marriage represents. Tanner (1979: 105) writes that love in the novel of adultery "is . . . the sexual drive that initiates the narration, without which the text would remain in a state of inert noncommencement."[52] Adulterous desires work in the same way to produce the conflict—and epic speeches—of the *Iliad*'s superplot.

The narrative importance of Helen's queerness explains why Homer largely avoids demonizing her for her adultery and, indeed, presents her as a rather sympathetic character. No one blames Helen except for the heroine herself during the *Iliad*'s story time,[53] and while her words do represent a narrative acknowledgment of the destructive consequences of her behavior,[54] they also rehabilitate her character, making her into a woman with a sense of shame. In her cognizance of social transgression and self-deprecating remorse, Helen appears virtuous, and thus her self-blame actually elicits the goodwill of others.[55] Moreover, her conduct in Troy is that of a modest and irreproachable wife insofar as she spends her time weaving at home and only emerges from the house veiled and with female attendants (3.141–44);[56] during the Teichoskopia, she is also respectful and obedient to her Trojan father-in-law, Priam. For all of these reasons, Helen is charming, inviting sympathy rather than condemnation from both the internal characters and the external audience.[57]

If Helen's appealing persona makes us care for her and desire her happiness, then we become more invested in the evolving superplot. We now desire more fervently to know the outcome of the duel that will decide her fate, especially since the Teichoskopia has delayed the confrontation, increasing our suspense. More importantly, the Teichoskopia has enabled and enticed us to read Helen's mind and see people and events through her eyes. This alignment, along with her painful emotions and sympathetic character, encourage our empathy with her conflicted erotic subjectivity. Such empathetic desire only deepens anticipation for the duel, which offers Helen reunification with the Spartan husband she now

[51] In the Greek world, the contract is between husband and father, guaranteeing the husband's ownership of the wife (Taillardat 1982: 12); in Homer specifically, the woman is usually exchanged for bridewealth (see Finley 1955; Lacey 1966; Snodgrass 1974; Perysinakis 1991; Lyons 2012: 19–22).

[52] See also Arthur 1981: 26, who calls Helen "a disruptive force."

[53] Helen predicts that the Trojan women will blame her if she joins Paris in their bedchamber after the duel (3.411–12), and she describes how Hektor used to defend her whenever one of her in-laws would rebuke her (24.768–70), but none of them actually criticizes her in the *Iliad* itself.

[54] Ebbott 1999.

[55] Worman 2001: 28–29; Roisman 2006: 13–14; Blondell 2010: 9–16; 2013: 63–69; 2018: 117.

[56] Blondell 2010: 11–12; 2013: 58; 2018: 117.

[57] The critic Martin West's response to Helen attests to her pull on the external audience. He writes (1975: 3), "Her personality is as captivating as her person . . . [Homer's] Helen is to my mind the most marvellous, sincere, sweet-natured woman in ancient literature, with the possible exception of Sophocles' Deianeira."

yearns for—or the confirmation of the new marriage with Paris that she chose. As the narrator turns back to the preparations for the duel, the audience is riveted, eager to find out how it will end.

The Triangle of Helen, Paris, and Aphrodite

The motivating desires of the superplot are most fully thematized in the final scenes of Book 3, during the duel and its aftermath. In the duel, after Paris' first spear-cast fails to penetrate Menelaos' shield, the Greek hero prefaces his own answering throw with an appeal to Zeus (3.351–54):

> *Ζεῦ ἄνα, δὸς τείσασθαι ὅ με πρότερος κάκ᾽ ἔοργε,*
> *δῖον Ἀλέξανδρον, καὶ ἐμῇς ὑπὸ χερσὶ δάμασσον,*
> *ὄφρα τις ἐρρίγῃσι καὶ ὀψιγόνων ἀνθρώπων*
> *ξεινοδόκον κακὰ ῥέξαι, ὅ κεν φιλότητα παράσχῃ.*
>
> Lord Zeus, grant me to exact retribution against he who first did me wrong,
> brilliant Alexandros, and subdue him under my hands,
> so that someone in later days may also shudder
> to commit wrongs against a host who has provided guest-friendship (*philotēta*).

Menelaos' prayer "to exact retribution" (*τείσασθαι*) clearly articulates his driving desire for vengeance, repeating the verb that the narrator had used twice previously to describe Menelaos' aggressive desire (2.590; 3.28). Moreover, once again Menelaos focuses all of his libidinal energy on Paris, whom he faults for violation of the *philotēs* that had united them when he entertained the Trojan in his house, avoiding any explicit reference to Helen and the corruption of his marriage.

Menelaos' citation of Paris' past transgression also connects anew this current episode with the war's origin story. The poet signals again that this duel is a narrative replay of past events when Menelaos fails to harm Paris first with spear, then sword (3.355–63); he seems as impotent to stop the Trojan prince as when Paris sailed away from Sparta with Helen. This repetition reaches its apex when the goddess Aphrodite breaks the chin-strap of the helmet with which Menelaos threatens to choke Paris (371–75),[58] and then, as Menelaos attacks a final time, "raging to kill" (*κατακτάμεναι μενεαίνων*, 379), snatches Paris away, hides him in a cloud of mist, and deposits him in his "fragrant marriage chamber" (380–82).

[58] This chin-strap is described as a "much-embroidered strap" (*πολύκεστος ἱμάς*), with *πολύκεστος* being a Homeric *hapax legomenon*. As Krieter-Spiro 2015: 137 observes, this decorated strap may be another marker of Paris' special relationship with Aphrodite, since later in the epic Aphrodite wears a similar "embroidered strap" (*κεστὸς ἱμάς*, 14.214), which is magically imbued with sex and desire.

With Aphrodite's help, Paris has again escaped from Menelaos, foiling the satisfaction of the Greek's aggressive desire.

After leaving Paris, Aphrodite summons Helen to reconsummate her Trojan marriage, continuing the poet's representation of the desires and actions at the root of the war. The goddess finds Helen still on Troy's walls, surrounded by a group of Trojan women, and approaches her disguised as a beloved old slave woman from Sparta (3.383–88). Thus, her visit to Helen recalls and inverts Iris' previous appearance: both goddesses masquerade as an intimate of Helen and encourage her to proceed from one place to another; however, whereas Iris, disguised as a Trojan woman, prompts Helen's movement from her house to Troy's walls, Aphrodite, disguised as a Spartan woman, bids her to reverse her course. Homer thus suggests that this scene will address for a second time the heroine's competing desires for different men and lead to an outcome unlike the Teichoskopia.

While Iris' speech had inspired Helen's yearning (*himeros*) for Menelaos, Aphrodite's words to Helen are similarly meant to arouse her desire—but this time for the Trojan prince. The goddess tells the heroine that Paris is asking for her, and that he is in bed in their marriage chamber (3.390–91), supplanting Helen's previous recollection of her marriage chamber in Sparta (174). Then Aphrodite figures Paris as especially desirable, "shining in his beauty and his garments" (392),[59] and to underscore his attractiveness, she asserts that Helen would think that Paris was going to dance in a chorus, or had just come from there, rather than from the battlefield (392–94).[60] The goddess's account of Paris seems to have the intended effect of provoking Helen's desire: "thus she spoke, and roused the passion (*thumon*) in her chest" (*ὣς φάτο, τῇ δ' ἄρα θυμὸν ἐνὶ στήθεσσιν ὄρινε*, 395).[61] Aphrodite's instigation of Helen's *thumos* recalls how Iris previously cast yearning in her *thumos* (139),[62] and is narrated with the same formula used to describe how Agamemnon's testing speech affected the Greek soldiers (2.142), making them "eager for home" (2.154).

Yet, unexpectedly, Helen does not silently obey her visitor and her own desire, as she had when Iris came to her. Instead, she recognizes Aphrodite through her

[59] Blondell 2010: 22. Cf. Hera's adornment in 14.170–86, when she prepares for her seduction of Zeus (Louden 2006: 77).

[60] Choral dancers are envisioned as erotic objects in the *Iliad*: Hermes desired and impregnated Polymele after seeing her dancing in a maiden chorus for Artemis (16.179–83), and the youthful (female *and* male) dancers on the Shield of Achilleus are described as erotically appealing to viewers (*ἱμερόεντα*, 18.603). See also *H.Aphr.* 117–20 and Alkman fr. 27 PGM. On the eroticization of the chorus in early Greek poetry more generally, see Boedeker 1974: 47–51; Muellner 1990: 80–82; Kurke 2013: 150.

[61] Kirk 1985: 322; Louden 2006; Blondell 2010: 22.

[62] Lendle 1968: 68–71 argues that Helen's desire for Paris (inspired by Aphrodite) is different in kind and much more powerful than the desire that Iris inspires in her. I think that the structural analogy of these two episodes precludes Lendle's interpretation, and he himself describes the overwhelming effect of both instances of desire in similar terms.

disguise, questions the goddess's motives, mocks her, and finally refuses to reunite with Paris (3.396–412). On the basis of her aggressive response, some scholars have argued that Aphrodite's incitement of Helen's *thumos* represents the arousal of anger rather than desire,[63] but I believe that Blondell (2010: 22 n. 84) is right to conclude that "The anger is a secondary emotion, as she resists the desire."[64] Helen seems to be stricken first by passion for Paris and then by fury at Aphrodite for inspiring that feeling.

In this scene, therefore, Homer explores Helen's complex desires by positioning her as subject in a new triangle of desire with Paris as object and Aphrodite as rival, which resembles Achilleus' triangular conflict with Agamemnon over Briseis in Book 1. Notably, Helen reproaches Aphrodite in ways that recall Achilleus' first long rebuke of Agamemnon. She asks the goddess, "why do you desire (λιλαίεαι) to beguile (ἠπεροπεύειν) me in this way?" and wonders to which Asian city Aphrodite will lead her next for liaison with one of her male favorites (3.399–402). With these rhetorical questions, Helen complains that Aphrodite's desire, not her own, has caused her to follow Paris to Troy. Similarly, Achilleus begins with a rhetorical question, asking how anyone could obey Agamemnon's orders given the commander's shameless and greedy design to appropriate another king's prize, and then he asserts that he has come to Troy not for his own sake but rather to make war on Menelaos' and Agamemnon's behalf (1.150–60).

Both Helen and Achilleus also bemoan how their rivals are threatening their honor. Near the end of her speech, Helen declares that she "will not go" (οὐκ εἶμι) to Paris because it would make her an object of the Trojan women's *nemesis* and blame (3.410–12); these are the women that surround Helen when Aphrodite comes to find her at the beginning of the scene, and they represent her community at Troy. Achilleus ends his speech by saying that he "will go" (εἶμι) back to Phthia, instead of staying at Troy, because he is "dishonored" despite his contributions to the war (1.163–71). In both cases, Helen and Achilleus assert that they "will go" their own ways in order to preserve their reputations.[65] With Helen's aggressive, status-conscious desiring subjectivity in this scene, the poet again marks out his heroine as Achilleus' analogue and also a queer actor, since this positionality is gendered masculine according to the epic's established norms of behavior.[66]

Differently from Achilleus, however, Helen's rival in this triangle is a goddess, not a mortal, who has inspired her sexual and aggressive desires by bringing the

[63] Leaf 1971: 147–48; Willcock 1978: 222; MacCary 1982: 170; Roisman 2006: 18.

[64] See also Worman 2002: 50.

[65] Reckford 1964 also makes the connection between Helen's words here and Achilleus' "expressed intention to return to Phthia" (17) and recognizes that "both Achilles and Helen strive for honor and force the issue" (20).

[66] See also Worman 2002: 48 on how Helen's fear of others' insults and concern with fame (as we shall see in Book 6) are characteristics that normally belong to male speakers, and, particularly, warriors.

beloved object closer, rather than taking him away: Helen lashes out at Aphrodite for (again) trickily inducing her to become Paris' intimate partner in Troy instead of allowing Menelaos to lead her "home" (3.403–5). Although the poet avoids giving Helen's passion a name, her desire for Paris is aroused by his beauty and availability, and for these reasons is probably meant to be identified with the urgent drives of *erōs* and *himeros*; Aphrodite's mythological association with these two forms of desire, as well as her narrative parallelism to Iris, who previously inspired *himeros* in Helen, support this assumption. Helen's passion thus contrasts with Achilleus' desire for Briseis, which is based in the beloved concubine's absence after she was appropriated by Agamemnon, and therefore seems to constitute a variety of *pothē* ("longing"), though it, too, is never named.

Given the erotic nature of her desire for Paris, Helen endeavors to best her rival by mockingly encouraging her to unite with the Trojan prince herself, in a reversal of Achilleus' warnings to Agamemnon not to remove Briseis. Helen imagines Aphrodite's sexual congress with Paris as a diminution in which the female divinity gives up her place among the gods and subordinates herself to a mortal man as his "wife" or "slave" (3.406–9). If Aphrodite were to snatch Paris for herself, as before she had "carried him away" (τὸν δ' ἐξήρπαξ', 3.380) for Helen,[67] then the heroine would triumph over her rival and be free from her own desires—both lustful and aggressive.

However, like Agamemnon in relation to Achilleus, Aphrodite exhibits a reciprocal desire to dominate Helen.[68] "Angered" (χολωσαμένη, 3.413), she responds to Helen's power-play with a threat of her own that affirms her superior position (414–17):

μή μ' ἔρεθε, σχετλίη, μὴ χωσαμένη σε μεθείω,
τὼς δέ σ' ἀπεχθήρω ὡς νῦν ἔκπαγλα φίλησα,
μέσσῳ δ' ἀμφοτέρων μητίσομαι ἔχθεα λυγρά,
Τρώων καὶ Δαναῶν, σὺ δέ κεν κακὸν οἶτον ὄληαι.

Do not provoke me, foolhardy woman, lest angered I reject you,
and be your enemy as much as I am now terribly close to you,
and in the middle of both sides, I will devise grievous hatreds,
of Trojans and Danaans, and you might perish with an evil fate.

Addressing Helen insultingly, she warns the heroine that she could destroy her, by, presumably, revoking her prophylactic charm. While Aphrodite's favor has

[67] The verb ἐξαρπάζω is used in the *Iliad* and elsewhere in early Greek hexameter poetry to describe sexual abduction: *Il.* 3.344 (Paris and Helen); *Od.* 15.250 (Eos and Kleitos); *H.Aphr.* 117 and 121 (Hermes and the fictional daughter of Otreus), 203 (Zeus and Ganymede), 218 (Eos and Tithonos); *H.Dem.* 3, 19, 81 (Hades and Persephone). On this verb, see Boedeker 1974: 71.

[68] Blondell 2010: 17 sees in this exchange "competitiveness and jealousy on the goddess's part."

made Helen a valued object of others' sexual desire, the goddess's enmity would make Helen a universal target of aggressive desire based on her adultery and the lives lost on her behalf, costing Helen both her status and her life.[69]

Aphrodite's words recall not only Agamemnon's aggression toward Achilleus but also the Greek leader's admonition to Chryses in the first triangle of desire of Book 1, when he similarly told the priest "go, do not provoke me" (ἴθι, μή μ' ἐρέθιζε, 1.32). Additionally, Aphrodite's threat of harming Helen echoes Agamemnon's implicit threat of violence toward Chryses (1.26–28) as well as Zeus's more explicit threat to lay his hands on Hera (1.565–67) in the third, divine triangle of desire at the end of Book 1. Homer thus suggests a parallelism between this conflict and all three of the analogous triangular conflicts in Book 1.

This parallelism is confirmed by Helen's submissive reaction to Aphrodite's warning. The narrator reports that Helen "was afraid" after Aphrodite's speech (ὣς ἔφατ', ἔδεισεν), employing the same formula that had characterized the desiring subjects Chryses' and Hera's fearful responses to their rivals' aggressive words in Book 1 (3.418 = 1.33 = 1.568). And, like Chryses, who then "went away silently" (βῆ δ' ἀκέων, 1.34), and Hera, who "sat down silently" (ἀκέουσα καθῆστο, 1.569), Helen "went . . . in silence" (βῆ . . . σιγῇ, 3.419–20) from the walls of Troy, wordlessly obeying her more powerful rival. Moreover, in so doing, Helen "escaped the notice of all the Trojan women" (420), avoiding blame but also becoming socially isolated in a parallel to Achilleus' withdrawal from the Greek army.[70] The narrator's closing comment that "the goddess led the way" (ἦρχε δὲ δαίμων, 420) draws attention to Aphrodite's final triumph over Helen in this confrontation.

Yet Helen remains resistant to the goddess's compulsion, just as her analogues in Book 1, Chryses, Achilleus, and Hera, maintain their aggressive desires to subdue their rivals although they (temporarily) submit to their authority. Even as Aphrodite endeavors to enable the sexual relationship of Helen and Paris by setting out a chair for Helen in front of the Trojan prince (3.424–25),[71] Helen averts her eyes (427), protecting herself from the erotic effect of visually apprehending Paris' beauty,[72] while at the same time signaling antipathy toward her Trojan husband.[73] Instead of welcoming Paris from the battlefield, Helen "rebukes" (ἠνίπαπε, 427) him for escaping the duel, and wishes that he had been

[69] Pironti 2007: 225 and Blondell 2010: 23–24.

[70] Reckford 1964: 19 observes (without specific reference to these lines) that both Helen and Achilleus "are cut off from the normal communal ties of a Hector or Andromache."

[71] Here the narrator gives Aphrodite the epithet, "smile-loving" (φιλομμειδής, 3.424), which Boedeker 1974: 32–35 has argued is used specifically in this instance and elsewhere to emphasize "Aphrodite's aspect as goddess of sexual love."

[72] Blondell 2013: 71. For the relationship between vision and sexual desire, see Müller 1980: 11–16. Cf. Zeus's experience of *erōs* at the sight of Hera, who has elaborately adorned herself to accomplish the successful seduction (*Il.* 14.293–294).

[73] Minchin 2010: 391.

killed by Menelaos, whom she calls "my former husband" (429), mentions by name three times in six lines (430, 432, 434), and mockingly suggests is a better warrior than Paris (432–36). With this speech, Helen critiques her Trojan spouse and distances herself from him,[74] while indicating her preference for Menelaos. She refuses to give in entirely to the domineering influence of Aphrodite and the desire for Paris that the goddess has aroused, instead verbally intimating her *himeros* for Menelaos.

This scene of triangular conflict between Helen and Aphrodite over Paris vividly dramatizes Helen's complex desiring subjectivity—directed first at Paris, then Menelaos—which had been introduced earlier in Book 3. Although this scene repeats the triangular dynamics of Book 1, it invites a metaphorical interpretation by pitching, for the first time, a mortal, Helen, against a goddess, Aphrodite, while also linking the two antagonists as daughters of Zeus (*Διὸς θυγάτηρ Ἀφροδίτη*, 3.374; *Ἑλένη Διὸς ἐκγεγαυῖα*, 418).[75] Aphrodite's divine character as goddess of desire and sex, as well as her likeness to Helen, suggests a psychological reading of Aphrodite as a personification of Helen's own transgressive desire for Paris, as a manifestation of a libidinous part of Helen's ego, against which the heroine's superego—her moral conscience—struggles.[76] Typically for ancient Greek conceptions of *erōs*, this desire *qua* Aphrodite is presented not as an internal drive but as an outside force overwhelming the resistant subject.[77] If Helen's aggression against Aphrodite—and by extension Paris—represents hostility toward an externalized aspect of herself, the heroine again resembles Achilleus, who inflicts pain upon himself through his punitive withdrawal, "withering in his heart" and melancholically "longing for the battle cry and war" (1.491–92).[78]

At the same time, Homer does not allow Aphrodite to be entirely assimilated to a psychological construct, since she has definite "reality" as the divine actor who miraculously saves Paris from being killed by Menelaos. Aphrodite's intervention in the duel and subsequent confrontation with Helen remind the audience that the gods too act as determinants of plot in the *Iliad*, as was made clear in Book 1. Aphrodite appears not only to preserve Paris but also to render the duel inconclusive and confirm the transgressive pairing of Paris and Helen, therefore ensuring, as we shall see, the protraction of the war. As Bouvier (2017: 197) observes,

[74] See also Minchin 2010: 392–93. Austin 1994: 49 suggests that "Helen displaces onto Paris the anger that she is forbidden to direct toward Aphrodite, who, as a god, is taboo."

[75] Aphrodite's epithet "daughter of Zeus" is metrically equivalent to her alternative epithet "smile-loving" (*φιλομμειδής*), and so the use of the first epithet in this situation may be interpreted as a poetic choice. Boedeker 1974: 31–42 identifies *Διὸς θυγάτηρ* as the "marked" epithet of the two alternatives, and argues that here it emphasizes Aphrodite's role as Paris' protectress—a traditional function of her Indo-European precursor the Dawn Goddess, who carried the same epithet.

[76] On the ego and superego, see Freud 1960 [1923]: 22–36. For similar psychological interpretations of this scene, see also Calhoun 1937: 24–25; Grube 1951: 74; Clader 1976: 12; Kirk 1985: 232; Worman 2002: 50; Blondell 2010: 22–23. Cf. Reckford 1964: 15–20.

[77] On this Greek conception of sexual desire, see further Carson 1998 and Pironti 2007.

[78] On this passage, see "Back to Achilleus—and Zeus" in Chapter 2.

"for the hour, it is she [Aphrodite] who directs the action."[79] Yet Aphrodite's involvement does not invalidate Helen as a subject *and* agent of desire. As Blondell (2010: 20–22) explains, Helen is not a blameless victim of the goddess's coercion but is ultimately responsible for allowing the triumph of the shameful desire for Paris that Aphrodite at once inspires and represents.[80] Helen and Aphrodite are therefore shown to be collaborators in the production of the *Iliad*'s Trojan War superplot, as Achilleus and Zeus together generate the *Iliad*'s main plot.

In sum, by positioning Helen as an analogue to the desiring subjects of Book 1—especially Achilleus—and enmeshed in a parallel, if primarily internal, triangular conflict, the poet indicates to the audience her similar narrative importance and authority in the *Iliad*'s superplot. Helen's desires are deeply consequential for the larger Trojan War story: her lust for Paris has led to the Trojan War, and her current resistance to that desire and *himeros* for Menelaos destabilize her presence in Troy and provide additional motivation—together with Menelaos' and the Greek soldiers' desires—for the perpetuation of the war.[81] Helen's assumption of an assertive, Achillean subjectivity in this scene further figures the heroine as a disruptive, queer character whose mobile sexual desire generates plot.

Despite this queerness, the poet encourages us to celebrate, rather than villainize, this foundational heroine. The very fact that Helen fights against her desire for Paris—her consciousness of its "wrongness"—like her earlier expressions of self-blame and remorse for coming to Troy, make her a sympathetic character; then again, the very human futility of her effort, literalized through her fear of Aphrodite, only deepens our feeling for her.[82] Additionally, Helen's vivid frustration with the goddess and contempt for Paris, articulated and foregrounded through her powerful speech in this scene, once more demand our alignment and invite our empathy with this woman who tries, but fails, to be good. Both sympathetic and empathetic identification with Helen ameliorate the negative valency of her queerness and the grievous war it has caused. Far from being repelled, we are now fully engaged with the heroine and her superplot—even though her partner Paris, as we shall see, continues to be less ethically attractive.

[79] Pucci 2018: 204–5 also suggests that Zeus is a force behind the scenes who approves of Aphrodite's interference in the duel, given his apparent rejection of Menelaos' prayer for victory over Paris (also manifested through the breaking of Menelaos' weapons).

[80] *Contra* Reckford 1964: 18, Lendle 1968: 69–71, Roisman 2006: 23, and Wilson 2021: 20–22, who argue for Helen's victimization by Aphrodite.

[81] Blondell 2013: 72 writes that this scene evokes a sense of "marital instability"; see also Lynn-George 1988: 34–35. Here, also, Homer may subtly predict Troy's fall for the first time. In Book 1, Chryses eventually reclaims his daughter Chryseis in a paradigmatic resolution of desire, and Helen's parallelism to Chryses gestures toward her post-Iliadic reunification with Menelaos—the satisfaction of her yearning.

[82] Roisman 2006: 19 writes that Helen shows "courage" by standing up to Aphrodite.

Paris' Desire, Again

After exploring the destabilizing complexity of Helen's desires, Homer returns to Paris to confirm his queerness and narrative power as an irresistible creature of pure sexual desire. As in his earlier conversation with Hektor, Paris is unconcerned with Helen's critique of his martial capability and confident in the gods' favor: he tells Helen to stop rebuking him and asserts that he will be the victor next time, "for we have gods on our side too" (3.438–40). Instead of defending himself further, Paris exhorts Helen (441–42),

> *ἀλλ' ἄγε δὴ φιλότητι τραπείομεν εὐνηθέντε·*
> *οὐ γάρ πώ ποτέ μ' ὧδέ γ' ἔρως φρένας ἀμφεκάλυψεν*
>
> But come now, let us take satisfaction, having gone to bed in sexual union (*philotēti*);
> for not ever yet before has lust (*erōs*) so shrouded my wits...

The only thing that seems to matter to Paris is his overwhelming desire in the presence of Helen. Again, in this scene, Paris disregards normative expectations for masculinity, and specifically represents *erōs* at the force that determines this subjectivity, overtaking his mind.[83] The image of desire "shroud[ing]" Paris' "wits" suggests that *erōs* keeps him from being motivated by shame, evoking a victory of libido over superego, and echoing Aphrodite's previous domination of Helen.

Paris' location, nearly alone with only Helen (and Aphrodite) in his bedroom, physically stages his separation from the normative masculine sphere of the battlefield and his alienation from a community that would impose its values on him. In his social isolation, Paris is similar to Helen: just as Aphrodite—sexual desire's personification—has compelled Helen to leave the other Trojan women, the goddess has snatched him from the masculine homosocial community of warriors, where he was fighting the duel. His withdrawal from battle also resembles the queer situation of Achilleus alone beside the ships, although Achilleus, as we have seen, is conflicted about his absence from the war, while Paris' *erōs* eclipses any attachment he might have to the battlefield.

Paris and Achilleus are also both queerly positioned as objects of desire. Aphrodite, as I have shown, constructs Paris as beloved object, the position that elsewhere in Books 2 and 3 belongs primarily to Helen herself. Similarly, Achilleus promises the Greeks that he will be an object of their *pothē* (1.240), replacing the female concubines who were previously the objects of male desire in the triangular conflicts of Book 1. Paris, Helen, and Achilleus are all linked together through

[83] See also Ransom 2011: 47–48, who observes, "For any other man who was concerned with the proper heroic ethos of *τιμή* and *αἰδώς*, and the desire to avoid reproach at all costs, such a comment [as Helen's] would be unbearably emasculating."

their deviations from normative gender roles, and in each case their queer behaviors disrupt the social fabric and thus initiate epic plot.

The rest of Paris' speech to Helen clarifies the generative nature of Paris' queer enthrallment by sexual desire. After encouraging her to have sex with him and proclaiming his *erōs*, Paris connects this current desire with his feelings when he took away Helen from Sparta. He says that he has never felt such powerful *erōs* (3.443–46),

> *οὐδ' ὅτε σε πρῶτον Λακεδαίμονος ἐξ ἐρατεινῆς*
> *ἔπλεον ἁρπάξας ἐν ποντοπόροισι νέεσσι,*
> *νήσῳ δ' ἐν Κραναῇ ἐμίγην φιλότητι καὶ εὐνῇ,*
> *ὥς σεο νῦν ἔραμαι καί με γλυκὺς ἵμερος αἱρεῖ.*
>
> not even when first from desirable (*erateinēs*) Lakedaimon
> I sailed, having carried you off in seafaring ships,
> and on the Kranean island I joined with you in sexual union (*philotēti*) and bed;
> so much do I now lust after (*eramai*) you and sweet yearning (*himeros*) seizes me.

Although Paris declares his present lust to be even stronger than his former, implicit in this comparison is his original desire's power. Paris' description of Helen's homeland, Lakedaimon, as "desirable" further thematizes this lust and suggests that *erōs* suffuses his entire recollection of Sparta—which may be understood as an objective correlative for Helen. Furthermore, the place where they actually consummate their union emphasizes the insistence of Paris' desire. The adjective *Kranean* may refer to an island immediately off Lakedaimon's port, which would indicate that the couple did not go far or wait long to have sex for the first time. More likely, *kranean* is a descriptive epithet meaning "rocky," underscoring Paris' sexual urgency despite forbidding circumstances and in contrast to the comforts of his bedroom in Troy, where he speaks these words.[84]

With this speech, Paris clearly depicts his intense sexual desire as the force driving his abduction of Helen, which disrupted her marriage with Menelaos as well as Paris' own guest-friendship with the Spartan king, and caused Menelaos to wage war against Troy. As Ingrid Holmberg (2014: 329) has observed, Paris' current desire is what elicits this narrative of the past, and his act of narration resembles the creation of the epic poet. Paris' *erōs* and *himeros*, then, are shown to be behind the Trojan War story that forms the basis of the *Iliad*, and the desiring Paris himself appears as a source of that epic narrative.

Paris' comparison of past and present lust also encourages the *Iliad*'s audience to understand this culminating episode in Book 3 as a re-enactment of the

[84] Krieter-Spiro 2015: 162.

significant first union with Helen that he describes.[85] Paris successfully deploys the narrative of their initial sexual encounter in the service of seducing Helen to his bed again, highlighting the desirable quality of narrative, while also suggesting the iterative aspect of his intimate relationship with Helen.[86] Previously "having carried off" (ἁρπάξας, 3.444) Helen from Sparta, now he likewise "led the way to the bed" (ἄρχε λέχοσδε κιών, 447). Paris' action recalls how Aphrodite "led the way" (ἦρχε, 420) for her to the marriage chamber, and, as before, the verb ἄρχω expresses the leader's dominance and Helen's submission. Indeed, the narrator concludes this scene by reporting that "his wife followed with him" (ἅμα δ' εἵπετ' ἄκοιτις, 447), in a representation of the mastering and directive quality of Paris' desire, which overcomes Helen's misgivings.

This final statement also invites a reinterpretation of Helen's confrontation with Aphrodite as a representation of her original internal conflict when leaving her Greek husband for Paris. Here the Trojan prince ultimately convinces her to "follow" (εἵπετ') him to bed, just as she originally "followed" (ἑπόμην, 3.174) Paris to Troy. If Paris' divinely mediated escape from Menelaos in the duel repeats his evasion of the Greek king when he absconded with Helen from Sparta, this scene retells, in the superplot's real time, Paris' queer erotic victory—which substitutes for a normative victory on the battlefield.[87]

With Helen confirmed as Paris' "wife" (ἄκοιτις), the stage is set for the reinitiation of Menelaos' war of revenge in Book 4. In this way, Paris' and Helen's consummated desires lie behind not only the war's beginning but also its continuation in the ensuing episodes of the *Iliad*'s superplot—and main plot.[88] Book 3 ends by confirming the narrative irresolution caused by Paris' disappearance from the duel and liaison with Helen. The scene shifts to Menelaos vainly searching for his adversary among the crowd of Greek and Trojan warriors (3.449–52), in what may be a replay of his unsuccessful attempt to pursue Paris and Helen after their elopement from Sparta.[89] Agamemnon declares Menelaos the duel's victor and orders the return of Helen with the Greeks' approval (455–61), but the narrator does not communicate the Trojans' response, leaving the duel's outcome unclear and likely contested.

[85] e.g. Owen 1946: 35; Whitman 1958: 268; Reckford 1964: 17; Lendle 1968: 70–71; Edwards 1987: 196; Blondell 2010: 21.

[86] Cf. Holmberg 2014: 329.

[87] Rabel 1997: 77–79. Lendle 1968: 67 observes that Paris' arming scene before the duel is a typical element that introduces a hero's *aristeia*, an *aristeia* that is inverted in Paris' case. Dragged in the dust, he is "almost made into a caricature of a hero" (*er wird fast zur Karikatur des heroischen Helden gemacht*). His triumph is not on the battlefield but in the bedroom (Arthur 1981: 23). Alden 2000: 43 understands this triumph as the victory over Menelaos that Paris had predicted in his conversation with Helen (3.438–40). Louden 2006: 74–79 analyzes Paris as a parody of Hektor.

[88] Holmberg 2014: 326 recognizes the renewal of Paris' relationship with Helen in Book 3 as "the basis for the perpetuation of the current conflict within the *Iliad*."

[89] Krieter-Spiro 2015: 163.

However, the narrator does emphasize again the queerness of Paris' behavior by explaining that the Trojans "would not be hiding him out of solidarity (φιλότητι) if anyone had seen him; for he was hated by them all as much as black death" (3.453–54). Paris is again marked as a socially deviant "other" through his rejection by his own countrymen, who seem to dislike him because his actions—past and present—result in the destructive war in which they fight. Therefore, this final scene showcases the disruptive effect of Paris' lust for Helen while also reminding the audience of Menelaos' still unsatisfied aggressive desire to kill Paris. This brings us back to the opening of Book 3, with the two armies facing each other on the battlefield, in a circle that concludes the poet's presentation of the triangular desires of Menelaos, Paris, and Helen as the sources of the *Iliad*'s Trojan War superplot.

4
The Desire for War and Its Discontents

In this chapter, I show how Homer thematizes aggressive desire as the proximate motivation for the Greeks' renewed conflict with the Trojans in *Iliad* Books 4–6, which feature the rekindling of the war and the epic's first battle narrative. The poet particularly marks out the goddesses Hera and Athene, and the Greek kings Agamemnon and Diomedes, as subjects of this desire to kill, which is represented by anger (*cholos*) and by a will (*ethelō*) or eager rage (*meneainō, memaōs, menos*) to wage war. While Homer initially invites the audience to sympathize and empathize with Greek aggression and inspires our narrative desire to find out how and when Troy will fall, in Book 6 we are offered a new perspective on the fighting through a narrative shift from the battlefield to the city. The poet reveals the anguished desiring subjectivities of Andromache and the other Trojan women, who attract our sympathetic and empathetic desires, causing cognitive dissonance.

The Divine Determinants of War

Whereas Book 3 emphasizes the role of desiring mortals in generating the epic's Trojan War superplot, *Iliad* 4 begins with a divine council that firmly establishes the gods as important co-determinants. In the previous book, Aphrodite already played a key part in the consequential reconsummation of Paris and Helen's relationship, and now the poet shifts the scene to Mt. Olympos in order to implicate additional divinities, namely Hera, Athene, and Zeus himself, in the following reinitiation of the war.

Homer prepares the audience for renewed focus on the gods' motivating desires by linking this scene with the significant episode of divine conflict and reconciliation that capped Book 1. The gods sit together beside Zeus drinking nectar and watching the city of Troy (4.1–4) in an echo of their communal imbibing of nectar during the feast that concluded the first quarrel between Hera and Zeus over the fate of the Greek army (1.597–600). When, in Book 4, Zeus interrupts the gods' celebration in an effort to "provoke Hera with sarcastic words, speaking out deviously" (*ἐρεθιζέμεν Ἥρην/ κερτομίοις ἐπέεσσι, παραβλήδην ἀγορεύων*, 4.5–6), the poet constructs the book's beginning as a reversal of the end of Book 1: the gods move from tranquility to conflict, and once again the main antagonists are Zeus and Hera. Moreover, it is Zeus who begins the quarrel this time, speaking "with sarcastic words" (*κερτομίοις ἐπέεσσι*), whereas in Book 1, Hera first

Desire in the Iliad: *The Force That Moves the Epic and Its Audience.* Rachel H. Lesser, Oxford University Press.
 DOI: 10.1093/oso/9780192866516.003.0005

confronted Zeus, addressing him "sarcastically" (*κερτομίοισι*, 1.539). With these reverberations, Homer signals a return to the *Iliad*'s divine plotting and positions the gods' involvement in the superplot as a mirror image of their role in the main plot.

In the first part of his provocative speech, Zeus sets out the precise divine configuration informing the Trojan War superplot (4.7–12):

δοιαὶ μὲν Μενελάῳ ἀρηγόνες εἰσὶ θεάων,
Ἥρη τ' Ἀργείη καὶ Ἀλαλκομενηῒς Ἀθήνη.
ἀλλ' ἤτοι ταὶ νόσφι καθήμεναι εἰσορόωσαι
τέρπεσθον· τῷ δ' αὖτε φιλομμειδὴς Ἀφροδίτη
αἰεὶ παρμέμβλωκε καὶ αὐτοῦ κῆρας ἀμύνει·
καὶ νῦν ἐξεσάωσεν ὀϊόμενον θανέεσθαι.

Two of the goddesses are helpers to Menelaos,
Argive Hera and Athene of Alalkomenai.
But surely now these two, sitting apart and watching,
take their pleasure; while, on the other hand, smile-loving Aphrodite
is always at the side of that one [Paris] and wards off from him the death spirits;
and now she has saved him, although he was expecting to die.

Here Zeus identifies Hera and Athene as divine partisans of Menelaos, and reminds us of Aphrodite's protection of Paris. He is significantly silent about his own mortal affiliation, and assumes an indeterminate posture by adopting the role of a third-party observer.

By having Zeus single out these three goddesses, and oppose Hera and Athene to Aphrodite, Homer evokes for the audience the traditional myth of the Judgment of Paris, and links that myth with the action of the superplot.[1] In that story, the Trojan prince, chosen to judge a beauty contest between the three goddesses, awards Aphrodite the prize of the golden apple in return for sexual possession of the most beautiful woman in the world. The result is Paris' adulterous liaison with Helen and Menelaos' war of revenge. Zeus here "implies that Aphrodite has won again" in her salvation of Paris and reinstatement of his union with Helen.[2] The poet therefore presents the beginning of the superplot as a replay of the divine dynamics, along with the mortal ones, that led to the war. Furthermore, Zeus's words allusively suggest that these goddesses' contending

[1] *Pace* Reinhardt 1997 [1938]: 183–84, who denies "an explanatory reference to the judgement of Paris" here because of how subsequently "The powerful hatred of the powerful goddess blazes out, lives and justifies itself in its own terms." Reinhardt, however, recognizes the Judgment of Paris as a key event lying behind the *Iliad*'s story and alluded to elsewhere, which explains not only Aphrodite's support of Paris and Hera's and Athene's hatred for the Trojans but also the contrasting ethical portrayals of Paris and Hektor.

[2] Pucci 2018: 207.

desires for the golden apple represent the fundamental cause of the Trojan War; nevertheless, Homer subtly intimates this original divine determination only after fully exploring the human desires behind the war, foregrounding mortal causality in the superplot as in the main plot.

Since Aphrodite has already re-enacted her part in Book 3, now the poet has Zeus incite Hera and Athene to demonstrate in real time their influence on the superplot. Zeus attempts to end these two goddesses' complacency through insulting reference to Aphrodite's previous and current triumphs—but also with his following musing about how the gods should respond to the aborted duel (4.13–19):

> *ἀλλ' ἤτοι νίκη μὲν ἀρηϊφίλου Μενελάου·*
> *ἡμεῖς δὲ φραζώμεθ' ὅπως ἔσται τάδε ἔργα,*
> *ἤ ῥ' αὖτις πόλεμόν τε κακὸν καὶ φύλοπιν αἰνὴν*
> *ὄρσομεν, ἦ φιλότητα μετ' ἀμφοτέροισι βάλωμεν.*
> *εἰ δ' αὖ πως τόδε πᾶσι φίλον καὶ ἡδὺ γένοιτο,*
> *ἤτοι μὲν οἰκέοιτο πόλις Πριάμοιο ἄνακτος,*
> *αὖτις δ' Ἀργείην Ἑλένην Μενέλαος ἄγοιτο.*
>
> But surely now the victory goes to war-loving Menelaos;
> and let us take thought how these affairs will turn out,
> whether again we should rouse up evil war and dreadful battle,
> or whether we should impose peace (*philotēta*) on both sides.
> And if somehow this might be dear and sweet to all,
> then surely now the city of lord Priam would remain inhabited,
> and Menelaos would lead back Argive Helen.

Zeus's provocation is to suggest that the gods, instead of restarting the devastating war, could recognize Menelaos as the duel's default victor and enforce the terms of the duel, which mandate the war's end, the preservation of Troy, and the return of Helen to Sparta.

Zeus's—and Homer's—purpose here is to make known Hera's and Athene's aggressive desire to destroy the Trojans and to establish that desire as the main divine motivation for the waging of war against Troy.[3] In response to the divine king's words, both goddesses mutter against Zeus (4.20), "plot evils for the

[3] Similarly, Marks 2016: 64, who understands Zeus in this scene to make Hera "assume responsibility" for the war's resumption, "while casting himself as a compassionate, or at least dispassionate, divinity" in contrast to her passionate aggression. Elmer 2013: 147–50 observes that this divine assembly, in which Zeus provocatively suggests ending the war, parallels the Greek assembly in Book 2, in which Agamemnon had ingenuously suggested that the troops return home and abandon the war effort. In the previous chapter, I showed how this testing speech of Agamemnon provides an opportunity for the poet to stage Nestor's re-arousal of the Greek soldiers' aggressive desires as motivation for the war. Now Homer employs the same narrative tactic to explore Hera's aggressive desire as a driving force, with the result that divine desires appear once again to parallel mortal desires.

Trojans" (κακὰ δὲ Τρώεσσι μεδέσθην, 21), and feel "anger" (χόλος, 23; χόλον, 24). Unable to contain her anger (*cholos*), Hera declares, "you want (ἐθέλεις) to make vain and unaccomplished my labor" and goes on to describe how she has sweated and her horses have toiled as she gathered an army to bring evils to Priam and his sons (26–28). With these words, she not only complains that Zeus wishes to thwart her will but also clarifies how that will is aimed at causing trouble for the Trojan royal family, against whom she claims to have raised the Greek army. She ends with an emphatic statement of the lack of divine consensus regarding the cessation of the war: "do it, but all we other gods will not approve of it" (29).

The first part of Zeus's reply further highlights Hera's desire to destroy the Trojans and positions the goddess as Menelaos' divine analogue. Disingenuously, he asks her what wrongs Priam's family has committed against her "so that you unceasingly rage (ἀσπερχὲς μενεαίνεις) to sack the well-built city of Ilion?" (4.31–33). Here, Zeus draws attention to Hera's aggressive desire with the verb *meneainō*, which is derived from the noun *menos* ("force," "drive," "rage"), and can mean both "to desire" and "to rage."[4] This is only the second time that this verb appears in the narrative; the first time was when the narrator described how Menelaos futilely attacked Paris at the climax of the duel, "raging to kill" (κατακτάμεναι μενεαίνων, 3.379). Next, Zeus suggests that Hera would only cure her anger (*cholos*) if she should eat Priam and his sons and the other Trojans raw (4.34–36). This vision of Hera eating uncooked human flesh not only vividly emphasizes the intensity of her aggression but also might recall the simile comparing Menelaos to a hungry lion, determined to devour his prey, as he eagerly prepared to engage with Paris for the first time in the *Iliad* (3.23–28). With these echoes, the poet links Hera's aggressive desire with Menelaos' and even suggests that her own desire is an extension of his,[5] in the same way that Zeus's will appears to be directed by Achilleus' desire in the main plot. All the same, Zeus's comment here that Hera "unceasingly" desires to sack Troy constructs the goddess's aggression as an enduring emotion that transcends mortal temporality.

Zeus goes on to signal that he will allow Hera's aggressive desire to control the direction of the superplot. He tells his wife, "do as you will (ἐθέλεις)," and declines to let this quarrel become a source of further strife between them (4.37–38). With the verb *ethelō* ("to will," "to want"), he clearly empowers Hera's desire as the divine determinant of the subsequent action on the battlefield. By staging this deference of Zeus's will to Hera's, the poet indicates to the audience how Achilleus' and Zeus's main plot is being suspended during the superplot. In a final reversal of the divine quarrel in Book 1, this time Hera gets her way.

[4] See further O'Brien 1993: 79–85 on the meaning of *menos* and *cholos*, and Hera's association with these emotions in this passage.

[5] Cf. Pucci 2018: 220, who writes that "The text, through its representation of Hera, shows the human reasons for the war, the feelings that frequently nourish the war, i.e. hatred and resentment."

All the same, Zeus's imperative for the divine queen to act as she wishes marks his own assent to the course of action that she intends. Zeus himself articulates the paradox of his desire when he asserts to Hera, "I have given [this] to you willingly, although with an unwilling heart" (*ἐγὼ σοὶ δῶκα ἑκὼν ἀέκοντί γε θυμῷ*, 4.43)—he is both "willing" and "unwilling" at the same time. In his following words, he focuses attention on the latter feeling, explaining how the Trojans, among all the peoples of the earth, have especially honored him, always satisfying his desire for sacrificial offerings (4.44–49).[6] Zeus's Trojan sympathies are consistent with his promise to Thetis to empower the Trojans in battle, yet he has just allowed his wife to pursue Troy's destruction.

But perhaps Zeus's will is more coherent than it appears. The war must begin again for Zeus to fulfill his pledge to Thetis, and the eventual fall of Troy is not irreconcilable with temporary Trojan dominance in battle; these two versions of Zeus's will are compatible, even if they do not initially seem so.[7] Indeed, his speech to Hera here is introduced with the same line that prefaces his response to Thetis' request in Book 1: "greatly troubled, cloud-gathering Zeus addressed her" (*τὴν δὲ μέγ' ὀχθήσας προσέφη νεφεληγερέτα Ζεύς*, 4.30 = 1.517). In each case, Zeus is disinclined to yield to his female interlocuter's desire, but ultimately does so; both the main plot and superplot are products of his reluctant acquiescence. Nevertheless, the complexity of Zeus's desires in this scene raises the question of what the divine king really wants, and his compliance with Hera, who wishes the Trojans defeated, strengthens doubts, which had already been encouraged in Book 1, regarding the complete congruity of Zeus's and Achilleus' wills. With this divine enigma, the poet arouses our narrative desire to follow the progression of the epic until we can grasp satisfactorily the nature of the will of Zeus (*Dios boulē*).

When he agrees to let Hera's will prevail, Zeus presents conditions for his submission that again thematize her aggressive desire and oblige her to acknowledge how this feeling predominates over all other concerns. He warns her, "whenever I, eager (*μεμαώς*), should want (*ἐθέλω*) to sack that city where there are men close to you, do not in any way thwart my anger (*χόλον*), but allow me [to do it]" (4.40–42). With these words, Zeus demands that Hera grant him in the future what he is granting her now, emphasizing the aggressive desire behind such actions with *ethelō* and *cholos* as well as *memaōs*, the participle of aggressive

[6] Zeus asserts, "for in no way was my altar lacking in equal feast" (*οὐ γάρ μοί ποτε βωμὸς ἐδεύετο δαιτὸς ἐΐσης*, 4.48), employing a modified version of a familiar formula that indicates satiety: "in no way was the heart lacking in equal feast" (*οὐδέ τι θυμὸς ἐδεύετο δαιτὸς ἐΐσης*, 1.468 = 602).

[7] Marks 2016: 64, who asserts that "Zeus' strategies here are, then, complex and covert, but clearly signposted and entirely rational." Cf. Pucci 2018: 206–22, who contends that Homer makes Zeus deflect responsibility from himself and suffer pain for a decision that he has already made (the destruction of Troy) in order to highlight both the misery of the loss of a "great and pious city" and the mortal inability to comprehend or control the providential forces behind such a loss.

eagerness.[8] Hera readily agrees to Zeus's stipulation and even offers three cities, instead of one, for potential annihilation: Argos, Sparta, and Mykenai (51–54). This bargain not only underscores the intensity of Hera's hatred of Troy but also reveals that she cares more about destroying Troy than she does about preserving her cherished Greeks, for whom she was so solicitous in Book 1.[9] Hera now not only lets pass the opportunity for Menelaos to take home Helen and prevent further loss of Greek life but also demonstrates her willingness to sacrifice Agamemnon's, Menelaos', and Diomedes' cities in order to prolong the war and ensure Troy's doom.

This helps confirm that Hera's aggressive desire is of the primary, competitive type, rather than the secondary type conceived in response to loss of a beloved object. While the divine queen clearly has an attachment to the Achaians, they are ultimately a vehicle by which she vies for status and power with her husband and the other gods. Hera's wish to annihilate Troy, then, would appear to be a displaced form of that same competitive desire that was disappointed when Paris deemed her less beautiful and with less to offer than her rival Aphrodite. The allusion to the Judgment of Paris earlier in the scene suggests that both Hera's and Athene's hatred of the Trojans is a redirection of the aggressive libido bound up in that contest, a scapegoating of the mortals associated with their status-loss.

The council closes with Hera taking charge and initiating a chain of events that end the peace, demonstrating the power of her aggressive desire to impact the course of the superplot. After declaring her authority on the basis of her divinity, her identity as Kronos' eldest daughter, and her status as Zeus's wife—thus claiming prestige nearly co-equal to her husband's—she tells the divine king to command Athene to go down to the battlefield and cause the Trojans to injure the Greeks in violation of their oaths; he immediately does so (4.58–72). The narrator notes how Athene's desire matches Hera's: Zeus incites her "already being eager" (πάρος μεμαυῖαν, 73). Taking on the guise of Antenor's son Laodokos, Athene convinces the Trojan archer Pandaros to shoot Menelaos (86–140); as Pandaros' arrow springs forth from his bow, the arrow is personified, "raging (μενεαίνων) to fall upon the crowd" (126), by which it seems to manifest the aggression of Hera, to whom Zeus had previously applied this same verb of raging desire (μενεαίνεις, 32). Pandaros' shot wounds Menelaos, and Agamemnon immediately recognizes this action as an oath-breaking that marks the end of the duel's truce and guarantees the future fall of Troy (157–68).

While this sequence securely positions Hera's and Athene's aggressive desires as the immediate cause of the *Iliad*'s Trojan War superplot, it also confirms Zeus

[8] *Memaōs* is from the verb *memona*, "to be eager," which is cognate with *menos* and appears here for the seventh time; in every prior case it is used to describe the desire to fight—either to protect (1.590, 3.9) or to destroy (2.473, 2.543, 2.818, 2.863).

[9] See also O'Brien 1993: 84–85.

as the supreme divine actor in this plot, as in the main plot. It is Zeus's prerogative to order Athene to begin the war anew, just as he had to assent to the realization of Hera's aggression. In her conversation with Zeus, Hera observes that he could destroy her favorite Greek cities even if she objected, "since surely you are more powerful by far" (*ἐπεὶ ἦ πολὺ φέρτερός ἐσσι*, 4.56). Hera's acknowledgment of the divine king's omnipotence is an adaptation of the same line-ending formula that Hephaistos had used to describe Zeus's might in Book 1: "for he is by far the most powerful" (*ὁ γὰρ πολὺ φέρτατός ἐστιν*, 1.581). Again, Zeus's will emerges as the dominant divine determinant, even as the poet focuses the audience's attention on the narrative force of Hera's aggressive libido.

Finally, this opening scene of Book 4 confirms authoritatively for the first time in the epic the audience's traditional knowledge of the Trojan War's ending. Zeus's agreement with Hera causes us to anticipate Troy's fall, inspiring our narrative desire to find out how and when the city's destruction will come about. In this way, the divine council invests us in the upcoming battle narrative that Hera sets in motion.

Allegiance and Alignment with the Greeks

Although Homer shows the gods engineering the Trojans' violation of the truce in Book 4, he nevertheless depicts the Trojans as culpable and encourages the audience to feel sympathy for the Greeks as the aggrieved party. This begins with the negative presentation of Pandaros, who shoots Menelaos with his arrow at Athene's prompting. The goddess encourages Pandaros by telling him, "among all the Trojans, you would earn gratitude and glory, and most of all from the prince Alexandros," and she claims that Paris would give Pandaros "shining gifts" if he should see that Menelaos had been killed (4.95–99); that is, she appeals to Pandaros' desire for status and his greed. The narrator reports that Athene "persuaded the wits of that foolish man" (*τῷ δὲ φρένας ἄφρονι πεῖθεν*, 104), thereby constructing Pandaros' arrow shot as a thoughtless, misguided act. At no point does he consider that he is violating the oath sworn by Agamemnon and ratified by the Greeks and Trojans prior to the duel (3.276–301), nor does he worry about the consequences of that oath-breaking; it is as if he had no regard for the gods invoked as witnesses and guarantors: Zeus, Helios, the Rivers, Earth, and the Erinyes.[10]

The clouding of Pandaros' mind recalls the psychology of Paris, who says that at the sight of Helen, "lust (*erōs*) shrouded my wits" (*ἔρως φρένας ἀμφεκάλυψεν*, 3.442). Like Paris, Pandaros forgets social norms and religious obligations when

[10] See Kirk 1985: 304–5 for identification and discussion of the deities.

faced with an object of desire. As scholars have recognized, Pandaros' wounding of Menelaos represents a second narrative re-enactment—the first being the duel and its aftermath in Book 3—of Paris' original abuse of Menelaos' guest-friendship; Pandaros shoots on Paris' behalf and to win rewards from him, and his shot once again expresses Paris' responsibility for initiating the Trojan War, while also signaling the Trojans' collective guilt in their support of Paris.[11] Pandaros' Trojan companions offer no objections to his treacherous shot and, rather, enable it by protecting him with their shields (4.113–15).

While, on the one hand, this heedless, impious, corporate oath-breaking casts the Trojans in a negative light, on the other hand, their unjustly targeted victim Menelaos is made especially sympathetic through the device of apostrophe and graphic description of his injury. After Pandaros has released his arrow, the narrator suddenly abandons his objective third-person narration to address Menelaos directly twice (4.127, 146). As the bT scholia to these passages observe, these apostrophes create the impression that the narrator pities Menelaos' suffering, and they also direct the audience to feel a similar sympathy for the injured hero.[12] Moreover, although Athene prevents the arrow from mortally wounding Menelaos, the poet depicts the injury in vivid terms that invite the audience to feel for the hero: with a simile, the narrator compares the blood running down the hero's thighs, shins, and ankles to the stain of red-purple dye on an ivory ornament (141–47).

The Atreidai's anguished reactions to the trauma reinforce this audience response. The narrator reports that first Agamemnon, then Menelaos "shuddered" (ῥίγησεν) at the sight of the wound (4.148–50). Agamemnon, furthermore, is described as "groaning heavily" (βαρὺ στενάχων) and holding Menelaos' hand, while their companions "groaned alongside them" (ἐπεστενάχοντο, 153–54). These depictions of fear and grief invite the audience's sympathy and also require the audience to experience the wounding of Menelaos through the perspective of the Greeks.[13] This focalization is strengthened by Agamemnon's following speech, in which he imagines that his organization of the duel was a death sentence for his brother (155–56), and later asserts that he will feel "dreadful grief" (αἰνὸν ἄχος) for Menelaos, should he die (169–70). Agamemnon's expressions of regret and sorrow suggest his genuine love for his brother, making him more sympathetic; this characterization, together with the foregrounding of his intense pain, may evoke our empathy as well.

The Greek commander's prediction that the Trojans will suffer divine punishment for their wrongdoing, which appears in the middle of his exclamations of

[11] Whitman 1958: 268; Mueller 1984: 76; Postlethwaite 1985: 2; Taplin 1992: 103–5.

[12] Block 1982: 9.

[13] Rabel 1997: 80 observes that the audience experiences Pandaros' shot through three different focalizations: the narrator's, Agamemnon's, and then Menelaos'. See also Kozak 2017: 41.

distress, focuses the audience's reaction to this scene. Agamemnon identifies "the Trojans" in the collective as the attackers of Menelaos and the violators of oaths (4.157), reiterating the poet's previous depiction of their shared culpability and impiety, and forecasts that they will consequently pay a great penalty "with their own heads, and their wives and children" (162), elaborating how Troy, Priam, and Priam's people will perish by the action of Zeus, who is "frustrated with their deception" (164–68). This prophecy reaffirms our anticipation of Troy's ruin, and our wish to know and understand its course. If we share the Greek leader's yearning for justice, this empathetic desire will amplify our narrative desire to comprehend the Trojans' defeat.

Yet, Agamemnon's declaration that *all* the Trojans will suffer indiscriminately—including "wives and children"—may give us pause. Do the Trojan noncombatants deserve this fate? Does Agamemnon's desire for retribution go too far? Though Agamemnon's confidence in Zeus's justice demonstrates a piety that contrasts with the Trojan warriors' apparent disregard of the gods, the audience may experience first pangs of pity for the Trojan civilians as well as a renewed distaste for the Greek leader, who was distinctly unsympathetic in Book 1. Should this occur, these feelings darken, if not dampen, our desire to discover how Troy will fall.

Nevertheless, Homer keeps the audience aligned with the Greeks as the epic continues,[14] further encouraging us to empathize with them. First, Menelaos reveals that his wound is not serious, and Agamemnon arranges for his treatment by the doctor Machaon (4.183–219). Then, the armies prepare for battle, and although the narrator begins with a brief observation that the Trojan ranks advanced, armed themselves, and "remembered the joy of battle" (221–22), they subsequently disappear for hundreds of lines while the poet focalizes the narrative through the perspective of Agamemnon and the Greek kings with whom he converses as he rouses the men to war. During this inspection of the troops ("Epipolesis"), we are compelled to see the war through the Greeks' eyes, and invited to share Agamemnon's desire to fight and kill Trojans—and capture their families—which the poet showcases during this scene.

The narrator introduces the Epipolesis with the following articulation of the Greek leader's aggressive desire (4.223–25):

ἔνθ' οὐκ ἂν βρίζοντα ἴδοις Ἀγαμέμνονα δῖον,
οὐδὲ καταπτώσσοντ', οὐδ' οὐκ ἐθέλοντα μάχεσθαι,
ἀλλὰ μάλα σπεύδοντα μάχην ἐς κυδιάνειραν.

Then you would not see brilliant Agamemnon dozing,
nor cowering, nor not wanting (*ouk ethelonta*) to fight,
but very zealous for battle that brings triumph to men.

[14] See also Kozak 2017: 42–43.

Agamemnon demonstrates this desire for war and instills it in his men by ranging on foot through the ranks and encouraging those already eager to fight while rebuking those who seem to be holding back (231–421). His encouragement includes expressing his conviction that Zeus will punish the Trojans for their oath-breaking and conjuring a vision of enslaved Trojan women and children after the sacking of their city (235–39); that is, he depicts Troy's destruction as divinely endorsed, and, like Nestor in Book 2, he arouses the Greeks' aggressive desire to contend with Trojan men by presenting their wives (and children) as prizes of war and potential objects of sexual desire.

The Epipolesis may be the only scene in the *Iliad* where Agamemnon practices effective leadership. His direct exhortation of the troops here is in stark contrast with his failed strategy of employing reverse psychology in Book 2—a strategy that Odysseus and Nestor were forced to correct. In this case, the narrator reports the success of Agamemnon's arousal of the Greeks' aggressive desire by using a dramatic simile of wind-blown waves to picture how "the phalanxes of the Danaans then moved one after another ceaselessly to war" (4.422–28). Agamemnon's relatively positive portrayal in the Epipolesis seems designed to elicit the audience's sympathy for and empathy with the Greek leader in his readiness to fight.[15]

When the armies finally engage near the end of Book 4, the poet continues to privilege the perspective of the Greeks. The first three killings follow a pattern: a major Greek hero (Antilochos, Aias, Odysseus) slays a minor Trojan figure, and then another Trojan kills a minor Greek warrior in return (4.457–526). In the initial two rounds of engagement, the Greek kings are the first to attack; the poet celebrates them as brave and triumphant aggressors, while the Trojans appear as victims and reactors, rather than actors, who are not able to stop the prominent Greek warriors. The third round, however, works somewhat differently. Odysseus engages with a Trojan adversary only after his companion Leukos has been laid low; the poet describes how Odysseus is inspired to make his first successful spear-cast when "angered" (χολώθη; χολωσάμενος) by the death of his companion (494–501). With this account of Odysseus' loss-fueled anger, Homer thematizes Odysseus' psychology and invites the audience to empathize with his aggression.

Odysseus' experience—as the culmination of this opening tricolon crescendo of Greek martial heroism—also represents an important paradigm for how war fuel aggressive desire in a self-perpetuating spiral. Through Odysseus, the poet demonstrates how the death of a male companion on the battlefield works in the same way as the loss of a female intimate off the battlefield to arouse the aggressive impulse that drives conflict. Homer thus establishes continuity of

[15] Agamemnon errs, however, in his exhortation of Odysseus, who is offended by the Greek leader's suggestion that he is shrinking from battle (4.338–55).

motivation within the *Iliad* before and after the reinitiation of battle, confirming triangular aggression as a core narrative dynamic.

Diomedes' *Aristeia*

In Book 5, the poet continues to glorify the Greeks and to explore their motivating aggressive desires through the heroic excellence (*aristeia*) of Diomedes. Book 5 represents the exact center of the superplot's narration in Books 3–7, and while the beginning of this sequence replays the origin of the Trojan War and the background to the *Iliad*'s main plot, its middle is a kind of microcosm of the war itself and of the main plot's key battle narratives. During Book 5, Diomedes becomes the chief representative of the Greek army, and much of the book is focalized through his perspective as he wreaks havoc on the Trojan forces. Even though Menelaos himself also participates in the fighting, Diomedes acts during his *aristeia* as Menelaos' surrogate and manifests his aggressive libido. He also stands in for Achilleus, foreshadowing the hero's psychology and actions in the main plot. The narrative emphasis on Diomedes' desire to wage war on the Trojans—and the Trojans' answering desire—thus underscores aggressive desire's driving force in the *Iliad* and further introduces its form and nature.

Diomedes is established as a proxy for Menelaos when Pandaros shoots and injures him with an arrow near the beginning of his *aristeia* (5.95–100), in a repetition of his attack on Menelaos. Just as Athene had interfered to mitigate Menelaos' injury, here the goddess renews Diomedes' strength, reassures him, and also gives him the special ability to recognize the immortal gods (121–28). Pandaros makes the connection between Menelaos and Diomedes explicit when he complains to Aineias that he has not managed to kill either of these men with his bow, despite hitting them and drawing blood (206–8).

The poet first prepares the audience to apprehend Diomedes as a substitute for Achilleus at the end of Book 4, when, after the initial onslaught of the three Greek kings, Apollo descends to the battlefield to rouse the Trojan forces. The god tells them not to yield to the Argives and encouragingly informs them that Achilleus is not fighting on the battlefield (4.509–13). Apollo's words remind the audience of Achilleus, and when Diomedes single-handedly kills a succession of Trojan warriors (5.144–65), he seems to render Apollo's reassurance null and void, assuming Achilleus' role as the most threatening Greek hero.

Even before Diomedes' rampage, Pandaros encourages this perception of Diomedes as a new Achilleus by boasting, after he shoots him, that "the best of the Achaians" (ἄριστος Ἀχαιῶν) has been hit (5.103). This epithet brings to mind Achilleus, who twice previously called himself "the best of the Achaians" (ἄριστον

Ἀχαιῶν, 1.244; 1.412).[16] Later, after Diomedes' *aristeia* in Book 5, the Trojan priest Helenos advises Hektor to arrange sacrifices to Athene so that she might protect the Trojans from Diomedes. Helenos asserts that Diomedes is "the strongest of the Achaians" (κάρτιστον Ἀχαιῶν), and testifies that the fear Diomedes inspires in the Trojans is even greater than the terror roused up to that point by Achilleus himself (6.98–101). The Trojans thus directly compare Diomedes to Achilleus, and their words indicate to the audience how Diomedes' fighting in the superplot is meant to anticipate Achilleus' martial heroism—and its underlying psychology—in the main plot.[17]

After Athene's revivification of the wounded Diomedes, the narrator prefaces the hero's *aristeia* with an emphatic exploration of Diomedes' unstoppable drive to fight that uses language of desire and a lion simile (5.134–43):

> *Τυδεΐδης δ' ἐξαῦτις ἰὼν προμάχοισιν ἐμίχθη,*
> *καὶ πρίν περ θυμῷ μεμαὼς Τρώεσσι μάχεσθαι·*
> *δὴ τότε μιν τρὶς τόσσον ἕλεν μένος, ὥς τε λέοντα,*
> *ὅν ῥά τε ποιμὴν ἀγρῷ ἐπ' εἰροπόκοις ὀΐεσσι*
> *χραύσῃ μέν τ' αὐλῆς ὑπεράλμενον οὐδὲ δαμάσσῃ·*
> *τοῦ μέν τε σθένος ὦρσεν, ἔπειτα δέ τ' οὐ προσαμύνει,*
> *ἀλλὰ κατὰ σταθμοὺς δύεται, τὰ δ' ἐρῆμα φοβεῖται·*
> *αἱ μέν τ' ἀγχηστῖναι ἐπ' ἀλλήλῃσι κέχυνται,*
> *αὐτὰρ ὁ ἐμμεμαὼς βαθέης ἐξάλλεται αὐλῆς·*
> *ὣς μεμαὼς Τρώεσσι μίγη κρατερὸς Διομήδης.*
>
> And Tydeos' son, going forth at once, mixed with the fore-fighters,
> and even before he was eager (*memaōs*) in his heart to fight with the Trojans;
> but now thrice so much rage (*menos*) seized him, as if he were a lion,
> whom a shepherd, among his woolly sheep in the field,
> wounded slightly as he leapt over the sheep-enclosure, yet he did not subdue him;
> instead, first he roused the lion's strength, and then fails to ward him off,
> rather the lion enters the farmstead, and the deserted sheep are put to flight;
> and close together, they crowd upon each other,
> but he, very eager (*emmemaōs*), leaps out into the deep enclosure;
> thus eager (*memaōs*), strong Diomedes mixed with the Trojans.

At both the beginning and end of this passage, the narrator characterizes Diomedes as desirous to fight the Trojans by attaching to him the participle

[16] Agamemnon also "boasts that he is much the best of the Achaians" (1.91, 2.82). On the Iliadic competition for this appellation, see Nagy 1979: 26–35.

[17] On the parallelism between Diomedes in Book 5 and Achilleus, particularly during his return to battle in Books 20–22, see further Bassett 1938: 216; Owen 1946: 47; Whitman 1958: 167; Edwards 1987: 198–99; Rabel 1997: 90; and especially Louden 2006: 14–30.

memaōs ("eager"), which was also used in Book 4 to describe the gods' aggressive desires. In the middle of this passage, the narrator compares Diomedes to an injured, yet even more determined lion to show how Pandaros' attempt to neutralize the Greek hero has only intensified his desire to do battle against his enemy. Diomedes has triple the *menos* of before, while the lion is "very eager" (ἐμμεμαώς), the marked, intensive version of *memaōs*, which appears here for the first time,[18] underscoring the lion's—and Diomedes'—aggressive impulse. This simile also links Diomedes again to Menelaos, who was first compared to a hungry lion in his desire to attack Paris (3.23–28).

In this passage, the realization of Diomedes' aggressive desire through hand-to-hand combat is depicted in terms that connect war with sex. The narrator describes how the Greek hero "mixed" (ἐμίχθη; μίγη) with the Trojans, employing the same verb of mixing used elsewhere to describe the consummation of sexual desire, such as in Paris' account of his original union with Helen (3.445). This shared language indicates an analogy between the aggressive "mixing" of bodies on the battlefield and the sexual "mixing" of bodies in bed, and between the desires that inspire both.[19] The similarity of aggressive and sexual desires suggests that they represent different manifestations of the same basic libidinal impulse, and encourages the audience to perceive a consistent pattern of desire—broadly conceived—as a key motivating force for the *Iliad*'s characters.

In the melee, Diomedes kills a number of Trojans, provoking answering aggressive desires in Pandaros and the Trojan prince Aineias. The two join forces to stop Diomedes, and the narrator characterizes them as "very eager" (ἐμμεμαῶτ') as they drive their shared chariot against him (5.240). Sthenelos, Diomedes' charioteer, echoes the narrator's words when he warns his companion that the two Trojans are attacking him, "eager to fight" (μεμαῶτε μάχεσθαι, 244). After Diomedes has killed Pandaros with a spear—finally exacting retribution for the Trojan's bow shots—Aineias protects Pandaros' corpse, "like a lion, trusting in his might" and "eager to kill (κτάμεναι μεμαώς) anyone who should come against him" (299–301). With this reappearance of the lion simile, and the Trojans' aggressive desires to fight and kill, the poet demonstrates the symmetry and universality of the Iliadic warriors' motivating psychology.[20] Although this section of the narrative privileges the perspective of the Greeks, here Homer demonstrates to the audience that both sides in the war are driven by equivalent aggression.

[18] This intensive participle appears only ten times (*Il.* 5.142, 5.240, 5.330, 13.785, 17.735, 17.746, 20.284, 20.442, 20.468, 22.143).

[19] Vermeule 1979: 101; MacCary 1982: 137–48; Monsacré 1984: 64–66; Vernant 1989: 138; Pironti 2007: 226–28.

[20] Ready 2011: 184 observes that "[e]ven though Aineias assumes a defensive posture he is described with a simile appropriate for a tenor on the offensive," which "asserts Aineias' ferocity."

Despite Aineias' valiant eagerness, he is no match for Diomedes, who wounds him and initiates a final sequence that showcases the extremity of the Greek hero's aggressive desire as he continues to act as a narrative surrogate for Menelaos. When Diomedes crushes Aineias' hip socket with a boulder, Aineias' mother Aphrodite swoops down to the battlefield and rescues her son (5.311–18). Aphrodite's intervention recalls her salvation of Paris during the duel in Book 3, when Menelaos was about to kill him; indeed, the narrator describes her perception of Aineias' and Paris' distress in identical terms (5.312 = 3.374).[21] This narrative echo positions Aineias as a second Paris and Diomedes as a stand-in for Menelaos. While Menelaos had no idea what had happened in Book 3 and could not pursue Paris, this time Diomedes, granted more-than-mortal vision, is able to see Aphrodite, and his aggression is such that he attacks and wounds the goddess (5.330–43). Aphrodite flees the battlefield, but Apollo takes her place as the injured Aineias' guardian (344–46).

Although Diomedes recognizes this god too, even Apollo's presence does not stop him, and he continues to rush at Aineias. The narrator draws attention to Diomedes' unrestrained aggressive libido here, reporting that "he constantly desired (*ἵετο δ' αἰεί*) to kill Aineias and strip his glorious armor" (5.434–35), and goes on to describe how Diomedes "thrice then rushed at him, raging to kill" (*τρὶς μὲν ἔπειτ' ἐπόρουσε κατακτάμεναι μενεαίνων*), in a variation on the formulaic line used to describe Menelaos' final unsuccessful assault on Paris in the duel (5.436 ~ 3.379). Here again the poet deploys the rare and marked verb *meneainō*, which had also characterized Hera's aggressive desire to destroy the Trojans (4.32). Apollo fends Diomedes off, but nevertheless the hero insistently attacks for a fourth time, "equal to a god" (*δαίμονι ἶσος*, 5.438), prompting Apollo to verbally admonish Diomedes, "do not wish to be high spirited on a level with the gods" (*μηδὲ θεοῖσιν/ ἶσ' ἔθελε φρονέειν*, 440–41), which seems to be a warning for Diomedes to moderate his aggressive desire to the level of mortals.[22] Apollo's warning penetrates Diomedes' battle-fury, and the warrior backs off, allowing the god to abscond with Aineias.[23] Although this episode concludes with the salvation of the Trojan prince, as had the duel in Book 3, the intervention of a second god, Apollo, amplifies this version of the Greek hero's futile attack on his Trojan adversary, highlighting Diomedes' aggressive desire and unyielding bravery.

[21] Kirk 1990: 51 calls this "a new version of the scene in bk 3 where she rescued her favourite Paris." See also Reinhardt 1961: 130–33 and Kirk 1990: 93 *ad loc.*

[22] The quadruple attack is a battlefield type-scene (see Fenik 1968: 46–48), which later appears three more times in the *Iliad*, twice featuring Patroklos (16.702–6, 16.784–86) and once featuring Achilleus (20.445–49). In each case, Apollo foils the hero on his fourth attack, when his aggression leads him to overstep boundaries. This type-scene links together Diomedes, Patroklos, and Achilleus, and establishes Diomedes as a paradigm of extreme aggressive desire.

[23] Later, Diomedes shows that he has learned humility, advising his fellow Greeks to yield before the Trojans and their divine allies: "do not desire to fight by force with the gods" (*μηδὲ θεοῖς μενεαινέμεν ἶφι μάχεσθαι*, 5.606).

The Gods' Involvement in the Battle

Besides emphasizing the mortal combatants' motivating desires, Diomedes' *aristeia* presents the gods as key players in the conflict between Greeks and Trojans. As we have already seen, Athene invigorates Diomedes, and he encounters both Aphrodite and Apollo as opponents on the battlefield. Following this episode, the war god Ares enters the battle on behalf of the Trojans, and then Athene, with Hera's assistance, comes to fight herself alongside Diomedes and the Greeks; together, the goddess and hero wound Ares. This sequence, which stretches over the course of Book 5, not only confirms the gods' desires as determinants of the battle itself, in parallel to mortal desires, but also demonstrates allegorically, through its treatment of Aphrodite and Ares, the way that sexual and aggressive desires work together to drive the *Iliad*'s Trojan War superplot.

The poet prepares for the involvement of the gods in Book 5 by vividly marking their galvanizing presence just before the armies engage on the battlefield for the first time in the epic (4.439–45):

ὦρσε δὲ τοὺς μὲν Ἄρης, τοὺς δὲ γλαυκῶπις Ἀθήνη
Δεῖμός τ᾽ ἠδὲ Φόβος καὶ Ἔρις ἄμοτον μεμαυῖα,
Ἄρεος ἀνδροφόνοιο κασιγνήτη ἑτάρη τε,
ἥ τ᾽ ὀλίγη μὲν πρῶτα κορύσσεται, αὐτὰρ ἔπειτα
οὐρανῷ ἐστήριξε κάρη καὶ ἐπὶ χθονὶ βαίνει·
ἥ σφιν καὶ τότε νεῖκος ὁμοίϊον ἔμβαλε μέσσῳ
ἐρχομένη καθ᾽ ὅμιλον, ὀφέλλουσα στόνον ἀνδρῶν.

And Ares urged on the Trojans, and glancing-eyed Athene the Greeks,
and Terror and Rout and Strife, incessantly eager (*memauia*),
the sister and companion of man-slaying Ares,
who first rears up small, but afterwards
fixes her head in the heavens while she strides upon the earth;
that one even then pitched among them, in the middle, indiscriminate conflict,
going through the crowd, increasing the groaning of men.

Here the poet establishes the divine partisanship that will be manifested on the battlefield: Ares encourages the Trojans and Athene the Greeks; both will later enter battle and personally fight with and for their side. Moreover, beyond these fully anthropomorphic Olympians, Homer also introduces personified emotional and relational aspects of battle, Terror (*Deimos*) and Rout (*Phobos*) and Strife (*Eris*), who seem to attend the battle universally, without partisanship. Their presence renders numinous the essential experiences of war, constructing them as part of the divine order and making battle "without them and apart from them, impossible, illegitimate, even unthinkable."[24] Strife, who receives an extended characterization, is described as "incessantly eager" (ἄμοτον μεμαυῖα); she possesses as an inherent, unchanging trait the desire for battle that had previously been attributed to Hera and Athene, and that will also drive the mortal Greek and Trojan heroes to fight in Book 5. The poet imagines her as a force that expands to encompass the whole world, in a divine personification of the spiraling aggression and violence that constitutes the *Iliad*. Moreover, the narrator presents Strife as an agent of war who has actively "pitched" (ἔμβαλε) wholesale conflict, thereby "increasing" (ὀφέλλουσα) mortals' pain.

Homer continues this explication of the divine agency behind the fighting with Athene's multiple interventions in the first part of Book 5. At the very beginning of the book, the narrator describes how Athene gives Diomedes "rage (μένος) and courage (θάρσος), so that he would be distinguished among all the Argives and win noble fame" and makes his helmet and shield shine with fire, like a luminous star (5.2–7); then she "urged" (ὦρσε) him into the middle of the fighting (8). Athene thus imbues Diomedes with aggressive libido and rouses him for his *aristeia*. When the Greek hero is wounded by Pandaros, he prays to Athene for help, and she not only strengthens him but also exhorts him, "now have courage (θαρσῶν), Diomedes, to fight against the Trojans; for in your chest I have injected your paternal rage (μένος), fearless, such as the shield-shaking horseman Tydeus used to have" (124–26); once again, Diomedes' *menos* is attributed to Athene, even as it is also represented as an innate patrimony. Finally, it is Athene who guides Diomedes' spear cast so that he fatally strikes Pandaros (290–91).

While Athene is shown to be the main divine force behind Greek aggression in Book 5, Aphrodite's appearance on the battlefield reminds the audience of her role in starting and perpetuating the war. Athene prepares us for Aphrodite's entrance by encouraging Diomedes to wound the goddess if he encounters her (5.129–32), and her antagonism toward Aphrodite already evokes the goddess's insulting triumph in the Judgment of Paris, which resulted in the Trojan prince's liaison with Helen and the retribution of aggrieved parties, both mortal and divine, currently playing out.[25] When Aphrodite actually joins the battle to rescue Aineias, her intervention recalls not only her salvation of Paris in Book 3 but also her subsequent arrangement of his sexual encounter with Helen. Diomedes, after wounding Aphrodite on her hand, taunts her with words that call to mind Aphrodite's erotically coercive meeting with Helen in Book 3: "Yield, daughter of Zeus, from war and battle; isn't it sufficient that you beguile (ἠπεροπεύεις) strengthless women?" (5.348–49). Indeed, the Greek hero employs the same

[24] Bouvier 2017: 180; see also 188.

[25] See also Reinhardt 1997 [1938]: 181–82, who identifies the entire scene of the wounding of Aphrodite followed by Athene and Hera's mockery of her on Olympos as an allusion to or replay of the Judgment of Paris.

verb "beguile" that Helen had used when she asked Aphrodite, "why do you desire (λιλαίεαι) to beguile (ἠπεροπεύειν) me in this way?" (3.399). Both interlocuters conjure up an Aphrodite who is intent on deceiving women—and specifically Helen—into entering illicit relationships.

Once the wounded Aphrodite has retreated to Mt. Olympos using Ares' chariot and has been comforted by her mother Dione, Athene mockingly characterizes her in the same way, again evoking the events of Book 3. She suggests that Aphrodite has pricked her injured finger on the pin of an Achaian woman's peplos as she was inciting her "to follow along with the Trojans, with whom she is now terribly close" (*Τρωσὶν ἅμα σπέσθαι, τοὺς νῦν ἔκπαγλα φίλησε*, 5.423). Athene's language calls to mind the previous accounts of Helen "following" Paris (3.174, 447), and echoes Aphrodite's own assertion of her intimacy with Helen (*νῦν ἔκπαγλα φίλησα*, 3.415).[26] By introducing Aphrodite as the first divine casualty in the battle narrative and by repeatedly bringing up her agency in uniting Helen with Paris, Homer acknowledges both the goddess and the sexual desire that she provokes as the prime source of the *Iliad*'s martial conflict. Moreover, Diomedes' wounding of Aphrodite is thus constructed as an "implicit retribution" for her role in starting the Trojan War, a retribution that is roughly parallel, on the divine level, to his earlier killing of the most recent mortal instigator of the war and Paris' surrogate, Pandaros.[27]

As this sequence suggests, Aphrodite herself is not aggressive, but her actions lead directly to the aggression of *others*, in a divine figuration of the connection between the sexual and aggressive desires motivating the war. Aphrodite enters battle only to rescue Aineias; she shows no interest in attacking the Greeks and retreats as soon as she is injured. In this way she is like her mortal favorite, the erotic hero Paris, who is queerly disinclined to fight, preferring intercourse in his bedroom to combat on the battlefield. Zeus indeed encourages Aphrodite to involve herself in sex rather than battle, when he gently admonishes her (5.428–30):

> *οὔ τοι, τέκνον ἐμόν, δέδοται πολεμήϊα ἔργα,*
> *ἀλλὰ σύ γ' ἱμερόεντα μετέρχεο ἔργα γάμοιο,*
> *ταῦτα δ' Ἄρηϊ θοῷ καὶ Ἀθήνῃ πάντα μελήσει.*
>
> Not to you, my child, have deeds of war been given,
> but rather attend to the lovely (*himeroenta*) deeds of marriage,
> and all these affairs will be the concern of rushing Ares and Athene.

Zeus's words here normalize Aphrodite's hasty flight, and they also construct a sequential division of labor between Aphrodite, on the one hand, and Ares and

[26] Kirk 1990: 105. [27] Currie 2016: 175, 177.

Athene on the other. Aphrodite does her part of initiating sexual desire—a role that is acknowledged even when she briefly appears in battle—and then Ares and Athene, working, as we have seen, on the side of Trojans and Greeks respectively, assume responsibility for inspiring the warriors' aggressive desire.[28] Like Paris on the mortal level, Aphrodite is not disposed to fight, but her erotic exploits cause others to wage war.

Homer dramatizes this causality when Ares, and then Athene, subsequently enter the battle and stir up the troops themselves. Apollo, after saving Aineias and fending off Diomedes, goes to Ares and asks him to participate in the battle to counteract Diomedes' aggression, citing the hero's wounding of Aphrodite and attack on himself (5.455–59); here Apollo directly links Aphrodite with Ares' entrance into the war. Ares immediately encourages the Trojans in disguise, and the narrator describes how the war god "roused the rage and passion of each" (ὄτρυνε μένος καὶ θυμὸν ἑκάστου, 470). Later, Ares and Enyo—another war goddess—lead the Trojan ranks into battle themselves (592–95), causing the Greeks to pull back and suffer losses. In turn, Hera, dismayed, summons Athene to arm for battle and asks Zeus permission to strike Ares and so remove him from the fighting, complaining of how Aphrodite and Apollo "have incited that senseless one" (ἄφρονα τοῦτον ἀνέντες, 763); again, Aphrodite (together with Apollo) is identified as the inspiration for Ares' violence. Zeus gives his assent, and Athene, wearing her aegis featuring the personified martial divinities Rout, Strife, Strength, and Pursuit (739–40), immediately goes to Diomedes and rouses him again to fight, this time with herself at his side. This sequence replays with an emphasis on divine actors the series of events at the core of the superplot: Paris' erotic liaison with Helen, facilitated by Aphrodite, and then Menelaos' war of revenge, facilitated by Athene (and Hera).

Athene and Diomedes' joint wounding of Ares, which recalls the previous wounding of Aphrodite, also suggests again the similarity of the sexual and aggressive desires determining this superplot, this time through their divine instigators and personifications. Just as Aphrodite before him, Ares is struck by Diomedes with Athene's support and then flees to Mt. Olympos to complain to his divine parent and be healed (5.855–906). Aphrodite's earlier borrowing of Ares' chariot to escape the battlefield also creates a link at the outset between the goddess of sex and the preeminent god of war, who are both partisans of the Trojans.[29] Later, when the gods again fight one another in Book 21, Ares faces up

[28] Cf. Currie 2016: 176–77, who argues that Aphrodite's appearance in *Iliad* 5 is based on the Babylonian goddess Ishtar's attempted seduction of Gilgamesh in the *Epic of Gilgamesh*, and that the "military aspects of Ishtar that are unsuited to the Greek Aphrodite are displaced onto Athene and onto the specialist male Greek god of war, Ares, who in being wounded by Diomedes appears as a narrative counterpart to Aphrodite."

[29] Aphrodite's and Ares' Trojan partisanship seems to reinforce the culpability of the Trojans, who are thus associated with the divine embodiments of both sexual seduction and war.

for a second time against Athene, and again she wounds him; now, in reverse order, Aphrodite appears to rescue Ares and Athene in turn pushes her to the ground and vaunts over the two of them, calling Aphrodite the "ally" (ἐπίκουρος) of Ares (21.391–433). Gabriella Pironti (2007: 218–31) has observed these repeated connections between Aphrodite and Ares, and argues that their Iliadic solidarity and shared physical vulnerability is part of a larger Homeric analogy between sex and war as experiences of bodily mixing and subjection.[30] The parallelism of Aphrodite's and Ares' experiences in Books 5 and 21 likewise seems to create a correspondence between the desire for sex and the desire to fight, which are linked together as motivating forces of the superplot through the triangle of Paris, Helen, and Menelaos.

The end of Book 5 rounds out Homer's depiction of the divine determination of the Trojan War with a return to the Olympian dynamics introduced at the beginning of Book 4. Just as Hera and Athene had collaborated to restart the fighting and ensure the eventual destruction of Troy in Book 4, the last part of Book 5 features the two goddesses again joining forces against the Trojans, this time descending together in Hera's chariot to the battlefield itself. And as when Zeus only reluctantly allowed Hera to act on her aggression and reinitiate the war in Book 4, here also Zeus shows ambivalence toward the violence and deflects responsibility onto Hera. After Athene has wounded Ares, Zeus responds to the injured god's complaints with an assertion that Ares, in his intimacy with strife and wars and battles, is "most hateful" to him of all the gods (5.890–91), which resonates with his own earlier suggestion for the divine family to maintain the truce and preserve Troy.[31] Moreover, Zeus blames Ares' suffering on Hera's *menos*, which he describes as "ungovernable and unyielding" (ἀάσχετον, οὐκ ἐπιεικτόν, 892); he claims, "[only] with difficulty do I subdue her with words" (τὴν μὲν ἐγὼ σπουδῇ δάμνημ' ἐπέεσσι, 893). However, as before, Zeus has explicitly given permission for Hera and Athene's attack (764–66), and Book 5 concludes with Zeus acknowledging Ares as his son, arranging for his healing, and allowing him to sit by his side (895–906). In this way, Homer confirms that the Trojan

[30] As Pironti (2007: 218–31) notes, Aphrodite and Ares are even more intimately linked in other early Greek hexameter poetry: in the *Odyssey*, they appear as lovers in Demodokos' song (*Od.* 8.266–366), and in Hesiod they are spouses and co-parents of Fear, Rout, and Harmonia (*Theog.* 933–37).

[31] Cf. Lowenstam 1993: 70–72, who observes how Zeus's condemnation of Ares' penchant for war echoes with almost identical formulaic language Agamemnon's disdain for Achilleus' warlikeness (5.890–91 ~ 1.176–77). This suggests again a parallelism between Zeus and Agamemnon, and constructs a new correspondence between Ares and Achilleus. Lowenstam notes that both Ares and Achilleus are unreliable in their alliances: Ares is described as abandoning a promise to help the Greeks in favor of fighting for the Trojans (5.832–84, 21.413–14), and Achilleus refuses to fight for the Greeks and devises a plot for honor that is based on the defeat of his own side. I think that Zeus's ambivalence toward Ares here foreshadows a similar ambivalence toward Achilleus despite his promise to bring him honor.

War—the conflict that Hera desires and Ares embodies—is part of Zeus's will, even as that will is shown to be complex and somewhat obscure.

The Trojan Women's Desires

After focalizing most of Books 4 and 5 through the eyes of the gods or the Greeks, Homer provides a different perspective on the war in Book 6, undermining the previous aggrandizement of heroic aggression. This change of perspective begins after another series of Greek kills on the battlefield, which causes the concerned Trojan seer Helenos to advise Hektor to go into Troy and arrange for the Trojan women to make offerings and promises to the goddess Athene so that she "might take pity on the city and the Trojans' wives and infant children" (*αἴ κ' ἐλεήσῃ/ ἄστυ τε καὶ Τρώων ἀλόχους καὶ νήπια τέκνα*) and keep the greatest Greek threat, Diomedes, away from the city (6.86–98). Now, finally, the poet begins to explicate the psychology of the beleaguered Trojans, and focuses the audience's attention on their mental experience, particularly the painful desires of the Trojan women whom Hektor encounters when he eventually enters the city.

While Trojan women and children had been mentioned previously in the narrative, they had been regarded through the Greeks' perspective as desired prizes and future victims of just retribution for Trojan wrongdoing. In Book 1, the Greek kings argue over their enslaved concubines, Chryseis and Briseis, whose own subjectivity is almost entirely ignored. In Book 2, Nestor introduces the idea of Trojan women as prizes of war in order to entice the Greek men to fight. In Book 3, during the oath-taking prior to Paris and Menelaos' duel, both Achaian and Trojan soldiers pray to the gods to punish those who break the truce *and* their families: "let the brains of them and their children run to the ground like wine, and let their wives be subdued by others" (3.300–1). Once Pandaros has violated the truce, Agamemnon, as we have seen, repeatedly asserts that Zeus will bring justice down on the heads of Trojan men, women, and children (4.160–62, 235–39). At the beginning of Book 6, moreover, Agamemnon advises Menelaos not to take any prisoners, telling his brother that after what the Trojans have done to him, none of them should escape a harsh doom, "not even the male child that a mother carries in her womb" (6.58–59).[32] Therefore, Helenos' hope that Athene "might take pity on the Trojans' wives and children" is the first time that Trojan civilians are imagined as deserving of compassion rather than (sexual) violence.

When Hektor arrives in Troy in order to fulfill Helenos' directive, Homer elaborates on this new perspective by depicting the Trojan women themselves

[32] See Kozak 2017: 55 on Agamemnon's words, and how they evoke for the audience the memory of the oath-taking before the duel, Trojan oath-breaking, and the Greek leader's own prediction of the Trojan women and children's future enslavement, drawing attention to their "vulnerability."

confronting their prince. At Hektor's advent, "the Trojans' wives and daughters" (*Τρώων ἄλοχοι . . . ἠδὲ θύγατρες*) rush around him asking about their "sons, brothers, kinsmen, and husbands"; after Hektor advises them all to pray to the gods, we learn that "cares gripped many women" (*πολλῇσι δὲ κήδε' ἐφῆπτο*, 6.238–41).[33] With this anxious mob, the poet has concretized for the first time the women who were before abstract concepts, and revealed their concern for their male intimates still on the battlefield. Now at last the Trojan women are presented as fully realized subjects,[34] who suffer in their longing for their absent and endangered male relatives. Their suffering attracts the sympathy of the audience, who up to this point have been encouraged to care mainly for the Greeks.

The next scene, Hektor's encounter with his mother Hekabe, represents a specific exploration of what initially has been portrayed in generality.[35] Hektor meets Hekabe together with Laodike (6.251–52): they are individual embodiments of the "Trojans' wives and daughters."[36] More exactly, Hekabe is the paradigmatic Trojan mother concerned about the wellbeing of her son Hektor, the paradigmatic Trojan warrior; she worries that the Achaians are "wearing down" (*τείρουσι*) the Trojans, frets about his battle exhaustion, and offers him wine as refreshment (255–62). Furthermore, she acknowledges the threat of the situation with her suggestion that Hektor pray and pour libations to Zeus (256–60). Her direct speech is an unmediated and detailed personal expansion of the Trojan women's corporate reported speech, and it further illuminates the women's mindset and elicits the audience's sympathy.

At Hektor's command, which largely repeats Helenos' original injunction, Hekabe gathers the Trojan women to make the offering and prayer to Athene, in a climax of the poet's elucidation of the Trojan women's collective subjectivity. When they enter Athene's temple, the women are led by the priestess Theano, whose identification as the "the wife (*ἄλοχος*) of horse-taming Antenor" (6.299) indicates how she is a representative of the "Trojans' wives" (*Τρώων ἄλοχοι*) as a whole. It is Theano who addresses Athene, in a third and final variation on Helenos' original words, promising the goddess sacrifices if she "might take pity on the city and the Trojans' wives and infant children" by breaking the spear of

[33] Cf. Graziosi and Haubold 2010: 146 on this formulaic phrase, which generally "ties men to death," and which therefore here links the suffering of female civilians with that of male warriors.

[34] In Book 3, the Trojan women are briefly mentioned twice as being on the walls of Troy with Helen (3.384, 420), and Helen alone imagines the Trojan women's subjectivity when she worries that they will all blame her if she returns to Paris (3.411–12).

[35] Schadewaldt 1944: 212 recognizes this progression and identifies it as a typical Homeric narrative technique.

[36] This explains Laodike's inclusion in this scene and her description as "best in form of [Hekabe's] daughters" (*θυγατρῶν εἶδος ἀρίστην*, 6.252). Graziosi and Haubold 2010: 149 suggest that Laodike, "as the most beautiful daughter of Priam and as someone who was last seen together with Helen," reminds the audience of Helen, whom Hektor is soon to visit. *Contra* Kirk 1990: 194, who says that Laodike "adds nothing here."

Diomedes and making him fall prone before the Skaian Gates (305–10). With this speech-act, Theano expresses both a wish to be safe from harm and an aggressive desire to eliminate the enemy posing the greatest threat. Her prayer departs slightly from that dictated by Helenos and Hektor, as she asks for Diomedes to die rather than merely be turned away from Troy. This stronger version, with its vivid evocation of Diomedes' death, underscores the intensity of the women's fear and hatred of their attacking enemy.[37]

The narrator's immediate report of Athene's refusal of Theano's prayer (6.311) makes the Trojan women into objects of pity for the audience, if not for the goddess. In an instance of dramatic irony, we, but not the women themselves, know that their effort to preserve themselves is futile—an eventuality that we may have suspected given Athene's Greek partisanship and support of Diomedes on the battlefield. This irony, together with the women's desperation, makes them pathetic and invites our compassion and anguish on their behalf. Now, for the first time, the audience is asked to consider what the destruction of Troy, willed by Hera and Athene, and validated by Zeus, means for the Trojans—particularly the female civilians. Therefore, while Theano's prayer for Troy's preservation and Athene's subsequent denial gesture toward the fall of Troy and therefore strengthen the audience's narrative desire to comprehend the epic's path to this devastating conclusion,[38] at the same time this sequence informs that desire with pity and fear for the Trojans, thus generating what George Duckworth (1933) has termed "dreadful anticipation."[39]

The poet juxtaposes this foreshadowing of the war's brutal end with a reminder of how it began when Hektor visits Paris and Helen in order to summon his brother back to the battlefield. Hektor finds the couple in their bedchamber, the same place where the poet left them at the end of Book 3, and so this episode immediately calls to mind Paris and Helen's previous sex scene and the narrative exploration of how their desires caused the Trojan War. What is more, Helen is supervising her slave women's weaving (6.323–24), which reminds the audience of her textile depicting the war—the symbol of Helen's creation of both conflict and poetry. Hektor's first words are a rebuke to Paris for not participating in the war being waged "for your sake" (σέο δ' εἵνεκα, 328),[40] in an echo of his reproach at the beginning of Book 3, when he critiqued Paris' seduction of Helen and queer

[37] Cf. Morrison 1991: 152–57, who argues that Homer strengthens Theano's prayer to include Diomedes' death so that Athene can refuse it while still arranging an end to Diomedes' onslaught when she assents to Apollo's later suggestion of a duel between Hektor and Aias to pause the general hostilities (7.29–42).

[38] *Pace* Morrison 1991: 155–56, who argues that Theano's refused request does not have the typical "anticipatory function" of prayers.

[39] Duckworth 1933: 53 and 60 uses this term to describe the audience's reaction to the predictions of Hektor's death, the fall of Troy, and the enslavement of Andromache.

[40] Hektor exhorts Paris to come and fight before the city burns (6.331), reminding the audience yet again of Troy's ineluctable fate.

reluctance to engage with Menelaos on the battlefield.[41] In these ways, the episode's beginning reintroduces the key elements of the earlier portrayals of Paris and Helen, and positions the two of them together as *casus belli.*

The couple's replies to Hektor present Helen as a powerful agent of war and epic, positioning her as a foil to the other Trojan women. Paris promises Hektor that he will indeed rejoin the fighting, explaining, "now my wife, having persuaded me with soft words, has stirred me to war" (*νῦν δέ με παρειποῦσ' ἄλοχος μαλακοῖς ἐπέεσσιν/ ὅρμησ' ἐς πόλεμον*, 6.337–38). Here Paris depicts Helen as a catalyst of aggression, rather like the gods who urged on the warriors in Book 5. The effectiveness of her speech is evidenced in Paris' newfound willingness to fight and his later sally onto the battlefield (6.503–14), and it contrasts with the inefficacy of the Trojan women's prayer to Athene. The poet invites this comparison by having Paris refer to Helen as his "wife" (*ἄλοχος*), recalling the "Trojans' wives" (*Τρώων ἄλοχοι*) whom Hektor had just encountered. Through Helen's ability to push even Paris into mortal combat, this scene emphasizes the heroine's potent agency in causing conflict between men—in opposition to the other Trojan women's failure to counteract the danger threatening their city.

In her address to Hektor (6.344–58), Helen herself both acknowledges and demonstrates her own power to cause trouble through her desiring subjectivity. Echoing her speech of self-blame to Priam during the Teichoskopia (3.172–80), she refers to herself as an "evil-working, chilling dog" (*κυνὸς κακομηχάνου ὀκρυοέσσης*, 6.344) and wishes that she had died before "these deeds happened" (348), that is, before she eloped with Paris and triggered the war. Even as Helen again claims responsibility for the Trojan War and gestures toward her destructive lust for Paris, she goes on to critique him and wish she had a better husband, recalling her previous reproaches of his behavior and her taunt that her former husband Menelaos might be a better warrior than he (3.428–36). Yet this time it is Hektor, not Menelaos, who seems to be the alternative object of Helen's desire. She evinces guilt-stricken concern for the Trojan leader, bidding him sit down in a chair, "since distress (*πόνος*) has especially enveloped your mind for the sake of me, a dog (*κυνός*), and for the sake of Alexandros' delusion" (6.355–56). The "double-seat" (*δίφρῳ*, 354) that she offers is apparently the same one that Aphrodite had pulled up for the heroine right before she went to bed with Paris (3.424–25)—and it has room for two.[42] The narrator suggests the seductive quality of Helen's speech by introducing it as "honeyed discourse" (*μύθοισι ... μειλιχίοισι*,

[41] The narrator introduces Hektor's speech to Paris in Book 6 using the same formula that preceded Hektor's rebuke to his brother in Book 3: "looking at him, Hector upbraided him with disgraceful words" (*τὸν δ' Ἕκτωρ νείκεσσεν ἰδὼν αἰσχροῖς ἐπέεσσι*, 6.325 = 3.38). Cf. Ransom 2011: 53–55 on Paris' "effeminacy" in this scene.

[42] Arthur 1981: 29 and Graziosi and Haubold 2010: 179. Arthur (1981: 29) observes that Helen's description of her ideal husband as better socialized—"one who knew people's *nemesis* and many reproaches" (*ὃς ᾔδη νέμεσίν τε καὶ αἴσχεα πόλλ' ἀνθρώπων*, 6.351)—sounds like Hektor, especially as he presents himself in the following scene with Andromache.

6.343).[43] As in Book 3, Helen's desire appears to be shifty, and dangerously so, since her inconstancy has initiated conflict and brought "distress" to Hektor.[44]

While Helen's fussing over Hektor may recall Hekabe's, her concluding triumphant reflection on the Trojan War—and her own role in starting it—definitively opposes her to the other Trojan women. Helen ends her speech to Hektor by asserting that upon her and Paris, "Zeus bestowed an evil destiny so that even in later times we may be a subject of song for future people" (*Ζεὺς θῆκε κακὸν μόρον, ὡς καὶ ὀπίσσω/ ἀνθρώποισι πελώμεθ' ἀοίδιμοι ἐσσομένοισι*, 6.357–58). Here most explicitly Homer presents Helen as a proud, self-conscious creator of epic poetry in collaboration with Zeus: according to Helen, her adultery and the consequent war are part of the divine king's will and are designed to provide material for epic song, that is, the *Iliad* itself.[45] Although Helen recognizes her destiny as "evil," she nevertheless seems to revel in it, glorifying the war as a divinely decreed source of epic fame—for herself, Paris, and, implicitly, Hektor too.[46] Unlike the other Trojan women, she does not agonize over either her own safety[47] or the fate of the soldiers on the battlefield, toward which, rather, she is urging Paris. Instead of resembling the anxious women, Helen appears once more to be like Achilleus, who in Book 1 worked pitilessly together with Zeus to plot out the *Iliad*'s story of suffering and death on the Trojan battlefield.

Though Hektor refuses Helen's offer to remain with her, he embraces the war that she has caused and celebrates. He tells her (6.360–62),

μή με κάθιζ', Ἑλένη, φιλέουσά περ· οὐδέ με πείσεις·
ἤδη γάρ μοι θυμὸς ἐπέσσυται ὄφρ' ἐπαμύνω
Τρώεσσ', οἳ μέγ' ἐμεῖο ποθὴν ἀπεόντος ἔχουσιν.

Do not make me sit down, Helen, although you are close to me (*phileousa*); you will not persuade me;
for already my heart is agitated to defend
the Trojans, who have a great longing (*pothēn*) for me while I am absent.

[43] See Worman 2001: 27, who writes "Both Nestor and the Sirens also speak in a honeyed manner, so that the term delimits a range of speech types from the authoritatively but gently persuasive to the dangerously seductive."

[44] On the implications of Helen's seduction here, see also Graziosi and Haubold 2010: 43 and Blondell 2013: 72.

[45] On the metapoetics of this passage, see also Graziosi and Haubold 2010: 6, 180. Helen implicates the gods in her adultery, not only here but also a few lines earlier in her speech, when she resignedly declares, "but since the gods thus ordained these evils, then I wish I were the spouse of a better man" (6.349–50).

[46] Graziosi and Haubold 2010: 43–44.

[47] Indeed, Helen is right not to be concerned. As Austin 1994: 24 observes, "Of all the women in the *Iliad*, Helen alone escapes the slavery in store for the others—Chryseis, Briseis, Andromache, Hecuba, the seven beautiful and gifted women of Lesbos whom Agamemnon gives to Achilles in book 19—the list is almost endless . . . To heighten the difference further, Helen . . . will be responsible, or held responsible at least, for the slavery that befalls the other women."

Hektor rejects Helen's solicitation—as he had rejected his mother Hekabe's—and instead asserts his desire to return to the battlefield. The longing (*pothē*) for himself that he attributes to his soldiers seems to reflect his own wish to join them, which he expresses as an internal compulsion to come to their aid.[48] With this assertion of his urge to fight, Hektor accepts Helen's positive valuation of the war as a path to fame, just as he acknowledges her intimacy—her status as his *philos*—even if he is not responsive to her seduction. In this way, the poet shows that Hektor is fundamentally committed to what Helen's presence in Troy represents.

Andromache's Proleptic Longing

Yet Hektor delays his return to the battlefield in order to visit his wife Andromache and baby son, in a culminating scene that challenges Helen's glorification of the war by dramatizing Hektor's concurrent desire for his family and Andromache's answering desire for her husband. When the Trojan leader leaves Helen, he tells her that he is going to see his "dear wife" (*ἄλοχόν τε φίλην*) and son since he does not know if he will ever return alive again from battle (6.365–68); his use again of the term *philos*, this time applied to his wife rather than Helen, establishes Andromache's competing claim to his intimacy. Homer underscores Hektor's yearning for his wife by having him persistently inquire after and seek out Andromache after he fails to find her in their home. The delay in their reunion also creates suspense, arousing the audience's narrative desire to discover how this meeting will play out.[49]

The introduction of Andromache establishes her as the final and most compelling narrative representative of the "Trojans' wives and daughters" (*Τρώων ἄλοχοι . . . ἠδὲ θύγατρες*) who are beset with anxious longing for their men fighting on the battlefield. Hektor's first mention of Andromache as his "wife" (*ἄλοχον*) already associates her with the "wives" (*ἄλοχοι*) who had met him at the gates of Troy. The narrator introduces Andromache "with her child and well-dressed attendant, standing on the wall, lamenting and wailing" (6.372–73), situating her in the same liminal space as the crowd of Trojan women, and attributing to her a similar, but amplified distress. Later, the housekeeper tells Hektor that she has gone to the wall of the city "because she heard that the Trojans were being worn down" (*οὕνεκ' ἄκουσε/ τείρεσθαι Τρῶας*, 386–87); this description of Andromache's motivation echoes Hekabe's apprehension that the Achaians

[48] Cf. Achilleus' *pothē* for war (1.492) while he sits out the battle in the hope of arousing the Achaians' *pothē* for himself.

[49] On the suspense established here, see Schadewaldt 1944: 215–16. On the various factors informing the audience's "anticipation" for Hektor's encounter with Andromache, see further Kozak 2017: 63–64.

may be "wearing down" (*τείρουσι*, 255) the Trojans in battle, thus linking the psychologies of Hektor's wife and mother. Finally, when Hektor finds Andomache near the Skaian Gates, the narrator cements her association with the "Trojans' wives and daughters" by referring to her as "wife" (*ἄλοχος*, 394) and the "daughter of great-hearted Eëtion" (*θυγάτηρ μεγαλήτορος Ἠετίωνος*, 395). At the same time, the persistent grouping of Andromache with her son Astyanax, who is repeatedly called "infant" (*νήπιον*, 366; 400; *νηπίαχον*, 408), also points to their unique narrative roles as particular embodiments of the endangered "Trojans' wives and infant children" (*Τρώων ἀλόχους καὶ νήπια τέκνα*, 310) whom the Trojan women ask the goddess Athene to pity in their vain appeal.

But Homer also distinguishes Andromache from the other Trojan women, drawing attention to the special force of her desiring subjectivity. As the housekeeper informs Hektor, Andromache is not with the other Trojan women on the mission to Athene (6.384–85), having stepped out of this homogenous group and away from normal feminine activities and locations.[50] The housekeeper describes Andromache as "like a raving woman" (*μαινομένῃ ἐϊκυῖα*, 389), employing a verb of madness (*μαίνομαι*) previously used four times to describe Diomedes' and Ares' aggression on the battlefield (5.185, 5.717, 5.831, 6.101). In this way, the poet suggests a similarity between Andromache's emotion and the extreme aggressive desire of these warriors, and underlines the unusual intensity of Andromache's feeling.[51] Furthermore, the hero Glaukos uses a unique prefixed version of this same verb (*ἐπεμήνατο*, 6.160) to describe Anteia's adulterous infatuation with his illustrious ancestor Bellerophontes near the beginning of Book 6. This occurrence establishes the potential of "raving" to describe a woman's erotic passion for a man and implies that Andromache is as obsessed with Hektor as Anteia was with Bellerophontes.

When husband and wife finally meet, Andromache's long speech to Hektor confirms her passionate attachment to her husband, which opposes Hektor's desire for war. She begins by rebuking Hektor for letting his aggressive desire determine his course of action, lamenting, "your battle-rage (*μένος*) will destroy you," and accusing him of lacking pity for her and Astyanax on the grounds that there will be no "comfort" (*θαλπωρή*) but only "griefs" (*ἄχε'*) for them once he is killed by the Achaians (6.407–13). Here Andromache predicts Hektor's death in battle and, with her mention of future "griefs," foresees her own painful and permanent longing for her dead husband.

She explains why her desire would be so acute by recounting how Achilleus killed or took captive all her other family members when he sacked her home city

[50] Arthur 1981: 30.

[51] See also Schadewaldt 1944: 216 and Arthur 1981: 30 on the use of this verb to characterize Andromache as out of her wits and straying from a normative female routine. The verb *μαίνομαι* appears one additional time before it is applied to Andromache to describe the god Dionysos (6.132).

of Thebe (6.413–28), providing a familiar battle narrative from a new, female perspective. As Elizabeth Minchin (2007: 263) observes, "This story is not about warfare, as are Nestor's tales, but about its social consequences. This is a woman's view of war, the destroyer of families." Andromache's extended and personal story of Thebe's destruction particularly contrasts with Achilleus' own brief narration of the event to his mother Thetis, where he simply states that "we went to Thebe, the sacred city of Eëtion, and sacked it, and carried away everything there; and the sons of the Achaians distributed well these things among themselves, and they chose out for the son of Atreus fair-cheeked Chryseis" (1.366–69). This is the victor's careless view, with no regard for the vanquished, who are assimilated to mostly nameless objects.

While Andromache's account radically differs from Achilleus', it echoes the narrator's practice during battle narratives of offering "obituaries" of fallen warriors, which often emphasize their families' bereavements.[52] This resonance lends her voice the narrator's authority, while recasting his storytelling in the more vivid terms of first-person experience. With her powerful narrative, which allows the audience to see the brutality of war—and especially the devastation caused by Achilleus—through her eyes, Andromache inspires our pity and invites our empathy, causing us again to re-evaluate the war, and especially Achilleus' part in it, in more negative terms.[53]

Andromache caps her speech with a culminating declaration of her need for Hektor, and with an urgent plea for him to stay with her and refrain from risking his life on the battlefield. She concludes her autobiographical narrative with the assertion that Hektor is now "father, mother, brother, and flowering husband" to her (6.429–30), emphasizing her utter reliance on the Trojan leader, who has taken the place of her other lost family members. She ends with an appeal for Hektor to "take pity and remain here on the wall" so that he does not make Astyanax an orphan and her a widow, and suggests that he array the army defensively in front of the part of Troy's fortifications most vulnerable to Greek attack (431–39). Andromache's last words express not only her desire to maintain the integrity of her marital family but also her focus on preserving Troy, which contrasts with the aggressive desires of the Trojan warriors—such as Pandaros and Aineias—to pursue and subdue their enemies.

Despite Andromache's keen entreaty, Hektor's response shows that his desire to fight has mastered his desire for family. He says that he would be ashamed before the Trojan men and women if he were to keep away from war, and asserts that his "passion" (*θυμός*) bids him not to shrink from fighting, explaining that he

[52] e.g. Phainops' grief at Diomedes' killing of his two sons, Xanthos and Thoön (5.152–58).

[53] Andromache's speech details Achilleus' murderous capacity for the first time, even if it portrays him as respectful of his dead enemy, the king Eëtion, and willing to release the captive queen, Andromache's mother, for ransom payment.

has learned to contend bravely in the front-lines, "winning great fame (μέγα κλέος) for my father and myself" (6.441–46). With these words, Hektor makes clear that he intends to re-enter the battle, motivated by competitive desire for both honor and glory.

This desire appears all the more powerful because he understands its implications. Hektor pairs his commitment to the war with a confident assertion that Troy will fall, and with a clear-eyed forecast of Andromache's destined slavery, which he identifies as a care greater to him than the pain or death of his mother, father, or brothers (6.447–55). That is, Hektor understands that the war will end in Troy's destruction and his wife's suffering, and he rates her suffering as his highest concern, mirroring Andromache's identification of him as her all-and-all,[54] yet he still chooses to fight. Hektor's desire for a good reputation is greater than his desire for his wife, and ultimately incompatible with their marital union.[55] His choice represents the triumph of the desire for war—on the Trojan as well as Greek side—and its power to determine the direction of the *Iliad*'s plot, heightening yet again the audience's narrative desire to know how and when Troy will come to grief.

At the same time, Hektor's detailed vision of Andromache's fate amplifies the audience's pity and fear in relation to that end. He describes her servitude in terms that echo and expand upon the previous treatments of the spear-won concubines Chryseis and Briseis, but this time with fuller acknowledgment of the female captive's painful subjectivity. Just as Agamemnon promises that Chryseis, who was taken from Andromache's hometown of Thebe, will be his house-slave in Argos, working the loom and serving his bed (1.30–31), Hektor imagines that Andromache will end up weaving and carrying water as a slave in Argos or another Achaian city (6.456–57). He says to Andromache that some Greek will "lead you away crying, having taken away your day of freedom" (δακρυόεσσαν ἄγηται, ἐλεύθερον ἦμαρ ἀπούρας, 455), also recalling how Briseis was given to the heralds to "lead" (ἄγειν, 1.338; 347) from Achilleus' tent, and how Agamemnon holds Achilleus' prize, "having taken [her] away" (ἀπούρας, 1.356 = 1.507 = 2.240).

Moreover, Hektor focuses on how Andromache will *feel* when "hard necessity lies upon her," developing upon the single brief depiction of Briseis' subjectivity in Book 1. As Briseis leaves Achilleus' tent "unwillingly" (ἀέκουσ', 1.348), so Hektor figures Andromache as "very unwilling" (πόλλ' ἀεκαζομένη) and "shedding a tear"

[54] On the repeated appearance of the "ascending scale of affections" motif and throughout Hektor's sojourn in Troy, see Kakridis 1949: 49–64 and Alden 2000: 262–66.

[55] Schadewaldt 1944: 218; Kakridis 1949: 58; Arthur 1981: 37; Lohmann 1988: 45–47. See also Clarke 1978: 395 n. 37 for a frank analysis of the limitations of Hektor's conjugal love for Andromache. Alden 2000: 317–18 argues that Homer presents Hektor's rejection of Andromache's plea as "wrong-thinking." Beck 2005: 128–29 observes that in this scene "husband and wife never *exchange* ideas and feelings," in contrast to the conversations between Odysseus and Penelope in the *Odyssey* (her italics). Cf. Mackie 1996: 119–23 on the contrasting styles and tones of the Trojan spouses.

(δάκρυ χέουσαν, 6.458–59).[56] He also imagines how Andromache will suffer when someone identifies her as the former wife of the heroic Hektor, "in the lack of such a man to ward off the day of slavery" (459–63). His words remind the audience of Andromache's recently articulated need for him, and her anticipation of feeling anguished longing in the event of his death. Selfishly, Hektor ends with a wish to die before he perceives "your shouting and being dragged away" (σῆς τε βοῆς σοῦ θ' ἑλκηθμοῖο, 465), vividly driving home for the audience the consequences of the war to which he and the other soldiers are dedicated.

With Hektor's subsequent leave-taking of Astyanax, the poet emphasizes the contrast between the warrior's fatalistic embrace of the conflict and the perspectives of his wife and son. When Hektor tries to take Astyanax into his arms, the child shies away, crying, afraid of his father's helmet plume (6.466–70). Even as this reaction causes the laughter of his parents (471), relieving the stress of their conversation, it also illustrates the fearsomeness of war through a child's eyes, animating Astyanax for the first time and eliciting the audience's sympathy for the scared infant. Despite his son's dread of the equipment of battle, Hektor prays to the gods that Astyanax will become a strong warrior, better than his father, and bring home bloody spoils after killing a man, and he also imagines that Andromache will "rejoice in her heart" at their child's martial success (475–81). His prediction of his wife's delight seems like a projection of his own values that does not reflect what we have learned of Andromache's subjectivity.[57] The narrator's following account of Andromache "tearfully laughing" (δακρυόεν γελάσασα, 484) while taking Astyanax back from Hektor seems to communicate her anxiety at the prospect of either husband or son going to war. For audience members familiar with the Trojan War tradition, Hektor's prayer is ripe with dramatic irony, since Astyanax is killed during the sack of Troy,[58] never growing up to become a warrior. This irony only deepens our pity for Astyanax and his soon-to-be bereaved mother, forcing us to consider war's consequences for children and their families.[59]

The end of Hektor's meeting with Andromache inextricably conjoins for the audience the heroic waging of war with the death of soldiers and the suffering of women. Hektor tells Andromache not to grieve, though he is returning to battle, because "no man in excess of fate will send me to Hades" (οὐ γάρ τίς μ' ὑπὲρ αἶσαν

[56] Cf. Dué 2002: 12–14, 67–73 for comparison between Briseis and Andromache, which relies especially on the autobiography Briseis relates during her lament in Book 19.

[57] As Schadewaldt 1944: 219 observes, Andromache is nothing like a Spartan wife or mother who urges on her husband or son into battle.

[58] Neoptolemos throws him off the wall in the *Little Iliad* Frr. 18 and 29 (West 2003: 136–37; 139–41) and Proclus records that Odysseus throws him off in the *Sack of Troy* (West 2003: 146). On this implicit allusion to Astyanax's death, see also Edwards 1987: 211 and Graziosi and Haubold 2010: 213–14.

[59] Cf. Morrison 1992: 70, who argues that Hektor's hopeful prayer for Astyanax and the narrator's lack of comment on whether or not it will be fulfilled make the audience question its traditional knowledge: "the narrator allows the audience to consider these contradictory pictures."

ἀνὴρ Ἄϊδι προϊάψει, 6.487). The formula "will send to Hades" (Ἄϊδι προϊάψει) echoes the end of line 3 of the *Iliad*, which promises the deaths of heroes; Hektor's words remind the perceptive listener of the proem's prediction of lives lost,[60] and suggest that he will be one of the heroic dead. Andromache is not consoled. When Hektor puts back on his helmet and rejoins the war, this separation seems to renew Andromache's intense longing for her husband, as she once again sheds a tear and also leads her attendants in lamentation (*goos*) even though Hektor is still living, induced by an intuition that their parting will be final (496–502).[61] The poet thus asks the audience to experience Andromache's pain once more before the battle narrative resumes.

In Book 6, therefore, Homer complicates the audience's allegiance with the Greeks and possible empathy with their desire to destroy Troy by encouraging a new attention to and sympathy for the experience of the Trojan women and children. Andromache's compelling desiring subjectivity, in particular, not only elicits our sympathy but also beckons our empathy, rivalling the narrative allure of Helen, the other mortal woman granted a fully-formed and enthralling psychology. If Helen's transgressive adulterous desire causes war, Andromache's normative desire for her husband opposes war; yet, unlike Helen, she is unable to realize her desire.[62] Throughout Books 4–6, the poet makes clear that the war will continue and Troy will fall, arousing the audience's narrative desire to track the Trojan War superplot to this conclusion. But with his arresting depiction of the Trojan women's distress, Homer definitively colors that narrative desire with the emotions of pity and fear, and encourages opposing sympathetic and empathetic desires for Troy's salvation. These conflicted and conflicting feelings force us to reflect on the nature and meaning of the war in all its devastation. This episode thus invests the audience more deeply in the developing narrative and offers a powerful corrective to the previously unproblematic glorification of the Trojan War and its martial heroism.[63]

[60] Graziosi and Haubold 2010: 221.

[61] Cf. Dione's threat that Diomedes' wife will wake up the household "lamenting" (γοόωσα) in her "longing" (ποθέουσα) for her dead husband (5.413–14).

[62] For the comprehensive opposition between Andromache and Helen in the *Iliad*, see Schadewaldt 1944: 214; Owen 1946: 64–65; Lohmann 1988: 57–59; Louden 2006: 55, 60–63.

[63] Therefore, I disagree with Gaca 2008: 164, who claims that the *Iliad* focuses almost exclusively on the experience of men on the battlefield, neglecting women's experiences: "with few exceptions, little epic memory is given to the ensuing brutality largely directed at women and girls." Gaca identifies epic similes as these "exceptions," failing to consider the narrative's portrayal of the Trojan women.

5
The Renewal of Achilleus' Destructive Desires

After his expansive treatment of the Trojan War superplot in *Iliad* 3–7, Homer returns in Books 8 and 9 to the epic's main plot, that is, Achilleus' plot for revenge and the redemption of his status. Focusing on *Iliad* 9, this chapter shows how Agamemnon's embassy to Achilleus offers the audience the prospect of narrative satisfaction, but instead prolongs Achilleus' plot by rekindling his driving aggressive desires. Along the way, the hero appears again as a queer narrative agent, who deviates from the masculine norm of solidarity with fellow fighters on the battlefield. Meanwhile, Zeus's prophecy of the unexpected denouement of Achilleus' plot makes the audience eager to follow its development, and our complex engagement with characters further invests us in the upcoming battle narrative and asks us to evaluate Achilleus' righteousness.

From the Superplot to the Main Plot

Iliad 7 concludes the narrative sequence explicating the Trojan War story by reprising or recalling its key events. Once Hektor and Paris have returned to the battlefield after their sojourn in Troy, Apollo and Athene engineer a second inconclusive duel between Hektor and Aias that echoes the duel between Paris and Menelaos at the outset of the superplot in Book 3.[1] Whereas the first duel presented the interpersonal dynamics at the Trojan War's origin, the second duel establishes Hektor and Aias as the most powerful warriors on the Trojan and Greek sides, excepting Achilleus. Even as it confirms Hektor's strength and boldness, the duel also exposes his potential weakness, as he nearly succombs to Aias, who regards himself as the victor after the duel is aborted (7.244–312).[2]

[1] Myers 2019: 118–25 argues convincingly that the opposing partisan feelings of Apollo and Athene in this scene, for the Trojans and Greeks respectively, dramatize the conflicted response of the audience to the ongoing war, given both our identification with the Greek warriors and the sympathetic portrayal of the Trojan civilians in Book 6.

[2] Aias is described "rejoicing in victory" (κεχαρηότα νίκῃ, 7.312). Hektor's near defeat at the hands of Aias repeats his brother Paris' worsting by Menelaos. Menelaos' willingness to fight again in Book 7, before the other Greek champions volunteer, clearly marks this second duel as a repetition of the first. On the duel and its significance for the audience, see further Kozak 2017: 72–78.

Desire in the Iliad: *The Force That Moves the Epic and Its Audience.* Rachel H. Lesser, Oxford University Press.
 DOI: 10.1093/oso/9780192866516.003.0006

In this way, the second duel is an epitome of the superplot's battle dynamics, like the epic's opening battle narratives in Books 4 and 5 featuring Greek dominance.

Book 7 also confirms the inevitability of continued war with another failed attempt to make peace. In a Trojan council, the elder Antenor suggests the return of Helen, only to have Paris flatly refuse to give up Helen and offer merely the goods stolen from Sparta and additional material recompense (7.345–64). This sequence reminds the audience of Paris' sexual reunion with Helen in Book 3 after his escape from the first duel, which nullified its peace treaty, and it makes clear that Paris' lust for Helen continues to motivate the Trojan War. When the Trojan herald conveys this proposal to the Achaians, he says he wishes that Paris had died before he sailed back to Troy, and asserts that all the Trojans are in favor of returning Helen (385–93); as in Book 3, the other Trojans' condemnation of Paris contributes to his construction as queer. Diomedes' rejection, on behalf of the Greeks, of Paris' offer—and of Helen too—on the basis that Troy is clearly fated for destruction (400–4) reminds the audience of Zeus's guarantee of Troy's fall in Book 4 and shows that once Paris has set the war in motion, nothing can now prevent its ruinous denouement. The two sides can only agree on a brief truce for burial, during which the Greeks also fortify their camp with a wall and ditch, foreshadowing a future when they will find themselves on the defensive.

This occurs in Book 8, when Zeus finally grants the Trojans the upper hand in battle, thereby resuming the progress of Achilleus' main plot and reintroducing it to the audience. Zeus first calls a divine assembly and directs the gods not to help either side in the battle, warning that he will throw any disobedient god into Tartaros, since he is "the strongest of all the gods" (*θεῶν κάρτιστος ἁπάντων*) and could prevail over their combined power (8.2–27). With these words, Zeus puts a stop to the partisan divine interference that had characterized the battle narrative of the superplot, and reclaims final authority over mortal affairs, even as he acknowledges the possibility of other gods' dissent.[3] He also echoes Hephaistos' warning to Hera of his preeminent might when she challenged his collusion with Achilleus and Thetis (*ὁ γὰρ πολὺ φέρτατός ἐστιν*, 1.581), signaling a return to the main plot and its divine power dynamics.

At midday, Zeus weighs the fates of the two armies and finds the Achaian doom-day to be heavier (8.68–74), then he repeatedly thunders to encourage the Trojans to pursue the Greeks toward their ships, and finally rouses "rage" (*μένος*) in them to push the Achaians back into the ditch surrounding their camp (335–36). In dismay, Athene complains to Hera that Zeus "has actualized the plots (*βουλάς*) of Thetis, who kissed his knees and took his chin in her hand, supplicating him to honor Achilleus the city-sacker" (370–72). Athene's words remind the audience of Zeus's promise in Book 1 to fulfill Achilleus' desire for

[3] On Zeus's assertion of authority here and in the following battle scene, along with the lurking potential of other gods' rebellions, see also Kelly 2007: 43–48.

honor by making the Trojans triumphant over the Greeks in his absence—and they also indicate that Zeus is now acting on that promise.[4]

Indeed, when Hera and Athene prepare to enter the battle to aid the Achaians, in contravention of Zeus's earlier dictum, the divine king prevents them with threats (8.350–456). The goddesses' attempted intervention is a doublet of the episode in Book 5 when they descend to the Trojan plain to fight at Diomedes' side, but in the superplot, Zeus allows Hera and Athene to help the Achaians, while here in the main plot, he intercedes.[5] As G. S. Kirk (1990: 327) explains, this scene shows by contrast that "Zeus' will is paramount." Moreover, Zeus's boast to Hera and Athene that he has "untouchable hands" (*χεῖρες ἄαπτοι*) and that none of the Olympian gods could defeat him (450–51) recalls his similar threat to Hera in Book 1, when he warned her that none of the other gods would help her "when I should lay my untouchable hands (*ἀάπτους χεῖρας*) upon you" (1.566–67). Thus, the divine king reaffirms the incontrovertability of his desire to subdue the Greeks in the face of Hera's opposition.

When Hera nevertheless continues in her effort to thwart Achilleus' and Zeus's plot, asking the divine king for permission to give advice to the Greeks (8.462–68), she provokes him to reassert and further define his will in the form of a prophecy (473–77):[6]

οὐ γὰρ πρὶν πολέμου ἀποπαύσεται ὄβριμος Ἕκτωρ,
πρὶν ὄρθαι παρὰ ναῦφι ποδώκεα Πηλεΐωνα,
ἤματι τῷ ὅτ' ἂν οἱ μὲν ἐπὶ πρύμνῃσι μάχωνται
στείνει ἐν αἰνοτάτῳ περὶ Πατρόκλοιο θανόντος,
ὣς γὰρ θέσφατόν ἐστι·

for mighty Hektor will not cease from war
until he stirs up the swift-footed son of Peleus
on the day when they are fighting beside the ships' sterns
in most dreadful straits over the dead Patroklos,
for thus it is decreed...

[4] See further Heiden 2008: 106–19, who catalogues an extensive series of "thematic analogies" that link together Book 1 and Book 8.

[5] Reinhardt 1961: 140–51 and Kirk 1990: 327.

[6] *Contra* Marks 2016: 65, who interprets Zeus's revelation to Hera as "a conciliatory gesture" that keeps his promise to her in Book 1 that she would be the first to know of his plans once he was ready to reveal them. Cf. Scodel 2017: 84, who notes that Zeus only explains his will when he is enraged at Hera (so too at the beginning of Book 15), and observes how it is possible to interpret his prophecy as a newly formulated plan in response to Hera rather than as the exposition of a previously hidden but fully conceived plan. If the former is the case, then Zeus's will—and the epic's plot—not only emerges but is also defined in dialectical opposition to or negotiation with Hera and the other gods (see further "Zeus's Revised Will" in Chapter 6). Alternatively, Bonnet 2017: 92 suggests that while Zeus knows the final outcome of events, the path to that outcome is open and influenced by the diverse wills of the other gods. Scodel 2017 (esp. 89–90) interprets Zeus as a figure for the epic poet/performer as he composes his narrative under pressure from his (potentially critical) audience as well as the existing poetic tradition.

While Zeus here verifies his promise of temporary Trojan predominance over the Greeks, this prophecy does more than simply confirm the course of the main plot as it was conceived by Achilleus in Book 1. For the first time, the poet foreshadows the death of Patroklos and connects this death with Achilleus' re-entrance into battle, indicating to the audience that Achilleus' desires for revenge and honor will have a deadly and presumably unintended consequence that will impel him to rejoin the war. This prophecy, therefore, reveals definitively that Achilleus' and Zeus's desires are not perfectly aligned. It also inspires our narrative desire to find out how, when, and why Patroklos will be killed in battle. Thus, even as Book 8 finally returns to Achilleus' main plot, it also gestures toward its complication and expansion.

Zeus confirms the efficacy of his words with a final boast of his supreme dominance. He says to Hera, "I do not care about you being angry (χωομένης)" and then insists that he would not even be worried if she should go wandering down to Tartaros where Iapetos and Kronos sit (8.477–82). With this vision of Hera journeying to the Underworld, Zeus seems to be imagining his wife freeing the conquered Titans and fomenting with them a rebellion against his hegemony. By conjuring up this potential challenge to his rule, Zeus reminds the audience again of Book 1, where Achilleus told the story of a nearly successful attempt to bind Zeus by Hera, Poseidon, and Athene (1.397–406), and where the poet first thematized Hera's antagonism with Zeus through their quarrel over the Greek army's fate. As at the end of Book 1, here also Zeus asserts his ultimate power, dismissing the revolutionary force of Hera's anger.

Yet at the same time, he recognizes its potential to disrupt his cosmic order, not only through reference to his regime-establishing war against the Titans but also with his closing insult, "since nothing is more doggish (κύντερον) than you" (8.483). The slur "more doggish," directed at a female, recalls Helen's repeated self-abuse as "dog-faced" (κυνώπιδος, 3.180) and "dog" (κυνός, 6.344; 6.356). This reverberation links Hera's rebellious behavior in the divine sphere with Helen's disruptive adultery in the mortal sphere, which led to the world-altering and epic-generating event of the Trojan War.[7] Therefore, while Zeus, in this scene, re-establishes his will as the determinant of the *Iliad*'s plot, the associations that Hera amasses in his discourse suggest her continued threat to his will's realization.[8]

[7] Pucci 2018: 170 n. 48 asserts that "'bitch' is an image that insults a traitor," and refers to Helen's use of the term to characterize herself as "betrayer of Menelaus and Sparta." Cf. Franco 2014: 118–19, who interprets Zeus's doggish characterization of Hera as a way of putting her in her place as his subordinate; this insult thus functions as "a demand for submission."

[8] Cf. Kelly 2007: 64, who argues that Zeus "is incautiously underestimating the extent to which Here will be able to frustrate his intentions," and Bonnet 2017: 96, who reads Zeus's mention of the imprisoned Titans as "inscrib[ing] his power in all the thickness of time and space" (*inscrit son pouvoir dans toute l'épaisseur du temps et de l'espace*).

Book 8 points backward and forward,[9] reminding us what came before and arousing our narrative desire for what is still to come. J. A. Davison (1965) and Bruce Heiden (1996) have suggested that the first day of the *Iliad*'s three-day performance ended with Book 8, while Keith Stanley (1993: 261–66) imagines that this book actually began the second day of the poem's performance. In either case, these models acknowledge how Book 8 is an inflection point that brings us back to Achilleus' main plot and entices us to make sense of newly predicted narrative twists and turns.

The Embassy to Achilleus: Reconciliation or an Insult Revisited?

The beginning of Book 9 suggests that Achilleus' plot for revenge and honor is working. At the close of Book 8, the Trojan army had camped on the plain after a successful day of battle, ready to launch a renewed assault against the Achaians the next morning. In Book 9, the narrative focalization switches from the confident Trojans to the beleaguered Greeks, who are beset with "panic" (φύζα) and "unendurable sorrow" (πένθεϊ δ' ἀτλήτῳ, 9.1–3). After providing this general picture of the Achaian army's state of mind, the narrator focuses on Agamemnon particularly, asserting his "great grief" (ἄχεϊ μεγάλῳ) and describing his tears, which are elaborated with a simile of a dark stream pouring water down a cliff (9–15). Zeus seems to have brought to fruition Achilleus' promise that Agamemnon would feel grief (*achos*) when all the Achaians experienced longing (*pothē*) for Achilleus in the face of Hektor's deadly attack (1.240–43).

The situation of the Greek army at the opening of Book 9 is also reminiscent of the previous time that the Achaians were in a dire state of affairs: when they were dying from the plague sent by Apollo (1.44–53),[10] which was caused by the priest Chryses' conflict with Agamemnon over Chryseis. In response to this crisis in Book 1, the Achaians came together in an assembly, which resulted in Agamemnon returning Chryseis to her father and sending recompense to Apollo, thereby stopping the plague. Now, in Book 9, Agamemnon calls another assembly and then takes counsel privately with the Achaian kings; these meetings parallel the assembly of Book 1 not only on a structural level but also with regard to theme and language.[11] Achilleus' plot thus continues to develop along the same lines of Chryses' paradigmatic triangular conflict with Agamemnon.

[9] For extensive discussion of the correspondences between Book 8 and both preceding and succeeding books, see further Reinhardt 1961: 138–89.

[10] Rabel 1997: 116 and Heiden 2008: 126–27.

[11] Lohmann 1970: 173–78, 214–27 and Louden 2006: 112–20.

Robert Rabel (1997: 116–17) argues that Chryses' paradigm creates an expectation that the assembly and council in Book 9 will lead to a reconciliation between Achilleus and Agamemnon. However, we know from Zeus's prophecy in Book 8 that Achilleus will not return to battle until after Patroklos' death; circumstances are not yet right for an end to Achilleus' quarrel with Agamemnon. Therefore, I believe that the poet evokes the resolution of Chryses' paradigmatic plot as a touchstone for interpreting Book 9, as an indicator to the audience of how things go wrong in the Greeks' attempt to reconcile with Achilleus.[12] The departure in Book 9 from the reconciliation model introduced in Book 1 thus begins this episode's renewal of the audience's narrative desire to find out how and when Achilleus' desires will be appropriately and satisfactorily met.

Though Agamemnon initially creates the impression that he regrets his conflict with Achilleus in the assembly of Book 9, that impression is quickly proved wrong. In Book 1, Achilleus had told Thetis to ask Zeus for help "so that Atreus' son, wide-ruling Agamemnon, might recognize his delusion" (ἄτην, 1.411–12), and here Agamemnon begins by acknowledging to the army that Zeus has afflicted him with "delusion" (ἄτῃ, 9.18). But as Agamemnon continues, it becomes clear that the delusion (*atē*) to which he refers relates to his decision to lead the expedition against Troy rather than to his mistreatment of Achilleus (19–22). Furthermore, Agammenon's claim of *atē* and his following suggestion that the army abandon the war and return home repeat exactly his ill-conceived words in the assembly of Book 2, when he had tested his troops' resolve (9.18–25 = 2.111–18; 9.26–28 = 2.139–41). Given that Agamemnon's misguided speech in Book 2 nearly caused the disbandment of the Achaian army, its repetition in Book 9 does not inspire confidence in the Greek commander's ability to solve the crisis at hand.[13]

After Diomedes vehemently and abusively rejects Agamemnon's proposal of flight (9.32–49), Nestor's intervention further signals this episode's divergence from the paradigm of the Greeks' reconciliation with Chryses. Nestor steps in to keep the peace, then identifies Agamemnon's insult to Achilleus as the problem needing to be addressed and advises, "let us take thought how we might persuade him to be conciliated with gifts and gentle words" (96–113). Though Heiden (2008: 127) suggests that the Pylian king here takes on the role of Kalchas, who intervened in the Chryses episode to diagnose the cause of the plague and propose the return of Chryseis and propitiation of Apollo (1.92–100), Nestor's entrance to mediate the dispute between Diomedes and Agamemnon recalls more directly his failed mediation between Achilleus and Agamemnon in Book 1. Not only is the

[12] See also Wilson 2002: 75.

[13] Cf. Hainsworth 1993: 61–62, who notes the repetition but rejects interpreting this passage as a pointed allusion to Book 2. See Wilson 2002: 72–73 for a more generous view of Agamemnon's rhetorical tactics.

situation similar,[14] but Nestor's treatment of the two antagonists is nearly identical.[15] Nestor tells Diomedes, "you are strong" (*καρτερός ἐσσι*, 9.53), repeating the same complement that he had previously paid Achilleus (1.280). Then he flatters Agamemnon with the statement, "you are kingliest" (*βασιλεύτατός ἐσσι*, 9.69), which recalls his assertion in Book 1 that Agamemnon "is superior, because he rules over more" (*φέρτερός ἐστιν, ἐπεὶ πλεόνεσσιν ἀνάσσει*, 1.281).[16] These resemblances suggest that the sequence of events in Book 9 is conforming to the quarrel between Achilleus and Agamemnon in Book 1 rather than the resolution of Chryses' plot.

During his intervention, Nestor also introduces an important theme of Book 9: the damaging nature of conflict between members of a community. He declares, "outside of brotherhood, law, and hearth is he who lusts after (*ἔραται*) chilling civil war" (9.63–64). Using the verbal cognate of *erōs*, Nestor warns that aggressively desiring to make war against one's own people leads to social ostracism, and he defines such conflict as a horror. His programmatic statement informs the audience's interpretation of Agamemnon here and Achilleus in the following embassy scene, and anticipates much of the discourse of Agamemnon's ambassadors.

Despite this wisdom, Nestor's intervention here is as ineffective as it was in Book 1, where he failed to mollify the aggrieved parties or resolve their differences. In both instances, Agamemnon picks up Nestor's assertion of his kingliness and doubles down on it. In Book 1, he responds to the Pylian king with the claim that Achilleus is trying to usurp his power (1.286–91), and Achilleus interrupts in outrage (292–96); thus, Nestor inadvertently heightens Agamemnon's and Achilleus' mutual animosity. In Book 9, Agamemnon finally admits his *atē* vis-à-vis Achilleus and promises to bestow on him numerous valuable gifts and honors along with Briseis herself if he should return to the battlefield (9.115–57); yet, as scholars have shown, this offer is itself an assertion of dominance over Achilleus, which would put him in the inferior position of debtor and subject to Agamemnon[17]—and it is conditional on him doing what the Greek leader wants. Indeed, Agamemnon ends his recital of the gifts with an outright call for Achilleus to "be tamed" (*δμηθήτω*), "submit" (*ὑποστήτω*) to him, and recognize how much

[14] Lohmann 1970: 217–24; Hainsworth 1993: 66; Louden 2006: 119–20.

[15] Lohmann 1970: 224–25 sees a difference between Nestor as impartial mediator in Book 1 and definitively on the side of Agamemnon in Book 9, but I think that his two interventions are functionally the same.

[16] Later, during his second speech in the council, Nestor continues his aggrandizement of Agamemnon's ruling power (9.96–99), even as he expands upon his former negative evaluation of Agamemnon's seizure of Briseis (compare 1.275–76 and 9.106–11). See also Lynn-George 1988: 85–86 on how Nestor's language reconstitutes Agamemnon's kingship in these scenes in Book 9.

[17] e.g. Lynn-George 1988: 89–91; Donlan 1993: 164–66; Redfield 1994: 15–16; Lateiner 1995: 76–77; Muellner 1996: 141; Wilson 2002: 78–80. Wilson 2002: 76–80 also argues that Agamemnon, by terming the gifts ransom (*apoina*) rather than recompense (*poinē*), elides his offense as well as the need to compensate Achilleus and positions himself instead as an innocent Chryses-figure attempting to recover the Achaians' lives, which Achilleus is symbolically holding hostage by his absence.

"kinglier" (βασιλεύτερος) he is (9.158–61). This speech certainly does not include the "gentle words" that Nestor advises; there is neither apology nor a statement of his need.[18] The Pylian king seems to have (unintentially) reactivated Agamemnon's aggressive desire to best his Greek compatriot. As Donna Wilson (2002: 80) summarizes, Agamemnon's approach to Achilleus here "conforms with his behavior in Book 1."[19]

The following failure of Agamemnon's embassy to Achilleus to replicate the narrative pattern set by the delegation to Chryse in Book 1 foreshadows the failure of its mission.[20] Nestor composes the embassy to convey the Greek leader's offer, and advises its members on how best to persuade Achilleus (9.167–81), but again Nestor's agency here does not presage a positive outcome, given both his lack of involvement in the paradigmatic reconciliation with Chryses and his bad record of mediating successfully between Agamemnon and Achilleus.[21] On the other hand, Odysseus' prominent inclusion in the embassy recalls his leadership of the delegation to Chryse and suggests at first their parallelism.[22] Yet, whereas Odysseus was the only named participant in the mission to Chryse, this embassy comprises five named ambassadors, including two heralds. The major disparity between the delegations, however, is the fact that the first returns the disputed girl (Chryseis) and brings in addition a hecatomb to sacrifice to Apollo (1.431–39), while the second brings nothing at all except speeches and promises. The delegation to Chryse immediately delivers a true reparation, but the embassy to Achilleus is all word and no deed.[23]

Moreover, the arrival of the embassy at Achilleus' tent constitutes a strange reversal of the reconciliation with Chryses and Apollo. Whereas in Book 1 it is Odysseus who first addresses Chryses concerning the reparation while delivering Chryseis into his hands (1.440–45), in Book 9 it is Achilleus who first speaks words of welcome and invites the ambassadors inside (9.196–200). Again, whereas Odysseus' delegation in Book 1 provides the animals for the sacrifice and thus the meat for the feast, as well as the wine (1.447–71), in Book 9, Achilleus and his companions provide the feast and perform the requisite sacrifice (9.201–21). The embassy is supposed to be conciliating Achilleus, yet the ambassadors come empty handed and are themselves greeted as well as wined and dined.

[18] Bassett 1938: 195–96; Thornton 1984: 126–27; Lynn-George 1988: 88; Wilson 2002: 81.

[19] See also Whitman 1958: 192–93. *Contra* Montanari 2017: 44, who interprets Agamemnon's offer as "a total about-turn."

[20] Cf. Louden 2006: 120–34 for another comparison between these two delegations. Reece 1993: 6 observes how here "the messenger scene is transformed into a scene of hospitality."

[21] Louden 2006: 122–23.

[22] Wilson 2002: 81–82 argues that Nestor's glance at Odysseus positions Odysseus as the real head of the delegation, despite the formal designation of Phoinix as leader.

[23] See also Lynn-George 1988: 87–91 on the embassy's conspicuous lack: "The gifts to be 'given all at once' are deferred, do not materialise as objects, are repeated as language in a drama which focuses on the materiality *and* insubstantiality of words" (his italics).

This reversal of the resolution to Chryses' plot also applies, in a different way, to the embassy's first vision of Achilleus in his tent. The ambassadors find him "taking pleasure in his mind with the clear-toned phorminx" (φρένα τερπόμενον φόρμιγγι λιγείῃ, 9.186), and the narrator elaborates that he "was pleasuring his heart, and singing the fames of men" (θυμὸν ἔτερπεν, ἄειδε δ' ἄρα κλέα ἀνδρῶν, 189). In contrast to Achilleus' initial posture, Chryses is described as "rejoicing" (χαίρων) only *after* receiving back his daughter Chryseis (1.446), and Apollo is said to have been "taking pleasure in his mind by listening" (φρένα τέρπετ' ἀκούων, 1.474) to the Achaian youths' song *after* the propitiatory sacrifice.[24] In the paradigmatic narrative, the delegation's reparation effects a positive change of mood in the compensated parties (Chryses and Apollo) as they all celebrate together. But in Book 9, Achilleus is enjoying himself apart from the larger body of the Greeks *before* the embassy even arrives.

Achilleus' happy tranquility at this moment contrasts strongly with his last appearance in the narrative in Book 1. There, before he disappears for seven books, we are left with an image of the hero in a frustrated state of desire, "being wroth" (μήνιε), "withering away in his dear heart," and "longing (ποθέεσκε) for the battle-cry and war" (1.488–92). Now, however, Achilleus seems to be content, to have found a new sense of ease and completeness in his own private world.[25] He lacks neither companionship nor material resources: Patroklos attends him while he makes music (9.190–91), and later Automedon helps serve the feast provided for the embassy (209). The ambassadors' initial view of Achilleus suggests that the hero is no longer concerned with accruing honor within the larger Greek community and also "conveys the idea that [he] has no need of repossessing Briseis."[26] Achilleus' unexpected serenity presages the futility of the embassy's mission of appeasement.

Achilleus' lyre playing and singing of "the fames of men" also mark him as a bardic figure, in a parallel to Homer himself, confirming the narrative productivity of his withdrawal from the army. Achilleus' performance of epic song recalls his repetition and expansion of the narrator's diegesis in Book 1 and reminds the audience of how his desires have generated the *Iliad*'s main plot—Zeus's subjugation of the Greeks on the Trojan battlefield. Moreover, by explaining how Achilleus' phorminx (lyre) was acquired as booty from his sack of Eëtion's city

[24] Cf. Apollo's own accompaniment of the Muses' song on the phorminx *after* the gods' feast on Olympos at the end of Book 1 (1.603–4), which is part of the divine conflict-resolution narrative that is an analogic confirmation of Chryses' paradigm.

[25] Cf. Hainsworth 1993: 88, who writes, "the poet allows us to assume that Achilleus' emotional turmoil... has given way to tedium." But the poet shows Achilleus in a state of pleasure, not tedium.

[26] Fantuzzi 2012: 198. See also Lohmann 1970: 229, who observes, "This Achilleus of Book 9 is no more dependent on the goodwill of others; he does not need them; on the contrary, they now need him" (*Dieser Achill des 9. Buches ist nicht mehr abhängig vom Wohlwollen der anderen, er braucht sie nicht, im Gegenteil, sie brauchen jetzt ihn*); and Lynn-George 1988: 138, who writes that "Achilles' singing of *klea* on the lyre within his tent seem[s] to mark the point of the hero's greatest self-sufficiency and autonomy."

(9.188)—the place where Chryseis was taken captive and Andromache's family was killed—the narrator emphasizes the hero's agency as prime perpetrator of violence and thus generator of martial epic.[27] Homer invites us to imagine that the heroic deeds and deaths just recounted in *Iliad* 8 are the subject of this song that Achilleus performs, and has authored, together with the epic poet.

And yet the fact that Achilleus sings of other men's fame while sitting at leisure in his tent, rather than earning his own glory on the battlefield (he is no longer fighting as he did when he conquered Thebe and acquired his phorminx), links him ambivalently with the queer poet-figures of the superplot, Helen and Paris. Achilleus' epic singing recalls Helen's weaving of the Trojan War being fought "for her sake" (3.125–28); both represent but remain outside of the conflict for which they are responsible.[28] Achilleus' playing of a stringed instrument away from the battlefield also calls to mind Paris, whom Hektor ridiculed for occupying himself with the kithara and "the gifts of Aphrodite."[29] Like Hektor, Achilleus' auditor Patroklos does not encourage Achilleus' musical activity, but rather seems to embody a subtle posture of critique; the narrator reports that Patroklos "was sitting alone opposite Achilleus in silence, waiting for the grandson of Aiakos, when he would leave off singing" (9.190–91).[30] Patroklos' less than enthusiastic response may construct Achilleus' music-making, like Paris', as deviant in the context of total war.[31] While Helen imagines herself and Paris as the subjects of epic song (6.358), it is not on account of their martial exploits. Their epic fame may better be termed "infamy," and Patroklos' attitude may suggest that Achilleus is himself achieving a similar reputation through his withdrawal. Later, in his long speech to the embassy, Achilleus confirms this assessment when he acknowledges that his "*good* fame" (*κλέος ἐσθλόν*) will be lost if he does not re-enter the war (9.414–15).[32]

[27] See also Lynn-George 1988: 151, who writes, "Won amidst spoils, the lyre remains to celebrate fame—and to signify loss."

[28] Cf. Griffin 1995: 98, who also connects Achilleus here with Helen, arguing that they both appear to be self-conscious of their places in the poetic tradition.

[29] Lowenstam 1993: 88 and Ransom 2011: 42 n. 24 note the similarity of Paris and Achilleus as lyre players.

[30] *Contra* Frontisi-Ducroux 1986: 11–13 (see also 23–25), who suggests that Patroklos as silent auditor provides a model for the audience of the *Iliad* itself. Patroklos is hardly an ideal audience since he neither desires the song nor experiences pleasure; rather, he waits for Achilleus to *stop* singing.

[31] At times of peace, conversely, male singing and dancing appear to be normative activities, as indicated by their positive representation on the portion of Achilleus' shield devoted to the seasons of peaceful life (18.494–95, 567–72, 590–606). In contrast to Achilleus, Odysseus tells, not sings, his heroic narratives in the *Odyssey*, and they are stories of his own exploits, not generic "fames of men." Cf. King 1987: 10, who argues that "[t]here is no opposition between lyre and battle here" because Achilleus has won the lyre as a spoil of war; and Ransom 2011: 42 n. 24, who suggests that Achilleus' lyre playing does not impute his masculinity since he has withdrawn from the world of war, but rather serves to emphasize "his separation from the other Achaians."

[32] The (ambivalent) *kleos* that the *Iliad* itself bestows on Achilleus ultimately extends beyond the fame of his martial heroism, but I think that Taplin 2001: 362 overstates the case when he says that "Achilles is not immortalized for his massacre of Trojans in Books 20 and 21 so much as for his impending death before his time, for his rejection of the embassy in Book 9, and for his treatment of Priam."

The queerness of Achilleus' singing apart from the Greek army indicates again to the audience the antisocial nature of his plot for revenge and honor. Moreover, Patroklos' prominent re-emergence in the narrative at this juncture, where he at once appears as Achilleus' closest intimate and seems to express tacit disapproval of Achilleus' behavior, also reminds the audience of Zeus's prophecy of Patroklos' death—and positions that death as the ultimate manifestation of the Greek devastation willed by Achilleus. More generally, the conspicuous presentation of Achilleus as a poet at the moment when the embassy arrives suggests that the ambassadors will be unsuccessful in their attempt to bring to an end the hero's plot to subdue the Greeks.

If Achilleus' placid music-making implies that the embassy will fail to effect a resolution in accordance with the paradigm of the Greek delegation to Chryse, we must look elsewhere to find the appropriate model for the embassy of Book 9. As many scholars have recognized, the embassy directly recalls another delegation from Book 1 of an entirely different kind: Agamemnon's dispatch of heralds to take Briseis away from Achilleus' tent. The narrator makes the link explicit between Agamemnon's two delegations to Achilleus by describing their progress to and arrival at his tent in similar terms (compare 1.327–45 and 9.182–205).[33] The narrator's ungrammatical use of dual forms for the embassy of five in Book 9 is likely a purposeful, marked echo of the earlier duals referring to Agamemnon's two heralds in Book 1, meant to link together the scenes in the minds of the audience.[34] Likewise, the delegation to Achilleus' tent in Book 1 provides a pattern for the embassy in Book 9 coming without gifts and being greeted by Achilleus.

The heralds' removal of Briseis in Book 1 marked the climactic moment in Achilleus' conflict with Agamemnon, and solidified the hero's painful longing for his concubine and aggressive desires to take revenge and restore his status. The similarity of the embassy of Book 9 to this delegation suggests that it will function identically to (re)instigate Achilleus' desires, which seem to have become dormant. Since Agamemnon's offer of gifts in Book 9 may be understood as a half-hearted and self-serving recompense, which, indeed, again insults Achilleus' honor, the embassy has the potential to remind Achilleus of Agamemnon's

[33] See Segal 1968: 104; Lohmann 1970: 228; Louden 2006: 123–24 for catalogues of the similarities. Cf. Taplin 1992: 74–82 on the visit type-scene in the *Iliad* and Heiden 2008: 127–31 for comparison of the embassy in Book 9 with "four embassies that were narrated in book 1, as well as a fifth narrated in book 8." Segal 1968: 106 also notes that the motif of walking by the sea recalls Chryses' retreat from Agamemnon in 1.34 as well as the heralds' journey in 1.327; in both cases Agamemnon's pattern of bad behavior is brought to mind.

[34] Boll 1917 and 1919–20; Schadewaldt 1966 [1943]: 138; Segal 1968: 105–6; Lohmann 1970: 227–30; Rabel 1997: 122–23. *Pace* Nagy 1979: 49–55, who argues that the duals refer to Phoinix and Aias, and, by excluding Odysseus, emphasize his traditional enmity toward Achilleus. Martin 1989: 236–37 more plausibly suggests that the narrator, taking on Achilleus' focalization, assumes the presence of Phoinix "as natural" and uses the duals to refer to Odysseus and Aias, who are not members of his household. For summary of scholarly approaches to the duals, see Griffin 1995: 51–53. Scodel 2002: 160–71 and Louden 2006: 120–34 represent more recent readings.

original slight. Now the audience can provisionally identify Agamemnon's seizure of Briseis as the true paradigm for the embassy of Book 9.

The Revival and Modification of Achilleus' Desires

The mere arrival of the embassy jolts Achilleus out of his pleasant serenity and reminds him of his anger and plot to recoup his honor. The narrator emphasizes Achilleus' shock at the ambassadors' appearance by describing how it displaces him from his previous posture of ease: "amazed, Achilleus sprang up with his phorminx, having abandoned the seat where he was sitting" (9.193–94). The hero's following greeting suggests that his grievance is again foremost in his thoughts (197–98):

> *χαίρετον· ἦ φίλοι ἄνδρες ἱκάνετον· ἦ τι μάλα χρεώ,*
> *οἵ μοι σκυζομένῳ περ Ἀχαιῶν φίλτατοί ἐστον.*
>
> Greetings! You come as men close (*philoi*) [to me]; surely there is some great need,
> you who are closest (*philtatoi*) of the Achaians to me, though I am angry.

Even as he welcomes the ambassadors, Achilleus reassumes his characteristic emotion from Book 1. Furthermore, with his speculation that the embassy has come because "there is some great need (*χρεώ*)," Achilleus appears to be thinking of his vow that the Greek army would have "need of me" (*χρειὼ ἐμεῖο*, 1.341) and to believe that his plot to make them feel his absence has now come to fruition.[35] Achilleus' identification of the ambassadors as *philoi* seems to be based in his expectation that they have come to make good the insult to his honor, re-elevating his status among the Greeks and so making it palatable for him to rejoin their community.[36]

Odysseus' plea that the hero give up his anger and his communication of Agamemnon's offer (9.225–306), however, disappoint Achilleus' expectation and definitively reignite his aggressive desire for revenge against the man who has caused his loss. Achilleus rejects Agamemnon's gifts and refuses to rejoin the war effort in a long speech (308–429) that both repeats and expands upon themes and language from his antagonistic exchange with the Greek commander in Book 1.[37] In both cases, Achilleus denounces Agamemnon's unfair distribution of booty, given his own oversized contribution to the war effort, and condemns the leader's

[35] See also Leaf 1971: 386. Cf. Lynn-George 1988: 123–25, who argues that these words also imply Achilleus' own answering need to be recognized by the Achaians.

[36] See also Muellner 1996: 139, who remarks that "the scene appears to be set for the transformation of his *mēnis* into *philotēs*."

[37] Lohmann 1970: 240 catalogues the parallelism of Achilleus' speeches (1.149–71 and 9.308–429). He also tracks how Achilleus' speech is a point by point rebuttal of Odysseus' speech conveying Agamemnon's offer (236–45).

humiliating appropriation of Briseis; he throws the same insults at Agamemnon, asserting that he is "clothed in shamelessness" (ἀναιδείην ἐπιειμένε, 1.149 ~ 9.372) and comparing him to a dog (κυνῶπα, 1.159; κύνεος, 9.373); he also reiterates his own lack of desire to wage war against the Trojans and talks about going back home to Phthia.[38] To begin with, then, Achilleus' great speech in Book 9 demonstrates how he has received Agamemnon's proposal as an expression of continuing disdain that in many ways resurrects his previous state of mind, squarely positioning Book 9 as a variation on Book 1.[39]

All the same, Achilleus' desiring subjectivity is now significantly altered. First, by refusing Agamemnon's offer to restore Briseis to him, Achilleus reveals how his aggressive homosocial desire to humble the Greek commander has fully subsumed the heterosexual desire he felt for his concubine. Achilleus' complaint of Briseis' seizure, during which he compares his own quarrel with Agamemnon to the Atreidai's war against the Trojans, clarifies how the libidinal energy previously invested in Briseis—which was expressed as grief at her loss in Book 1—has been redirected at the perpetrator of her removal. He says (9.335–43),

τοῖσι μὲν ἔμπεδα κεῖται, ἐμεῦ δ' ἀπὸ μούνου Ἀχαιῶν
εἵλετ', ἔχει δ' ἄλοχον θυμαρέα· τῇ παριαύων
τερπέσθω. τί δὲ δεῖ πολεμιζέμεναι Τρώεσσιν
Ἀργείους; τί δὲ λαὸν ἀνήγαγεν ἐνθάδ' ἀγείρας
Ἀτρεΐδης; ἦ οὐχ Ἑλένης ἕνεκ' ἠϋκόμοιο;
ἦ μοῦνοι φιλέουσ' ἀλόχους μερόπων ἀνθρώπων
Ἀτρεΐδαι; ἐπεὶ ὅς τις ἀνὴρ ἀγαθὸς καὶ ἐχέφρων
τὴν αὐτοῦ φιλέει καὶ κήδεται, ὡς καὶ ἐγὼ τὴν
ἐκ θυμοῦ φίλεον δουρικτητήν περ ἐοῦσαν.

[The prizes] lie intact for those [other kings], but from me alone of the Achaians
he seized and he keeps the wife fitted to my heart; lying beside her,
let him take pleasure! But why is there need for the Argives to make war with the
Trojans? Why did Atreus' son gather the men and lead them here?
Was it not for the sake of white-armed Helen?
Do Atreus' sons alone among mortal men love (*phileous'*) their wives?
Since whoever is a good and sensible man
loves (*phileei*) and cares for his wife, just as I
loved (*phileon*) her from my heart, even though she was won by the spear.

[38] On the dog insult in these cases as an expression of Agamemnon's brazen disrespectfulness, see Franco 2014: 130–31. In Book 9, Achilleus explicitly denies aggressive desire vis-à-vis the Trojans: "now I do not want (οὐκ ἐθέλω) to make war with godly Hektor" (9.356).

[39] Muellner 1996: 142 similarly argues that Odysseus' speech "exacerbates Achilles' *mēnis* instead of arousing his *philótēs*."

At the beginning and end of this passage, Achilleus asserts his emotional intimacy with Briseis, calling her "the wife fitted to my heart" (ἄλοχον θυμαρέα) and saying "I loved her from my heart" (ἐκ θυμοῦ φίλεον), yet his use of the past tense of the verb *phileō* indicates how that intimacy has been disrupted. His transfer of libido away from Briseis and toward Agamemnon is confirmed by his focus on Agamemnon's appropriation of her, and his sardonic acquiescence to her continued sexual possession by the Greek leader: "lying beside her, let him take pleasure!"

In the center of this passage, Achilleus compares his previous closeness to his "wife" Briseis with the feelings of the Atreidai for their "wives,"[40] and by bringing up the fact that Agamemnon ("Atreus' son") is waging war against the Trojans in reaction to Helen's abduction, Achilleus implies that he is responding in a similar fashion to the seizure of Briseis. Here Achilleus makes explicit for the first time in the epic the analogy between the triangular conflicts of the *Iliad*'s main plot and superplot.[41] And he casts himself in the roles of Menelaos and Agamemnon in the superplot, whose aggressive desires to dominate their Trojan adversaries had been thematized by the poet. Meanwhile, Achilleus' antagonist in the main plot, Agamemnon, is assimilated to Paris, the one-time guest-friend turned mortal enemy.[42]

This analogy helps to explain the hostility that Achilleus expresses toward Agamemnon throughout his speech. Bruce Louden (2006: 127–30) makes the convincing case that the lying man whom Achilleus calls "hateful" (ἐχθρός) to him at the beginning of his speech (9.312–13) is none other than Agamemnon. Later, Achilleus explicitly describes Agamemnon's gifts as "hateful" (ἐχθρά) and says that he honors the leader "not a whit" (378). Richard Martin (1989: 173) has tracked how Achilleus speaks as if Agamemnon had carried out a raid against him, "us[ing] the conventions normal for speaking about one's relations with outsiders when he talks about his own commander." Achilleus clearly regards Agamemnon no longer as a leader, ally, or friend, but as an enemy.

By comparing himself vis-à-vis Agamemnon with the Atreidai vis-à-vis the Trojans Achilleus also illuminates his understanding of Agamemnon's embassy as a final betrayal that makes reconciliation unthinkable. As Menelaos, in the superplot, expected the return of Helen and recompense from the Trojans after Paris disappeared from the duel (3.456–61) but was insidiously shot by Pandaros

[40] By including both Menelaos *and* Agamemnon in this equation, Achilleus perhaps alludes to and repeats Agamemnon's similar comparison of *his* concubine Chryseis—who was reclaimed by her father Chryses—to his wife Klytaimnestra (1.113–15).

[41] See also Collins 1988: 41, 58; Suzuki 1989: 22–23; Dué 2002: 39–43; Wilson 2002: 44–51; Felson and Slatkin 2004: 93–95; Fantuzzi 2012: 109; Lyons 2012: 56–60. Cf. Athenaeus, *Deipnosophistae* 13.560.

[42] Cf. King 1987: 33–34, who argues that the parallel implies that Agamemnon is a rapist no different than Paris, and that his war of vengeance for Helen's sake has thus lost moral justification; from Achilleus' perspective, "there remains not even a principle to fight for."

(4.124–47), so Achilleus was disappointed of the reparation that he anticipated from the embassy and simultaneously reinjured by Agamemnon's insulting offer of gifts. An implicit analogy in Achilleus' mind between Pandaros' sneak attack and Agamemnon's embassy would explain why Achilleus repeatedly accuses Agamemnon of deceit (9.344, 371, 375–76). Consequently, just as the Greeks will no longer accept recompense from the Trojans—not even the return of Helen—and will contemplate no *philotēs*, pressing on for the utter destruction of Troy (7.400–4), Achilleus now rejects Briseis' return, says that he will accept no material recompense (9.378–86), and definitively refuses to rejoin the army until Agamemnon should "pay back to me all the heart-grieving outrage" (ἀπὸ πᾶσαν ἐμοὶ δόμεναι θυμαλγέα λώβην, 387). As Wilson (2002: 92) has shown, this final condition represents a demand for suitable compensation (*poinē*) for the harm inflicted, which Achilleus probably envisions in the form of the Greek leader's own degradation through "the humiliation of defeat or the torching of the ships." Achilleus' stance toward Agamemnon is thus equivalent to the Greeks' intention to continue fighting until Troy is sacked.

Though Achilleus persists here in his vengeful desire to inflict pain on Agamemnon, a new impulse to pursue a comfortable life at home seems to have preempted both his former longing for Briseis and competitive desire to earn honor at Troy. He asserts in this speech that he will leave for Phthia the next morning (9.356–63), explaining "there very much my proud passion (θυμὸς ἀγήνωρ) urges me to marry a wooed wife, a fitting spouse, and to enjoy the possessions that old Peleus acquired" (398–400). Achilleus refocuses his heterosexual desire from the spear-won Briseis to a putative home-grown, legitimate bride. He goes on to declare that no material possessions he might acquire at Troy are worth his life (401–3), and elucidates how he is destined to die young but achieve "imperishable fame" (κλέος ἄφθιτον) if he stays at Troy or lose his "good fame" (κλέος ἐσθλόν) but enjoy a long life if he returns to Phthia (410–16). Honor (*timē*) and it extension in fame (*kleos*) are no longer Achilleus' primary concerns; he now contemplates the satisfaction of longevity. Accordingly, the hero indicates a newfound apathy toward his plot to redeem his status through the worsting of the Greeks, advising the rest of the army to go home too, and exhorting the elders to find a fresh plan that will save their ships and army from destruction (417–25). He ends by underscoring his determination to return to Phthia through an invitation for his compatriot Phoinix—one of the ambassadors—to remain in his tent overnight so that he can accompany him back home the next morning if he so wishes (427–29).

Even though Achilleus articulates a new lust for life and abnegates—or at best, devalues—the triangular desires previously motivating his actions, he does not question the heroic pursuit of *timē* and *kleos* on an a priori basis. Rather, he does so because he feels that the system has malfunctioned, that his heroic efforts have gone unrewarded and unappreciated: "there was no gratitude (χάρις) for fighting always and ceaselessly against enemy men" (9.315–17). In the past, as he explains (325–29), he did not hesitate to risk life and limb in triangular conflict, fighting with men "for the sake of their wives" (ὀάρων ἕνεκα σφετεράων, 327). Now, however, he understands that Agamemnon's offer of women and other gifts on the condition of his return to battle is not the remuneration that it appears to be. With his inclination to abandon his plot for honor and sail away to Phthia, Achilleus expresses his deep disappointment with the embassy and his conviction that Agamemnon and his army have failed to fulfill his triangular desires and cannot be trusted to do so in the future.[43]

Yet his initial reception of the embassy indicated his openness to reconciliation, and his emotional response to Agamemnon's proposal marks it as an unanticipated affront. Achilleus' great speech of refusal therefore leaves an opening for the other two ambassadors, Phoinix and Aias, who have not yet spoken, to refute Achilleus' perception of the Greeks and thereby persuade him to revise his position. As we shall see in the final sections of this chapter, these ambassadors do successfully change Achilleus' mind, but not in the way that they hope.

Phoinix's Speech

Throughout his long speech to Achilleus, Phoinix deploys three main arguments to persuade the hero to alter his evaluation of the Greeks and rejoin the army: (1) Achilleus is at odds with those closest to him; (2) if he continues fighting with his community, the results will be disastrous; (3) however, if he accepts Agamemnon's offer, he will not only get back Briseis but also achieve great honor among the Greeks—along with fame. These arguments insist on Achilleus' solidarity with the Greek army and warn him of the dangerous consequences of his continued animosity while also promising the satisfaction of his original triangular desires.

Phoinix begins his speech by emphasizing his ties with Achilleus' family in an attempt to establish the legitimacy and authority of his discourse, and also to signal his focus on maintaining good relations between *philoi*. He declares his loyalty to Achilleus, asserting that he will follow him wherever he goes, and he

[43] *Contra* Nagler 1974: 134, who argues that "Homer has Achilleus reject the supplicants who offer him the fulfilment of his own desires as he stated them." Cf. Rabel 1997: 117–32, who contends that Achilleus realizes his desires are unsatisfiable on existential grounds. Drawing on Lacan, Rabel differentiates between "need" as an "impulse to attain defined goals (material, sexual, and egotistical) and to be content once they are attained" and "desire," which is when "demands exceed need." Rabel argues that Achilleus here feels a "desire" that cannot by its nature be satisfied, unlike Chryses' paradigmatic "need," which was satisfied by the return of Chryseis. It is undeniable that Achilleus' frustration has escalated to such a degree that his stated desire—for Agamemnon to "pay back to me all the heart-grieving outrage"—has become imprecise and expansive. On the other hand, Agamemnon actually sends Chryseis back to Chryses, while he merely offers to return Briseis and at the same time reiterates his superiority to Achilleus through the proffered gifts. Later, as we shall see, Achilleus does anticipate the Greeks' satisfaction of his triangular desires (11.609–10, 16.84–86).

reminds the hero that his father Peleus sent him to Troy as Achilleus' mentor and teacher (9.434–43). In this way, Phoinix establishes himself as a surrogate parent to Achilleus (a role that he expands upon when he later describes how he cared for him as an infant), and one whose instruction has been mandated by Achilleus' real father.

Phoinix's words also evoke Odysseus' earlier account, in his speech to Achilleus, of Peleus' admonition to his son on his leave-taking for Troy. Odysseus had reminded Achilleus how Peleus told him, "restrain the great-hearted passion (μεγαλήτορα θυμόν) in your breast; for an attitude of solidarity (φιλοφροσύνη) is better; and leave off from strife that causes evils, so that both young and old among the Argives honor you more" (9.255–58). Odysseus there drew on the clout of Achilleus' father to suggest the destructiveness of internecine quarrels, in an echo of Nestor's earlier pronouncement, while promising Achilleus greater honor if he adopts a cooperative posture. Now Phoinix similarly positions himself as a stand-in for the absent Peleus, meant to emphasize for Achilleus the desirability of harmony between *philoi*.

Phoinix then tells an autobiographical narrative of conflict among *philoi* (9.447–84) that highlights its damaging consequences. Phoinix's story of his quarrel with his father Amyntor over the sexual possession of a concubine represents a clear parallel to Achilleus' conflict with Agamemnon over Briseis.[44] Ruth Scodel (1982: 132–33) argues that Phoinix's autobiography is too comic to be taken as a positive heroic paradigm, especially given the fact that Phoinix loses his fertility due to his father's curse,[45] and I believe that she is right to read this narrative as a negative *exemplum*. The end result of Phoinix's conflict with his family is total alienation from his natal community and no hope of future heirs, even though Achilleus' father Peleus takes Phoinix in as a *philos* and gives him wealth and status. With his autobiographical story, Phoinix communicates to Achilleus that he might also have a sufficient life should he return to Phthia, but that he will have similarly cut himself off from his true family, the Greek army, and, implicitly, lost his own chance of (symbolic) self-perpetuation through heroic fame. Indeed, as Gregory Nagy (1979: 184–85) has shown, "Phthia" evokes the idea of wasting away with its relation to *phthi-* verbs ("to wither").[46]

[44] See Rosner 1976: 318–19 and Schein 1984: 111–12 for point-by-point comparison of the two situations. Cf. Alden 2000: 220, who notes the parallels but also differences between Achilleus' and Phoinix's experiences.

[45] Cf. Bassett 1938: 199, who calls Phoinix an "ethically low-grade character" based on how he sleeps with his father's concubine and contemplates parricide.

[46] Cf. Alden 2000: 221–24, who analyzes Phoinix's message as "inconsistent: he wants to present the choice of departure/exile as simultaneously a bad thing, and a good thing." According to Alden, Phoinix is trying to convince Achilleus to "stay at the scene of the quarrel," instead of leaving as he had, while also encouraging him to take Agamemnon's gifts and accept the Greek leader as a surrogate father(-in-law) just as he himself had received wealth and status from Peleus as his surrogate father.

Phoinix's autobiography also reminds the audience again of how Iliadic conflict is motivated by triangles of desire. This story represents a curious melding of the libidinal dynamics at work in the main plot and the superplot. Two men quarrel over a concubine, but Phoinix does not himself desire the concubine. Rather, it is Phoinix's mother's desire for revenge in response to her husband Amyntor's dishonoring liaison with another woman that leads to the quarrel, as she convinces Phoinix to have sex with Amyntor's concubine. Homer doubles the female in this erotic triangle, with one woman representing the silent and disempowered Chryseis or Briseis and the other representing Helen as disruptive desiring subject and agent.[47]

With his following allegory of the Prayers (9.502–14), Phoinix expands upon the idea of the bad that could come if Achilleus continues to reject the embassy's effort to reconcile him with Agamemnon. First, he describes how the Prayers follow upon harmful Delusion (*Atē*), providing a remedy; Phoinix must intend Delusion to refer to Agamemnon's dishonoring seizure of Briseis (which Agamemnon himself, as we have seen, admits was the result of *atē* in 9.115–19) and the Prayers to represent the embassy itself.[48] Then, Phoinix warns that if the Prayers go unheeded, they entreat Zeus to inflict Delusion on the inflexible party, so that he may suffer harm in turn. Judith Rosner (1976: 321) has noted that Agamemnon's rejection of Chryses' entreaty provides a paradigm for this negative result, since it leads to the plague that kills many Achaians.[49] Finally, Phoinix admonishes Achilleus too to honor the Prayers, making explicit the analogy between his allegory and the hero's situation. Thus, as Maureen Alden (2000: 199–205) has explained, Phoinix's allegorical narrative constitutes a vague threat of divine retribution should Achilleus refuse the embassy's entreaty.

Now, at last, at the center of his speech, Phoinix makes his big "ask" of Achilleus to renounce his anger on the grounds that he is being appropriately compensated by *philoi*. First, he implies that Agamemnon's offer of gifts represents a legitimate reparation, asserting that he would not bid Achilleus to give up his wrath if the Greek leader were not "bringing gifts" (9.515), but "now at once he is giving many things, and has promised other things later" (519); Phoinix overlooks how the embassy has not actually brought gifts "now" as well as Achilleus' declaration that he is not interested in material recompense. Then, Phoinix observes that Agamemnon "has sent the best men to entreat you, having chosen from the Achaian host those of the Argives closest (φίλτατοι) to you yourself" (520–22). With this statement, he not only echoes Achilleus' own opening identification of the ambassadors as *philtatoi* but also asserts that they are representatives of

[47] Phoinix's mother also recalls the libidinous Anteia from the story of Bellerophontes (6.156–66).

[48] Rosner 1976: 320.

[49] While up to this point Achilleus has been presented in opposition to Agamemnon, here Phoinix brings to the audience's attention how Achilleus, like Agamemnon before him, is causing harm to the Achaians.

Agamemnon and the Greek army, thereby collapsing any distinction between the two categories. He is trying to claim that *all* of the Greeks with whom Achilleus is at odds are his *philoi*.

Phoinix's mythological *exemplum* of Meleagros (9.524–99) is his capstone attempt to convince Achilleus to reconcile with his own community. Phoinix introduces this story as an example of the "fames of men" (κλέα ἀνδρῶν, 524), usurping creative control from Achilleus, who himself had been singing the "fames of men" when the embassy arrived at his tent (189). By appropriating Achilleus' bardic role, Phoinix tries to change the direction of Achilleus' plot, to make it the story of the hero's participation in the war as an honored Greek rather than of his withdrawal. In addition, Phoinix's words respond to Achilleus' own contemplation of the mortal cost of "imperishable fame" (κλέος ἄφθιτον, 413). He offers the fame of Meleagros as an example for Achilleus, even if he ultimately urges Achilleus to return to battle sooner than Meleagros in order to accrue more honor (600–5). In so doing, Phoinix subtly dismisses the idea that Achilleus might go home and forfeit honor and fame altogether.

Meleagros' story contains a series of parallels to Achilleus' situation,[50] and Phoinix recounts this myth to make the point to Achilleus once and for all that he is quarreling with his own people to destructive effect and that he ought to redirect his aggression toward his real enemies. The opening of the narrative features Oineus, the king of the Aitolians, angering Artemis through delusion (*atē*) and thus causing the Kalydonian boar to ravage his land, after which Oineus' son Meleagros kills the boar and saves his people—in a prescriptive analogy to Agamemnon's *atē* and Achilleus' desired re-entrance into battle, which positions the two men as father and son. Two proscriptive parallels of devastating conflicts between allies or kin follow: the Kouretes and Aitolians, neighboring peoples who had hunted the boar together, now fight a war over the boar's trophies, in analogy to Agamemnon and Achilleus' quarrel over the war prize Briseis; then Meleagros' mother Althaie curses her son to die for killing her brother, and Meleagros withdraws from the war in anger, in a familial analogy to the conflict between Agamemnon and Achilleus.

Phoinix offers the second part of Meleagros' myth as a more immediate negative parallel to Achilleus' current situation. With the Aitolians losing the war in the absence of Meleagros, a sequence of ambassadors—community elders and priests, then family members, then friends—offer gifts and entreaties to the angry hero for his return to battle. After these appeals are unsuccessful, when the Kouretes are about to sack the city, Meleagros' wife Kleopatra makes a final plea, recounting all of the horrible things that happen when a city falls: the men are killed, the city is burned, and the women and children are enslaved. Phoinix must

[50] These are catalogued by Rosner 1976: 323.

mean this as a warning to Achilleus of the harm that could come to his own Greek compatriots—first and foremost, the death of his male companions—if he continues to leave them at the mercy of the Trojans.[51] Kleopatra's entreaty finally convinces Meleagros to fight again, and he saves his city from destruction but forfeits the gifts promised by the ambassadors. Thus, Phoinix ends with an exhortation to Achilleus not to delay his re-entrance into battle, but to take the gifts offered, "for equally to a god the Achaians will honor (τείσουσιν) you" (9.603); on the other hand, "if without gifts you enter the man-destroying war, no longer in the same way will you be honored (τιμῆς ἔσεαι) in war, though having defended [the army]" (604–5). Phoinix's closing argument is that Achilleus' Achaian community desperately needs the hero to avoid annihilation, and that his people are eager to give Achilleus all the honor that he desires, but that he must accept the embassy's offer and rejoin the army at once—and not later—in order to attain that honor.

While Phoinix here doubles down on his portrayal of the ills of internecine conflict and on his promise to satisfy Achilleus' desire for honor among the Greeks, he also expands on his theme of the Achaians' *philotēs* with Achilleus. Johannes Kakridis (1949: 19–23) famously observed how Phoinix alters the traditional "scale of affections" in his description of the groups who visit Meleagros: instead of blood relatives, he makes Meleagros' "companions, who were the most cherished and closest (φίλτατοι) to him of all" (9.585–86) the penultimate party to entreat him, just before his wife Kleopatra. According to Kakridis, these non-kin companions appear in this culminating position because Phoinix wants Achilleus to heed the embassy of his Greek friends.[52] Additionally, with this rhetorical tactic Phoinix suggests that Agamemnon's ambassadors are "closest" to Achilleus not only among the Greeks but absolutely—more intimate than even his blood relatives, such as the father, mother, and sisters who appeal to Meleagros. Phoinix thus elevates relationships between unrelated *philoi*, particularly between the Greek warriors, above blood kinship relationships,[53] building on his earlier implication in his autobiographical narrative that Achilleus belongs more with the Achaians at Troy than with his own father Peleus in Phthia.

But solidarity between Achilleus and the Greeks is not the only non-blood-kinship relationship that Phoinix promotes in his telling of the myth of Meleagros.

[51] Kleopatra's desire for Meleagros' protection and description of the sack of a city also recall Andromache's anguished desire for Hektor, and Hektor's prevision of Troy's fall in Book 6, reminding the audience of the devastating cost of war and suggesting again that Achilleus' main plot will develop along lines similar to the superplot. Cf. Kakridis 1949: 60, who detects a contrast between Kleopatra's desire for Meleagros to fight and Andromache's desire for Hektor not to fight.

[52] Cf. Lohmann 1970: 258–59, Rosner 1976: 324, and Alden 2000: 244–46, who argue that each group of suppliants to Meleagros represent one of Agamemnon's ambassadors, and that they come to him in the same order as the ambassadors deliver their speeches to Achilleus: the elders and priests are Odysseus (and Nestor, who arranges the embassy), the blood relatives (or particularly Meleagros' father) represent Phoinix, and the companions stand in for Aias.

[53] Muellner 1996: 148.

Kleopatra is the final and successful petitioner, and she is introduced at the start of the narrative of Meleagros' anger, when Phoinix describes Meleagros, in his withdrawal, "lying beside his wooed wife (ἀλόχῳ), the beautiful Kleopatra" (9.556). Phoinix goes on to describe her parentage at length before returning to remark again on how she shares a bed with Meleagros (557–65). While Kleopatra may be a traditional figure in Meleagros' story,[54] Phoinix's emphasis on her as Meleagros' "wife" and attractive sexual partner seems designed to remind Achilleus of Briseis, whom the hero has just described as his "wife" (ἄλοχον, 336). With focus on Kleopatra, and on her deciding role in convincing Meleagros to re-enter the war, Phoinix seems to be subtly attempting to inflame Achilleus' desire for Briseis, and submitting reunion with her as a final reason—if he disdains Agamemnon's other proffered gifts—for him to accept the leader's bargain and rejoin the Greek army.

At the same time, Kleopatra evokes Achilleus' companion Patroklos, and her pivotal role in Meleagros' story reminds the audience that Zeus has already linked Patroklos—in his death—with Achilleus' return. Just as Kleopatra alone remains beside Meleagros during his angry withdrawal, Patroklos attends Achilleus when he is apart from the other Greeks in his tent. Moreover, Kleopatra's name is built from the same roots as Patroklos', and Wolfgang Schadewaldt (1966: 140) has influentially argued that Homer invents her name to refer to Patroklos and foreshadow his role in causing Achilleus to rejoin the war. Therefore, Kleopatra serves a double function, on two levels of narration: the intradiegetic level, between Phoinix and Achilleus, and the extradiegetic level, between the poet and his audience. Phoinix appears to invoke Kleopatra to remind Achilleus of Briseis, while Homer uses Kleopatra to confirm for the audience that Agamemnon's embassy will fail and to signal again that Achilleus will actually re-enter battle through Patroklos' agency. Yet how and when this might come to pass remains unknown to the audience, and so Kleopatra provokes anew our narrative desire to plot out Patroklos' enigmatic part in Achilleus' return.

Achilleus' reply shows that Phoinix has been successful in reinvigorating the hero's competitive desire for honor but unsuccessful in his attempts to rehabilitate Agamemnon's gifts, position Agamemnon and his army as *philoi* to Achilleus, and convince the hero of the danger of his internecine aggression. In response to Phoinix's closing words linking Agamemnon's gifts with Achilleus' status among the Greeks, the hero asserts (9.607–10),

> *οὔ τί με ταύτης*
> *χρεὼ τιμῆς· φρονέω δὲ τετιμῆσθαι Διὸς αἴσῃ,*
> *ἥ μ' ἕξει παρὰ νηυσὶ κορωνίσιν, εἰς ὅ κ' ἀϋτμὴ*
> *ἐν στήθεσσι μένῃ καί μοι φίλα γούνατ' ὀρώρῃ.*

[54] Kakridis 1949: 23–31.

I do not have any need of that honor (*timēs*);
but I think that I have been honored (*tetimēsthai*) by the allotment of Zeus,
which will hold me beside the curved ships while breath
remains in my chest and my own knees are in motion.

With these words, Achilleus sarcastically rejects "that honor" associated with Agamemnon's proposal, while at the same time indicating his renewed interest in accumulating honor through another avenue—"the allotment of Zeus." In Book 1, Achilleus had wished that Zeus might honor him precisely because Agamemnon had dishonored him (1.353–56), and asked the divine king to do so by empowering the Trojans in battle against the Greeks until Agamemnon regretted his failure to honor him as "best of the Achaians" (408–12). Now again Achilleus looks to Zeus for honor, apparently recommitting to his original plot for the subjugation of the Greeks. His change of mind is evident in his statement that "the allotment of Zeus" will keep him beside the ships as long as he lives; Achilleus has abandoned his plan to return to Phthia and his desire for a long life, and decided instead to remain at Troy, since only under these circumstances will he realize his plot to achieve honor through Zeus's agency.

Achilleus' following words underscore Phoinix's failure to mitigate the hero's inimical aggression toward Agamemnon and his army.[55] He chastises Phoinix (9.612–14),

μή μοι σύγχει θυμὸν ὀδυρόμενος καὶ ἀχεύων,
Ἀτρεΐδῃ ἥρωϊ φέρων χάριν· οὐδέ τί σε χρὴ
τὸν φιλέειν, ἵνα μή μοι ἀπέχθηαι φιλέοντι.

do not confuse my heart by mourning and grieving,
doing a favor for the hero Atreus' son; you must not in any way
be close to (*phileein*) him, lest you become an enemy to me who is
close to (*phileonti*) you.

While Achilleus here acknowledges Phoinix as his personal *philos*, he orders him to stop advocating for Agamemnon and flatly warns him that he cannot simultaneously be a *philos* to both himself and the Greek leader, making clear his enmity toward Agamemnon. He continues to insist on Phoinix's exclusive identification

[55] *Contra* Schadewaldt 1966: 135–36, who attributes Achilleus' newfound resolve to remain at Troy to a characteristic "mildness," that is, a sensitivity toward others' suffering that tempers his self-assertion. For similar interpretations, see Schein 1984: 112–15, who argues that Achilleus' change of mind is motivated by tenderness and desire for the Greeks' solidarity, and Kim 2000: 103, who writes that Achilleus stays at Troy because "the sufferings, *κήδεα*, of his friends have been brought home to him by the embassy."

as his intimate by differentiating him with a μέν-δέ construction from the other ambassadors, whom he treats as representatives of Agamemnon and the Greeks: they will bring his message to the army, but Phoinix will stay and sleep in Achilleus' tent and make a final decision with him in the morning whether to stay or go (617–19). Achilleus then signals to Patroklos to make a bed for Phoinix in order to indicate to the other ambassadors that they are no longer welcome (620–22).[56]

Achilleus' Obstinacy

Aias, however, seizes this moment to make a final appeal to Achilleus to accept Agamemnon's offer of gifts and rejoin the army, combining a harsh critique of the hero's antisocial aggressive desire with Phoinix's strategy of positioning the Greeks as Achilleus' honoring *philoi*. Aias opens by complaining to Odysseus that "Achilleus has put a wild, arrogant passion (θυμόν) in his breast, merciless!" (9.628–30). Then, he counters Achilleus' own assertion that he has been honored by Zeus "beside the curved ships" with the claim that it is the Greeks who have honored him especially as their *philos* "beside the ships": "he does not care for his companions' solidarity (φιλότητος), how we honored him beside the ships beyond others, pitiless!" (630–32). With these words, Aias identifies the Greeks, not Zeus, as Achilleus' *philoi* and the source of honor, while also reproaching the hero for his lack of regard for the Greek army.

Aias then recommends to Achilleus an alternative model for responding to injury. He invokes the man who takes compensation for the murder of his brother or son—"whose heart and proud passion (θυμὸς ἀγήνωρ) is checked when he receives recompense" (9.635–36)—and contrasts that man's mollification after the killing of a male blood-relative with Achilleus' "implacable and evil passion…for the sake of a girl only" (ἄλληκτόν τε κακόν τε/ θυμὸν…εἵνεκα κούρης/ οἴης, 636–38). He goes on to remind Achilleus that Agamemnon has offered him seven superlative women and many other gifts, and urges him to "adopt a propitious temperament" (ἵλαον ἔνθεο θυμόν, 639).

Barbara Graziosi and Johannes Haubold (2003: 65–68) have shown how the adjective "proud" (ἀγήνωρ), which they define as "excessively manly," and its related noun ἀγηνορίη, "characterize individualistic, anti-social, and often self-destructive behaviour on the part of an isolated warrior," which departs from the normative Iliadic masculinity of acting in solidarity with other men on the battlefield. With his positive paradigm of the man who restrained his "proud

[56] See also Muellner 1996: 150, who summarizes, "While Phoenix has been trying to reintegrate Achilles among the Achaeans, Achilles has been trying to detach Phoenix from them, and he eventually succeeds."

passion" (θυμὸς ἀγήνωρ), Aias seems to respond to Achilleus' earlier statement that his θυμὸς ἀγήνωρ urged him to find a wife and enjoy his father's wealth in Phthia (9.398–400). Thus, Aias confirms the hero's own previous characterization of his desire as overstepping the masculine norm and as motivating the gender-deviant and antisocial behavior of abandoning comrades-in-arms,[57] and bids him to moderate it. He ends his speech by emphasizing the ambassadors' opposing desire for solidarity with Achilleus: they are under his roof and, beyond the other Achaians, "are eager (μέμαμεν) . . . to be dearest and closest (φίλτατοι)" to him (640–42).

Although Achilleus appears to allow Aias' critique of his behavior ("you seem to have spoken everything in accordance with my judgment," 9.645), he nevertheless reaffirms and defends his aggressive desires for revenge and honor. He explains (646–48),

> *ἀλλά μοι οἰδάνεται κραδίη χόλῳ, ὁππότε κείνων*
> *μνήσομαι, ὥς μ' ἀσύφηλον ἐν Ἀργείοισιν ἔρεξεν*
> *Ἀτρεΐδης, ὡς εἴ τιν' ἀτίμητον μετανάστην.*
>
> but my heart swells with anger whenever I remember those things,
> how Atreus' son made me foolish among the Argives,
> as if I were some dishonored migrant.

As Jonathan Ready (2011: 34–39) demonstrates, with his self-comparison to a migrant, Achilleus recalls again how Agamemnon excluded him from receipt and retention of the prestige wealth that he should have earned by fighting with the Greek army. While Achilleus seems to acknowledge the queerness of his continued withdrawal, he asserts the righteousness of his antisocial rage, as when Paris had acknowledged Hektor's rebuke of his lack of martial valor but refused to disavow the divine "gifts of Aphrodite" near the beginning of the superplot (3.59–66).

Consequently, he tells the ambassadors to announce his intention to stay out of battle until Hektor, killing Greeks and burning their ships, has reached the tents and ships of his own Myrmidons (9.649–55). With these words, Achilleus confirms his reinvestment in his original plot for honor through Greek death and suffering, articulating an explicitly destructive stance toward his erstwhile *philoi*. He seems to have been inspired by the story of Meleagros to seek a similar fame, rather than avoid his example: his promise to enter battle only when the Greek ships are burning recalls how Meleagros returned to the war only when the

[57] Therefore, somewhat paradoxically, Achilleus' excessive masculinity—or, in contemporary parlance, "toxic masculinity"—causes him to act in unmasculine ways, isolating himself from his fellow men and occupying a feminine position on the sidelines of the war.

Kouretes had set the city on fire.[58] Achilleus has been convinced by Phoinix and Aias to pursue again his aggressive desires for satisfaction from the Greeks at Troy,[59] but he has remained unmoved by their protestations of *philotēs* and by Phoinix's warnings of the negative consequences of conflict with one's own community.

At the end of Book 9, once Odysseus has communicated Achilleus' refusal of the embassy to the Greek kings,[60] their closing resolve to prepare themselves for battle the next day, and to fight as best as they can without Achilleus, leaves the audience looking (or listening) forward. This final scene, together with Achilleus' recommitment to his original plot, arouses anew our narrative desire to find out what will transpire on the battlefield and how Hektor will reach the ships, as Zeus has prophesied.

Our investment with the ongoing narrative is further informed by how we respond to the epic's characters in Book 9. On the one hand, Achilleus may continue to command our sympathy, as he is at once so gracious to the ambassadors and so aggrieved by Agamemnon's offer. In addition, his complex desiring subjectivity and sophisticated rumination on heroic values, which encourage the audience to devote sustained attention to reading his mind, may help to evoke both our admiration for and empathy with the conflicted hero. If this is the case, as we anticipate renewed battle, we may sympathetically desire to see Achilleus' wrongs righted and share his aggressive desire for the worsting of the Greeks and their humbling before him.

On the other hand, the ambassadors' repeated articulations of the Greeks' desperation may elicit our sympathy for the beleaguered Achaians. Achilleus' aggression may be alienating in its relentlessness. If this is so, we may feel a sympathetic wish for the Greeks' success against their Trojan adversaries that conflicts with our narrative desire to find out how Achilleus' plot will come to its realization, and that colors that desire with pity and fear for the Achaians. This cognitive dissonance, in turn, may cause us to question the justice of Achilleus' driving desire to make the Greeks pay in blood for Agamemnon's slight. In any

[58] Lynn-George 1988: 151. Lynn-George (1988: 151) also observes that Achilleus picks up on Phoinix's account of how anger "swells" (*οἰδάνει*) the mind of Meleagros (9.553–54) when he says to Aias that his heart "swells" (*οἰδάνεται*) in anger (646).

[59] See also Staten 1995: 39, who recognizes that these ambassadors begin the process of drawing Achilleus back "into the matrix of social valuations," and Alden 2000: 260, who observes, "Although it meets with refusal, the embassy succeeds in arousing Achilles' interest in such approaches."

[60] While Odysseus states Achilleus' rejection of the embassy, he misrepresents Achilleus' final position, conveying Achilleus' earlier threat to return to Phthia but passing over his concluding promise to re-enter battle once Hektor has fought all the way to his own ships. Many different explanations have been offered for Odysseus' omission (see Griffin 1995: 145–46), but I think Hainsworth 1993: 148 is correct in noting that only Achilleus' immediate absence is relevant to the Achaians; they care about fending off the Trojans now, not later, in order to protect themselves from defeat, so Odysseus only tells them the pertinent information that Achilleus will not presently be coming to their aid.

case, the ambassadors' warnings of the suffering caused by unremitting strife between *philoi*, taken together with Zeus's earlier prophecy of Patroklos' death, are foreboding, provoking the audience's dreadful anticipation on behalf of *both* the Greek army *and* Achilleus himself.[61] Therefore, no matter where our allegiance lies, the narrative of Book 9 re-engages us with Achilleus' renewed plot for honor and revenge.[62]

[61] See also Kozak 2017: 91–92, who focuses on how Achilleus' ignorance of Patroklos' death as he articulates his conditions for return in Book 9 "increases emotional investment and anticipation" by drawing the audience's attention to their own gaps in knowledge of what is to come.

[62] Thus Book 9, like Book 8, is appropriate as either the end to the first day of the *Iliad*'s performance (Wade-Gery 1952: 13–16, Schadewaldt 1975: 24, and Taplin 1992: 11–31) or the beginning of its second day (Davison 1965 and Heiden 1996 and 2008); the latter makes the most sense to me.

6
The Oppositional Desires of Hera and Patroklos

This chapter shows how competing desires prolong the *Iliad*'s "Great Day of Battle" for almost eight full books and set the stage for the epic's grand finale. Though Zeus asserts his will (*boulē*) to advance Achilleus' plot for the worsting of the Greeks in *Iliad* 11–12, Hera subdues that will and asserts her own through a deceptive seduction of her husband in Book 14, enabling the Achaians to rally under Poseidon's leadership. Even after Zeus reassumes control, Hera's desire for Troy's destruction informs the divine king's prophecy of a second arc of the epic's main plot featuring Greek success on the battlefield. In Book 16, Zeus's revised will manifests in Patroklos' wish to help the Achaian army and aggressive desire to defeat the Trojans, in another challenge to Achilleus' plot that leads to Patroklos' death in battle and catalyzes the main plot's new arc.

The Progression of Achilleus' Plot through Zeus's Will

At dawn on the day after the embassy to Achilleus, Zeus continues to move forward the hero's plot to humble the Achaians in battle. First, Zeus ensures that the Greeks are ready to fight again despite their defeat the previous day and Achilleus' refusal to come to their aid: the divine king sends forth the goddess Strife (*Eris*) into the Greek camp, who casts "great strength" into each Achaian heart "to make war and fight ceaselessly," thus causing war to become "sweeter" than a return home (11.3–14). Consequently, Agamemnon, who had initially advised giving up the war the evening before, now prepares himself for battle in an extended arming scene, and the other Greeks follow suit. The scene closes with a return to the divine plane in a ring that confirms Zeus as the divine motivator and makes clear his destructive intention: "Kronos' son urged on among them the evil din of battle, and sent down from on high dew wet with blood from the air, because he was about to send many powerful heads to Hades" (πολλὰς ἰφθίμους κεφαλὰς Ἄϊδι προϊάψειν, 11.52–55). The final line of this passage repeats almost exactly the programmatic third line of the *Iliad*, which recounts how Achilleus' wrath "sent many powerful souls to Hades" (πολλὰς δ' ἰφθίμους ψυχὰς Ἄϊδι

Desire in the Iliad: *The Force That Moves the Epic and Its Audience.* Rachel H. Lesser, Oxford University Press.
 DOI: 10.1093/oso/9780192866516.003.0007

προΐαψεν, 1.3), thus linking Zeus's will here with Achilleus' aggressive desires and the main plot of the epic as prefigured in the proem.[1]

After a brief account of the Trojans' preparations for battle and the joining of the two armies, the poet emphasizes the narrative predominance of Zeus's will to subdue the Greeks with a telling glimpse of the society of the gods. Strife is the only divinity present on the battlefield; the other gods sit without interfering in their Olympian homes, "and they were all censuring Kronos' son of the dark clouds, because he wished (ἐβούλετο) to grant victory to the Trojans" (11.78–79). This divine scene recalls Zeus's prohibitions in Book 8 against the gods' further involvement in the mortal conflict (8.2–27, 397–408, 447–56), confirming that these prohibitions are still in effect and that the king of the gods is firmly in control. Moreover, the verb ἐβούλετο connects Zeus's wish for Trojan martial dominance with the "will" (βουλή)—or "plot"—of Zeus that was nebulously invoked in the proem (1.5).

At the same time, the description of the gods' chagrin reminds us of Hera's and Athene's frustration at Zeus's intention to bring harm to the Greeks, and foreshadows future challenges to his will. However, just as Zeus twice before declared that he did "not care" (οὐκ ἀλεγίζω, 8.477; οὐ . . . ἀλέγω, 8.482–83) about Hera's anger, again here the narrator reports that Zeus "did not care" (οὐκ ἀλέγιζε) about the other gods' disapproval, and was sitting apart from them "glorying in his triumph" while watching the deadly battle between Trojans and Greeks (11.80–83). In this way, Book 11 is positioned from its outset as a continuation of Book 8, which featured the execution of the will of Zeus (*Dios boulē*) for Trojan success on the battlefield.

Although the poet first glorifies Agamemnon and builds suspense by featuring the Greek leader's triumphant *aristeia*, the controlling force of the *Dios boulē* is soon confirmed as the battle progresses. First, Zeus sends Iris to inform Hektor that he will turn the tide in his favor once Agamemnon has been wounded, granting Hektor power to kill Greeks until he reaches the ships and the sun goes down (11.191–94). Agamemnon is wounded almost immediately, and retreats; Hektor, accordingly, rallies the Trojans with assertion of Zeus's support and they begin to push the Achaians back toward their ships. When other Greek warriors take a stand, they are injured one by one—first Diomedes, then Odysseus, then the physician Machaon, and finally Eurypylos—and compelled to retire from battle; only Aias fights on unscathed, but is gradually pressed back toward the camp. Thus, over the course of Book 11, Zeus's will for Trojan dominance is incrementally actualized.

Homer reminds the audience how Achilleus' desires have helped to determine Zeus's will by featuring the hero's reaction to the Greek casualties. When Achilleus

[1] See also Hainsworth 1993: 225 and Myers 2019: 30–31.

sees Nestor's chariot go by carrying a wounded Achaian, he sends Patroklos to discover if the injured man is Machaon, first exclaiming, "now I think that the Achaians will stand at my knees entreating; for a need has come that is no longer bearable" (*νῦν ὀΐω περὶ γούνατ' ἐμὰ στήσεσθαι Ἀχαιοὺς/ λισσομένους· χρειὼ γὰρ ἱκάνεται οὐκέτ' ἀνεκτός*, 11.609–10). He seems to imagine that the Achaians are in such dire straits that they will actually supplicate him for help, debasing themselves before him and finally granting him the honor he craves.[2] His speculation about the Greeks' "need" (*χρειώ*) echoes his previous greeting to the embassy (9.197), when he had also seemed to anticipate a reparation of his status. In this case, he dispatches Patroklos to confirm that the Achaians have lost someone as important as the doctor Machaon, whose absence would further undermine efforts to repel the Trojans without his aid. His inquiry regarding the wounded man's identity is therefore motivated by his competitive desire for honor,[3] rather than by pity for the Greek army, as some scholars have conjectured,[4] and it functions to reintroduce this aggressive desire behind the plot of Greek defeat that Zeus is bringing about.

The poet pairs this reminder of Achilleus' driving desire with another prediction of the personal harm it will cause, continuing the ominous foreshadowing of Books 8 and 9. When Patroklos first responds to Achilleus' command, the narrator portentously remarks, "and indeed for him it was the beginning of evil" (*κακοῦ δ' ἄρα οἱ πέλεν ἀρχή*, 11.604). With these words, the narrator alludes to Patroklos' future death, which was prophesied by Zeus (8.476), and positions Achilleus' desire for status as the source of his companion's doom. Even as this pronouncement stimulates anew the audience's narrative desire to find out how and when Patroklos will die, it also enables us to securely identify his death as one of the devastating consequences of internecine conflict forewarned by the elders Nestor, Odysseus, and Phoinix in Book 9, encouraging us to anticipate his demise with pity and fear.

In Book 12, Zeus definitively empowers the Trojans in the battle, though he also indicates that their victory will be fleeting. Near the opening of the book, the Greeks retreat toward their ships, "dominated by the whip of Zeus" and fearing Hektor (12.37–39), who then leads the Trojans in pursuit across the ditch surrounding the Greek encampment. The narrator reports that Zeus "charmed the mind of the Achaians and bestowed triumph (*κῦδος*) on the Trojans and Hektor" (254–55). With the divine king's continuing support, the Trojans attack the wall protecting the Greek tents and ships, and Book 12 ends with Hektor breaking the wall's gates open, enabling the Trojans to pour through the gate and over the wall.

[2] Alden 2000: 181–85. As Alden observes, such a posture contrasts with the approach of Agamemnon's embassy in Book 9, which never offered Achilleus a ritual supplication (on this failure, see also Schadewaldt 1966: 81; Rosner 1976: 322; Wilson 2002: 99–100).

[3] Thornton 1984: 133; Hainsworth 1993: 289; and Wilson 2002: 111.

[4] Whitman 1958: 95 and Kim 2000: 103–6. Cf. Lynn-George 1988: 167.

However, before Hektor crosses the ditch to launch this assault, a portent appears in the form of a flying eagle carrying a live snake, which the eagle eventually drops after being bitten (12.200–7). The Trojan seer Poulydamas interprets this omen as a warning to the Trojans not to pursue the Greeks to their ships, since they will eventually be driven back in a rout and lose many men (210–29). This portent and its elucidation recall how Zeus promised Hera in Book 4 that Troy would fall; Zeus's will for Trojan dominance is only temporary and derived from his promise to grant Achilleus honor rather than from a true commitment to Trojan victory. When Hektor rejects Poulydamas' interpretation as an admonition to "forget the counsels (βουλέων) of thundering Zeus," and exhorts his men, "let us trust in the will (βουλῇ) of great Zeus" (12.235–41), he appears deluded by Zeus's assurances of his martial success, unable to grasp how the king of the gods has promised him triumph for that one day only. Therefore, while in Book 12 the poet progressively satisfies the audience's narrative desire to find out how the worsting of the Greeks will occur, the eagle and snake omen gestures toward events after the realization of Achilleus' plot, inspiring the audience's desire to discover what will happen once Hektor's day of glory is over.

Homer marks Book 13, which begins the second half of the *Iliad*'s narrative, as the start of something new through the sudden relaxation of Zeus's vigilance and the subsequent intervention of Poseidon in the ongoing battle. At the opening of Book 13, with Hektor and the Trojans drawing near to the Greek ships, Zeus turns his attention from Troy to Thrace in the expectation that none of the gods will interfere in the mortal conflict (13.1–9). Yet, Poseidon, pitying the Greeks and "strongly indignant at Zeus" (Διὶ δὲ κρατερῶς ἐνεμέσσα), immediately takes advantage of the situation and descends to the battlefield (15–31). In disguise, he repeatedly encourages the Greeks and imbues them with newfound strength and courage to defend their ships. At this point, the narrator draws attention to the competing wills of Zeus and Poseidon, describing how their "intentions were divided" (ἀμφὶς φρονέοντε); Zeus "was wishing" (βούλετο) victory for the Trojans on Achilleus' behalf, while Poseidon "was grieved" (ἤχθετο) at the Greeks being dominated (345–53), with this grief seeming to represent his longing to preserve the beleaguered Achaian army. Because of Zeus's seniority and greater knowledge, however, Poseidon avoids openly helping the Greeks, preferring to be "always rousing them secretly throughout the army, in the likeness of a man" (354–57).

With Poseidon's support, the Greeks halt the Trojans' deadly advance, but his secret encouragement is not enough to turn the tide of battle. Indeed, the narrator ends his account of the opposing wills of Zeus and Poseidon by figuring their competition as a destructive but inconclusive tug-of-war (13.358–60), which Noriko Yasumura (2011: 64) has compared to the inconclusive mortal duels of Books 3 and 7. Even as the Greeks rally, the Trojans remain confident in Zeus's favor and fight on valiantly. At one point, Menelaos invokes the divine king to wonder at his support for the Trojans and the force of their aggressive desire (13.633–39):

οἷον δὴ ἄνδρεσσι χαρίζεαι ὑβριστῇσι,
Τρωσίν, τῶν μένος αἰὲν ἀτάσθαλον, οὐδὲ δύνανται
φυλόπιδος κορέσασθαι ὁμοιΐου πτολέμοιο.
πάντων μὲν κόρος ἐστί, καὶ ὕπνου καὶ φιλότητος
μολπῆς τε γλυκερῆς καὶ ἀμύμονος ὀρχηθμοῖο,
τῶν πέρ τις καὶ μᾶλλον ἐέλδεται ἐξ ἔρον εἶναι
ἢ πολέμου· Τρῶες δὲ μάχης ἀκόρητοι ἔασιν.

How you gratify, indeed, these violent men,
the Trojans, whose rage is always reckless, nor are they able
to sate themselves of the din of indiscriminate war.
There is satiety of all things, of sleep and sex (*philotētos*)
and sweet celebration and noble dancing;
one would rather wish (*eeldetai*) to put away the lust (*eron*) for these things
than for war; but the Trojans are insatiate of battle.

Menelaos, reminding the audience of the epic's analogy between desire for war and desire for sex,[5] here remarks on the tenacity of the Trojans' aggressive desire when they might instead be pursuing satisfaction in other, more peaceful, activities. Indeed, such is the stalemate beside the ships, despite Poseidon's intervention, that, at the beginning of Book 14, the injured Greek kings watching from the sidelines are distraught, with Agamemnon again suggesting that they sail away and abandon the war (14.65–81). After Odysseus strongly condemns Agamemnon's idea, Diomedes' rather desperate solution is for the wounded leaders to return to the battlefront and rouse the other Greeks (128–32). Poseidon, still in disguise, does his best by reassuring Agamemnon and by instilling courage in the Achaians with an enormous yell (135–52), yet Zeus's will to honor Achilleus is still clearly operative on the Trojan battlefield.

Hera's Plot

It is at this juncture that Hera brings to bear her own will in support of Poseidon's. The poet reintroduces Hera into the narrative with a clear statement of her loyalties. Looking out from Olympos she recognizes "her own brother and brother-in-law," that is, Poseidon, going about the battle and "rejoiced in her heart" (*χαῖρε δὲ θυμῷ*), but she also sees Zeus sitting on Mt. Ida and "he was

[5] See further MacCary 1982: 143–48.

hateful to her in her heart" (στυγερὸς δέ οἱ ἔπλετο θυμῷ, 14.153–58). These lines are focalized through Hera's perspective:[6] the description of Poseidon as Hera's kinsman reflects her identification with him and his desire, while her even closer ties with Zeus, whom she finds "hateful," go unacknowledged. This Hera is immediately recognizable as the subject of familiar triangular desires: a longing for the Greek army's welfare—now being partially satisfied by Poseidon—is paired with a competitive desire to dominate her husband, who has been working against the Achaians and on the side of her enemies, the Trojans.

In order to thwart Achilleus' and Zeus's plot and thus fully realize her desires, Hera immediately conceives her own competing plot to subdue Zeus's controlling will. Since her previous efforts in Books 1 and 8 to defy that will openly have been unsuccessful, now she deliberates on "how she might deceive the mind of aegis-bearing Zeus" (ὅππως ἐξαπάφοιτο Διὸς νόον αἰγιόχοιο, 14.160).[7] The narrator reports (161–65),

> *ἥδε δέ οἱ κατὰ θυμὸν ἀρίστη φαίνετο βουλή,*
> *ἐλθεῖν εἰς Ἴδην εὖ ἐντύνασαν ἓ αὐτήν,*
> *εἴ πως ἱμείραιτο παραδραθέειν φιλότητι*
> *ᾗ χροιῇ, τῷ δ' ὕπνον ἀπήμονά τε λιαρόν τε*
> *χεύῃ ἐπὶ βλεφάροισιν ἰδὲ φρεσὶ πευκαλίμῃσι.*
> This plot (*boulē*) seemed best to her in her heart:
> to go to Ida, having prepared herself,
> so that somehow he might yearn (*himeiraito*) to lie in sexual union (*philotēti*)
> beside her body, and then pour sleep, free from cares and gentle,
> over his eyelids and sharp wits.

Hera's plot is to inspire in Zeus a sexual yearning (*himeros*) that overmasters his desire for Trojan victory, and then to complete her conquest of his will through a sexual encounter that leads directly to his full mental incapacitation in sleep. The formula that introduces Hera's plot, "this *boulē* seemed best to her in her heart," was used in reference to a divinity only once before, when it prefaced Zeus's plot at the beginning of Book 2 to send a destructive Dream to Agamemnon in order to begin actualizing his will to honor Achilleus and destroy many Greeks (14.161 = 2.5).[8] This repetition signals how Hera is preempting the *Dios boulē*—now focused on fulfilling Achilleus' main plot—with her own deceptive *boulē*, taking control of the *Iliad*'s narrative and propelling it in a new direction.

[6] Janko 1992: 172 and Krieter-Spiro 2018: 78.

[7] See also scholia T on 14.160 and bT on 14.166.

[8] Cf. Pironti 2017: 66–67, who observes the repetition of the line and links Zeus's deployment of Dream against Agamemnon with Hera's deployment of Sleep against her husband in their respective plots. She notes, however, that Hera must also draw on *himeros* and *philotēs* in order to induce sleep since she is manipulating the king of the gods rather than a mere mortal.

First, Hera grooms herself for seduction in a bathing and dressing scene that assimilates her to a hero preparing for his martial *aristeia*. She goes to her private bedroom, washes and anoints herself with ambrosial perfume, arranges her hair, dresses in a garment fashioned by Athene, pinning it with golden brooches and fastening it with a belt, puts on earrings, and, finally, dons a headdress and binds sandals on her feet (14.166–86). Scholars have observed the parallelism between this scene of feminine adornment and the traditional masculine type-scene of arming in its linguistic highlighting of individual items and sequential progression ending with the assumption of headgear, as well as in its strategic function of making the subject ready to exercise power over another.[9] Indeed, her final look is described with heavenly light imagery that anticipates the celestial shining of Achilleus' shield and helmet after he has donned them in Book 19.[10]

This likeness between Hera's toilette and a warrior arming for battle underscores the aggressive purpose of her seduction—dominance over Zeus and control of the ongoing war—and also suggests once again a similarity between sex and fighting and the desires that motivate them. The detail that Athene wove Hera's "fine dress" (ἑανόν, 14.178) calls to mind Hera and Athene's shared hatred of the Trojans and their the alliance to help the Greeks in Books 4–8,[11] and also Athene's own scene of arming in Book 5 before she descended to fight on the Trojan battlefield (5.733–47).[12] The most significant difference between Hera's adornment and a hero's arming is that hers is done inside, behind closed and locked doors (14.167–69), which emphasizes the clandestine and deceptive nature of Hera's tactics for besting Zeus,[13] in contrast to the open warfare of the battlefield.

This toilette scene also seems to connect Hera from the outset with the goddess Aphrodite, anticipating their subsequent encounter. Scholars have long recognized that this passage is similar to multiple other instances of female adornment in preparation for erotic encounters in early Greek epic, and most have understood it as an example of a traditional and generic type-scene.[14] However, more recently P. Brillet-Dubois (2011: 110–12) and Bruno Currie (2016: 151–56) have argued convincingly that this scene "belongs" to Aphrodite in the Greek epic

[9] See Janko 1992: 173–74 and Krieter-Spiro 2018: 85–86, with bibliography. See also Brillet-Dubois 2011, who argues specifically for a link between Aphrodite's seduction of Anchises in the *Homeric Hymn to Aphrodite* and Iliadic *aristeiai*.

[10] After Hera's dressing and adornment, "great charm was shining forth" (χάρις δ' ἀπελάμπετο πολλή, 14.183) and her headdress "was white like the sun" (λευκὸν δ' ἦν ἠέλιος ὥς, 14.185). Similarly, the narrator repeatedly describes the "brightness" (σέλας) of Achilleus' shield (19.374, 375, 379) and compares it to the "moon" (μήνης, 19.374), while the crest of his helmet "was shining forth like a star" (ἡ δ' ἀστὴρ ὣς ἀπέλαμπεν, 19.381).

[11] See Janko 1992: 176, who writes that "By weaving Here's dress even the virgin Athene aids her plot, with which she would sympathize."

[12] Athene, in a reversal of Hera's dressing, begins by taking off her feminine peplos, which is also described as "fine" (ἑανόν, 5.734), and dons instead a masculine chiton, and then armor and Zeus's fearsome aegis.

[13] Janko 1992: 174 and Krieter-Spiro 2018: 83.

[14] e.g. Forsyth 1979; Janko 1992: 170, 173; Krieter-Spiro 2018: 85.

tradition, and is particularly associated with her seductions of the Trojan princes Anchises and Paris on Mt. Ida (insofar as she "seduces" Paris to secure victory during the Judgment); therefore, as they contend, this *Iliad* passage alludes to these traditional Aphroditean stories.[15] In the Judgment of Paris, Aphrodite wins the golden apple by promising (and then delivering) Helen to Paris, causing the union that initiates the Trojan War, which is celebrated in the *Iliad*'s superplot. Hera's assumption of an Aphroditean role in this passage indicates that she will similarly use eroticism to generate mortal conflict and epic narrative. It also figures Hera appropriating Aphrodite's particular *modus operandi* in the service of ultimately harming Aphrodite's Trojan favorites, making Hera's seduction plot not only a deceptive assault on Zeus but also a sly gesture of dominance over Aphrodite and an act of revenge in kind—and with the goddess's own "arms"—for Aphrodite's previous triumph in the Judgment.[16]

Hera's cunning attack on Aphrodite becomes apparent in the following scene, when she deceitfully convinces her rival to grant her special erotic and sexual powers. Hera's opening words to Aphrodite immediately evoke their competition as she asks whether the goddess will be receptive to her or bear a grudge against her, "since I help the Danaans and you the Trojans" (14.190–92). When Aphrodite graciously indicates her willingness to help and proclaims, "say what you intend" (αὔδα ὅ τι φρονέεις, 195), Hera replies "with the intention to deceive" (δολοφρονέουσα, 197); her discourse is thus marked as "devious" and manipulative from the start, concealing her true will.[17] Hera then asks for "sex and yearning, by which you dominate all immortals and mortal men" (φιλότητα καὶ ἵμερον, ᾧ τε σὺ πάντας/ δαμνᾷ ἀθανάτους ἠδὲ θνητοὺς ἀνθρώπους, 198–99), explicitly requesting the goddess's own powers and also intimating how she really plans to use them—as tools of domination. Sex (*philotēs*) and yearning (*himeros*) are thus figured as the two "weapons" that would complete Hera's "arming."[18]

But the rest of her speech is a lie that at once veils and alludes to her true intentions. Hera claims that she will use Aphrodite's powers to bring the estranged divine couple Okeanos and Tethys, her foster-parents, back to bed together and so earn their closeness and respectful gratitude (14.200–10). The epithets "origin of gods" (θεῶν γένεσιν) and "mother" (μητέρα), which she applies to Okeanos and Tethys respectively (201), position these sea divinities as a cosmogonic couple responsible for producing the earlier (pre-Olympian) generation of gods; thus, her desire to facilitate the reconsummation of their union seems to suggest her interest

[15] See also Pironti 2017: 67, who notes how this scene is reminiscent of Aphrodite's seduction of Anchises in the *Homeric Hymn to Aphrodite* and also detects Aphrodite's immanence in the *himeros* and *philotēs* that are part of Hera's plot (14.163).

[16] Brillet-Dubois 2011: 111–12 and Currie 2016: 154–55.

[17] Janko 1992: 180 and Beck 2005: 131–34. Beck shows that this participle is deployed only when Hera speaks deceptively, replacing more neutral formulas normally used to introduce Hera's speech.

[18] Krieter-Spiro 2018: 100.

in challenging Zeus and his divine order.[19] Indeed, her account of how Okeanos and Tethys took care of her "when widely-seeing Zeus set Kronos below the earth and the fruitless sea" (202–4) specifically refers to Zeus's violent establishment of his hegemony through the overthrow of his father Kronos, and creates a link between her relationship with Okeanos and Tethys and divine opposition to Zeus's rule.

Aphrodite, however, does not appear to detect this sinister subtext, declaring that she cannot refuse Hera, "for you lie in the arms of Zeus, who is best" (14.212–13).[20] The goddess immediately bestows her own powers on the divine queen in the form of a special embroidered strap (*kestos himas*) that she removes from her breasts and gives to the divine queen. The narrator describes the *kestos himas* in the following way (215–17):

> *ποικίλον, ἔνθα τέ οἱ θελκτήρια πάντα τέτυκτο·*
> *ἔνθ' ἔνι μὲν φιλότης, ἐν δ' ἵμερος, ἐν δ' ὀαριστὺς*
> *πάρφασις, ἥ τ' ἔκλεψε νόον πύκα περ φρονεόντων.*
>
> intricate, and in it have been crafted all enchantments:
> in it there is sex (*philotēs*) and yearning (*himeros*) and intimate converse (*oaristus*)—
> enticement, which steals the mind even of those with shrewd intentions.

This strap contains the *philotēs* and *himeros* that Hera had requested, as well as *oaristus*, all attributes traditionally associated with Aphrodite in early Greek hexameter poetry;[21] it thus materializes Hera's appropriation of Aphrodite's divine identity.[22] Together, these powers are characterized as "enticement" that distracts one's mind, in a further elucidation of Hera's strategy to best Zeus by redirecting his desire from the Trojan battlefield toward herself.

The *kestos himas* also recalls Aphrodite's first consequential intervention in the *Iliad*'s narrative in Book 3. Aphrodite initially appeared in the epic during the duel between Paris and Menelaos, when Menelaos was choking Paris with the embroidered strap (*polukestos himas*) of the warrior's own helmet (3.370–72). Aphrodite

[19] Janko 1992: 180–81 and Pucci 2018: 181; cf. Pironti 2017: 75. See further Janko 1992: 181–82 and Krieter-Spiro 2018: 102–3 on Okeanos and Tethys as cosmogonic progenitors, rather than Ouranos and Gaia (as in Hesiod's *Theogony*), and on their potential derivation from the Babylonian primordial parents Apsu and Tiamat in the *Enuma Elish*. However, Kelly 2008: 274–85 argues against any direct link between Okeanos and Tethys and the Babylonian creation myth, and contends that Okeanos' description as "origin of gods" (*θεῶν γένεσιν*) refers only to his parentage of divine rivers and streams.

[20] This image of Hera and Zeus together suggests Aphrodite's ignorance of their antagonism, while her description of Zeus as "best" (*ἀρίστου*) positions him securely in charge. As Krieter-Spiro 2018: 96 observes, Aphrodite's lack of suspicion, especially given that she herself is a master of deception, foreshadows Hera's success in similarly duping Zeus. Cf. Pironti 2017: 68, who argues that Aphrodite perceives Hera's true intentions with this remark, and that her words allude to the denouement of the episode, which features Hera in Zeus's embrace.

[21] These powers accompany her in *Theog.* 201–6.

[22] Pironti 2017: 68–69.

rescued Paris by breaking the chin-strap and then spiriting him away in a cloud of mist (3.374–82), after which she engineered the sexual reunion between Helen and Paris at the basis of the epic's superplot. Aphrodite's *kestos himas* in Book 14, therefore, may remind the audience of her salvific, erotic, and narrative powers in Book 3, and its transfer to Hera represents the divine queen's assumption of Aphrodite's function and connects the present episode with the events of the superplot—rather than Achilleus' and Zeus's main plot.

The poet ends this scene with foreshadowing of Hera's imminent manipulation of Zeus. After handing over the strap, Aphrodite promises the realization of Hera's will: "I say that it will not be unaccomplished, whatever you are anxious for (μενοινᾷς) in your mind" (14.220–21). As Hera dons the *kestos himas* of the goddess who had just been named with her signature epithet "smile-loving" (φιλομμειδής, 211), she too smiles (μείδησεν; μειδήσασα, 222–23). This smile at once confirms Hera's appropriation of Aphrodite's powers and seems to indicate her satisfaction in victory over her rival and in the progress of her plot.[23] Furthermore, it recalls her identical smile at the end of Book 1 (14.222–23 ~ 1.595–96), when she stood down from her challenge to Zeus's will to grant Achilleus honor, accepting her son Hephaistos' mediation. There her smile appeared to conceal a persistent desire to dominate Zeus, and its recurrence here signifies her adoption of the same deceptive amity. It also suggests that Hera is now finally approaching the fulfillment of the competitive desire that she suppressed in Book 1.

Hera's subsequent meeting with Sleep (*Hypnos*) on the island of Lemnos enables her to acquire the remaining "weapon" that she needs to overpower Zeus's will, while emphasizing the cosmically threatening nature of her plot and demonstrating the efficacy of her newly assumed erotic power. The aggression immanent in Hera's attempt to secure Sleep's cooperation is indicated by his introduction as "the brother of Death" (14.231); Hera's plan to use Sleep against her divine adversary Zeus is parallel to the way that a mortal warrior deals death to his enemy: both subdue the mind and body, rendering the subject senseless.[24] Indeed, when Hera addresses Sleep, she calls him "lord of all gods and men" (233), in an acknowledgment of his universal power to dominate, which she had also attributed to Aphrodite (199). In her plot against Zeus, Hera takes care to win over the divinities who are capable of overcoming everyone, including the king of the gods. This time, in her eagerness, she eschews deception and directly asks Sleep to induce Zeus's slumber after they have had sex in return for her eternal gratitude and a golden throne (235–41).

[23] Krieter-Spiro 2018: 112.

[24] See also Krieter-Spiro 2018: 117, who finds "entirely imaginable" an allusion here to the fact that Hera's plan "is clearly dangerous, albeit mostly for human beings, and contains the seed of a theomachy."

Sleep's initial refusal underscores the stakes of Hera's challenge to Zeus's authority. His opening address to her as "daughter of great Kronos" and assertion that he would easily put to sleep any other god, even "Okeanos, though he is the origin to all" (14.243–46) recall Hera's lying story to Aphrodite and again associate the divine queen with gods predating or opposing Zeus's regime. Sleep goes on to say that he will not use his powers against Zeus because of his negative experience the last time he did so, when he enabled Hera's persecution of Herakles in opposition to Zeus's will (247–56). Then, Sleep escaped Zeus's subsequent wrath only by obtaining the protection of his mother Night, "the dominator (δμήτειρα) of gods and men" (256–62). This narrative proves Hera's capacity to master Zeus through alliance with Sleep and positions another potent older divinity (Night) on their side, but it also suggests the temporary and perilous nature of any victory that Hera might win.

The divine queen does convince Sleep to work on her behalf, however, once she remembers to deploy Aphrodite's powers against him. In response to his refusal, she protests, "Sleep, why are you anxious over these things in your mind?" (Ὕπνε, τίη δὲ σὺ ταῦτα μετὰ φρεσὶ σῇσι μενοινᾷς, 14.264), echoing the language of Aphrodite, who had just promised her the accomplishment of "whatever you are anxious for in your mind" (ὅ τι φρεσὶ σῇσι μενοινᾷς, 221). She then attempts to arouse overmastering sexual desire in Sleep by offering him one of the Graces as his wife (267–68), testing out the erotic tactic she will use against Zeus. The divine queen's assumption of an Aphroditean role with this proposition is marked by her promise of a Grace—traditionally linked with Aphrodite[25]—and also by the way that her sexual bribe of Sleep recalls Aphrodite's bribe of Paris with Helen during the Judgment.[26]

Drawing on desire and sex, Hera is irresistible, as Aphrodite had assured her she would be: Sleep immediately rejoices and tacitly assents to help her, demanding Hera's oath that she will give him the Grace Pasithea as his bride, for whom "I myself have wished (ἐέλδομαι) for all time" (14.270–76). Sleep's long-standing desire for Pasithea seems to make him forget his fear of Zeus's wrath. The oath that Sleep stipulates and Hera at once swears on the river Styx, with the Titans in the underworld as witnesses (277–79), ends the episode with a final reminder of the cosmic implications of the rebellion that Hera is plotting, and is now close to accomplishing, with Sleep's assistance.[27]

[25] The Graces help Aphrodite prepare for the Judgment of Paris in *Cypria* Frr. 5–6 (West 2003: 85–87); a Grace appears as the wife of Hephaistos in *Iliad* 18, while Aphrodite is Hephaistos' wife in *Odyssey* 8.

[26] Janko 1992: 185.

[27] See also Krieter-Spiro 2018: 136, who contends that reference to the Titans here is meant "to remind the audience of earlier dangers posed to Zeus' rule, to which his wife does not want to submit completely once again." According to Hesiod (*Theog.* 361, 776–77), Styx is the daughter of Okeanos and Tethys, who have already featured prominently in Hera's plot.

The Deception of Zeus

When Hera finally approaches Zeus on the Gargaron peak of Mt. Ida, the divine king's intensely erotic response indicates that her plot is working, and recalls the sexual encounter between Paris and Helen in Book 3. Instead of recounting how Hera "found" (εὗρε) Zeus, which is the usual way of describing the visit of one Homeric character to another, the narrator twice relates how Zeus "saw" (ἴδε; ἴδεν, 14.293–94) Hera, dramatizing the process by which Zeus conceives desire at the sight of her.[28] The narrator explains (294–96),

> *ὡς δ' ἴδεν, ὥς μιν ἔρως πυκινὰς φρένας ἀμφεκάλυψεν,*
> *οἷον ὅτε πρωτόν περ ἐμισγέσθην φιλότητι,*
> *εἰς εὐνὴν φοιτῶντε, φίλους λήθοντε τοκῆας.*
>
> and, as soon as he saw her, lust (*erōs*) shrouded his shrewd wits,
> as when first the two mixed in sexual union (*philotēti*),
> going to bed, having escaped the notice of their parents.

Zeus's immediate *erōs* for Hera overmasters his mind, inhibiting his ability to maintain, much less pursue, any other intentions. The account of how "lust shrouded his shrewd wits" echoes Paris' assertion to Helen that "not ever yet before has lust so shrouded my wits" (*οὐ γάρ πώ ποτέ μ' ὧδέ γ' ἔρως φρένας ἀμφεκάλυψεν*, 3.442), suggesting a parallelism between Hera's seduction of Zeus and the queer union of Helen and Paris, with its socially disastrous but narratively generative effect. While Paris' desire makes him disregard normative expectations of masculinity, Zeus's desire causes him forget his own hegemonic will (*boulē*), which is itself normative within the divine community and the epic's narrative. As Janko (1992: 198) has observed, the narrator's addition of "shrewd" (*πυκινάς*) to describe Zeus's "wits" (*φρένας*) in this variation "aptly stresses the intelligence that is overcome." Ingrid Holmberg (2014: 328) explains further: "The fatal danger of Paris' sexual attraction to Helen, whose result is being played out in the *Iliad*, is magnified in the cosmic danger of Zeus' sexual attraction to Hera, an attraction that not only upsets the traditional sexual hierarchy of male dominance but also threatens the cosmic political order, just as Paris' attraction threatens mortal political order."

What is more, just as Paris' sexual liaison with Helen in Book 3 is represented as a re-enactment of the first consummation of their desire, here also the encounter between Hera and Zeus is portrayed as a symbolic repetition of their initial union. The account of the divine couple, on that first occasion, "having escaped the notice of their parents," juvenilizes Zeus in his lust, and thus links his overwhelming

[28] Janko 1992: 198.

sexual desire for Hera with a cosmic temporality when he was not yet lord of the universe, when the Titans still ruled.[29] The connection between present and past liaisons also suggests that the competitive and deceptive dynamic of this episode is an essential, universal, iterative fact of the divine couple's relationship—that Hera is always contesting Zeus's power and that Zeus is always dangerously susceptible to deception through *erōs*.[30]

The couple's initial dialogue underscores the devious nature of Hera's seduction through its echo of her earlier disingenuous conversation with her rival Aphrodite. As Aphrodite had asked Hera what she wanted from her (14.194–96), now Zeus inquires of Hera, "going where, eager (*μεμαυῖα*), have you come here from Olympos?" (298–99). In both cases Hera replies "with the intention to deceive" (*δολοφρονέουσα*, 197; 300) and tells the same lie about reconciling Okeanos and Tethys (200–2 ~ 301–3; 205–7 = 304–6), although when speaking to Zeus she strategically omits mention of his overthrow of Kronos—presumably not wanting to put him on his guard. In addition, Hera says that she has come to inform Zeus of her journey so that he does not become angry at her for going to Okeanos' home without his knowledge (309–11), in a deceptively submissive gesture meant to (a)void Zeus's suspicion along with his wrath, and position him—rather than herself—as the seducer.[31]

Zeus's subsequent speech confirms that he has fallen victim to Hera's erotic plot. He orders his wife to delay her journey and exhorts her (14.314–16, 328),

> *νῶϊ δ' ἄγ' ἐν φιλότητι τραπείομεν εὐνηθέντε.*
> *οὐ γάρ πώ ποτέ μ' ὧδε θεᾶς ἔρος οὐδὲ γυναικὸς*
> *θυμὸν ἐνὶ στήθεσσι περιπροχυθεὶς ἐδάμασσεν,*
> ...
> *ὡς σέο νῦν ἔραμαι καί με γλυκὺς ἵμερος αἱρεῖ.*
>
> And come, let the two of us take satisfaction, having gone to bed in sexual union.
> For not ever yet before has lust (*eros*) for a goddess or woman
> so dominated the heart in my breast, having poured around it,
> ...
> as now I lust after (*eramai*) you and sweet yearning (*himeros*) seizes me.

[29] See also Pucci 2018: 186, who writes, "Suddenly Zeus is no longer the monarch of the gods and the lord of fate, no longer the immortal being untouched by the phases of age: he appears as the lucky youth accomplishing what his parents ought not to know, his first intercourse with Hera."

[30] Cf. Pironti 2017: 73–79, who interprets this episode as an epic articulation of cultic myths that feature a cycle of estrangement and reunification between Hera and Zeus, and of a traditional mythology that presents Hera as, eternally, "the redoubtable antagonist of Zeus, who often throws challenges at him, opposes his decisions, and tests his authority" (*la redoutable antagoniste de Zeus, qui souvent lui lance des défis, s'oppose à ses décisions et met à l'épreuve son autorité*, 78).

[31] See Krieter-Spiro 2018: 147–48.

Zeus's diction explicitly frames his lust as an aggressive force accosting him and dominating his person, in an indication of how he has lost control of himself and the world around him. Moreover, his account of his own sexual desires once more repeats Paris' words to Helen in Book 3, stressing their narrative parallelism (14.314–15 ~ 3.441–42; 14.328 = 3.446). Just as the intensity of Paris' *erōs* and *himeros* prompts recollection of similar feelings during his first sexual encounter with Helen (3.443–45), now, in between his declarations of desire, Zeus positively compares his current lust with his previous desires for multiple mortal women and goddesses, and finally, again, for Hera herself (14.317–27). In his tactless account to his wife of his past adulteries, Zeus expands upon Paris' example, underscoring his own particular thoughtlessness under the power of desire[32] as well as his special status as divine progenitor of heroes and gods.[33]

Despite this difference, Paris and Zeus are similarly motivated by their sexual desires to narrate story material that does not properly belong to the *Iliad*'s main plot,[34] symbolizing their generation of additional plots as desiring subjects. As we have seen, Paris' lust, aroused by Aphrodite through her proxy Helen, catalyzes the *Iliad*'s superplot, which in Books 3–7 replaces Achilleus' main plot and causes a narrative expansion; likewise, Zeus's lust, aroused by Hera, is now causing a suspension of that main plot and the emergence of a counter-plot. Hera's aggressive desire is, of course, the ultimate force behind that counter-plot.[35]

The poet emphasizes Hera's control through her reply to Zeus's articulation of his desire. Speaking again "with the intention to deceive" (δολοφρονέουσα, 14.329), she objects to immediate intercourse with Zeus on Mt. Ida out of worry that the other gods will see them, which "would be a thing of *nemesis*," and suggests that they return to the privacy of their bolted bedroom if Zeus insists on having sex (330–40). Hera here deceitfully adopts a posture of modest reluctance in order to stoke Zeus's desire and strengthen his mistaken impression that he is the sexual aggressor. Indeed, she focuses attention on his lust and attempts to increase it by repeatedly naming it with additional expressions of desire: "if now you desire to go to bed in sexual union..." (εἰ νῦν ἐν φιλότητι λιλαίεαι εὐνηθῆναι, 331), and "but if indeed you want [it] and it is close to your heart..." (ἀλλ' εἰ δή ῥ' ἐθέλεις καί τοι φίλον ἔπλετο θυμῷ, 337).

This response also confirms Hera's parallelism with Helen. With her simulation of reluctance, Hera appears to mimic Helen's resistance to sleeping with Paris, a resistance that only seemed to augment Paris' desire. Likewise, Hera's pretended

[32] As Alden 2000: 46 articulates, "Zeus' clumsiness arises from his condition: he cannot wait." See further Krieter-Spiro 2018: 150–51.

[33] Pironti 2017: 72.

[34] Holmberg 2014: 329.

[35] Cf. Pucci 2018: 185, who writes, "Hera does not merely symbolically restore the order of the Titans; she also displaces the *Iliad*'s narrative and replaces it with other mythical stories. It is not that these stories are not true, but they have been buried by the *Iliad* under Tartaros with their characters and do not have any relevance for the Zeus of the *Iliad*."

anxiety about being seen with Zeus by the divine community recalls Helen's worry about the Trojan women observing her going to Paris; both of them say that it "would be a thing of *nemesis*," in the same line-end position (νεμεσσητὸν δέ κεν εἴη, 14.336 = 3.410). However, whereas Helen's resistance seemed to be authentic, dramatizing a real internal conflict between her lust for Paris, imposed by the goddess of love, and her sense of propriety and yearning for Menelaos, Hera's is entirely feigned and meant to disguise her true desire—to subdue Zeus's will. Thus, while Helen openly displays anger toward both Aphrodite and Paris, Hera merely teases Zeus, cleverly concealing her aggression. Yet even so, Hera's similarity to Helen helps to figure the divine queen as a desiring subject in her own right and as a co-producer with the lustful Zeus of the counter-plot that she has concocted, just as Helen is complicit with Paris in generating the superplot in Book 3.[36] In this way, Homer confirms the link between Helen, who calls herself "dog" (κυνός, 6.344; 356), and Hera, about whom Zeus says, "nothing is more doggish (κύντερον) than you" (8.483), as generators of Iliadic narrative.

Zeus is entirely taken in by Hera's protestations of modesty, and collaborates in his own undoing by creating the circumstances for the subjugation of his will. He promises his wife that he "will shroud" (ἀμφικαλύψω) them with a golden cloud (14.343–44), ironically literalizing the way that "lust shrouded (ἀμφεκάλυψεν) his shrewd wits" (294): with his vision obscured by a cloud, Zeus will be fully insensate to the larger world. Indeed, after he produces the cloud and finally takes Hera in his arms, the narrator concludes, "thus the father slept motionless on the Gargaron peak, dominated by sleep and sex" (ὕπνῳ καὶ φιλότητι δαμείς, 352–53). In a final summation of the successful execution of Hera's plot, Sleep himself subsequently reports to Poseidon, "Zeus lies sleeping (εὕδει), since I shrouded (περὶ... κάλυψα) him with a soft slumber, and Hera enticed him to go to bed with her in sexual union" (ἐν φιλότητι παρήπαφεν εὐνηθῆναι, 358–60).

With Zeus incapacitated, Poseidon is finally able to turn the tide of battle in the Greeks' favor, prolonging the epic's "Great Day of Battle." After Sleep exhorts Poseidon to protect the Greeks and give them glory while Zeus is still sleeping (14.357–58), the sea god immediately encourages the Achaian army with words that signal the stalling of Achilleus' and Zeus's plot. He acknowledges how Hektor has become emboldened due to Achilleus' withdrawal, but asserts, "there will not in any way be excessive longing (ποθή) for him, if we others are roused to protect each other" (368–69). Here Poseidon appears to refer to Achilleus' vow in Book 1

[36] In Book 3, despite her resistance, Helen ultimately follows Aphrodite to the "marriage chamber" (θάλαμον, 3.423) and then has sex with Paris. Hera's suggestion that she and Zeus retire to their "marriage chamber" (θάλαμος, 14.338) again follows the model of Helen's sexual encounter with Paris, but may also imply Hera's intention to sequester Zeus inside where he cannot see the Trojan battlefield and even, possibly, to keep him trapped there under lock and key, since the room she describes seems to be the same one where she prepared herself for the seduction, and which she alone is able to open (Janko 1992: 205).

that there would be a longing (*pothē*) for him among the Achaians (1.240), but promises that the Greeks can dispense with that longing, essential to Achilleus' plot for revenge and honor, through collaborative effort.

This suspension of the *Iliad*'s main plot is initiated by Poseidon's command for the army to redistribute their armor, with the best soldiers wearing the best armor (14.371–77); when the Greeks do so, they have in effect prepared for a group *aristeia*.[37] Now Poseidon himself leads them into battle, holding a sword, while Hektor marshals the Trojans; the face-off between god and mortal as champions of their respective armies (390–91) is far from the nearly balanced clash of Poseidon's and Zeus's wills in Book 13. Soon Aias wounds Hektor with a stone and the Trojans start to withdraw, crossing back over the river Xanthos toward the city (409–39). Book 14 ends with the Greeks in pursuit and Aias slaughtering many Trojans.

Zeus's Revised Will

The realization of Hera's and Poseidon's desires is, however, short lived. When Zeus wakes up from his post-coital nap at the start of Book 15, he immediately observes how the Trojans are in retreat and understands that he has been duped by Hera. In response, he reasserts his dominance, first with a threat that he will hang Hera with golden chains and anvil from Olympos, as he did when he discovered how she had arranged for Herakles to be blown to the island of Kos (15.16–33).[38] Hera reacts with a shudder, indicating her frightened acknowledgment of Zeus's supremacy, in a variation on the formulaic line that described her compliant fear after her husband similarly warned her not to continue challenging his will in Book 1 (15.34 ~ 1.568). She then attempts to assuage his anger with a technically accurate oath that Poseidon helped the Greeks "not through my will" (μὴ δι' ἐμὴν ἰότητα), but rather because "his passion (θυμός) urged and bid him" out of pity for the Achaians (36–44). Moreover, she demonstrates her submission by stating that she "would encourage" (παραμυθησαίμην) Poseidon to go wherever Zeus orders (45–46). In turn, the divine king smiles (μείδησεν, 47), signaling how the power hierarchy in Book 14 has been reversed; now Zeus, and not Hera, seems to feel triumphal satisfaction, but his smile may, like his wife's, conceal aggression, in this case fueled by knowledge of Hera's treachery.[39]

[37] Janko 1992: 208.

[38] As Yasumura 2011: 39–57 has shown, it was Hera's attempt to keep Herakles from aiding Zeus's faction in his war against the Giants that resulted in her previous punishment by hanging. Zeus's recollection of that series of events here confirms how Hera's deceptive seduction in Book 14 constituted a similar challenge to his cosmic supremacy.

[39] Cf. Pironti 2017: 81, who interprets Zeus's smile as evidence of his understanding that Hera's conflict with him "is part of the order of things" (*fait partie de l'ordre des choses*), and also Janko 1992: 233, who writes, "It is one of the charms of Homer's style that we are left to wonder whether Zeus smiles because Here agrees, or because he sees through her wiles, or for both reasons."

Indeed, Zeus's subsequent speech seems initially to constitute a hegemonic reaffirmation of his will to accomplish Achilleus' plot for Greek debilitation. He commands Hera to summon Iris and Apollo from the divine ranks in order for the former to direct Poseidon to leave the battlefield and the latter to heal and empower Hektor (15.54–61). He then delivers a prescriptive prophecy that repeats and expands upon his previous articulation of his will to Hera after her provocation in Book 8. He confirms Hektor's lethal pursuit of the Greeks to their ships and his killing of Patroklos, but adds the detail that Achilleus "will rouse to action his companion" (61–66). Now, for the first time, Zeus explicitly positions Achilleus as an agent in his friend's death, in a confirmation of the link, suggested in Book 11, between Achilleus' plot and Patroklos' demise. This forecast, even as it arouses again the audience's narrative desire to comprehend the exact course of events resulting in Patroklos' death, also functions to re-establish Zeus's authoritative power after his will had been temporarily subdued by Hera.

But Zeus does not stop there: he goes on to temper his self-assertion with prophetic concessions to Hera's desire for the destruction of the Trojans. First, he predicts that Patroklos, before dying, will kill many adversaries, including his own son Sarpedon (15.66–67), indicating his willingness to grant glory to a Greek other than Achilleus and to see the Trojan side suffer losses—even to tolerate the death of his own heroic progeny. He then prophesies that Achilleus, angered by Patroklos' death, will kill Hektor in turn, and lead a counter-attack against Troy that will last "until the Achaians take steep Ilion through the plots (βουλάς) of Athene" (68–71). That is, Zeus predicts a second arc of the *Iliad*'s main plot that extends beyond Achilleus' original plot against the Greeks, featuring the hero's return to battle, the death of Hektor, and even the sack of Troy. Significantly, this arc accords with the desires of Hera, Poseidon, and Athene (here singled out) for the supremacy of the Achaians and, ultimately, for Troy's fall. Insofar as Zeus only expresses this expanded plot in reaction to Poseidon's and, especially, Hera's challenges, Homer creates the impression that Zeus is modifying or even formulating for the first time his own will in consideration of the other gods' desires.[40] At the same time, his apparent indulgence of his wife is familiar from Book 4, when he had agreed, despite his own disinclination, to allow the eventual realization of Hera's and Athene's aggressive desires for the sack of Troy.

[40] Scodel 2017: 84 admits this as one possible interpretation, with the other being that Zeus announces a pre-conceived plan in these situations "in order to insist that he will do as he chooses"; thus, Janko 1992: 229 and 234 argues that Zeus's prophecy reveals how Hera's "intrigues are in vain" since his will has always been directed toward the eventual destruction of Troy. For more recent modifications of Janko's position, see also Marks 2016: 67–68 and Pironti 2017: 82–83, who writes that here everything is shown to be pre-determined according to "a well thought-out and wise strategy" (*une stratégie réfléchie et avisée*) even as she recognizes "the productive antagonism" (*l'antagonisme productif*) of Hera and Zeus through which the latter's will is realized. See also Chapter 5, note 6.

What Zeus prophesies, therefore, is his integration of the *Iliad*'s superplot and main plot in cooperation with his wife. Although Hera only briefly dominated Zeus's will through her deceptive seduction, her ability to redirect Zeus's desire toward herself confirmed her narrative agency, and her adoption of Aphrodite's and Helen's roles from Book 3 foreshadowed the superplot's imminent reappearance, as she united in her own person *all* its female agents. Before proclaiming the epic's future course, Zeus declares to Hera how powerful their conjoined wills could be: "if indeed hereafter you, ox-eyed lady Hera, should sit among the immortals with intentions the same as mine (ἶσον ἐμοὶ φρονέουσα), then certainly Poseidon, even if he very much wishes (βούλεται) otherwise, would at once twist his mind in accordance with your and my heart" (15.49–51).

This statement, though delivered as a potential conditional that acknowledges the historical divergence between Hera's and Zeus's "intentions," has prophetic force, setting up the divine dynamics informing the remainder of the poem. After Zeus has finished speaking, Hera grudgingly advises the other gods not to defy him (15.104–9),[41] and Poseidon ultimately stops helping the Achaians, although he warns of his rebellious anger should Zeus, in opposition to the desires of Troy's divine antagonists, "not be willing" (οὐδ' ἐθελήσει) to eventually bring about Troy's destruction (211–17). Poseidon's words show that his obedience is dependent upon Zeus's agreement with the anti-Trojan faction regarding the sack of Troy, and again suggest the dialectical formation of Zeus's will and the *Iliad*'s plot through competition and compromise between Zeus and his Olympian kin.[42] This series of events securely inspires our narrative desire not only to find out how Achilleus' original plot will come to fruition but also to discover how the newly revealed second arc of the main plot—authored by Zeus in conjunction with the other gods—will unfold.

[41] Hera, however, provokes Ares to defy Zeus's command of non-interference by informing him that his son Askalaphos has been killed in battle (15.110–12). Ares is greatly upset and immediately prepares to descend to the battlefield, but Athene intervenes to convince him to endure his pain and avoid Zeus's wrath (119–42). As Janko 1992: 225 argues, Ares' aggressive desire to avenge his son's death, which is stymied by Athene, prefigures Patroklos'—and ultimately Achilleus' own—aggrieved aggression against the Trojans, which is finally delimited by the interventions of Apollo (and Zeus). Ares' experience also, as Janko recognizes, anticipates Zeus's grief at the death of his mortal son Sarpedon, and his obligation to accept that death despite the pain it brings him.

[42] See also Elmer 2013: 162–66, who argues that Book 15 begins a movement toward consensus between the *Iliad*'s conflicting divine wills, which have been represented not only through the confrontations between the opposing divine factions but also in the heretofore ambivalent mind of Zeus himself. Cf. Bonnet 2017: 100–3, who interprets the *Iliad*'s divine dialectic as a social model wherein crises are resolved "through collective exchange and debating of authority, which often takes advantage of the opportunity to reaffirm itself" (*par un échange collectif et par une mise en débat de l'autorité, qui souvent en profite pour se raffermir*); and Friedman 2001 and Bergren 2008: 54, who contend that the challenges to Zeus's will in Books 13–15 show how it is really the poet, not Zeus, who controls the direction of the epic.

Patroklos' Challenge to Achilleus' Plot

According to Zeus's prophecy, Patroklos' involvement in the battle is the connecting link on the mortal level between the main plot's first and second arcs, that is, between Achilleus' familiar plot for revenge and honor, and what comes after.[43] Since Achilleus has so far kept all of the Myrmidons on the sidelines with him, his plot must be altered for Patroklos to rejoin the war. Patroklos' visit to Nestor's tent in Book 11, where he is sent by Achilleus to inquire whether Machaon was wounded in battle, creates the circumstances for him to conceive new desires that oppose Achilleus' will and challenge his plot.

Nestor seizes the opportunity of Patroklos' separation from Achilleus to recruit him to the greater Greek cause. The old king detains him with a long speech during which he describes the recent Achaian casualties, recounts his own youthful exploits in battle, and exhorts Patroklos to persuade Achilleus to re-enter the war or, failing that, to lead the Myrmidons into battle himself, dressed in Achilleus' armor (11.656–803). His speech seems designed to elicit Patroklos' sympathy for the beleaguered Greek army and to arouse an empathetic longing for Achilleus' return as well as an aggressive desire to achieve heroic glory, in competition with Nestor's example.[44] The effect of Nestor's words on Patroklos indicates their success: "thus he spoke, and roused the passion (*thumon*) in his breast" (ὧς φάτο, τῷ δ' ἄρα θυμὸν ἐνὶ στήθεσσιν ὄρινε, 804). In Book 3, the narrator had used the same formula to express the effect of Aphrodite's exhortation for Helen to join Paris in their marriage chamber (11.804 = 3.395); then, the goddess seemed to inspire in the heroine both a sexual desire for Paris and an aggressive desire to best herself. Now Nestor appears to have similarly affected Patroklos, since he immediately sets off among the ships in search of Achilleus (11.805).[45]

Before he can reach Achilleus, however, Patroklos is detained a second time by the wounded Eurypylos (11.809–48), in an encounter that deepens his identification with the Greeks. When he comes upon Eurypylos, the man's suffering arouses his pity and inspires him to ask about the state of affairs on the battlefield. In response, Eurypylos describes once again the dire straits of the Achaian soldiers and asks him for medical assistance. Patroklos confirms that he is on his way to speak with Achilleus as Nestor had enjoined him, yet also agrees to help Eurypylos and goes with him to his tent, thereby indicating his sympathy for the suffering

[43] Thus, Janko 1992: 310 calls Achilleus' decision to send Patroklos into battle "the linchpin holding the poem's two halves together."

[44] See further Alden 2000: 88–99 on Nestor's autobiographical story as a paradigm for Patroklos.

[45] Each of the five times this formula appears in the *Iliad* (2.142, 3.395, 4.208, 11.804, 13.468) it indicates how an exhortation literally moves the speech's recipient: following this formula, the addressee always (eventually) goes wherever directed by the speaker. See also Alden 2000: 256, who asserts that Patroklos "has fallen completely under the influence of Nestor."

Greeks in general and this representative injured warrior in particular. With this stop, Patroklos becomes even further embedded in the Achaian community as he lengthens his separation from Achilleus.

When Zeus finally brings Achilleus' destructive plot close to realization in Book 15, Patroklos is provoked to entreat the hero on the Greeks' behalf. Zeus had ended his great prophecy with a declaration that he would not stop his anger, nor allow any other god to protect the Greeks, until he accomplished Achilleus' "wish" (*ἐέλδωρ*) and fulfilled his promise to Thetis to honor the hero (15.72–77). Accordingly, working through Apollo, he immediately resuscitates Hektor and inspires him to lead the Trojans back over the Achaian rampart and toward their ships (236–389). When Patroklos, still tending to Eurypylos, perceives the increasingly desperate situation of the Greeks, he groans and announces his intention to return at once to Achilleus and convince him to rejoin the battle, after which he sets off for the hero's tent (390–405). While he is in transit, the danger becomes even more extreme: Hektor and his Trojans begin setting the ships on fire, with only Aias attempting to beat them back (716–46).

Patroklos' weeping as he confronts Achilleus at the opening of Book 16 confirms not only his sympathy for but also his empathy with the Achaians and their suffering. His crying is compared to a dark stream pouring water down a cliff in a precise echo of the simile that had characterized Agamemnon's tearful anguish at the beginning of Book 9, just before he sent the embassy to Achilleus (16.3–4 ~ 9.14–15); this repetition immediately characterizes Patroklos as a surrogate for Agamemnon and his army.[46] Achilleus' comparison of the weeping Patroklos to a girl begging to be picked up by her mother (16.7–10) acknowledges Patroklos' empathetic longing for the angry hero: as a distressed child looks to her mother for comfort and safety,[47] Patroklos, on the Achaians' behalf, looks to Achilleus to deliver the army from ruin. Yet, inasmuch as the girl in the simile is holding back a mother whose intent is focused elsewhere (*ἐσσυμένην κατερύκει*, 9), Achilleus already recognizes that Patroklos' desires are at odds with his own.[48]

[46] Lynn-George 1988: 168. *Pace* Hainsworth 1993: 60, who writes "No other connexion between the passages is made explicit and it is hard to imagine that an *audience* would make one, unless it were well trained in the nuances of the epic style." I counter that the implied audience is *de facto* "trained in the nuances of the epic style." Moreover, the openings of Book 16 and 9 both respond to a situation of mortal danger for the Achaians. Indeed, this scene in Book 16 makes repeated reference to Book 9, as Schadewaldt 1966: 128–30 has shown. Cf. Ready 2011: 173, who argues that this is a traditional simile deployed when "a character faces a terrifying situation and is willing to resort to measures he never would have considered before."

[47] Gaca 2008 argues that this simile evokes the scenario of a panicked mother and child, bereaved of their defending male kin, fleeing from invading soldiers, "in which a young daughter prevents her mother from outpacing her and compels her to pick her up" (151). Ready 2011: 174–77, however, does not find textual support for such a specific vehicle.

[48] As Warwick 2019a: 22 explains, this image "reflects Achilles' frustration with the fact that his personal pursuit of honor is being hindered by the Achaeans' and Patroclus' need for his protection" even as the simile as a whole acknowledges how Achilleus is failing to perform his proper protective role of "mother" toward his Greek "children." Cf. Ready 2011: 177–82, who maintains that Achilleus'

When Achilleus asks why he is crying, Patroklos himself makes clear that he is sharing in the miserable longing of the Greek army. He explains that grief (*achos*) has overcome the Achaians because many of their best men have been wounded and he critiques the anger that keeps Achilleus from "warding off shameful destruction from the Argives" (16.22–32).[49] In a final demonstration of his assumption of the other Greeks' mindset, Patroklos goes on to articulate to his companion the exact plea dictated to him by Nestor (*mutatis mutandis*): failing Achilleus' own return, to don the hero's armor himself and lead the Myrmidons into battle in order to push the Trojans away from the Greek ships and tents (16.36–45 ~ 11.794–803). The poet reminds the audience that this plan of action is not in Patroklos' own interest with the narrator's subsequent comment: "thus he spoke in entreaty, greatly foolish; for indeed he was destined to pray for his own evil death and doom" (46–47).

Achilleus' response reveals how Patroklos' appeal represents a challenge to his will. The narrator introduces his reply with the report that he was "greatly troubled" (μέγ' ὀχθήσας, 16.48), deploying a restricted formula that had previously been used to describe Zeus's and Poseidon's reactions to another divinity's statement or request that was contrary to their own immediate desires.[50] Achilleus' first words are an exclamation of dismay: "Oh my, god-born Patroklos, what a thing you have said!" (49). The hero goes on to indicate how he still feels a competitive desire for status among the Greeks. He reiterates his losses—of Briseis and of honor—and resulting heartache, recounting how Agamemnon's abduction of the "girl" (κούρην), his *geras* that the army selected for him, has caused him "dreadful grief" (αἰνὸν ἄχος) and "pains" (ἄλγεα) (55–59), and complaining again that Agamemnon has treated him "as if I were some dishonored migrant" (16.59 = 9.648). Although he then says "let us allow these things to be over and done with; it was not somehow in my mind to be unceasingly angry (ἀσπερχὲς κεχολῶσθαι)," he also recalls his promise not to renounce his "wrath" (μηνιθμόν) until the fighting comes to his own ships (60–63). Since Hektor has now reached the ship of Protesilaos (15.704–6), but not his own, Achilleus implicitly refuses to re-enter the war, demonstrating that he remains committed to his plot for honor—even if he is no longer bent on revenge—and that he cares more about holding his position than about the army's welfare.[51]

simile is meant to comfort Patroklos by reassuring him that his distress is as easily remedied as the girl's: if the Greeks should give Achilleus the honor he desires, he would save them as quickly as the mother in the simile would console her child by picking her up.

[49] On the Achaians' *achos* here, see Nagy 1979: 89–90.

[50] Zeus vs. Thetis (1.517), Zeus vs. Hera (4.30), Zeus vs. Poseidon (7.454); Poseidon vs. Hera (8.208), Poseidon vs. Iris/Zeus (15.184). Cf. Scully 1984: 21 on how this formula associates Achilleus with Zeus.

[51] See also Wilson 2002: 112, who writes that Achilleus "does not abandon his objective of taking *poinē* and gifts or his struggle for domination." Cf. Whitman 1958: 198; Schein 1984: 118–19; Lynn-George 1988: 168; Redfield 1994: 17–18; Alden 2000: 258; Warwick 2019a: 23–24.

Achilleus' persistent aggression toward the Greeks stands in sharp relief to Patroklos' empathetic tears, and underscores how Patroklos' physical separation from Achilleus has led to a psychical disconnect. The man who was formerly Achilleus' closest and most loyal subordinate in his Phthian retinue, who previously acted as an agent of Achilleus' will,[52] has taken the side of his current antagonists, Agamemnon and the Greek army. In so doing, Patroklos has become the Greeks' new ambassador, assuming Phoinix's double identity as agent of the Greek army and intimate of Achilleus, and thus reproducing the tense dynamic between Phoinix and Achilleus in Book 9.

Achilleus cannot, however, dismiss Patroklos' plea on the Greeks' behalf as easily as he had Phoinix's. While there is no evidence that the hero pities the Achaians as they suffer defeat on the battlefield, he "pitied" (ᾤκτιρε) Patroklos when he saw him come weeping to his tent (16.5). Achilleus' compassion for his friend as well as Patroklos' powerful entreaty seem to compel the hero to grant his request: Achilleus orders Patroklos to lead the Myrmidons into battle dressed in his own armor (64–65).[53] In so doing, he follows the precedent of Zeus and Poseidon, who, when "greatly troubled" (μέγ' ὀχθήσας), also ultimately cede to the will of their interlocuters.[54]

Nevertheless, just as these gods' concessions are delayed or conditional, Achilleus' acquiescence comes with limitations that are meant to reconstruct Patroklos' return to battle into a move that serves his own interests. After he has directed Patroklos to protect the Greek ships from destruction,[55] Achilleus commands his friend to "obey" (πείθεο, 16.83) a final injunction: once he has saved the ships, he must not lead the Greeks against the city of Troy, but rather come back and let the two armies make war without him on the plain (87, 95–96). Achilleus explains that this limitation is meant to further his plot for honor: "so that you may win great honor and glory for me from the Danaans, and so that they send back the very beautiful girl and give many shining gifts in addition" (84–86). Achilleus intends Patroklos and the Myrmidons to assist the Achaians up to a point, but not enough to render him superfluous; that is, he decides to give the Greeks a taste of himself through Patroklos but leave them wanting the real thing. He reconceives of Patroklos' intervention as a fresh means to recoup his status

[52] See Fantuzzi 2012: 206–7. This relation is emblematized by the formula used repeatedly to describe Patroklos' subservience: "thus he [Achilleus] spoke and Patroklos obeyed his dear companion" (ὣς φάτο, Πάτροκλος δὲ φίλῳ ἐπεπείθεθ' ἑταίρῳ, 1.345 = 9.205 = 11.616).

[53] *Pace* Bassett 1938: 200 and Schadewaldt 1966: 136, I regard Achilleus' concession as a demonstration less of care for the Achaian army and more of respect and pity for Patroklos.

[54] On Achilleus' conflicted feelings, see also Macleod 1982: 24, Schein 1984: 118–19, and Brügger 2018: 17, 41.

[55] Even as Achilleus gives in to Patroklos' desire to help the Greek army, he reframes that desire as an act of simple self-preservation, telling him to protect the ships from the Trojans "lest they burn up the ships with shining fire and take away our own homecoming" (16.81–82).

among the Greeks, as another way to force their deference by showing them how vital the Myrmidons and their commanders are to the war effort.[56]

In Book 9, Achilleus had warned Phoinix that he could not simultaneously be a *philos* both to himself and to Agamemnon (9.613–14), insisting on Phoinix's exclusive and submissive solidarity, and now Achilleus has imposed a similar demand on Patroklos, requiring his companion to make his own honor his primary concern. Indeed, Achilleus explicitly orders him not to conceive an independent will lest it foil his own plot: "do not, certainly, apart from me desire (λιλαίεσθαι) to wage war against the war-loving Trojans; you will make me more dishonored" (16.89–90). Here and throughout his speech, Achilleus attempts to reassert dominance over Patroklos and realign his companion's desires with his own. Dressing Patroklos in his own armor is symbolic of this effort. In Achilleus' armor, Patroklos goes into battle not as himself, but as Achilleus, becoming Achilleus' alter ego;[57] Achilleus' armor literally and metaphorically encompasses Patroklos, erasing his individual identity.

Furthermore, Achilleus ends his speech by imagining himself and Patroklos as a unified pair in opposition to both Trojans *and* Greeks, in an "us against the world" scenario. Calling on Zeus, Athene, and Apollo, he wishes for every Trojan and Achaian to die except for the two of them; he wishes that he and Patroklos alone might conquer Troy (16.97–100).[58] As Marco Fantuzzi (2012: 207–9) has observed, Achilleus' use of the dual pronoun *νῶϊν* (99) positions Patroklos as his second self, on his side and opposed to everyone else. He thus negates Patroklos' solidarity with the Achaians and pre-empts Patroklos' and the Greeks' longing for his help with his own desire for total domination, making clear how little he cares about the wellbeing of the other Achaians.[59]

The problem, however, with Achilleus' attempt to reposition his companion as his faithful retainer is that Patroklos and the Myrmidons are going into battle without him as part of the Greek collective. With this action, they are aligning themselves with the Achaians, who are driven by aggressive desire to defeat the Trojans. In fact, sharing this aggressive desire is necessary for their successful participation in combat, as Achilleus himself recognizes when he takes it upon himself to "rouse" (*ὀτρύνων*, 16.167) the Myrmidons. Before his men go into battle, Achilleus tells them to remember their earlier desire to

[56] Devereux 1978: 5 and Crotty 1994: 56. See also Wilson 2002: 113, who explains, "Patroklos must do only enough to advance Achilleus' strategy and allow the Achaians an opportunity to return the woman and offer gifts."

[57] Whitman 1958: 200–1; Nagy 1979: 33–34, 292–95; Sinos 1980: 35.

[58] Zenodotus and Aristarchus athetized these lines.

[59] Achilleus' wish, however, is self-defeating, since there would be no one to honor him, at least in the world of mortals, if everyone else were dead. The scenario that Achilleus has conjured up points to the problem of controlling the damage he has wrought. Once he has unleashed his aggression against the Greeks, where will it stop? See also Nagler 1974: 145, 155 and Schein 1984: 120, who calls this a "nihilistic wish."

fight, a desire that they had expressed when he was keeping them back although they were "unwilling" (ἀέκοντας, 16.204). Indeed, he explicitly invokes their *erōs* for war: "now is manifest the great work of battle, which before you lusted after" (ἐράασθε, 207–8). Following these admonitory words, the narrator reports that he "roused the rage and passion of each" (ὄτρυνε μένος καὶ θυμὸν ἑκάστου, 210), testifying to his success in inspiring the Myrmidons' aggressive desire.

Achilleus' subsequent prayer to Zeus, and the divine king's ambivalent response, confirm the hero's inability to maintain control over Patroklos and remind the audience of Zeus's will. Achilleus asks Zeus to give Patroklos "triumph" (κῦδος) and a brave heart, and also to ensure that he returns back to the ships unscathed, with all his weapons and his fighting companions (16.240–48). The narrator reports that Zeus assented to Achilleus' first request but refused his second—that Patroklos come back safe from the fighting (250–52). By dramatizing the divergence between Achilleus' and Zeus's desires at this moment in the epic, Homer marks Patroklos' entrance into battle as a turning point that begins the transition between the main plot's first arc, motivated by the conjoined wills of Achilleus and Zeus, and its second arc, which is initiated by the parallel wills of Patroklos and Zeus, working in opposition to Achilleus' desires. In addition, the narrator's foreshadowing of Patroklos' heroism and imminent death arouses our narrative desire to discover how this sequence will unfold in the upcoming battle scene.

At the same time, however, the entire opening of Book 16 may inspire our opposing sympathetic and empathetic desires for Patroklos' survival. Patroklos appears kind in his care for the injured Eurypylos and concern for the army as a whole; moreover, in his identification with the Greeks' suffering, Patroklos elicits not only Achilleus' sympathy but also our own. Thus, we may wish Patroklos well as a "good" character who is in pain. Furthermore, we may continue to empathize with Achilleus, particularly in his compassion and concern for Patroklos, sharing his desire for his companion's safe return. But we may also be alienated by his stubborn pursuit of honor at the cost of Greek lives, including, as he fails to see, Patroklos' own. Inasmuch as we know that our desire for Patroklos' welfare is futile, such desire makes us ponder the fatal meaning of Achilleus' plot and may cause us to critique the hero, even as we pity him for his self-harming delusion.[60] Whatever frustration and pity we may feel, these emotions color our narrative desire and keep us even more riveted as Patroklos leads the Myrmidons into battle.

[60] On Achilleus' delusion (*atē*) here, see Alden 2000: 261–62. On the audience's response to Achilleus' prayer to Zeus, see also Kozak 2017: 150–51.

Patroklos' *Aristeia*

Despite the poet's ominous revelation of Achilleus' failure to determine Patroklos' future, as long as Patroklos is within Achilleus' sphere of influence he continues to operate as the hero's surrogate. Dale Sinos (1980: 30–33) has observed how Patroklos' designation as Achilleus' *therapōn* ("attendant") indicates his subservience or subordination to Achilleus, who is the primary figure.[61] The narrator calls Patroklos Achilleus' *therapōn* after he has put on the hero's armor and is preparing to lead the Myrmidons into battle (16.165), and Achilleus himself names Patroklos his *therapōn* as he prays for his success and safe return (244). Accordingly, Patroklos' exhortation to the Myrmidons before they fight show that he has taken on Achilleus' desires—and even his discourse—as his own. He tells his men to be courageous so that they may honor Achilleus, and "so that the wide-ruling son of Atreus, Agamemnon, may recognize his delusion, that he did not honor the best of the Achaians," repeating Achilleus' own earlier words to his mother Thetis (16.273–74 = 1.411–12).[62] The narrator also describes the efficacy of Patroklos' exhortation in the same language used previously to characterize Achilleus' successful rousing of the troops (16.275 = 210). Indeed, when Patroklos first enters battle, the poet emphasizes his close identification with Achilleus by having the Trojans mistake him for his master. Seeing Patroklos, they initially think that Achilleus has "thrown off his wrath (μηνιθμόν) and chosen solidarity (φιλότητα)" (16.282), and they scatter in retreat.

The complete identification of the two men, however, turns out to be just as illusory as Achilleus' putative *philotēs* with the Greek army. As soon as Patroklos advances farther from Achilleus, he becomes fully integrated into the Achaian army and escapes Achilleus' control. During his *aristeia*, Patroklos ceases to be called a *therapōn*, functionally *separating* from Achilleus.[63] After he has led the Achaians to reverse the tide of battle in a first successful round of kills, the narrator groups Patroklos with the other Greek fore-fighters in his summation: "these leaders of the Danaans, each of them, took a man" (16.351).

Now Patroklos begins to pursue his own desires, in solidarity with the Greeks and in transgression of Achilleus' command that he do no more than drive the Trojans away from the ships. When Hektor in his chariot crosses back over the

[61] As van Wees 1992: 42–43 explains, in general *therapontes* are those who serve a social superior, performing "personal services for him, such as preparing and serving his food or grooming and driving his horses; and they follow him to war." This service relationship can be permanent or a temporary arrangement during a military campaign.

[62] See also Pucci 2018: 94, who writes "At this point, Achilles and Patroclos seem to be two faces of the same person. But it is a unity undergoing separation."

[63] Sinos 1980: 34, 55–57. Cf. Nagy 1979: 293–95, who observes that Patroklos is compared to Ares when he rashly attacks Apollo (16.784) as well as when he first leaves Achilleus' tent to go to Nestor's (11.604). Nagy suggests that Patroklos, in his death, ceases to be Achilleus' *therapōn* and becomes the *therapōn* of Ares, that is, a victim of the war god.

ditch surrounding the Greek camp and flees toward Troy (16.367–69), Patroklos follows him, "intending evils for the Trojans" (*Τρωσὶ κακὰ φρονέων*, 373). A few lines later, the narrator expands upon this revelation of the aggressive psychology driving Patroklos: "his passion (*thumos*) had called him against Hektor, for he desired to strike him" (*ἐπὶ δ' Ἕκτορι κέκλετο θυμός·/ ἵετο γὰρ βαλέειν*, 382–83). Although Patroklos does not kill Hektor, he satisfies this eruption of aggressive desire by killing the Lykian champion, Zeus's son Sarpedon.

Patroklos' own desires are stimulated once again when Hektor kills one of the Myrmidons, Epigeus, as the Lykians and Trojans rally to rescue Sarpedon's corpse (16.570–80). The narrator reports that "grief (*ἄχος*) came to Patroklos because of the death of his companion" (581), and then continues, "thus straight at the Lykians, horse-riding Patroklos, you sped, and at the Trojans, and you were angered (*κεχόλωσο*) at the doom of your companion" (585). Here the poet presents the familiar triangle of desire in which the subject (here Patroklos) feels grief (*achos*) because of his longing for his lost companion and anger (*cholos*) toward those rivals who have deprived him of his loved one.[64] This aggression continues to carry him forward to engage with the Achaians' enemies—in violation of Achilleus' prohibition.

Zeus's deliberation on the timing of Patroklos' death positions his will as a double determinant of Patroklos' belligerence. As battle rages for possession of Sarpedon's corpse, Zeus wonders whether he should have Hektor kill Patroklos immediately, or else allow Patroklos to push the Trojans all the way back toward the city, taking the lives of more enemy combatants; he chooses the second option (16.647–55). This window into Zeus's psychology reinserts into the narrative the divine king's desire as a motivating force, and suggests that Patroklos' aggressive desire to continue killing Trojans is in accordance with—and, indeed, a product of—Zeus's will. The narrator confirms this causality when he remarks that Patroklos "was greatly deluded" (*μέγ' ἀάσθη*) and "foolish" (*νήπιος*) for ignoring Achilleus' limitations, and then concludes that "the mind (*νόος*) of Zeus is always stronger than that of men, he who routs even a stalwart man and takes away his victory easily, when he himself urges him on to fight; it was he who, also then, incited the heart in his breast" (685–91). Zeus's will is identified as the force behind Patroklos' fatal aggressive impulse.[65]

With this foreshadowing, the narrator also provokes again the audience's dreadful anticipation of Patroklos' demise, and he further intensifies that feeling by apostrophizing Patroklos in the very next lines and seven other times over the

[64] Shay 1994: 87–88 also flags the death of Patroklos' Myrmidon companion as a trigger point that alters his psychology, propelling him into a "berserk" state in which he ignores Achilleus' restraints and attempts to storm Troy. Cf. Wilson 2002: 114, who similarly notes that Patroklos "loses his own sense of limits."

[65] On the double motivation here, see further Pucci 2018: 108–10.

course of Book 16.[66] As Homeric critics have long recognized, these apostrophes create the impression that the narrator feels sympathetic compassion for Patroklos as he moves inexorably toward his death.[67] The narrator's attitude draws the audience's attention to Patroklos[68] and "develops and confirms an answering sympathy in the audience."[69] Thus, our pity for Patroklos is augmented even as we continue desiring to find out how he will die. Apostrophe also links Patroklos with the only other character addressed multiple times by the narrator, Menelaos (4.127, 4.146, 7.104). He was apostrophized during the superplot at moments when his life was endangered, just as Patroklos is now at risk,[70] and these later apostrophes therefore help to indicate how Patroklos' *aristeia* represents the re-emergence of the superplot within the epic's narrative.

Indeed, before his death, Patroklos leads a deadly Greek attack on Troy, this time assuming Diomedes' role from the superplot. The narrator reports that the Greeks would have taken the city under Patroklos' leadership had not Apollo intervened (16.698–701). He goes on to describe how Patroklos assaults Troy's walls three times, and is thrice repelled by Apollo; on the fourth try, when he rushes forward "equal to a god," Apollo verbally admonishes Patroklos, telling him to give way since it is not his destiny to take Troy, and he yields before the god (702–11). Patroklos' foiled attack repeats Diomedes' ferocious, yet ultimately futile quadruple assault on Aineias during the superplot (5.436–44), and Apollo's decisive intervention in each case is nearly identical. This narrative echo signals to the audience how the epic's main plot is converging with its superplot through the person and agency of Patroklos. The Greeks are again on the offensive and menacing Troy, even if it is not yet time for the city to fall.

Homer drives home the superplot's recurrence by figuring Patroklos' last moments of martial glory and subsequent death as a third variation on this same narrative pattern. Patroklos, "intending evils for the Trojans" (*Τρωσὶ κακὰ φρονέων*), rushes against his enemy three times, killing nine men in each assault (16.783–85). Finally, he attacks the Trojans a fourth time, rushing forward "equal to a god," and once more Apollo intervenes, this time physically, striking Patroklos and knocking off his helmet, breaking his spear, and denuding him of his shield and armor; with Patroklos exposed and confused, the Trojan Euphorbos injures him with a javelin and then Hektor finishes him off with a spear (786–828).

[66] See also Kozak 2017: 159. The eight apostrophes are at 16.20, 584, 692f., 744, 754, 787, 812, 843.

[67] e.g. scholion ad 16.787; Parry 1972: 9; Block 1982: 16–17; Allen-Hornblower 2015.

[68] Frontisi-Ducroux 1986: 21.

[69] Block 1982: 16. See also de Jong 2009: 95, who argues that apostrophe increases the vividness (*enargeia*) of the narrative, bringing it alive for the audience.

[70] Allen-Hornblower 2015 observes this correspondence and, building on Mueller 1984: 55–56 and Martin 1989: 235–36, suggests that the apostrophes represent Agamemnon's and Achilleus' focalizations respectively; the narrator's voice merges with that of the heroes, each concerned for the welfare of his male *philos*. I prefer to understand the narrator anticipating, rather than expressing, the responses of Agamemnon and Achilleus.

Patroklos' long-anticipated killing comes in the context of yet another quadruple attack foiled by Apollo.

While Patroklos' *aristeia* changes the balance of the war and presages a shift in the epic's main plot, his death is part of Zeus's accomplishment of his original promise to honor Achilleus. In Achilleus' absence, Patroklos, like Diomedes before him, has taken the Phthian hero's place as the most fearsome Greek warrior. Thus, Patroklos' aggression threatens not only the integrity of Troy but also Achilleus' own indispensability. Patroklos' continued glory would garner him the honor that Achilleus himself aims to attain, as the hero has recognized (16.89–90). Zeus, by ordaining Patroklos' death, keeps him from entirely wrecking Achilleus' plot, from obviating the Greeks' longing for Achilleus. The divine king's refusal to grant Achilleus' prayer for Patroklos' safety is thus in the service of fulfilling his earlier wish for honor.[71] This means that Achilleus shares responsibility for Patroklos' death—at one level, Hektor's killing of Patroklos is the ultimate realization of Achilleus' plot for the worsting of the Greeks. From this perspective, Patroklos' death is the negative consequence, predicted repeatedly in Book 9, of Achilleus' persistent internecine aggression.[72]

However, Achilleus never meant for Patroklos to truly join the Greek collective and become their champion; it was Zeus who inspired Patroklos to disregard Achilleus' limitations on his fighting and pursue the Trojans away from the Greek camp, then attempt to storm Troy.[73] The desires of Zeus and Patroklos, working together in opposition to Achilleus' desires, cause Patroklos' death, thus generating more epic. Not only does Patroklos' killing further prolong the "Great Day of Battle" as the two armies contend over his corpse in Books 17–18,[74] but, more significantly, as I will follow in the next chapter, it is the catalyst for Achilleus' return to battle and for the second arc of the main plot constituted by the hero's mourning and revenge—and Greek triumph.

Therefore, it could be said that Patroklos is a mortal equivalent to Hera and Poseidon, the divine agents who instigate the development and prolongation of the *Iliad*'s narrative in Books 13–14. Just as these gods are motivated by desires in opposition to Zeus's controlling will, so also Patroklos is driven by desires contrary to Achilleus' will. Thus, Patroklos emerges as an important desiring

[71] Nimis 1987: 87–93 tracks how Achilleus' second prayer to Zeus is in opposition to his original prayer and thus creates textual confusion.

[72] Achilleus, in his responsibility for his retainer Patroklos' death at Apollo's hand after refusing the embassy's offer of compensation, appears to resemble Agamemnon, who brings destruction on his own men through Apollo's plague after his refusal of Chryses' ransom offer. Thornton 1984: 135–36 observes this parallelism, and interprets both Patroklos' death and the plague as divine punishments that mark the impropriety of Achilleus' and Agamemnon's rejections of the respective embassies.

[73] Significantly, the same formula is used to describe Patroklos' aggressive desire at the critical junctures when he pursues Hektor across the ditch and launches his fatal quadruple attack against the city (*Τρωσὶ κακὰ φρονέων*, 16.373 = 783).

[74] On how the fight over Patroklos' body slows down the pace of the narrative, see Purves 2019: 128–31.

subject and narrative agent, and the causative dynamics of the mortal and divine worlds once again mirror one another. At the same time, insofar as Zeus causes Patroklos' deadly desires to serve his own dual purpose of honoring Achilleus *and* giving victory to the Greeks in the end, the divine king is confirmed as the final director, if not the unilateral motivator, of the *Iliad*'s plot.

7

Achilleus' Mourning and Revenge

Achilleus, waiting for news from the Greek camp, finally learns of Patroklos' death at the opening of Book 18. This chapter shows how Achilleus' consequent longing (*pothē*) for Patroklos manifests itself in melancholic mourning and in an aggressive desire to take revenge on Hektor that drives the hero back into battle. Achilleus' new triangular desires both parallel and supersede his previous ones, motivating a second and final arc of the *Iliad*'s main plot and preventing his reconciliation with Agamemnon in Book 19 from providing narrative resolution. Meanwhile, the queerness of Achilleus' attachment to Patroklos explains and highlights the socially destructive and narratively generative nature of the new desires his loss provokes. Homer keeps the audience engaged as the epic continues by arousing our narrative desire to find out how and when Achilleus will kill Hektor, and by encouraging our empathy with the desiring hero and sympathetic wish for the alleviation of his pain. Yet our sympathies may shift as the hero conceives and enacts his brutal vengeance, eliciting reflection on the morality of Achilleus' new plot.

Achilleus' New Triangular Desires

When Antilochos informs Achilleus of Patroklos' killing (18.16–21), the hero's intense sorrow and gestures of mourning reveal his self-destructive new desire for his lost companion. After receiving the news, "a black cloud of grief (*acheos*) covered him" (*τὸν δ' ἄχεος νεφέλη ἐκάλυψε μέλαινα*, 22); he defiles his face and clothing with dust and lies stretched out on the ground "tearing" (*δαΐζων*) his hair (23–27). Achilleus' grief seems to indicate his longing for Patroklos, and his actions suggest that he is identifying with his beloved companion and turning against himself the anger associated with his loss in an experience of "melancholia." He not only punishes himself but also mimics the position and appearance of his companion's corpse, fallen to the ground (16.822) and later twice described as "torn (*δεδαϊγμένον*) by the sharp bronze" (18.236, 19.283).[1] Antilochos restrains

[1] Book 18, lines 26–27, where the narrator describes how Achilleus "in the dust was lying, massive and massively stretched out" (*ἐν κονίησι μέγας μεγαλωστὶ τανυσθεὶς/ κεῖτο*), recall the previous narrative of how the dead Kebriones, Hektor's charioteer, "in a whirl of dust was lying, massive and massively, having forgotten his horsemanship" (*ὁ δ' ἐν στροφάλιγγι κονίης/ κεῖτο μέγας μεγαλωστί, λελασμένος ἱπποσυνάων*, 16.775–76). This echo makes clear to the audience the death-like quality of

Desire in the Iliad: *The Force That Moves the Epic and Its Audience.* Rachel H. Lesser, Oxford University Press.
 DOI: 10.1093/oso/9780192866516.003.0008

Achilleus' hands in the fear that he will cut his own throat (18.33–34); he understands that Patroklos' death has made Achilleus suicidal.[2]

Achilleus' response to Patroklos' killing recalls his reaction to Briseis' appropriation, though it is more powerful. In both cases, at the first perception of loss, grief (*achos*) afflicts the hero (1.188, 18.22), yet the "black cloud" metaphor here indicates Achilleus' magnified, enveloping anguish over Patroklos' death. Both losses initiate "melancholia": after Briseis was taken away, Achilleus identified with his concubine in his feminine withdrawal from battle, and inflicted pain on himself, "withering away in his own heart" while "longing (ποθέεσκε) for the battle-cry and war" (1.491–92); now the hero goes further, assuming the posture of a corpse and physically assaulting his own person. This escalation appears to reflect not only the absolute permanence of this second loss but also the greater intensity of Achilleus' libidinal connection with his dead companion, which seems to combine deep love with a frustration engendered by the circumstances of his death.

As we saw in the previous chapter, Achilleus sends Patroklos into battle with mixed feelings. He is "greatly troubled" (μέγ' ὀχθήσας, 16.48) when Patroklos entreats him on behalf of the Achaians, taking the side of his current adversaries. Yet he is unable to refuse his closest companion's request to fight off the Trojans, and he demonstrates his exceptional love for Patroklos with his wish that they might storm Troy alone together (16.97–100)[3] and with his prayer to Zeus for his safe return (16.233–48). Though Achilleus allows Patroklos to enter the war, the latter loses his life only after he has defied Achilleus' command not to pursue the Trojans beyond the ships (16.89–96). The poet reminds the audience of this sequence when he reintroduces Achilleus at the very opening of Book 18 observing with unease how the Greek army has been driven into confusion on the field of battle. The hero is again "troubled" (ὀχθήσας, 18.5), fearing that Patroklos may have died while also recalling his order for his companion to refrain from attacking Hektor (6–14). All of this sets the stage for Achilleus to be angry at the dead Patroklos for desiring to fight and disobeying him, and at himself for not protecting his beloved companion. Thus, Achilleus' severe "melancholia" seems to

Achilleus' mourning. Moreover, the couplet that was applied to Kebriones also occurs in *Od.* 24.39–40 in the description of Achilleus' own corpse by Agamemnon's shade, and Neo-analytic critics have interpreted this epic language as traditionally associated with Achilleus' death in pre-Homeric narratives (for discussion and bibliography, see Edwards 1991: 145–46 and Rutherford 2019: 98–99). If this is the case, then appearance of this formula in Homer's marked initial account of Achilleus' mourning would help to indicate Achilleus' deep identification with his dead companion and establish a link between Patroklos' and Achilleus' deaths. Cf. Shay 1994: 51–53, who argues that Achilleus' mourning reflects a feeling of being already dead typical of soldiers who suffer from post-traumatic stress disorder, often after being bereaved of a friend-in-arms.

[2] For defense of these lines' authenticity, see Rutherford 2019: 100–1. On Achilleus' self-punishment and suicidal intentions here, see also Shay 1994: 50.

[3] See Warwick 2019b: 119–20 on the powerful and exclusive passion implied by these lines, which differs from the normal "warrior friendship" and troubled ancient commentators.

manifest the extreme ambivalence of his longing for Patroklos, which is defined at once by great affection and resentment. Homer's focus on Achilleus' complex grief, and the mind reading that this activates, may encourage us anew to empathize with the suffering hero.

The subsequent arrival of Achilleus' mother Thetis securely connects the hero's loss of Patroklos with his previous loss of Briseis and begins to establish this scene as a parallel, yet amplified, desire-fueled narrative beginning.[4] In both Book 1 and Book 18, Thetis emerges from the sea in reaction to her son's grief and asks, "child, why do you weep? What pain has come to your heart? Speak it out, do not hide it" (1.362–63 = 18.73–74). And in each case, the narrator introduces Achilleus' reply with an identical formulaic line: "Then swift-footed Achilleus addressed her, groaning heavily" (1.364 = 18.78). On this second occasion, however, Thetis' own distress is augmented: she laments her son's pain and mortality in the company of her numerous Nereid sisters before coming to his side (18.35–64), and she takes her son's head in her arms (18.71) rather than merely stroking him by the hand (1.361). Thetis' acute pity for Achilleus may provide a model for the audience's response and help to engender our own sympathy for the hero whose suicidal impulse has already testified to the particular power and authenticity of his new suffering.[5]

The ensuing conversation between Thetis and Achilleus shows how the hero's grievous longing for Patroklos has eclipsed his original triangular desires. After asking Achilleus to explain his sorrow, Thetis observes that Zeus has accomplished his prayer for the worsting of the Greeks during his absence from battle (18.74–77); she wonders why Achilleus is still in pain though his desire for revenge against the Achaians for Briseis' removal has been fulfilled. Achilleus explains that the enormity of his new loss keeps him from deriving satisfaction from making the Greeks suffer: "truly the Olympian has accomplished these things, but what pleasure do I have of them, since my close companion has perished (ὤλεθ'), Patroklos, whom I honored above all my companions, equally to myself? I have lost (ἀπώλεσα) him..." (79–82).[6] This interchange not only draws attention to Achilleus' overriding new libidinal focus on Patroklos but also invites us to

[4] On the modified parallelism of Thetis' encounter with Achilleus in Books 1 and 18 and its implications, see also Reinhardt 1961: 368–73 and especially Rutherford 2019: 2–3. On the common "libidinal structure" informing Achilleus' relationships with both Briseis and Patroklos, see generally Staten 1995: 30.

[5] See also Edwards 1991: 44, who writes "it is essential that we appreciate the depth of Achilleus' grief for [Patroklos] so that we may understand, and perhaps sympathize with, his later barbaric behaviour toward Hektor's corpse."

[6] The verb ἀπώλεσα could mean either "I have lost him" (as rendered above) or "I have destroyed him"; the latter would constitute a clear admission of responsibility on Achilleus' part for Patroklos' death. Both Edwards 1991: 155 and Rutherford 2019: 112 agree that it may be going too far to assume the second meaning here, particularly given Achilleus' more neutral use of the un-prefixed version of the verb (ὤλεθ') above; I would add that Achilleus immediately brings up Hektor's culpability in his next phrase, reporting that Hektor stripped Patroklos' armor, "having slayed him" (δῃώσας, 18.83). At

contemplate how the hero's present grief ironically derives from the realization of his previous aggressive desire,[7] in yet another extension of the spiral of loss and desire introduced in Book 1. Comprehending this causality may augment the audience's pity for Achilleus, insofar as he appears now as a "tragic" character who suffers through his own error.

In this speech to his mother, Achilleus also articulates how his new longing for Patroklos is paired with an aggressive desire for revenge against his companion's killer. Immediately after acknowledging Patroklos' death, he introduces Hektor by name and declares that he slew and stripped Patroklos (18.82–83), and a few lines later he asserts, "my heart does not bid me to live, nor to remain among men, unless Hektor first loses his life, struck by my spear, and pays retribution for the slaughter of Patroklos" (90–93). Achilleus now positions himself as the desiring subject in a second, exclusively homosocial triangle with Patroklos as the beloved object and Hektor in the position of the rival who has, in this case, permanently separated subject and object of desire.

While Achilleus' description of Hektor's violence against Patroklos parallels his earlier account to Thetis of Agamemnon's seizure of Briseis (1.387–92), here we are given greater insight into the mechanism and meaning of his consequent desires. In Book 1, he at once requests his mother's aid in taking revenge upon Agamemnon and his army, but in Book 18 he meditates on the psychic genesis of his desire for vengeance. When he tells Thetis that killing Hektor is his only way of going on, of side-stepping his melancholic will to die,[8] he elucidates his revenge wish as an external displacement of the aggressive libido associated with Patroklos that he otherwise directs against himself.[9] As Judith Butler (2004: 41) has explained, violence against others is an attempt to reconstitute a self injured by loss. The subject denies his own vulnerability to suffering by imposing that pain and vulnerability on others; he tries to repair himself by undoing another.[10]

While revenge, then, allows for Achilleus' immediate survival, at the same time it represents a path toward the ultimate fulfillment of his death wish. He tells Thetis that she will soon grieve him, never receiving him back home (18.88–90),

the same time, I think that Edwards is right to note the ambiguity of ἀπώλεσα, and Rutherford accurately observes that Achilleus clearly accepts a degree of responsibility for Patroklos' death in his subsequent speeches.

[7] Rutherford 2019: 3. On the relationship between Achilleus' aggression against the Achaians and Patroklos' death, see "Patroklos' *Aristeia*" in Chapter 6.

[8] He reiterates that melancholic desire later in his speech, when he says "may I die at once, since I was not of the mind to keep my companion from being killed" (18.98–99).

[9] See also Murnaghan 1999: 211, who observes, "With Achilleus, the mourner's characteristic wish to die is modified into a resolution to avenge his loss." Cf. Devereux 1978: 9, who declares that "the *only* way Achilleus could cope with his guilt feelings over the death of Patroclus (in which he had connived 'accidentally on purpose') was to put *all* the blame on Hector" (his italics).

[10] Cf. Austin 2021: 64, elucidating the meaning of Achilleus' later comparison in his mourning to a grieving and angry lion pursuing a hunter who has stolen his cubs (18.318–22): "such anger is not necessarily the hope of redressing a wrong, but a response to the inability to redress that wrong, a kind of translation of the inner longing for what is lost into outward action."

gesturing toward the fate that his mother subsequently confirms (95–96): he is destined to die at Troy soon after Hektor is killed, and so slaying the Trojan prince also means setting in motion his own death. Therefore, Achilleus' aggressive desire to avenge himself on Hektor is at once a displacement *and* expression of his self-punishing libidinal response to Patroklos' loss, which both alleviates and serves his self-destructive grief.

Achilleus' second speech to Thetis in Book 18 confirms that his new driving triangular desires supersede his former ones. First, he draws attention to the seductive force of his anger (*cholos*) toward Agamemnon, reflecting on how it led him to abandon his men to be subdued by Hektor and describing it as "much sweeter than honey" (18.102–11). Then, however, Achilleus dismisses that anger together with its concomitant grief in favor of a fresh compulsion (112–15):

> ἀλλὰ τὰ μὲν προτετύχθαι ἐάομεν ἀχνύμενοί περ,
> θυμὸν ἐνὶ στήθεσσι φίλον δαμάσαντες ἀνάγκῃ·
> νῦν δ' εἶμ', ὄφρα φίλης κεφαλῆς ὀλετῆρα κιχείω,
> Ἕκτορα·
>
> But let us allow these things to be over and done with, although we grieve,
> having subdued our own passion (*thumon*) in our breasts by necessity;
> and now I will go so that I may reach the destroyer of my own self,
> Hektor...

Achilleus is ready to master his aggressive desire toward Agamemnon and his sorrow over Briseis' loss in order to pursue his new desire for revenge against Hektor.[11]

When Achilleus goes on to wish that he may bring lamentation to some Trojan woman (18.122–25), he demonstrates how he has thoroughly reoriented his aggression from his Greek male compatriots to the Trojan community writ large. Achilleus intends to transfer his own grief to a female Trojan civilian,[12] just as he has redirected some portion of his aggressive libido from himself toward Hektor. This plan to elicit another's mourning recalls and replaces Achilleus' similar plot in Book 1 to visit back upon Agamemnon and the Greeks the painful desire that they had aroused in him, which he expressed through his vow that the Achaians would experience *pothē* and *achos* because of his withdrawal from battle (1.240–44). Now the Trojans are his new targets.

[11] See also Taplin 1992: 199–200, who recognizes that Achilleus transfers his anger from Agamemnon to Hektor in this speech.

[12] Pucci 1987: 224 and Murnaghan 1999: 211. See also Staten 1995: 38, who observes generally that "Achilleus weeps, and makes women weep, for himself and his loss. To wreak vengeance in the *Iliad* means finally: to be the cause of mourning, to transform the passive affect of grief into the active, compensatory pleasure of inflicting grief upon others and most conclusively upon women."

Achilleus' transformed purpose is also evident when he articulates to Thetis a sudden interest in winning "good fame" (*κλέος ἐσθλόν*) through his return to the war, though imminent death should follow (18.115–21). These remarks recall Achilleus' speech to the embassy in Book 9, when he cited his mother's prophecy of his twin fates: either short life and "imperishable fame" (*κλέος ἄφθιτον*) or a long but obscure life (9.410–16). While Achilleus' earlier alienation from the Greeks and their war effort had left his choice between these destinies ambiguous, here he explicitly chooses death and glory, driven by his fresh desire to destroy his Trojan enemy.[13]

Achilleus' decision constitutes a narrative turning point and represents the initiation of a new arc of the *Iliad*'s plot. While the main plot's first arc had followed the worsting of the Achaians in battle during Achilleus' withdrawal, its second arc relates Achilleus' return to fighting and triumph over the Trojans. Achilleus' new set of triangular desires—aimed at Patroklos and Hektor—motivate this final section of the narrative, just as his original triangular desires—focused on Briseis and Agamemnon—had been the prime impetus for the action up until this juncture. By pointing forward to the hero's re-entrance into the war, Achilleus' new aggressive desire arouses in turn the audience's narrative desire to find out how his glorious revenge will unfold. Our engagement in this final arc of plot will be even stronger if we empathetically share Achilleus' driving desires, and if we sympathetically wish for him to relieve his grief and anger. However, as Pietro Pucci (1987: 224) observes, Achilleus' vision of a weeping Trojan woman is a "crude image." Its brutality may begin to erode our sympathy for Achilleus, and its piteousness may evoke an opposing feeling for his putative Trojan victims, particularly if it reminds us of the sympathetic Andromache longing for Hektor in Book 6. Should this be the case, the audience will already begin to regard Achilleus' new plot with an apprehension that provokes moral reflection.

While this fresh plot is conceived by the desiring hero, it also reflects Zeus's will as enunciated in his second prophecy to Hera (15.68–71), and requires divine cooperation to be actualized. As Thetis reminds Achilleus (18.130–32), he has no armor to wear into battle since Hektor has stripped his old armor from Patroklos' body. In Book 18, Thetis overcomes this obstacle by going to the smith god Hephaistos on her son's behalf and procuring splendid new armor so that Achilleus can re-enter the war. This visit recalls Thetis' successful supplication of Zeus in Book 1, when the divine king agreed to honor her son by empowering the Trojans on the battlefield. Once again, the main plot's second arc parallels its

[13] Taplin 1992: 194 writes that Achilleus' encounter with Thetis in Book 18 "is crucial to the entire poem, and marks his irrevocable turning toward death." See further Rutherford 2019: 5–9 for excellent general discussion of Achilleus' "choice" of an early death.

first arc, and is likewise formulated and realized through the concerted resolve of Achilleus, his immortal mother, and her divine male allies.

But this time Hera also helps Achilleus to accomplish his aggressive desire rather than working against him, since now he wishes to destroy her enemies instead of her friends. Before Thetis returns with new armor, Hera arranges, with the aid of Iris and Athene, for Achilleus to frighten the Trojans from the sidelines so that the Greeks can beat off Hektor and recover Patroklos' body (18.166–242). Hera's intervention on Achilleus' behalf signals to the audience once again that this second narrative arc constitutes a convergence of the *Iliad*'s main plot with its Trojan War superplot. While Zeus's divine will has been responsible for bringing to fruition the first arc of Achilleus' main plot, Hera's desire for Troy's fall has been the main divine motivator of continued Greek aggression in the superplot; now the wills of the king and queen of the gods definitively coalesce.

Homer highlights this development with a brief scene in which Zeus observes that Hera has "roused up Achilleus," and Hera responds with a defense of her prerogative as angry divine queen "to stitch together evils for the Trojans" (18.356–67). In this interchange, Zeus acknowledges how Hera's desire is helping to drive Achilleus' return, while Hera connects her intervention with her hostility toward the Trojans, familiar from the superplot. While Zeus's tone is antagonistic, he does not censure Hera, nor does he take any action to reverse her involvement in this new narrative arc. Zeus has tacitly consented for Hera to facilitate the fulfillment of Achilleus' plot for revenge against Hektor and thus to ensure the final defeat of the Trojans.

An Incomplete and Unsatisfactory Resolution

Once Thetis arrives with freshly fashioned armor at the beginning of Book 19, she tells Achilleus to call an assembly of the Achaians and publicly repudiate his anger against Agamemnon before preparing for battle (19.34–36). In addition to the help of the gods, Achilleus needs the backing of his Greek army in order to pursue his revenge plot—he cannot, after all, attack the Trojans singlehandedly and hope for success, even if he is "the best of the Achaians." He must, therefore, reconcile with the leader of the Greek army, Agamemnon.[14] This reconciliation (19.40–275), during which Achilleus renounces his wrath and Agamemnon returns Briseis and provides the gifts promised by the embassy in Book 9, resolves the conflict between Achilleus and Agamemnon that began in Book 1 and constituted the first arc of the *Iliad*'s main plot.

[14] On expediency rather than newfound solidarity as motivation for Achilleus' reconciliation with Agamemnon, see also Sinos 1980: 42–44; Schein 1984: 139–40; Nimis 1987: 35; Coray 2016: 37, 43.

The poet formally signals this long-desired resolution to his audience in two ways. First, as many scholars have observed, Book 19 repeats in reverse key events from Book 1. Achilleus and Agamemnon quarrel during the Achaian assembly in Book 1, but make peace during the parallel assembly in Book 19, both of which are called by Achilleus; Agamemnon sends a delegation to take Briseis from Achilleus' tent in Book 1, and a delegation to bring her back to the tent in Book 19.[15]

Second, this successful reconciliation—unlike the failed embassy of Book 9[16]—replicates in many ways the Greek army's paradigmatic reconciliation with Chryses and appeasement of Apollo (1.430–87).[17] In both cases, Odysseus, at Agamemnon's direction, leads a group of young Achaians in returning an abducted woman and providing additional reparation to the injured party; in Book 19, they bring Briseis and Agamemnon's compensatory gifts to the middle of the agora, the center of the Achaian community, in a secular variation on how in Book 1 they had led Chryseis and a hecatomb to the altar of Apollo's temple in Chryse. The cores of both reconciliation scenes rest on the performance of appropriate ritual: in Book 1, Chryses prays to Apollo to end the plague while presiding over the sacrifice of the hecatomb, after which those present feast on the offering; in Book 19, Agamemnon swears that he was not physically intimate with Briseis over the sacrifice of a boar, after which Achilleus formally absolves Agamemnon of wrongdoing and bids the Achaian army to eat in preparation for battle. This mirroring in Book 19 of the reconciliation pattern in Book 1 satisfies the audience's narrative desire for the end of the main plot's first arc.

Yet this scene's lack of other important elements of Chryses' paradigm indicates the incompleteness of this narrative resolution. First, Achilleus diverges from the pattern of Chryses in his treatment of Briseis. In Book 1, the priest joyfully receives his daughter Chryseis into his hands (1.446–47), but in Book 19 Achilleus repudiates and all but rejects Briseis. He begins his speech during the assembly by rhetorically asking whether it was good for him and Agamemnon "to rage (μενεήναμεν) in heart-devouring strife for the sake of a girl," and then wishes that Artemis had killed Briseis when he first took her as his slave so that so many Achaians had not died while he was angry (19.56–62). With these words, Achilleus "scapegoat[s] the female Other" as the cause of Greek deaths in order to reconcile with Agamemnon and thus pursue his revenge against Hektor.[18] In so doing, he regrets and essentially gainsays his desire for Briseis, and clarifies this

[15] Lohmann 1970: 173–74; Edwards 1991: 239; Rabel 1997: 178–79. Cf. Arend 1933: 117, who notes that the assembly in Book 19 is an "augmentation" (*Steigerung*) of the assembly in Book 1.

[16] Schadewaldt 1966: 131–34 argues for an intimate connection between Books 9 and 19 in opposition to the Analytical view that Book 9 is a late interpolation. Louden 2006: 124 suggests that Book 19 presents the ideal because most efficacious version of the delegation motif exhibited in Books 1, 9, and 19.

[17] See also Edwards 1991: 263, Louden 2006: 123–25, and Coray 2016: 110 on the similarities of the two episodes.

[18] Suzuki 1989: 26.

position by demanding neither her return nor compensation for her loss. When Agamemnon, unprompted, offers Achilleus both Briseis and the many gifts previously promised by the embassy (19.138–44), the hero declares that he does not care whether he is awarded the gifts or not (147–48); Odysseus has to insist that Achilleus allow the ritual reparation (172–83), that is, fulfill Chryses' paradigm.[19] All the same, the hero refrains from personally receiving or acknowledging Briseis in Book 19. She is brought with the other gifts to the assembly (243–49) and then led by Myrmidons to his tent (278–80) without interaction with Achilleus himself. Even more significantly, Achilleus does not have sex with Briseis despite her return. He sleeps with her again only at the moment of his narrative exit just before the end of the *Iliad* (24.675–76).

Achilleus' second departure from the reconciliation paradigm comes in his refusal of food. In Book 1, Chryses participates fully in the Achaians' sacrifice, including the cooking of the meat (1.462), and there is no reason to suspect that he does not also eat the meal; the narrator seems to include everyone there as subjects of the third-person verb denoting the sharing of the feast (δαίνυντ', 468). In contrast to this commensality, Achilleus pointedly declines to eat with—or without—the Greeks in Book 19. When Odysseus bids Achilleus to allow the Achaian soldiers to take food before battle (19.160–70) and to share a "feast" (δαιτί) provided by Agamemnon (179–80), Achilleus argues that the Greeks should fight first and eat later, and declares that he will not consume food or drink before resuming battle (205–10). Odysseus' subsequent insistence that they all take sustenance before fighting (225–33) results in Achilleus sending the men to their meal (275). But he refuses again to eat himself when the Achaian elders beg him to do so (303–8). Ultimately, the concerned gods fortify the hero with ambrosia and nectar (340–54).

The *Iliad*'s emphasis on Achilleus' rejection of both Briseis and nourishment suggests the symbolic importance of these twin self-denials.[20] One way to understand Achilleus' asceticism is in terms of the epic's thematics of desire.[21] In the

[19] Cf. Wilson 2002: 118–20, who argues that Achilleus never actually accepts the gifts because he does not want to "accept a dependent position in relation to Agamemnon." He does, however, get the gifts, and according to Wilson, their receipt restores his status without rendering him subordinate to the giver.

[20] Thetis will later link together these two acts of abstinence when she asks Achilleus, "my child, until when, mourning and grieving, will you eat out your heart, remembering neither food nor bed at all?" (24.128–30). See "Approaching the End" in Chapter 8.

[21] Other scholars plausibly interpret Achilleus' abstentions as signs of his departure from normal humanity during his mourning and revenge. Nagler 1974: 174–80 identifies food and sex (along with sleep and bathing) as basic human needs, and reads Achilleus' self-denials as indications of his inhumanity in his inconsolable grief over Patroklos' death. Schein 1984: 139–40 links Achilleus' refusal to eat in Book 19 with his superhuman, "daimonic" characterization in Books 18–22. Edwards 1987: 58 suggests that Achilleus' eventual retirement to bed with Briseis in Book 24 shows "that he has accepted the normal standards of human behavior, urged on him by his doting mother." Grethlein 2005 shows how Achilleus' fasting is associated with his narrative assimilation to both the divine and the beastly: instead of participating in the civilized sharing of agricultural products, he is fed nectar and ambrosia and also acts like a wild animal on the hunt for raw meat.

Iliad, Homer repeatedly connects sex and the consumption of food with desire's resolution. Afflicted by overwhelming lust (*erōs*) and yearning (*himeros*), Paris and Zeus propose, and then achieve, the satisfaction of sexual union (*philotēs*) (3.441–47; 14.314–53). The formula that commonly concludes the description of a Homeric meal expresses how eating fulfills—or, more specifically, negates—desire: "but after they put away their lust (*eron*) for drink and food..." (αὐτὰρ ἐπεὶ πόσιος καὶ ἐδητύος ἐξ ἔρον ἕντο).[22] Achilleus explicitly conceives of eating as a kind of satiation when he tells the Greek elders, "do not bid me beforehand with food nor drink to sate my heart (ἄσασθαι φίλον ἦτορ) since horrible grief (ἄχος αἰνόν) has come to me; rather, I will hold out and endure all the same until the sun sets" (19.306–8). I suggest that Achilleus' unwillingness to satisfy or "put away" desires for sex and food is meant, first, to underscore the narrative irresolution of his reconciliation with Agamemnon and, second, to highlight the ongoing motivating force of his longing for Patroklos and desire to kill Hektor.

Achilleus' reply to the Greek elders communicates how his abstinence from nourishment is connected with his intense mourning and aggressive desire for revenge: his "horrible grief" (ἄχος αἰνόν) keeps him from eating until he has spent the day fighting. Likewise, when he refuses sustenance during the assembly, Achilleus explains that he is preoccupied by Patroklos' unburied body and consumed by a thirst for blood (19.209–14):

> πρὶν δ' οὔ πως ἂν ἔμοιγε φίλον κατὰ λαιμὸν ἰείη
> οὐ πόσις οὐδὲ βρῶσις, ἑταίρου τεθνηῶτος,
> ὅς μοι ἐνὶ κλισίῃ δεδαϊγμένος ὀξέϊ χαλκῷ
> κεῖται ἀνὰ πρόθυρον τετραμμένος, ἀμφὶ δ' ἑταῖροι
> μύρονται· τό μοι οὔ τι μετὰ φρεσὶ ταῦτα μέμηλεν,
> ἀλλὰ φόνος τε καὶ αἷμα καὶ ἀργαλέος στόνος ἀνδρῶν.
>
> Beforehand, there is no way it would pass down my throat,
> neither drink nor food, with my companion dead,
> who, in my tent, torn by the sharp bronze
> lies turned toward the doorway, and around him my companions mourn;
> therefore, these things are of no concern to me in my mind,
> but rather slaughter and blood and the painful groaning of men.

Here Achilleus testifies that anguish over Patroklos' death and craving for brutal vengeance dominate his psyche, pushing aside and replacing his other appetites. As Rana Liebert (2017: 97) explains, Achilleus "sustains himself on the painful emotions that in turn 'feed' on him by co-opting all of his desires and directing

[22] The line-formula appears seven times in the *Iliad* (1.469, 2.432, 7.323, 9.92, 9.222, 23.57, 24.628).

them at substitute nourishment: blood and gore."[23] Until he can begin killing Trojans, the mourning hero brooks no satisfaction of any kind.

Later, Achilleus confirms that we should understand his abstinence as a sign of unfulfilled desire. In his lament over Patroklos following the assembly—which he speaks instead of turning his attention to Briseis—Achilleus declares, "my heart is fasting from drink and food, though they are within, because of longing (*pothēi*) for you" (ἐμὸν κῆρ/ ἄκμηνον πόσιος καὶ ἐδητύος, ἔνδον ἐόντων,/ σῇ ποθῇ, 19.319–21). Now, finally, the hero explicitly acknowledges his desire for his lost companion and pinpoints it as the reason for his refusal to eat. Thus, Achilleus reveals his fasting to be another melancholic mourning practice that manifests how he is identifying with Patroklos and self-destructively turning against himself the aggressive libido that is tied up with his love for his companion.

Achilleus' dramatic naming of his *pothē* not only draws attention to this desire as the force underlying his mourning but also makes it intelligible. It now has substance and shape as a protracted longing for Patroklos' unique person that dwells in absence, feeds on memory of a shared life, and has no end in sight[24]—unlike Achilleus' more insubstantial and undefined desire for Briseis, which remained unnamed and implicit. This identification also gives the hero's desire context: it is the kind of longing men feel in the *Iliad* for a leading warrior who is missing or dead, and specifically recalls the *pothē* that Achilleus promised to inflict upon the Achaian army through his withdrawal from battle (1.240). That *pothē* has now rebounded reciprocally back on himself since it has resulted—through Patroklos relieving the Greeks' longing by fighting in his place—in his own *pothē* for his lost companion. Thus, this term marks Achilleus' desire for Patroklos as thematic within the *Iliad* and lays bare the ironic causality of that longing.

Achilleus' desire-fueled grief, and the single-minded focus on joining battle that accompanies it, are elements foreign to Chryses' reconciliation paradigm. In Book 1, after the sacrificial feast, the Achaian youths celebrate and propitiate Apollo all day with dance and song, then go to bed (1.472–76). In Book 19, although the Greeks do "rejoice" (ἐχάρησαν, 19.74) when Achilleus first renounces his wrath,[25] after Agamemnon's sacrifice and their meal, they arm for battle and muster brilliantly before the ships (351–64). Here preparation for fighting in the service of Achilleus' revenge takes the place of peaceful festivities and repose. In Book 1, Apollo "took pleasure" (τέρπετ') hearing the Achaians' music (1.474). Likewise, after the assembly in Book 19, Nestor, Idomeneus, and Phoinix try to

[23] Liebert 2017: 95 writes further, "Homeric anger desires revenge as an appetitive need . . . Anger hungers for blood and flesh rather than water and food, which are typically rejected by the aggrieved and bereaved in favor of this more gruesome sustenance." See also Monsacré 1984: 189–90 and Coray 2016: 97; 141.

[24] See Austin 2021: 17–32 on the meaning of *pothē* in the *Iliad*.

[25] See also Nagy 1979: 92 on how the Achaians' "mirth" here constitutes the reversal of their thematic grief (*achos*), which was brought upon them by Achilleus' wrath.

"pleasure" (τέρποντες, 19.312) Achilleus, but they are unsuccessful: "*in no way* did he take pleasure in his heart before entering the mouth of bloody war" (οὐδέ τι θυμῷ/ τέρπετο, πρὶν πολέμου στόμα δύμεναι αἱματόεντος, 312–13). Instead of enjoying himself after the reconciliation, Achilleus returns to mourning and gives the speech of lamentation where he articulates his *pothē* for Patroklos. Then he joins the Achaians in arming to pursue his aggressive desire for vengeance (364–98). Even as Achilleus' lack of pleasure once again signals his dissatisfaction and the irresolution of this reconciliation scene, the thematization of his newfound driving triangular desires throughout Book 19 further encourages our empathy with and sympathy for the hero, and activates our narrative desire to comprehend the contours and meaning of his mourning and revenge.

The Queerness of Achilleus' Attachment to Patroklos

Just as Homer portrays Achilleus as a queer subject in his deviant withdrawal from battle over Briseis' loss, the poet also marks him as queer in the unheroic, antisocial, and feminized mourning that Patroklos' loss provokes. This non-normative mourning extends the epic's larger portrayal of Achilleus' relationship with Patroklos as queer in its realization off the battlefield and away from the other Greeks, and in its resemblance to and replacement of a heterosexual conjugal bond. The queerness of Achilleus' attachment to Patroklos accounts for why his second set of triangular desires are even more socially destructive—and generative of martial epic—than the first.

The queerness of Achilleus' longing for Patroklos begins to be thematized in relation to the hero's grief-stricken rejection of food in Book 19. During the assembly, Odysseus critiques Achilleus' refusal to eat as incompatible with normative heroic masculinity (19.225–33):

> *γαστέρι δ' οὔ πως ἔστι νέκυν πενθῆσαι Ἀχαιούς·*
> *λίην γὰρ πολλοὶ καὶ ἐπήτριμοι ἤματα πάντα*
> *πίπτουσιν· πότε κέν τις ἀναπνεύσειε πόνοιο;*
> *ἀλλὰ χρὴ τὸν μὲν καταθάπτειν ὅς κε θάνῃσι,*
> *νηλέα θυμὸν ἔχοντας, ἐπ' ἤματι δακρύσαντας·*
> *ὅσσοι δ' ἂν πολέμοιο περὶ στυγεροῖο λίπωνται,*
> *μεμνῆσθαι πόσιος καὶ ἐδητύος, ὄφρ' ἔτι μᾶλλον*
> *ἀνδράσι δυσμενέεσσι μαχώμεθα νωλεμὲς αἰεί,*
> *ἑσσάμενοι χροῒ χαλκὸν ἀτειρέα.*

> There is no way for the Achaians to lament a corpse with their bellies;
> for too many, one after another, fall every day.
> When would one take a breath from labor?

> But they must bury the one who dies,
> having pitiless hearts, after weeping for one day;
> and as many as survive the hateful war
> must remember drink and food, so that still more
> we may fight our enemies ceaselessly, always,
> having drawn weariless bronze about our skin.

Here Odysseus argues that Greek warriors properly limit the extent and nature of their mourning over dead companions in order to fulfill their imperative to continue fighting. Since he cannot long afford to refrain from battle, the normative hero grieves only briefly before burying his companion, and makes sure to eat and drink so that he is physically sustained for further combat.[26] Therefore, when Achilleus insists on fasting, he privileges mourning above performing optimally on the battlefield, in a departure from normative masculinity.

Achilleus' abstention from food is also queer insofar as it represents his continued social detachment from the community of Achaian warriors. Stephen Nimis (1987: 33) explains that "sharing a meal functions as an expression of social harmony, the physical and spiritual continuity of a group which is dedicated to some concerted action." As he elucidates further, commensality "reaffirms one's commitment to a community against the claims of some other attachment which conflicts with the best interests of the group."[27] Achilleus' refusal to eat with the other Achaians, then, signals not only his persistent dissatisfaction but also his ongoing alienation from the Greek army as he is consumed by his personal longing for Patroklos and desire to kill Hektor. As we have seen, solidarity between fellow warriors is an heroic norm; in its self-involvement and self-isolation, Achilleus' fasting is deviant.

Achilleus' separation from the rest of the army in his abstinent mourning for Patroklos is consistent with the epic's larger representation of the two men's relationship as a queer alternative to Achilleus' participation in the Greek collective. Patroklos is first introduced into the *Iliad* at the very moment when the angry Achilleus leaves the Greek assembly after his quarrel with Agamemnon: "the son of Peleus went to the tents and balanced ships with the son of Menoitios [Patroklos] and his companions" (1.306–7). When Agamemnon's heralds appear to take away Briseis, Achilleus orders Patroklos to hand her over (1.337–38);

[26] With this speech, Odysseus expands on his earlier contention that a man grows weak without food "even if he desires (*μενοινάᾳ*) in his heart to make war," but "whoever satiates himself (*κορεσσάμενος*) on wine and food makes war all day against his enemies" (19.164–68). Coray 2016: 86 observes that *κορεσσάμενος* "denotes the purely physical process of sating oneself, in contrast to expressions with *τέρπεσθαι*." Odysseus, then, seems to be arguing that physical satisfaction can coincide with the raging of mental desire, a proposition that Achilleus rejects.

[27] Nimis 1987: 39. See also Schein 1984: 139 and Grethlein 2005: 257–58.

Patroklos thus comes to the fore in the moment of Briseis' departure, the event that cements Achilleus' alienation from the other Achaians.

Patroklos appears with Achilleus again, as we have seen, in Book 9, when Agamemnon's embassy finds him listening to the hero playing the lyre and singing in his tent. Cloistered together away from the rest of the army, the two men seem to constitute a society unto themselves, and this alternative social world feels both self-contained and complete.[28] Later, Achilleus confirms this perception with his wish that all the other Trojans and Greeks might perish, and that he and Patroklos alone might storm Troy (16.97–100). In that passage, Achilleus imagines fighting with Patroklos at his side, and elsewhere he suggests that they have fought together in the past (16.243–45, 24.7–8), but in the *Iliad* the two men never go into battle as a pair.[29] Their relationship is realized away from the normative Iliadic masculine space of the battlefield, in Achilleus' private quarters.

In this and several other ways, their tie is more similar to conjugal bonds in the *Iliad* than to the typical pairing of Homeric warriors.[30] In their intimate seclusion, Achilleus and Patroklos mirror the queer spouses Paris and Helen, who appear together in their bedroom in Books 3 and 6, as well as the husband-and-wife pair Meleagros and Kleopatra, who sit out the war together in Phoinix's tale from Book 9. As we have seen, Homer seems to intend for Kleopatra to evoke Patroklos in the minds of the audience, and for her pivotal role in convincing Meleagros to re-enter battle to foreshadow Patroklos' agency in bringing Achilleus back into the war. Indeed, Patroklos' plea to Achilleus to go out and fight (16.21–45) recalls not only Kleopatra's similar entreaty of Meleagros (9.590–94) but also Helen's urging of Paris to return to the battlefield (6.337–38, 363). In addition to resembling Kleopatra and Helen vis-à-vis their husbands, Patroklos, in his oppositional stance toward Achilleus in Book 16, is functionally parallel to the divine queen Hera in her challenge to her husband Zeus. Insofar as Achilleus' relationship with Patroklos is the only male–male bond that resembles these spousal pairs, it appears to depart from the norm for masculine ties.

Moreover, their relationship not only recalls heterosexual couplings in the *Iliad*—it also replaces them. As we have seen, Patroklos appears with Achilleus when Briseis, whom Achilleus describes as his "wife" (*ἄλοχον*) and compares to Menelaos' wife Helen (9.336–43), is absent. In the Greek camp at Troy, Patroklos

[28] Fantuzzi 2012: 196–98. Despite the narrowing of narrative focus onto Achilleus and Patroklos, the two men are not completely alone, since other members of Achilleus' household appear later in the embassy scene: Automedon, another heroic attendant, is mentioned once (9.209), and, at the end of the episode, Achilleus and Patroklos go to sleep with their respective concubines (9.663–68).

[29] Cf. Austin 2021: 40, who writes "It is a peculiar beauty of the poem that we never see Achilles and Patroklos fighting together, yet we are constantly aware that such was their normal state. Thus, when Patroklos goes out to fight without Achilles, we feel the absence of what should be there."

[30] See Warwick 2019b, whose powerful argument I augment here with additional evidence and discussion. On men in pairs as a standard feature of the epic's battlefield landscape, see MacCary 1982: 129–34. A hero generally relies on a companion while fighting, whether that companion is a subordinate attendant (*therapōn*) driving his chariot or a peer providing support.

oversees the operation of Achilleus' household, directing male comrades and slave women to make up a bed for Phoinix on Achilleus' orders (9.658–59). In so doing, he performs a duty that at home might be the responsibility of the hero's wife—if he had one.[31] Later, for example, Hektor's wife Andromache bids her slave women to prepare a bath for her husband's return from battle, unaware that he will never come back alive (22.442–46).

Patroklos takes Briseis' place not only living, but also dead. As we have seen, Achilleus, overwhelmed by his grievous longing for Patroklos and aggressive desire to take revenge on Hektor, renounces the similar triangular desires he had previously directed at Briseis and Agamemnon. As Celsiana Warwick (2019b: 125) has observed, Achilleus thus positions Patroklos at the top of his "ascending scale of affections," the place normally occupied by a hero's wife, "thus flouting the natural order of things." Patroklos' loss is what clarifies the queer dominance of Achilleus' same-sex bond over the heterosexual relationship to which it is compared. While Patroklos was alive, Achilleus also engaged in sexual relations with women,[32] but after he dies, the hero eschews a sexual reunion with Briseis in favor of mourning his companion.

Although Patroklos seems to play the role of Achilleus' wife in the hero's tent, once Patroklos enters battle and is killed, Achilleus takes the gender-deviant feminine part. Watching ambivalently from the sidelines as his companion sallies forth to defend the camp, Achilleus resembles Helen and Andromache, willingly and unwillingly sending off their husbands to battle at the end of Book 6. After Patroklos dies, Achilleus likewise seems to adopt a feminine role when he delivers spoken laments for his companion.[33] He is the only man in the *Iliad* whose mourning speeches are prefaced with the formula "began the lament" (*ἐξῆρχε γόοιο*, 18.316; 23.17);[34] elsewhere women lead lamentation, specifically mothers (Thetis and Hekabe),[35] a wife (Andromache), and a sister-in-law (Helen).[36] Homer draws a particular parallel between Achilleus' mourning over Patroklos

[31] Clarke 1978: 390 and Halperin 1990: 84. Warwick 2019b:120 suggests that it is normative for a male attendant to perform such duties during a campaign (when the wife remains at home), observing that Automedon takes on this role after Patroklos' death (24.625–26), but it is noteworthy that Homer only portrays this quasi-domestic heroic practice in association with Achilleus. When Agamemnon entertains the kings in his tent (2.402–32, 23.35–56), no male attendant is singled out.

[32] Achilleus presumably had sexual relations with Briseis before her seizure by Agamemnon. After Briseis is taken away, Achilleus sleeps with a different concubine, Diomede, while Patroklos beds down with his own concubine, Iphis (9.663–68).

[33] Clarke 1978: 389; Staten 1995: 43; Warwick 2019a: 8. See also van Wees 1998: 14–15, who observes that formal lamenting is usually done by women, and Tsagalis 2004: 68, who calls the lament "a female-dominated genre."

[34] Murnaghan 1999: 210 and Tsagalis 2004: 61.

[35] As Warwick 2019a explores, Achilleus has implicitly set himself up as a mother figure already through maternal similes (9.323–27; 16.7–10). See also Pucci 2018: 86 on how the maternal simile of Book 16 "implies a domestic context and feminization of both characters."

[36] *Il.* 18.51, 22.430, 24.723, 24.747, 24.761. See also *Il.* 6.500 and 22.476 for Andromache's spoken laments described with the verb *γοόω*.

and Andromache's mourning over her husband Hektor: both cradle the heads of their deceased loved ones during their respective funerals (23.136–37; 24.724).[37]

Briseis' own lament over Patroklos after she has returned to Achilleus' tent (19.287–300) puts into relief the queerness of Achilleus' grieving. Briseis' speech is marked since it is the first and only time we hear her voice in the epic; the fact that her unique utterance comes in the form of lamentation helps to associate this genre with the feminine. Moreover, Briseis speaks here not only for herself: she is also made to stand in for Andromache, the *Iliad*'s paradigmatic mourning wife. Along with Patroklos' death, Briseis laments the prior deaths of her husband and three brothers, and the sacking of her city; and she specifies Achilleus as the killer of her husband. As many critics have observed, this autobiographical narrative echoes Andromache's own recital to Hektor of how Achilleus slew her father and seven brothers when he sacked her home of Thebe (6.414–23).[38] The only substantive difference in Briseis' and Andromache's life stories is that Achilleus has killed Briseis' *husband*, but Andromache's *father*. Yet this discrepancy serves to remind the audience of Andromache's fear for her *husband* Hektor's safety and her anticipatory mourning for him in Book 6. Briseis' evocation of Andromache[39] in her lament over Patroklos therefore invites the audience to compare the similarly mourning Achilleus with both women.

Through Briseis, furthermore, Homer links Achilleus' transgressive mourning with his coming ravaging of the Trojan social fabric. Briseis' recital of her grievous personal history thematizes Achilleus' destructive potential, revealing how he is capable of wrecking marriages, families, and cities when he fights. At the same time, her similarity to the anguished Andromache reminds the audience of Zeus's prophecy of Hektor's death at the hands of Achilleus (15.68) as well as Achilleus' own recently expressed intention to take revenge on Hektor and so make a Trojan woman lament (18.114–15, 122–25). Briseis' speech augments our narrative desire to see how Achilleus' violence will unfold and our countervailing dread regarding Hektor's death, even as it suggests the queerness of the mourning that produces his epic revenge.

Briseis' lament also highlights for a final time how Achilleus' longing for Patroklos has supplanted his parallel desire for her. Briseis' marked speaking emphasizes her return to Achilleus' household and brings into focus Achilleus' failure to acknowledge her presence. This failure is underlined by the narrator's alluring description of Briseis as "like to golden Aphrodite" (*ἰκέλη χρυσέῃ*

[37] Halperin 1990: 84 and Warwick 2019b: 121. See also van Wees 1998: 15, who notes the abnormality of how "it is men, led by Achilleus himself, who are the most prominent mourners" of Patroklos.

[38] Reinhardt 1961: 52; MacCary 1982: 108; Dué 2002: 12–14, 67–72; Tsagalis 2004: 141–42; Coray 2016: 135–36.

[39] As Suzuki 1989: 29 observes, Briseis, in her renewed identity as Achilleus' slave, also evokes Andromache's future slavery as it was imagined by Hektor in Book 6.

Ἀφροδίτῃ, 19.282).[40] During her lament, Briseis remembers how Patroklos promised that he would make her Achilleus' "wedded wife" (κουριδίην ἄλοχον), a comment that underscores by contrast Achilleus' present indifference to her,[41] even as it may constitute an attempt to re-entice him. In this way, Briseis articulates her own marginalization as Achilleus' new triangular desires consume him and dominate the narrative.

Indeed, the narrator indicates the movement of narrative focus away from Briseis even as he introduces her speaking subjectivity: her name "Briseis" is replaced by "Patroklos," the object of her vision and lamentation, in the next line (19.282–83). Achilleus' following antiphonal lament over his companion (315–37) not only corresponds structurally and thematically to Briseis' lament,[42] but it also coopts, answers, and overwhelms Briseis' voice.[43] At the same time, it represents a return to his posture in Book 18 and the beginning of Book 19, where he lay weeping over Patroklos' body; Achilleus' queer mourning over Patroklos thus envelops and ultimately obscures the narrative reappearance of Briseis. In this way the poet firmly dismisses Briseis as desired object of both Achilleus and the audience, while redirecting the audience's empathetic and narrative desires toward the completion of the hero's mourning and avenging of Patroklos.

Although Homer never portrays Achilleus' bond with Patroklos as explicitly sexual, Warwick (2019b) argues that Achilleus' supreme valuation of Patroklos and their relationship's association with conjugal ties imply its eroticism.[44] Whether or not we accept this, their bond, as Warwick recognizes, clearly deviates in its form and intensity from normative male homosociality. As she (2019b: 134) concludes, Achilleus' attachment to Patroklos is "part of a larger pattern of

[40] This epithet also sets up Briseis' similarity to Helen and Hera, who respectively inspire Paris' and Zeus's desires through the help of Aphrodite. The narrator's suggestion of Briseis' resemblance to Helen recalls how in Book 9 Achilleus compared his desire for Briseis with Menelaos' desire for Helen, throwing into relief the hero's current lack of interest.

[41] Coray 2016: 137.

[42] Lohmann 1988: 13–21; Pucci 1993; Tsagalis 2004: 49–50, 149–50; Coray 2016: 131–32.

[43] Lohmann 1988: 19 describes Achilleus' lament as "more fully dynamic, more active, more dramatic" (*voller Dynamik, aktiver, dramatischer*) than Briseis' speech. He argues that Achilleus appears to want to "one-up" (*übertrumpfen*) Briseis' lament (20). Murnaghan 1999: 210, however, prefers to regard Achilleus' lamentation as an echo of Briseis', and an expression of his feminization in his withdrawal from the male homosocial world of the battlefield.

[44] Differently, many—if not all—classical Athenians seem to have regarded Achilleus' relationship with Patroklos as an heroic paradigm for their own practice of pederasty, even as they disputed which erotic role (*erastēs* or *erōmenos*) each partner played (on which, see Clarke 1978: 381–386; Barrett 1981: 88–89; Hubbard 2013: 146; Austin 2021: 33–34). Modern scholars, however, have tended to agree that Homer does not represent Achilleus' tie with Patroklos in the age-differentiated, erotically asymmetrical terms of pederasty, even as consensus remains elusive about whether we should understand their relation as homosexual, homoerotic, or as a uniquely intimate—even familial—friendship (see e.g. Clarke 1978; Barrett 1981; Halperin 1990: 83–87; Mauritsch 1992: 115–20; Davidson 2007: 255–84; Hubbard 2013: 146; Austin 2021: 35–38).

Achilles displaying excessive and transgressive affect, which is in keeping with Achilles' violations of social norms elsewhere in the poem." Achilleus consistently feels and acts in queer ways that make him uniquely disruptive of the social order, and, at the same time, especially productive of heroic narrative, as becomes evident during his *aristeia*.

Achilleus' *Aristeia*

After uttering his lament over Patroklos in Book 19, Achilleus pauses his melancholic and deviant mourning, and redirects his aggressive libido almost exclusively at his Trojan enemies for the epic's next three books (20–22). He thus appears to enter into a state of "mania," in which, according to Freud (1957 [1916]: 254–55), the ego has "mastered" or "pushed aside" the complex of mourning, releasing energy and "seeking like a ravenously hungry man for new object-cathexes." Melanie Klein (1994 [1940]: 100–6) has also associated the manic state with denial of psychic pain and guilt, and feelings of omnipotence and triumph over "bad" objects. During this manic period, Achilleus demonstrates his heroic excellence (*aristeia*) on the battlefield, routing the Trojans and killing many of them, including, ultimately, his rival Hektor. By concentrating the narrative on Achilleus and by repeatedly drawing attention to his aggressive desire for revenge, Homer presents that desire as the force driving the *Iliad*'s plot to this climax. Although Achilleus' fighting is more normative than his withdrawal or mourning, his *aristeia* nevertheless also has a queer cast that underscores its violent extremity and confirms the importance of queer behaviors to the generation of the *Iliad*'s devastating epic narrative.

Achilleus' transition from mourning to waging war is marked first by Athene's nourishment of the hero on Zeus's orders with nectar and "desirable" (*ἐρατεινήν*) ambrosia, "so that the hunger that leaves one unsatisfied might not afflict his knees" (*ἵνα μή μιν λιμὸς ἀτερπὴς γούναθ' ἵκοιτο*, 19.352–54). With this act, the gods undo Achilleus' queer fasting, effectively satisfying his desire for food so that he is fit to fight. Yet since this divine sustenance comes irrespective of Achilleus' will, without the hero accepting any satiation, the poet indicates that Achilleus' longing for Patroklos continues unabated.

The following arming scene shows, however, that the aggressive component of his desire is being refocused more normatively away from himself. The hero no longer self-isolates apart from his Achaian compatriots but rather joins them in preparing for battle: "and in the middle of them (*ἐν δὲ μέσσοισι*) brilliant Achilleus put on his helmet" (19.364). As Achilleus dons his armor, Homer explicitly indicates the hero's channeling of his painful longing into aggression with the narrator's successive account of his sorrow and anger: "and unendurable grief (*ἄχος ἄτλητον*) entered into his heart; but, then, raging (*μενεαίνων*) at the Trojans, he put on the gifts of the god" (19.366–67).[45] The reappearance of *meneainō*, the relatively restricted verb of aggressive desire that was last used by Achilleus during his reconciliation with Agamemnon, when he declared "now I am stopping my anger (*χόλον*), since I must not always unceasingly rage (*μενεαινέμεν*)" (19.67–68), underscores how the hero's desirous fury has now found a new target. Moreover, it links Achilleus with Menelaos and the goddess Hera, the first two subjects of this verb in the *Iliad*, who similarly "rage" at Trojans in the epic's superplot (3.379 and 4.32), pointing toward the convergence of the second arc of Achilleus' main plot with the epic's superplot during his coming *aristeia*.

After an extended narration of Achilleus' splendid arming, yoking of his chariot, and conversation with his divine horses about his looming death, which invests the audience in the hero's re-entrance into battle,[46] the narrator begins Book 20 with a neat summary of Achilleus' new positioning and mentality: "Thus beside the curved ships they armed around you, son of Peleus, insatiate of battle, the Achaians" (*ὣς οἵ μὲν παρὰ νηυσὶ κορωνίσι θωρήσσοντο/ αμφὶ σέ, Πηλέος υἱέ, μάχης ἀκόρητον Ἀχαιοί*, 20.1–2). The hero's location in the middle of the sentence, between the article and proper name of the Achaians, textually expresses his reintegration into the Greek collective while also prefiguring his narrative centrality during the impending battle. At the same time, the apostrophe of Achilleus singles him out as a character with especial affinity to the narrator, and suggests the way that he—like the poet himself—will direct the course of the upcoming narrative as lead warrior.[47] Finally, the descriptor "insatiate of battle" constructs Achilleus as a subject of unbounded aggressive desire, thematizing his motivating psychology.[48]

As the Greek and Trojan armies join in battle, spurred on by gods who themselves fight on opposing sides, the poet again features Achilleus' desire and specifies Hektor as its particular focus. After describing the gods facing up against one another, the narrator declares (20.75–78),

> *αὐτὰρ Ἀχιλλεὺς*
> *Ἕκτορος ἄντα μάλιστα λιλαίετο δῦναι ὅμιλον*
> *Πριαμίδεω· τοῦ γάρ ῥα μάλιστά ἑ θυμὸς ἀνώγει*
> *αἵματος ἆσαι Ἄρηα ταλαύρινον πολεμιστήν.*

[45] See also Coray 2016: 165, who recognizes that these lines "create a special atmosphere of aggression that emerges around Achilleus," and Austin 2021: 89, who writes "Throughout this arming scene and entry into war, the listener is actively reminded that this enormous anger has its roots in grief for Patroklos."

[46] Kozak 2017: 185–86.

[47] Frontisi-Ducroux 1986: 23. Patroklos is the character most frequently apostrophized in the *Iliad* (see "Patroklos' *Aristeia*" in Chapter 6), and so this apostrophe may also connect Achilleus with Patroklos. Both men are objects of the narrator's special interest and solicitude. Kozak 2017: 187 suggests that the apostrophe of Achilleus here may "increase the audience's concern for him going into battle, so soon after his horses' prediction of his impending death."

[48] The textual variant *ἀκόρητοι* makes the Achaians "insatiate of battle" instead, taking some of the emphasis away from Achilleus and his desire.

> But Achilleus
> especially desired (*lilaieto*) to enter the throng against Hektor
> son of Priam; for especially his passion (*thumos*) bid him
> to sate (*asai*) the shield-enduring warrior Ares with blood.

The verb *lilaiomai* is a fairly rare and thus notable expression of desire in the *Iliad* that takes both war and sex as its objects;[49] here it emphasizes Achilleus' aggressive wish to engage with Hektor, whose name and patronymic both appear prominently in line-opening position in the Greek text. The poet also highlights Achilleus' aggressive libido with graphic figurative language. The idea of sating Ares with blood metaphorically represents violence in terms of the satiation of hunger or thirst, continuing the substitution of aggressive for alimentary desire that began in Book 19. Here Achilleus' "passion" is conflated with the war god's blood thirstiness, and Hektor's injury or death is established as the circumstance of his satisfaction.

These lines, just before Achilleus begins fighting, not only pinpoint desire to kill Hektor as the basis of his *aristeia* but also establish him as the primary narrative focalizer in the upcoming scenes. In this way, the poet encourages the audience to read Achilleus' mind and see the action through his eyes, and thus invites our empathy with the desiring hero. Empathetic desire will invest us in the upcoming battle narrative and intensify our narrative desire to discover how and when Hektor will die, which is reinvigorated by this account of Achilleus' fervor to fight him.

Homer heightens that narrative desire further by delaying the ultimate encounter between Achilleus and Hektor. In Book 20, Apollo twice foils Achilleus' wish to engage his Trojan rival, in scenes that stress the driving force of Achilleus' aggressive desire and reveal how his *aristeia* constitutes the definitive reemergence of the *Iliad*'s superplot. First, disguised as Lykaon, Apollo goads Aineias into attacking Achilleus (20.79–110). When the two men initially engage, the narrator reports that they "came together, eager to fight" (συνίτην μεμαῶτε μάχεσθαι, 159); the dual participle *memaōte* indicates their mutual aggressive impulse, while the dual main verb signifies the violent joining of two bodies that is the goal of that desire. After Achilleus has pinned Aineias' shield with his spear, the narrator specifically makes note of Achilleus' aggressive libido as he prepares to finish off his enemy: "very eager, he rushed at him, having drawn his sharp sword" (ἐμμεμαὼς ἐπόρουσεν ἐρυσσάμενος ξίφος ὀξύ, 284). Here the poet applies to Achilleus for the first time the more restricted and marked intensive version of

[49] It appears only nine times in the *Iliad*. For war or fighting as objects of *lilaiomai*, see also 3.133, 13.253, 16.89. For its use in sexual contexts, see 3.399 and 14.331. In addition, the verb's participle appears three times in a formulaic phrase that metaphorically describes a spear's desire to sate itself with flesh (11.574, 15.317, 21.168).

the same participle of eagerness that had characterized both men at the beginning of their encounter. The intensive *emmemaōs* will appear three more times in the epic, always as a descriptor of Achilleus at key moments in his *aristeia*. Before Achilleus can strike the fatal blow against Aineias, however, Poseidon takes pity on the Trojan and spirits him away (290–339). Once he realizes what has happened, Achilleus himself voices his frustrated desire using the marked verb *meneainō* ("to rage"): "I do not see at all the man whom I attacked, raging to kill" (κατακτάμεναι μενεαίνων, 345–46).

This whole opening sequence—and particularly its language of desire—is strongly reminiscent of Diomedes' *aristeia* in Book 5. Homer introduced Diomedes' *aristeia* with a simile comparing him to a "very eager" (ἐμμεμαώς) lion (5.142), in the first occurrence of this intensive participle in the epic. Diomedes too encounters Aineias, together with the Trojan Pandaros, early in his *aristeia*, and predicts that one of them will fall and "sate the shield-enduring warrior Ares with blood" (αἵματος ἆσαι Ἄρηα, ταλαύρινον πολεμιστήν, 5.289). His warning constitutes the only appearance of this formulaic expression of sating Ares until the beginning of Achilleus' *aristeia*. Diomedes goes on to kill Pandaros and then wound Aineias, but before he can slay the Trojan prince, Aineias is rescued by the gods (Aphrodite and Apollo), as he will be again in Book 20. Nevertheless, Diomedes attacks three times "raging to kill" (κατακτάμεναι μενεαίνων, 5.436), in an anticipation of Achilleus' psychology, and only yields when Apollo admonishes him on his fourth sally, as he charges "equal to a god" (δαίμονι ἶσος, 438).[50] Achilleus' echo of Diomedes at the outset of his re-entrance into the war signals to the audience that the *Iliad*'s superplot of Greek ascendancy on the Trojan battlefield has returned. But now the main plot's hero, Achilleus, is finally taking his rightful place—formerly occupied by Diomedes and then Patroklos—as the preeminent Greek warrior leading the troops and wreaking havoc on their Trojan enemies. Through the person of Achilleus, the main plot and superplot have merged, to the detriment of the Trojans.

Homer makes this convergence even clearer through the narrative of Achilleus' first, unsuccessful attempt on Hektor's life, which is a doublet of his previous encounter with Aineias. After Achilleus has killed Hektor's brother Polydoros, Hektor's desire for revenge impels him to approach the Greek hero, despite Apollo's earlier command that he avoid Achilleus (20.375–78). Achilleus jumps at the chance to engage with Hektor, articulating how his longing for Patroklos motivates his aggression: "near is the man who especially affected my heart (μάλιστ' ἐσεμάσσατο θυμόν), who killed my honored companion" (425–26). In the following description of Achilleus' attack, the narrator combines in one forceful and dynamic dactylic line the two articulations of aggressive desire

[50] See "Diomedes' *Aristeia*" in Chapter 4.

from Diomedes' *aristeia* that had appeared separately during Achilleus' fight with Aineias: "very eager, he rushed at him, raging to kill" (ἐμμεμαὼς ἐπόρουσε κατακτάμεναι μενεαίνων, 442).

When Apollo, however, snatches Hektor away and covers him in a mist, Achilleus charges at his Trojan adversary three times; on the fourth attempt, attacking "equal to a god" (δαίμονι ἶσος), he recognizes that Apollo has saved Hektor and verbally derides his opponent, promising that he will finish him off when they meet again (20.445–54). This abortive quadruple attack is the final instance of the significant type-scene that appeared not only during Diomedes' *aristeia* (5.436–44)[51] but also twice during Patroklos' *aristeia* (16.698–711; 16.784–93). In each case, Apollo stops the foremost Greek hero from utterly destroying his Trojan enemy. Here this type-scene emphasizes how Achilleus is now leading the Greeks to victory, while also indicating that he has not yet reached the climax of his *aristeia* and the *Iliad*'s narrative. Hektor survives to fight again, and so this episode is a tease that delays the narrative satisfaction of Achilleus' revenge.

It also begins the representation of the Phthian hero as super-human during his *aristeia*. Twice more in his rampage, he is compared to divinity with the formula "equal to a god" (δαίμονι ἶσος, 20.493; 21.18). Additionally, Achilleus seems closer to element than man by way of the fire, light, and star imagery that is repeatedly applied to him as he prepares for and enacts his vengeance against the Trojans.[52] This portrayal of the hero as godlike or a force of nature may help the audience to empathize with him despite the extent and brutality of his violence because it marks him as "larger than life," as an epic character who does not exist in our "real" world. At the same time, in his transcendence of normal humanity—and thus normative masculinity—Achilleus again appears rather queer.[53]

Homer emphasizes this queerness and further encourages the audience's empathy with the hero by presenting him during his *aristeia* as if he were doing battle alone, in isolation from the Greek collective. After Achilleus exhorts every Achaian to "be eager to fight" (μεμάτω δὲ μάχεσθαι, 20.355) and the army joins in battle with the Trojans, the other Greeks all but disappear from the narrative until after the death of Hektor.[54] Jonathan Shay (1994: 86) argues that their absence emphasizes Achilleus' "social detachment" as he is entirely consumed

[51] Moreover, Achilleus' taunting words at Hektor's disappearance repeat exactly Diomedes' speech when Hektor also escapes his attack in Book 11 (20.449–54 = 11.362–67).

[52] *Il.* 18.205–14; 19.359–86; 20.371–72; 20.480–94; 22.25–32; 22.134–35; 22.317–19. On the association of this imagery with Achilleus, see Whitman 1958: 137–44 and King 1987: 15–19.

[53] See also Warwick 2019b: 134, who writes, "Achilles' socially anomalous attachment to Patroclus resonates with his characterization elsewhere in the *Iliad* as an essentially transgressive half-mortal/half-god hybrid who exceeds normal human social boundaries."

[54] The "Achaians" are mentioned once, when the narrator describes them approaching the walls of Troy with their shields (22.3–4).

by the desire to kill.[55] Even as he rejoins the war, then, Achilleus seems to retain his queer alienation from his fellow soldiers and to become something other and greater than they, endowed with extraordinary will and power to destroy. Additionally, the narrowing of narrative vision keeps the audience focused exclusively on Achilleus as the battle narrative progresses and underscores the hero's key role in generating this second arc of plot.

As Achilleus fights on in pursuit of Hektor, slaughtering a series of Trojans, Homer continues to emphasize the hero's aggressive desire, presenting it now as an overwhelming force that masters the will of every mortal who challenges him. When the Trojan warrior Tros approaches Achilleus with the intention of asking him to spare his life, the narrator remarks on the futility of his desire, given Achilleus' psychology: "for he was in no way a sweet-hearted man nor kindly, but so very eager" (οὐ γάρ τι γλυκύθυμος ἀνὴρ ἦν οὐδ' ἀγανόφρων,/ ἀλλὰ μάλ' ἐμμεμαώς, 20.467–68). This is the third application of the participle *emmemaōs* to Achilleus, and the narrator's gloss clarifies how the term signifies an aggressive drive that defines the hero's character—at least during his *aristeia*. Therefore, as Tros grasps Achilleus' knees in supplication, "desiring to entreat him" (ἱέμενος λίσσεσθ'), Achilleus' eagerness for slaughter engulfs Tros's opposing will to live, and he pierces the man's liver with his sword (468–69).

The same dynamic is at play in Achilleus' encounter with Hektor's half-brother Lykaon (21.34–135).[56] When Achilleus overtakes the fleeing Lykaon, the narrator introduces the Trojan prince as one whom Achilleus has already once taken "not willing" (οὐκ ἐθέλοντα, 36) from his father's orchard and then returned for ransom; now Achilleus is about to send him to Hades, "even though he is not willing to go" (καὶ οὐκ ἐθέλοντα νέεσθαι, 48). This preface establishes from the start the total dominance of Achilleus' desire over Lykaon's. At this second meeting, Lykaon, like Tros, chooses to supplicate rather than fight Achilleus, and so approaches "eager (μεμαώς) to grasp his knees, for he exceedingly wished (ἤθελε) to escape evil death and dark doom" (65–66). Achilleus, on the other hand, hefts his spear, "eager to strike him" (οὐτάμεναι μεμαώς, 68), yet his spear flies over Lykaon and fixes in the earth, "desiring to sate itself with human flesh" (ἱεμένη χροὸς ἄμεναι ἀνδρομέοιο, 70). Here Achilleus' spear metonymically expresses the hero's own frustrated desire, and its phallic shape suggests the similarity between aggressive and sexual urges.[57] Lykaon thus obtains the opportunity to plea for his life, but Achilleus remains intent on his death—as an

[55] Shay 1994: 77–99 recognizes this single-minded indifference to others as characteristic of the berserk state into which he believes Achilleus enters during his *aristeia*.

[56] As Richardson 1993: 56 observes, Tros's unsuccessful supplication anticipates this scene.

[57] See also Vermeule 1979: 157. Likewise, the narrator's description of how Achilleus perceives Lykaon "naked" (γυμνόν) without helmet, shield, or spear (21.49–51) seems to construct Lykaon as a sexualized object of Achilleus' gaze (see Vernant 1989: 137–38 on the "feminine implications" [*valeurs féminines*] of the adjective γυμνός).

unavoidable counterpart, so he says, to Patroklos' death and his own ineluctable mortality (99–113). After refusing Lykaon's supplication, Achilleus kills him with his sword and throws him to the fishes in the river Skamandros (Xanthos). Homer reminds the audience that the loss of Patroklos, enabled by Achilleus' own withdrawal, is at the root of the hero's aggression with his subsequent boast that all the Trojans will perish in this way until "you have paid back the slaying of Patroklos and the destruction (λοιγόν) of the Achaians whom you killed by the swift ships apart from me" (134–35).[58]

Although Achilleus' next opponent, Asteropaios, tries to match the hero's aggressive desire with his own, his effort is likewise futile. Achilleus leaps at Asteropaios with his spear, "raging to kill" (κατακτάμεναι μενεαίνων), and this time the Trojan stands up to his adversary, having been infused with a mirroring "rage" (μένος) by the river god Xanthos, who is angry at Achilleus (21.139–47). Asteropaios throws his spear first, but only grazes Achilleus; now it is his spear that ends up vainly fixed in the earth, "desiring to sate itself with flesh" (λιλαιομένη χροὸς ἆσαι, 168). In turn, Achilleus hurls his spear, yet again "raging to kill" (κατακτάμεναι μενεαίνων, 170), but when that misses as well, he draws his sword and jumps at him, "eager" (μεμαώς, 174). While Asteropaios "rages" (μενεαίνων, 176) to draw Achilleus' own spear from the river bank and "wished in his heart" (ἤθελε θυμῷ, 77) to break it, Achilleus kills him before he is able to do so. The Greek hero's desire has yet again overpowered the will of his enemy.

Only a god can counter Achilleus' aggression. Xanthos takes it upon himself to "ward off destruction from the Trojans" (Τρώεσσι δὲ λοιγὸν ἀλάλκοι, 21.138 = 250),[59] and his waves threaten to overcome the hero, despite Achilleus' swift-footedness. Although Achilleus prays to Zeus for help, instead he is saved through the will of Hera, who rouses her son Hephaistos to burn the river's waters until "the rage (μένος) of Xanthos was tamed" (383), after which she restrains the two "though she was still angry" (χωομένη περ, 384). As Joan O'Brien (1993: 85–87) has recognized, Hera's intervention underscores how Achilleus is now aligned more directly with her than with Zeus, sharing and enacting her aggressive desire to destroy the Trojans. Indeed, later, as Achilleus attempts to fight Apollo in his disguise as the Trojan Agenor, the god remarks to the hero, "you unceasingly rage" (ἀσπερχὲς μενεαίνεις, 22.10), echoing Zeus's own critique of Hera earlier in the epic (4.32).[60] Achilleus' association with the unremittingly ireful *female* divinity Hera during his *aristeia*, rather than with the less partisan and more

[58] See also Kozak 2017: 192, who observes that Achilleus' words invite the audience to "judge his actions against the background of Patroklos's death."

[59] Achilleus is now threatening the Trojans with the same destruction (*loigos*) that the Achaians suffered when he withheld himself from battle in his earlier expression of aggressive desire (see *Il.* 9.495, 13.426, 16.32, 16.75, 16.80, 18.450, 21.134 and Nagy 1979: 74–76). By describing in identical terms the damage to both Achaians and Trojans because of Achilleus' desires, the poet again asserts the parallelism of Achilleus' conflicts with Agamemnon and with Hektor.

[60] O'Brien 1993: 82–83. On this passage, see "The Divine Determinants of War" in Chapter 4.

moderate *male* king of the gods, may help to construct his re-entrance into battle as queer.

After Achilleus escapes from the river, Homer prepares the audience for his final deadly confrontation with Hektor by emphasizing the super-human and manic quality of the hero's pursuit of the Trojans toward the city of Troy. First, Achilleus' affliction of pain and suffering on the Trojans is compared with the "gods' wrath" (θεῶν ... μῆνις) causing a city to burn (21.522–25); thus the hero, in his aggression, is once again assimilated to an angry divinity. Then the narrator contrasts the all-too-human parched and dusty fleeing Trojans with the eagerly chasing Achilleus, who is possessed by mania: "a powerful madness was continually gripping his heart, and he raged to obtain triumph" (λύσσα δέ οἱ κῆρ/ αἰὲν ἔχε κρατερή, μενέαινε δὲ κῦδος ἀρέσθαι, 542–43). The narrator drives home the desiring hero's destructive otherness by describing how, as he approaches Troy in his glittering armor, he looks to King Priam like the malignant Dog Star, brightest in the sky (22.25–32).

Achilleus Meets Hektor

While the other Trojan warriors escape into the city, Hektor stays behind to face the attacking Greek hero. Despite the entreaties of his panicked parents, Hektor is "vehemently eager to fight with Achilleus" (ἄμοτον μεμαὼς Ἀχιλῆϊ μάχεσθαι, 22.36).[61] Hektor's aggressive desire, however, is of a different nature than that of Achilleus. In a soliloquy before the walls, Hektor, echoing his justification to Andromache for leaving Troy to fight in Book 6, explains that shame compels him to confront Achilleus[62]—this time, fear of the Trojans' blame for recklessly leading his army to defeat (22.104–7). This socialized competitive desire is essentially defensive rather than offensive, and does not seem to be as powerful as aggressive desire predicated on loss. While Achilleus' vengeful desire drives him forward relentlessly to ever greater feats of martial heroism, Hektor's desire is merely sufficient to inspire him to stand his ground. This asymmetry defines the following contest between the two adversaries.

This same soliloquy dramatizes Hektor's decision to fight in terms that identify and characterize the desires animating this culminating contest. First, he rethinks his will to engage Achilleus in battle, and considers approaching him unarmed to offer back Helen and the possessions stolen by Paris, "which were the beginning of

[61] The narrator also notes Hektor's aggressive desire with a simile comparing him to a snake with "dreadful anger" (χόλος αἰνός, 22.94). Later, Athene calls Hektor "insatiate of battle" (μάχης ἄατόν, 22.218).

[62] 22.105 = 6.442. On this correspondence, see de Jong 2012: 86. On Hektor's motivating shame, i.e. desire for a good reputation, see also Arieti 1985: 202; Redfield 1994: 115–19, 157–58; Alden 2000: 272–74. Mackie 1996: 97–125 demonstrates Hektor's consistent preoccupation with *kleos*.

the conflict," as well as half the wealth of Troy (22.111–21). Hektor's putative treaty reminds the audience of the triangle of desire at the root of the Trojan War superplot, and connects it—as first cause—to the upcoming fight.[63] The Trojan leader imagines that if he could negate the union of Paris and Helen, then he could neutralize Achilleus' aggression and escape a violent confrontation.

But he immediately discounts the feasibility of this plan, recognizing the intractable and dominating nature of Achilleus' driving desire (22.123–28):

> *ὁ δέ μ' οὐκ ἐλεήσει*
> *οὐδέ τί μ' αἰδέσεται, κτενέει δέ με γυμνὸν ἐόντα*
> *αὔτως ὥς τε γυναῖκα, ἐπεί κ' ἀπὸ τεύχεα δύω.*
> *οὐ μέν πως νῦν ἔστιν ἀπὸ δρυὸς οὐδ' ἀπὸ πέτρης*
> *τῷ ὀαριζέμεναι, ἅ τε παρθένος ἠΐθεός τε*
> *παρθένος ἠΐθεός τ' ὀαρίζετον ἀλλήλοιιν.*

> He will not pity me
> nor respect me, but he will kill me naked,
> just like a woman, after I have taken off my armor.
> It is not possible now from oak or rock
> to converse intimately with him, like a maiden and a youth,
> a maiden and a youth conversing intimately with one another.

When Hektor concludes, "he will kill me naked, just like a woman," he acknowledges Achilleus' unstoppable aggression and imagines himself as a vulnerable and passive victim. Moreover, by imaginatively denuding and then feminizing himself, Hektor implicitly conflates Achilleus' martial dominance with sex. In so doing, he draws attention to the similar desire that motivates sexual unions and Achilleus' violence.

But then Hektor introduces another image of desire that he identifies as a site of difference, reflecting that it is *not* possible for him to "converse intimately" with Achilleus, "like a maiden and youth." Again, Hektor imagines himself as a female, but now she is a maiden, not a mature woman, and she appears in a courtship scene, not a sexual encounter. He seems to envision an equality, mutuality, and reciprocity between maiden and youth, who are both subjects of the dual verb "conversing intimately" (*ὀαρίζετον*), which derives from the Homeric word for "wife" (*ὀάρ*). E. T. Owen (1946: 221–22) argues that Hektor's words evoke his encounter with Andromache in Book 6 and represent his own subconscious memory

[63] See also Owen 1946: 220–21, who observes that the idea of giving up Helen "takes us back to Bk. III, and the circumstances surrounding the duel between Paris and Menelaus. The poet is reminding us of the broken faith on which the cause of Troy rests, and, just where it is most telling, of Hector's own condemnation of it." Hektor's description of Troy as the "lovely city" (*πτολίεθρον ἐπήρατον*, 22.121) characterizes it as an object of (Achaian) desire since *ἐπήρατον* derives from *erōs*.

of that event; there the narrator says that Hektor "was conversing intimately with his wife" (ᾗ ὀάριζε γυναικί, 6.516). Oliver Taplin (2001: 352–53) connects this image with the scene of innocent maidens and youths picking grapes and dancing on Achilleus' shield (18.567–72). These passages confirm the association of Hektor's putative young couple with marriage and romance rather than with sex, which is inherently asymmetrical and subjugating. Hektor's repetition of "maiden and youth" draws special attention to this simile and suggests the speaker's wistfulness. Whereas Hektor might wish for this kind of amiable and peaceful rather than hostile and destructive relation between Achilleus and himself, he realizes that it is unattainable.[64]

Throughout the extended martial engagement between Hektor and Achilleus, the poet repeatedly focuses attention on Achilleus' motivating aggressive desire, which now reaches its highest pitch. He advances toward Hektor not only "equal to a god" but equal to the war god himself (ἶσος Ἐνυαλίῳ, κορυθάϊκι πτολεμιστῇ, 22.132). When Hektor flees, Achilleus rushes to pursue him like a hawk hunting a dove, whose "passion (*thumos*) bids him to seize her" (ἑλέειν τέ ἑ θυμὸς ἀνώγει, 142). This bird simile again depicts Achilleus as the male aggressor and Hektor as his female victim, and it is capped off with a characterization of Achilleus, for the fourth and final time, as "very eager" (ἐμμεμαώς, 143). Once Hektor gives up his flight and confronts the Greek hero, Achilleus refuses to make any burial agreement with his Trojan adversary before one of them "sates Ares with blood" (αἵματος ἆσαι Ἄρηα, 267), deploying the now familiar metaphor that equates deadly violence with the satisfaction of alimentary desire. After the two men trade ineffectual spear casts, they charge one another, and the narrator describes how Achilleus "was filled in his heart with savage rage" (μένεος δ' ἐμπλήσατο θυμὸν/ ἀγρίου, 312–13). He then plots where to strike, "intending a dire thing for brilliant Hektor" (φρονέων κακὸν Ἕκτορι δίῳ, 320).

At this juncture, Homer provides a window into Achilleus' psychology that supports the interpretation of Achilleus' libidinal fixation on Hektor as an external displacement of his ambivalent longing for Patroklos. The narrator describes Achilleus scrutinizing Hektor to find a weak spot in the beautiful bronze armor covering his body, armor "which he stripped after he destroyed the strength of Patroklos" (22.322–23). The account of the armor seems to be a moment of embedded focalization, representing Achilleus' perspective. If this is the case, when Achilleus looks at Hektor, he sees him wearing the armor that Patroklos

[64] Cf. Ormand 2014: 144–45, who argues that the narrative of Atalanta's competition and marriage with Hippomenes in the Hesiodic *Catalogue of Women* alludes to this passage, and "renders literal" Hektor's erotic fantasy. As Vernant 1989: 137–38 notes, the metaphor of warriors on the front line of battle being engaged in intimate converse (*oaristus*) is evoked twice before this by Idomeneus (13.291) and Hektor himself (17.228). In those cases, which perhaps anticipate the actual dynamic between Achilleus and Hektor, *oaristus* seems to have aggressive valence, perhaps suggesting the competitive boasting and threatening that often precedes physical violence.

had worn and remembers how Hektor killed Patroklos.[65] He thus identifies the two men with one another, while differentiating Hektor as the "bad" libidinal object who has perpetrated his loss and at whom he may therefore channel his aggression.[66]

The long-desired death of Hektor evokes a sexual consummation.[67] Achilleus' spear point "passes through" Hektor's "tender" (ἁπαλοῖο) neck (22.327); thus, a phallic object enters a part of the anatomy that some ancient Greeks believed was connected to the vagina in women's bodies.[68] After Hektor breathes out his last, Achilleus withdraws his spear and strips his enemy naked (367–68); in this martial mixing, divestment follows rather than precedes intercourse. When Achilleus is done with the body, other Achaians marvel at its "stature and shining appearance" (φυὴν καὶ εἶδος ἀγητὸν, 370) and remark on its softness (373). Then, as if it were a gang rape, they proceed to have their way with the corpse, each striking and penetrating it (371, 375). The sexualization of Hektor's death draws attention to the role of desire in motivating Achilleus' violence, and shows again how that violence has preempted and replaced any other kind of intercourse.

Yet, unexpectedly, killing Hektor does *not* satisfy Achilleus' aggressive desire. Even though the Trojan prince has now "sated Ares with blood," Achilleus refuses again Hektor's dying supplication for the release of his body to his family (22.345–54):

μή με, κύον, γούνων γουνάζεο μηδὲ τοκήων·
αἲ γάρ πως αὐτόν με μένος καὶ θυμὸς ἀνείη
ὤμ' ἀποταμνόμενον κρέα ἔδμεναι, οἷα ἔοργας,
ὡς οὐκ ἔσθ' ὃς σῆς γε κύνας κεφαλῆς ἀπαλάλκοι,
οὐδ' εἴ κεν δεκάκις τε καὶ εἰκοσινήριτ' ἄποινα
στήσωσ' ἐνθάδ' ἄγοντες, ὑπόσχωνται δὲ καὶ ἄλλα,
οὐδ' εἴ κέν σ' αὐτὸν χρυσῷ ἐρύσασθαι ἀνώγοι
Δαρδανίδης Πρίαμος· οὐδ' ὧς σέ γε πότνια μήτηρ
ἐνθεμένη λεχέεσσι γοήσεται, ὃν τέκεν αὐτή,
ἀλλὰ κύνες τε καὶ οἰωνοὶ κατὰ πάντα δάσονται.

[65] De Jong 2012: 139. Achilleus' following vaunt over the dying Hektor strengthens this reading, since his opening reference to Hektor "stripping Patroklos" (*Πατροκλῆ' ἐξεναρίζων*, 22.331) indicates that he is thinking about their shared armor.

[66] An intimate association between Hektor and Patroklos is confirmed at the narrative level after Hektor's death with an account of his *psychē* leaving his body that also appeared in Patroklos' death-scene (22.361–63 = 16.855–57). In addition, both men die prophesying the future doom of their killers. For a catalogue of these and other similarities between the two men's deaths, see de Jong 2012: 140.

[67] See also Monsacré 1984: 72–73 and Vernant 1989: 138, who identify the eroticization and feminization of Hektor's body; and Rabel 1997: 194, who asserts that the narrator "stylize[s] the death of the trapped and powerless Hektor as the violation of the female by the male, the very conclusion the hero himself most feared."

[68] See Dean-Jones 1991: 124 on the ancient Greek medical idea of a tube linking the mouth to the vagina.

> Do not, dog, beg me by my knees or parents;
> if only my rage (*menos*) and passion (*thumos*) would drive me
> to cut apart your flesh and eat it raw, such things have you done,
> so that there is no one who would keep the dogs from your head,
> not even if ten and twenty times the ransom
> they should bring and weigh out here, and also promise other things,
> not even if he should bid your body to be redeemed against gold,
> Dardanian Priam. Not even so will your revered mother
> lay you on a bier and lament you, whom she herself bore,
> but dogs and birds will divide every part of you.

Achilleus' fantasy of eating Hektor's corpse raw links him once more with the ceaselessly raging goddess Hera, to whom Zeus attributes a nearly identical desire to consume Priam, his sons, and all the other Trojans raw (4.34–36).[69] It represents a denial of human civilization that also equates the hero with the dogs and the birds whom he promises will feed on Hektor's body.[70] Achilleus' would-be omophagia signifies how he continues to desire the sustenance of violence rather than normal human food.

Furthermore, his adamant refusal of future ransom (*apoina*) for Hektor's body recalls his earlier rejection of Agamemnon's compensatory *apoina* in Book 9.[71] In both instances, his refusal seems to indicate the force of his desire for revenge and his difficulty in conceiving terms for its satisfaction. It also echoes his previous rejections of Tros's and Lykaon's supplications on the battlefield, which reflected his relentless aggression. Indeed, Achilleus expresses his continued desire to inflict harm on Hektor through his subsequent mutilation of the Trojan's corpse: he pierces Hektor's ankles and then ties him to the back of his chariot and drags him through the dust before the city of Troy (22.395–404).

The hero's abuse of Hektor's body violates social norms regarding the respectful treatment of corpses,[72] capping off his destruction of the social order during his *aristeia*. It is the culmination of his carnage on the battlefield, which acknowledges no limits and honors no human connections beyond shared mortality. But this same carnage is what earns Achilleus, in his own words, "great triumph" (μέγα κῦδος, 22.393). Although it is the norm for a warrior to avenge the death of his

[69] O'Brien 1993: 89.

[70] See Segal 1971c: 38–41; Redfield 1994: 196–99; Shay 1994: 82–84; Grethlein 2005: 264, 269.

[71] Macleod 1982: 20–21; Seaford 1994: 69; Wilson 2002: 122. There Achilleus says in almost the same language that he would not accept Agamemnon's gifts even if he offered "ten times and twenty times so many" (οὐδ' εἴ μοι δεκάκις τε καὶ εἰκοσάκις τόσα δοίη, 9.379). Moreover, here Achilleus derisively calls the dying Hektor "dog" (κύον, 22.345), as in their first encounter (20.449), evoking his address to Agamemnon as "dog-faced" (κυνῶπα, 1.159, cf. 9.373). As Franco 2014: 114–18 explains, "dog" as applied to Hektor is a generalized insult expressing Achilleus' complete dominance.

[72] As Segal 1971c: 13, writes, "the exposure and mutilation of a dead warrior's corpse does indeed arouse in Homer repugnance and even some measure of moral outrage."

companion,[73] the special quality and intensity of Achilleus' queer attachment to Patroklos and his consequent aggression produce heroic feats that far outstrip the standard vengeance. These feats confirm the hero's reputation as the greatest warrior among the Greeks and constitute the *Iliad*'s epic climax. Achilleus' queerness, therefore, makes him, like Paris and Helen, an especially potent source of battlefield heroism and the poetry that memorializes it.

While Achilleus' queer triangular desires bring him imperishable *kleos*, the social devastation that they cause also makes him a less sympathetic character. His continued violence against Hektor's lifeless corpse may particularly alienate the audience. The hero's unremitting aggressive desire thus prepares us to conceive new sympathies even as it denies narrative resolution, driving the *Iliad*'s newly unified plot onwards beyond its climax.

[73] Van Wees 1988: 6 and Austin 2021: 78–79.

8
Desire for Lamentation

This last chapter demonstrates how newly conceived Trojan desires together with Achilleus' existing desires prolong the *Iliad*'s narrative and keep the audience engaged until they are remediated in Book 24. Hektor's killing arouses the Trojan royal family's longing for their lost champion, and in their desirous anguish, Priam, Hekabe, and Andromache attract the audience's sympathy and empathy, complicating and extending our investment in the epic. Though Achilleus celebrates Patroklos' funeral, his aggressive attachment to Hektor's corpse keeps both himself and the Trojans from satisfying their yearning (*himeros*) or lust (*erōs*) for lamentation (*goos*) and relieving their underlying longings, and establishes a final triangle of desire with Priam as subject, Hektor as object, and himself as rival. I explain how Priam's supplication of Achilleus in the *Iliad*'s final book resolves the desires of both the Greek hero and the Trojans, and how the poem's closing scenes gratify the audience, even as they also provoke our desire for more epic narrative.

Priam's and Hekabe's Desires

Near the beginning of *Iliad* 22, as Achilleus approaches Troy and Hektor stands outside the Skaian Gates awaiting him, Homer switches the narrative perspective from the battlefield to the city walls. Now, for the first time since Book 6, the poet reintroduces in a developed way the points of view of the Trojan non-combatants, exploring the thoughts and feelings of Hektor's father Priam and mother Hekabe as they behold their son in mortal danger and beg him to retreat to safety. This scene represents the start of Homer's repeated thematization of Trojan longing for Hektor in the final books of the epic. While the pathetic representations of Achilleus' Trojan victims during his brutal *aristeia* may have already elicited the audience's pity,[1] the distressed desiring subjectivities of the Trojan royal family are even more compelling. The foregrounding of their painful emotions demands our

[1] The poet evokes our sympathy, e.g. by presenting the touching and ironic personal histories of Hektor's half-brothers, Polydoros and Lykaon, before Achilleus kills them (20.408–12, 21.35–46), and through the graphic accounts of how Lykaon's and Asteropaios' bodies are thrown into the Skamandros to be food for the eels and fishes (21.120–27, 202–4).

Desire in the Iliad: *The Force That Moves the Epic and Its Audience.* Rachel H. Lesser, Oxford University Press.
 DOI: 10.1093/oso/9780192866516.003.0009

sympathy and also invites our empathy, investing us in their plight and keeping us fully engaged with the *Iliad*'s narrative until its very end.

The Trojan desire for Hektor first becomes manifest in Book 22 through Priam's pitiful appeal to his son not to remain outside Troy. The narrator introduces Priam's desiring subjectivity even before he speaks with vocal and physical expressions of his anguished longing: the Trojan king cries out (ᾤμωξεν; οἰμώξας, 22.33; 34) and strikes his head with his hands, then stretches them out while "entreating his dear (*philon*) son" (λίσσομενος φίλον υἱον, 35). The adjective *philos* draws attention to the men's intimacy, which is now threatened by Hektor's choice not to re-enter the city.

In his speech of entreaty, Priam anticipates his grievous longing for Hektor if his son should lose his life, and articulates the personal and communal need that informs that desire "in pitiful terms" (ἐλεεινὰ προσηύδα, 22.37). He begs Hektor not to fight Achilleus lest the Greek warrior kill him, "since he is much more powerful" (38–40), and declares that he would only be free from "grief" (ἄχος) if Achilleus, who has deprived him of many good sons, should himself die (41–45). Priam then speculates about the fate of his missing sons Lykaon and Polydoros, asserting his "pain" (ἄλγος) if they are dead (46–53); the Trojan king's response to their loss demonstrates, to a lesser degree, the way he will feel if he loses Hektor. Moreover, the dramatic irony of his words—Priam is woefully ignorant that they have died by the hand of Achilleus—makes the Trojan king especially pitiable, as a scholiast observes.[2] He then asserts the whole city's particular reliance on Hektor, reminding him that the Trojan people's "pain" (ἄλγος) will be less if he survives, and exhorting him to come inside Troy "in order to save the Trojan men and women" (54–57). In the last part of his speech, Priam focuses on the royal family's own need for Hektor, urging his son to "pity" him because of the many evils that he will see and experience (implicitly, in Hektor's absence): sons killed, daughters and daughters-in-law enslaved, bedrooms ransacked, infants thrown to the ground, and himself killed, then torn apart and devoured by his own palace dogs (59–76).

While Priam's words do not seem to touch his son ("he did not persuade Hektor's heart," 22.78), the vivid and ugly scenes that he imagines cannot but prompt the audience's pity and make us anticipate Hektor's imminent death with dread. At the same time, the intensity and singularity of Priam's fear of Achilleus' deadly force, ignorance of his sons' death, and foresight of his entire family's destruction,[3] invite the audience to empathize with the Trojan king. If we feel that empathy, it will disrupt, at least for the moment, any empathetic identification with Achilleus during his *aristeia* and will work in opposition to narrative and empathetic desires for Hektor's killing. We are given pause—as we were during

[2] "The ignorance of the father is very pitiable" (ἐλεεινὴ λίαν ἡ ἄγνοια τοῦ πατρός, b *ad* 22.49).

[3] See de Jong 2012: 73 on how Priam foresees Troy's fall "in terms of the dissolution of his family."

Andromache's encounter with Hektor in Book 6—and made again to take stock of the human cost of the Trojan War in general, and Achilleus' aggression in particular.

After Priam's failed appeal, Hekabe likewise calls upon Hektor's pity—and our own—through gestures and words that assert her maternal claim on her son, and her urgent desire for his return to Troy. First she expresses that painful longing by weeping (ὀδύρετο δάκρυ χέουσα, 22.79; δάκρυ χέουσ', 81), and then bares her breast and holds it out, telling Hektor to respect the bond that it represents and pity her who nursed him (80–83). This self-exposure and verbal plea are meant to remind Hektor not only of his debt to the one who gave him life[4] but also of their intimacy as mother and child,[5] which has already been disrupted by his position outside of the walls. Hekabe then explicitly begs Hektor to take refuge from Achilleus inside city (84–85), driving home their endangered intimacy by addressing her son twice as "child" (τέκνον, 82; 84) and twice with the adjective *philos* (84; 87).

Moreover, she warns him that if he dies, neither she nor his "much-gifted wife" (ἄλοχος πολύδωρος) will be able to lament over his body, declaring, "very far apart from the two of us, swift dogs will eat you beside the ships of the Achaians" (22.86–89). With this closing image, Hekabe foresees not only her permanent longing for her dead son but also her inability to mourn him properly because of her separation from his corpse. She thus evokes the audience's proleptic sympathy for both herself and her unburied son while also introducing the problem that will animate the driving desires of characters and audience until it is resolved: Achilleus' abusive attachment to the body of his enemy.

With her powerful subjectivity, Hekabe provides a maternal counterpart to Priam's paternal perspective. Homer's presentation of both male and female desiring minds can be understood as a further strategy to elicit the audience's empathy with the Trojans, since perceived similarity is associated with empathetic response, and the royal couple offers the opportunity for both men and women to identify with a Trojan character of their own gender. Of course, a gender mismatch between audience and character by no means precludes identification, and not all listeners are fathers or mothers. On that account, Hekabe refers to a third member of the Trojan royal family, Hektor's wife, as a partner in her prospective mourning. This brief mention reminds the audience of Andromache and her anxious desire for her husband, which were vividly portrayed in Book 6. Since Andromache's subjectivity was introduced at length earlier, she does not entreat Hektor here—it would be redundant and anticlimactic; however, Hekabe's speech brings her back into the audience's ken and prepares us for her dramatic reaction to Hektor's death at the end of Book 22.

After Achilleus has killed Hektor and begun to mutilate his corpse, Homer builds toward Andromache's reintroduction by depicting again the grief and

[4] De Jong 2012: 78.

[5] See also Crotty 1994: 74–75 and Alden 2000: 271.

lamentation of Hektor's parents as well as of the Trojan community at large. When Hekabe sees her dead son being dragged through the dust, she tears her hair, throws off her veil, and "wails" (κώκυσεν, 22.407). Priam "cries pitifully" (ᾤμωξεν δ' ἐλεεινά, 408), repeating his earlier response to Hektor's endangerment. The Trojan people echo both queen and king with "wailing" (κωκυτῷ) and "crying" (οἰμωγῇ) that make it sound as if the entire city were burning (408–11), in a prevision of what the lack of Hektor will mean for Troy.[6] As E. T. Owen (1946: 231) observes, the Trojans' sorrow "drowns out all other feeling. The voice of lamentation fills the poem." Homer deepens the audience's sympathy for and (possible) empathy with the Trojans through this overwhelming portrayal of their initial mourning.

As before, the poet then focuses on Priam's subjectivity, revealing how his longing for Hektor has taken the shape of a desire to reclaim his son's body—the only part of the hero that is now recoverable. According to the narrator, the Trojan people can scarcely hold back Priam, "impatient" (ἀχαλόωντα) and "eager" (μεμαῶτα), from exiting the city (22.412–13); as he subsequently explains, the Trojan king intends to entreat Achilleus personally for the return of Hektor's corpse (416–20). When his concerned subjects keep him from pursuing this desired reunion with his dead son, Priam gives himself up to melancholic mourning, identifying with Hektor and turning against himself his anger at this fresh loss: he rolls in the dung (414) and declares that his "sharp grief" (ἄχος ὀξύ) for Hektor will bring him down to Hades (425–26).

Priam ends his speech of lamentation with an unattainable wish that nevertheless points a way forward: "if only he had died in my hands; then the two of us would have sated ourselves (κορεσσάμεθα) with weeping and bewailing, his mother, who, ill-destined, gave birth to him, and I myself" (22.426–28). Here the king suggests that the bereaved parents could achieve a form of satiation—resolving, or, at least, mitigating their grievous longing—through protracted lamentation over Hektor's body. When the Trojan citizens groan in antiphonal responsion (429), we are left with the impression that Priam speaks and feels not only for himself and his wife but for the broader community.

Once again, Homer follows up Priam's lament with the complementary female perspective of Hekabe: "and among the Trojan women, Hekabe began the thick lament" (ἁδινοῦ ἐξῆρχε γόοιο, 22.430). While Priam's desire to recover his son's corpse had echoed Hekabe's earlier fears that she and Andromache would not be able to tend to Hektor's body, now Hekabe reiterates a main theme of Priam's previous entreaty to Hektor: the hero's status as preeminent defender of Troy. She remembers how Hektor, while alive, was a "boast" (εὐχωλή) throughout the city, a "benefit" (ὄνειαρ) to all the Trojan men and women, and a "very great triumph"

[6] Richardson 1993: 150.

(μάλα μέγα κῦδος) for them (433–35). Priam's and Hekabe's reverberations of one another cause their voices, though at first distinct, to merge together as a unified articulation of Trojan loss. Their overlapping desiring subjectivities encircle the narrative of Hektor's fatal encounter with Achilleus and emotionally overwhelm it, insistently beckoning the audience away from the battlefield.

Andromache's Melancholic Mourning

The poet completes the audience's investment in the Trojan civilians' bereavement through the following 78-line narrative capstone of Andromache's apprehension of Hektor's death and subsequent lament.[7] From the outset, Homer emphasizes the particularity and importance of her perspective by distinguishing her from Hekabe and the other Trojan women who listen to the queen's lament: "thus [Hekabe] spoke, crying, but Hektor's wife (ἄλοχος) had not yet in any way learned of [his death] . . . " (22.437–38).[8] Andromache, as we soon discover, is not on the city walls with the rest of the women, but is at home weaving a textile and supervising her slaves' preparation of bathwater for Hektor on his return (440–44), following his closing instructions at their last meeting (6.490–91).[9] Indeed, in many respects Andromache's appearance in Book 22 recalls her previous encounter with Hektor in Book 6, where she expressed her need for him and vainly begged him to stay out of harm's way,[10] just as Priam's and Hekabe's reactions to Hektor's killing echo their earlier entreaties for him to save himself. This resonance brings to the audience's mind Andromache's fierce attachment to Hektor and her proleptic grief and longing at their final farewell, making her suffering after Hektor's death more meaningful and poignant. Homer also "increases *pathos*"[11] from the start through the dramatic irony of Andromache's hopeful and ignorant preparation of Hektor's bath. The narrator's comment, "oblivious woman (νηπίη), she did not perceive how, very far from the baths, glancing-eyed Athene had dominated him through the hands of Achilleus" (22.445–46), draws attention to this irony and models for the audience a sympathetic response.[12]

[7] Cf. Kozak 2017: 210, who writes, "This chain of emotional responses to Hektor's death, from the other Achaians on the battlefield, Achilles himself, Priam and Hekabe, and finally Andromache, works to amplify and affect audience response mirroring, as it does, a kind of 'scale of affection.'"

[8] Segal 1971a: 37–38 observes how Andromache is introduced as "wife" (22.437) and how this status defines her mourning.

[9] Segal 1971a: 40; Richardson 1993: 53; de Jong 2012: 175.

[10] Segal 1971a *passim*, Lohmann 1988: 63–69, and Richardson 1993: 152–53 catalogue the correspondences.

[11] AbT scholia *ad* 22.445. See also bT scholia *ad* 17.401.

[12] AbT scholia *ad* 22.445 observe that "the poet exclaims sympathetically . . . as if pitying her ignorance."

As Andromache gradually realizes that Hektor has been killed, Homer reveals her profound emotional agitation through an escalating series of physical movements and symptoms that deepen our sympathy for the heroine and invite our empathy. When Andromache first apprehends the wailing of the Trojans from the wall, "her limbs were shaken and her shuttle fell to the ground" (22.448). She calls to her slave women to follow her and find out what has happened, saying that at the sound of her mother-in-law's voice, "the heart in my chest is shaken right up into my mouth, and my knees are stuck beneath me" (452–53). After she speculates that Achilleus has "indeed stopped [Hektor] from his grievous boldness" (*δή μιν καταπαύσῃ ἀγηνορίης ἀλεγεινῆς*, 457),[13] the narrator recounts that "she rushed from the marriage chamber like a maenad, shaken in her heart" (460–61). Finally, when she peers down onto the battlefield and she sees her husband's corpse being dragged away from the city, she suddenly faints: "dark night covered her eyes, and she fell backward, and gasped out her breath" (466–67). Andromache is in turn startled, then paralyzed, then frantic, and ultimately stunned. The embodiment of her anxiety and pain is both vivid and familiar; it activates not only our pity but also our own remembered experiences of adrenaline rush or paralytic shock, encouraging us to feel with the heroine as she recognizes her loss.

Homer hints that desire is at the core of Andromache's visceral response through this passage's evocation of previous moments in the epic. Her trajectory from bedroom, where she has been placidly weaving, to Troy's walls, where she views the battlefield below, recalls our first vision of Helen in Book 3. There the goddess Iris interrupts Helen's similar weaving by inspiring her with a sudden yearning (*himeros*) for her former husband Menelaos, which impels her to view the upcoming duel from the rampart.[14] Helen's prototype suggests that Andromache too is driven by desire for her husband, but, differently, this is not a new feeling for her, nor must it be aroused through divine intervention. In Book 6, Andromache had also gone to Troy's walls on her own impetus because she heard rumors of Trojan hardship on the battlefield, and, in the intensity of her passion, was then described as "like a raving woman" (*μαινομένῃ ἐϊκυῖα*, 6.389);

[13] De Jong 2012: 179 observes how Andromache cannot quite bring herself to articulate her presentiment of Hektor's death explicitly: "Andromache describes what she fears has taken place.... However, she still does not spell out the idea of Hector's death but instead uses a euphemistic expression."

[14] On the resonance between Andromache in Book 22 and Helen in Book 3, see Lohmann 1988: 59–62. Both women weave a "web" (*ἱστόν*) that is "double-folded and purple" (*δίπλακα πορφυρέην*) (3.125–26; 22.440–41), although Andromache weaves in innocuous designs (*θρόνα ποικίλ'*) while Helen portrays the Trojan War itself. Following Lohmann, I think that this formulaic link between the two heroines asks the audience to compare and then contrast the loyal and soon-to-be grief-stricken Andromache with the faithless, destructive, and relatively carefree Helen.

now, similarly, she is "like a maenad" (μαινάδι ἴση, 22.460) when she rightly suspects that she has lost her husband forever.[15]

Indeed, Homer forces us to confront the unmitigated rawness of Andromache's longing for her dead husband by emphasizing the hostile aspect of her feelings surrounding his loss. Already when she guesses that Hektor has been killed, she reflects on how he insists on fighting in the front lines, "yielding to no one in his battle-rage" (ὃν μένος οὐδενὶ εἴκων, 22.459), and characterizes this action, as we have seen, as "grievous boldness" (ἀγηνορίης ἀλεγεινῆς, 457). These words betray a frustration with Hektor for putting himself at risk and ignoring her entreaties for him to preserve himself for the sake of his family and city.[16] Once Andromache has confirmed Hektor's death, her subsequent spoken lament is full of implicit reproach of her husband for abandoning herself and their son.[17] Calling upon Hektor, she exclaims, "you leave me behind in hateful sorrow, widowed in our halls" (483–84), and then asserts that he will be no "benefit" (ὄνειαρ) to Astyanax (485–86) before detailing the difficult life with which the boy is now confronted, bereft of his princely father (487–506).

Andromache's anger also manifests itself in "melancholia," as she identifies with her lost husband, saying that she and Hektor share the same evil fate (22.477–78, cf. 485), and turns her resentment toward Hektor inwards, at herself, wishing that she had never been born (481). Homer seems to introduce Andromache's melancholic response to loss through his depiction of her embodied experience as she becomes aware of Hektor's killing; much of the language describing Andromache's physical dysfunction is appropriated from the world of war, and the same formulas used to communicate her faint elsewhere refer to a warrior's death in battle.[18] Moreover, as Dieter Lohmann (1988: 61) has observed, Andromache's divestiture of veil and headdress as she loses consciousness (468–70) parallels the nakedness of Hektor's corpse below, stripped of his armor (376). In her mourning, Andromache briefly becomes like and then wishes to be like her dead husband.

In this and other ways, Andromache's loss of Hektor mirrors Achilleus' loss of Patroklos. War deprives both of the person closest to them. Both are frustrated that their loved one did not heed their bidding for him to restrain his aggression

[15] On the erotic nature of Andromache's first comparison to a "raving woman," see "Andromache's Proleptic Longing" in Chapter 4. On this narrative echo, see also Segal 1971a: 47–48 and de Jong 2012: 180–81. Cf. Lesser 2021: 146–55 on the possibility that Andromache here is a paradigm for the speaker in Sappho's Fragment 31.

[16] Graziosi and Haubold 2003 show that ἀγηνορίη, "boldness" or "excessive manliness," indicates transgressive, problematic behavior (see "Achilleus' Obstinacy" in Chapter 5), and explain that here Andromache "feels that [Hektor] went beyond the call to which all men were responding" (71). *Pace* Richardson 1993: 156, who understands Andromache's words as an expression of "admiration for [Hektor's] courage."

[17] With this passage as her prime example, Alexiou 1974: 183 identifies blame of the dead—which reverses the standard praise speech—as a traditional feature of lament.

[18] Segal 1971a: 43–48. On Andromache's death-like fainting, see also Richardson 1993: 156; Tsagalis 2004: 57; de Jong 2012: 182–83.

on the battlefield—at the cost of his life and their own futures. Both identify with their lost beloved and internalize that anger, at least at first. When Achilleus redirects his aggressive desire externally, toward Hektor as substitute object, he also fulfills his promise to transfer his own suffering over Patroklos' loss to a Trojan woman (18.122–25). Andromache's lamentation functions, within the larger structure of the main plot's second arc, as an antiphonal refrain responding to Achilleus' lamentation and created by Achilleus for this very purpose. The spiraling, retributive chain of loss and desire that began in Book 1, when Agamemnon's loss of Chryseis led to Achilleus' loss of Briseis, reaches its climax with the Trojans' loss of Hektor.[19]

By foregrounding the desiring subjectivities of the bereaved Trojans, and especially Andromache, Homer engages the audience in this loss. Whether we only sympathetically wish for the alleviation of their suffering, or also empathetically share their grievous longing for Hektor, we have become invested in their pain. We now require resolution of the Trojans' mourning in order to achieve narrative satisfaction.

At the end of Book 22, however, Homer leaves the Trojans' desire unprocessed in all of its ambivalence, their loss unresolved. The Trojans are unable to mourn Hektor properly: his body remains with Achilleus, mutilated and deprived of funeral rites. Andromache reminds us of this fact near the end of her lament, emphasizing Hektor's distance from his family: "but now, beside the curved ships, far from your parents, the wriggling worms will eat you after the dogs are sated" (κορέσωνται, 22.508–9). Instead of Priam, Hekabe, and Andromache satiating themselves through mourning, only the beasts will be sated, having consumed Hektor's corpse in a perversion of burial ritual. When Andromache stops her lament, the Trojan women groan in antiphonal responsion (515), indicating that they too share her unmitigated desire.

Achilleus' Persistent Mourning

Though Achilleus' killing of Hektor and abuse of his corpse make the Trojans feel grief and longing similar to the Greek hero's, these actions fail to alleviate his own

[19] While Andromache's and the other Trojans' longing for Hektor might well be called *pothē*, Homer reserves this term in the latter part of the epic to refer exclusively to Achilleus' and other Greeks' longing for Patroklos. Austin 2021: 119–49 contrasts Achilleus' *pothē* as intensely personal, fueling angry revenge, and focusing on the present of bereavement with the Trojans' grief as civic, passive, and forward-looking, anticipating Troy's future destruction. Yet, as Austin acknowledges, Andromache's and Priam's individual mourning resembles that of Achilleus in many ways, and, conversely, Achilleus is not the only Greek to grieve for Patroklos. I find that the poet emphasizes more the similarity of Achilleus' and the Trojans' painful losses than their difference. That said, the restricted language of *pothē* certainly brings special attention to Achilleus' desire for Patroklos, marking it as the engine of the second arc of the *Iliad*'s main plot.

longing for Patroklos. On the contrary, they seem to sustain it. In Book 23, Homer thematizes Achilleus' ongoing desire for Patroklos as he mourns his companion and celebrates his funeral, and repeatedly links that desire with his continuing aggression toward Hektor. Moreover, the poet confirms that Achilleus' fixation on Hektor represents a displacement of the aggression associated with his libidinal attachment to Patroklos by connecting the two bodies as objects of his obsessional tendance.

Homer relates Achilleus' relentless aggressive drive to the renewal of his mourning from the moment that he has killed Hektor. After the Trojan is vanquished, the hero turns to his fellow Greek soldiers and suggests that together they attempt to storm Troy itself "since Hektor is no longer alive" (Ἕκτορος οὐκέτ' ἐόντος, 22.384), but then immediately backtracks (385–90):

ἀλλὰ τίη μοι ταῦτα φίλος διελέξατο θυμός;
κεῖται πὰρ νήεσσι νέκυς ἄκλαυτος ἄθαπτος
Πάτροκλος· τοῦ δ' οὐκ ἐπιλήσομαι, ὄφρ' ἂν ἔγωγε
ζωοῖσιν μετέω καί μοι φίλα γούνατ' ὀρώρῃ·
εἰ δὲ θανόντων περ καταλήθοντ' εἰν Ἀΐδαο,
αὐτὰρ ἐγὼ καὶ κεῖθι φίλου μεμνήσομ' ἑταίρου.

But why has my own passion (*thumos*) dictated these things to me?
He lies beside the ships, a corpse unmourned and unburied,
Patroklos; I will not forget him so long as I
am among the living and my own knees are in motion;
and if one forgets among the dead in Hades,
I, at least, even there will remember my close companion.

In this speech, contemplation of Hektor's killing seems to trigger the thought of Patroklos, reminding Achilleus of the truer object of his desire and reactivating the impulse to mourn.[20] Indeed, it prompts him to declare his eternal memory of Patroklos, to be sustained uniquely in both life and death.[21] Achilleus again ties his longing for Patroklos to his aggression against Hektor when he subsequently leads his men back to the ships, where his companion lies, while dragging his enemy's body in the dust behind his chariot (391–404).

[20] Cf. Kozak 2017: 207, who writes "This flip, away from the corpse *here* to the corpse *there* connects the two as cause and effect, justifying one with the other, just as the narrative did by recapping Hektor's killing Patroklos just before Achilles kills Hektor (22.321–8)."

[21] When Achilleus says that he will not forget Patroklos as long as "my own knees are in motion" (μοι φίλα γούνατ' ὀρώρῃ) he uses the same formula that he had employed when he promised Agamemnon's embassy that he would stay at Troy as long as he lives and earn honor from Zeus (22.388 = 9.610), linking his longing for Patroklos with his previous desire to redeem his status among the Greeks. Yet here he adds that he will remember Patroklos when he is dead too, indicating again how his attachment to his companion is the strongest of his feelings in the epic.

After portraying the Trojans' reactions to Hektor's death in the remainder of Book 22, the poet turns back to Achilleus and his Myrmidons at the beginning of Book 23 to depict the hero's urgent desire to lament Patroklos. In an echo of his previous impatience to pursue revenge against Hektor, now Achilleus insists on mourning immediately, without even unharnessing the horses from their chariots: "let us cry for Patroklos, for that is the honor of the dead. And after we have taken satisfaction of woeful lamentation (ὀλοοῖο τεταρπώμεθα γόοιο), then we will all release the horses and take our meal here" (23.9–11). By looking to lamentation for satisfaction and putting off eating still longer, Achilleus indicates that the desires provoked by Patroklos' loss continue to preempt normal physical needs, such as the *erōs* for food and drink.

Homer focuses attention on these overriding desires, and elucidates their nature with his following account of the Myrmidons' mourning (23.12–16):

> *ὣς ἔφαθ', οἱ δ' ᾤμωξαν ἀολλέες, ἦρχε δ' Ἀχιλλεύς.*
> *οἱ δὲ τρὶς περὶ νεκρὸν ἐΰτριχας ἤλασαν ἵππους*
> *μυρόμενοι· μετὰ δέ σφι Θέτις γόου ἵμερον ὦρσε.*
> *δεύοντο ψάμαθοι, δεύοντο δὲ τεύχεα φωτῶν*
> *δάκρυσι· τοῖον γὰρ πόθεον μήστωρα φόβοιο.*
>
> Thus he spoke, and, gathered together, they cried out, with Achilleus taking the lead.
> And they drove their well-groomed horses around the corpse three times,
> weeping; and among them Thetis roused up a yearning for lamentation (*himeron goou*).
> The sands were wet, the equipment of the men was wet
> with tears; for so greatly were they longing (*potheon*) for the bringer of rout.

Here the poet not only declares explicitly that the men's mourning is motivated by a longing (*pothē*) for Patroklos but also links that *pothē* with a yearning (*himeros*) for lamentation: desire to lament emerges as a corollary to and expression of unresolved desire for a lost love object.[22]

Achilleus' spoken lament (*goos*) and treatment of Hektor's body confirm the intimate relationship between these mournful desires and his enduring aggressive impulse. In his lament, Achilleus tells Patroklos that he is fulfilling his vengeful promises to give Hektor's body to the dogs to be consumed raw and to cut the throats of twelve Trojan prisoners-of-war "in anger (χολωθείς) over your killing" (23.19–23). He then "devise[s] disgraceful deeds against brilliant Hektor," but instead of immediately throwing him to the dogs, he lays him prone in the dust

[22] Austin 2021: 74, drawing on Aristotle's *Rhetoric*, argues that the link between the two desires rests in lamentation's invocation of memory of the beloved, concluding "In grief, one longs for a missing presence, and in weeping, one achieves a shadow of that presence."

beside the bier of Patroklos (24–26). By joining together the corpses of Hektor and Patroklos, Achilleus shows that his libidinal attachments to the two are inextricably bound together, even if he differentiates them as "bad" and "good" objects respectively.[23] Indeed, in the narrator's subsequent account of how Achilleus sacrifices numerous animals for Patroklos' funeral feast, the two bodies seem to merge into one: "everywhere around the corpse the streaming blood rushed forth" (34).

As Achilleus' conjoined grief and anger continue to overwhelm his mind, he only reluctantly and in a limited way rejoins the larger community of Greeks and attends to his long-deferred desire for normal sustenance. The Achaian kings lead him to Agamemnon's tent "with effort having cajoled him, angered in his heart over his companion" (*σπουδῇ παρπεπιθόντες ἑταίρου χωόμενον κῆρ*, 23.37). Once there, he refuses to wash the bloody gore from his body before Patroklos has been placed on his funeral pyre, "since not a second time will grief (*ἄχος*) enter my heart in this way, so long as I am among the living" (42–47). That is, while Achilleus still holds on to the material remains of Patroklos, he similarly clings to the blood of his enemies, including Hektor, again linking together the two dead men. Although the hero then bids everyone to share the celebratory meal, he indicates his own abiding disinclination to eat with the ambivalent and "odd"[24] expression, "let us submit to the hateful feast" (*στυγερῇ πειθώμεθα δαιτί*, 48). While the narrator reports that all the Greeks satiated their hearts with the feast and "put away their lust (*ἔρον*) for drink and food" (56–57), he immediately emphasizes how Achilleus has still *not* satisfied his yearning for lamentation: in contrast to the other Greeks, who go to sleep in their tents, he lies on the seashore, "groaning heavily" (58–60).

Although sleep does finally overtake Achilleus, he continues to remember and long for Patroklos in his dreams. While asleep, he is visited by Patroklos' shade, who rebukes him for not yet consigning his body to the funeral pyre, prophesies Achilleus' death, and asks that the two of them be buried together, as before they had grown up together in Peleus' house (23.65–92). Patroklos' words bring our attention to Achilleus' unwillingness to give up his lifelong emotional and physical attachment to his companion, and represent for Achilleus a kind of "compromise" wherein he can give Patroklos his due rites, yet also look forward to bodily reunion after his own death.

Having agreed to follow Patroklos' instructions, Achilleus tries to alleviate his desire for his companion by reuniting with him briefly and engaging in joint mourning: "but stand closer to me, and embracing one another, if only for a little while, let us take satisfaction of woeful lamentation" (*ὀλοοῖο τεταρπώμεθα γόοιο*,

[23] See also Nagler 1974: 165, who describes Achilleus' "selfish attachment to his friend, which mirrors, in Homer's brilliant psychology, his attachment to his enemy. The former is an attachment of attractions and the latter of aversion, but they are inevitable concomitants." Cf. Segal 1971c: 48, who remarks how Book 23 develops a contrast between the handling of Hektor's and Patroklos' corpses, the first mutilated and the second granted extravagant funerary rites.

[24] Richardson 1993: 170.

23.97–98). This effort to find satisfaction, however, is futile, as Patroklos' insubstantial shade slips through the hero's hands and vanishes under the earth (99–101). Thus, Achilleus' longing persists unabated: he wakes up lamenting the fleeting dream appearance of Patroklos to those around him, and the narrator describes how his words "roused up in all of them a yearning for lamentation" (*τοῖσι δὲ πᾶσιν ὑφ' ἵμερον ὦρσε γόοιο*) that keeps them mourning through daybreak (101–10).[25]

That day, during the funeral that Patroklos' shade had demanded, the entire Greek army joins Achilleus and his Myrmidons in their desire to lament. When Achilleus, denying that he will ever return to Phthia, dedicates to Patroklos a lock of his hair that Peleus had promised to the river Spercheios on his son's arrival home (23.144–53), he "rouse[s] up in all of them a yearning for lamentation" (*τοῖσι δὲ πᾶσιν ὑφ' ἵμερον ὦρσε γόοιο*, 153).[26] The narrator reports that the sun would have set on the Achaians' mourning if Achilleus had not intervened (154–55). He tells Agamemnon (156–60),

> *Ἀτρεΐδη, σοὶ γάρ τε μάλιστά γε λαὸς Ἀχαιῶν*
> *πείσονται μύθοισι, γόοιο μὲν ἔστι καὶ ἆσαι,*
> *νῦν δ' ἀπὸ πυρκαϊῆς σκέδασον καὶ δεῖπνον ἄνωχθι*
> *ὅπλεσθαι· τάδε δ' ἀμφὶ πονησόμεθ' οἷσι μάλιστα*
> *κήδεός ἐστι νέκυς· παρὰ δ' οἵ τ' ἀγοὶ ἄμμι μενόντων.*
>
> Son of Atreus—for the Achaian host will especially
> obey your orders—of lamentation one can also be sated,
> but now disperse [the men] from the pyre and order them to prepare a meal;
> we will labor at these matters, those of us with special
> obligation toward the corpse; and let the leaders remain with us.

Achilleus here attempts to relieve unsatisfied yearning (*himeros*)—and its attendant narrative suspension[27]—in two ways. First, he releases the body of the Greek army to sate themselves with food and drink, for which, as we have seen, men quickly "put away their *erōs*." Second, he continues to seek satiety through lamentation with a more intimate group by completing Patroklos' funeral rites.

But that satiety remains elusive as Achilleus' aggression is again linked to the prolongation of his mourning. After building the pyre, Patroklos' friends lay his

[25] See also Flatt 2017: 390, who concludes "Clearly the satiety of lamentation to which Achilles has twice referred is still some way off."

[26] This yearning for lamentation may be interpreted as a manifestation of longing for Patroklos, proleptic longing for Achilleus (who here implicitly forecasts his own death at Troy), and/or desire for the family and home that each Greek warrior has left behind to join the war.

[27] Flatt 2017: 389 describes the "threat posed by open-ended lamentation to the resolution of the epic story, and thus to the consummation of narrative desire." On Achilleus' intervention in this passage, where he "sets events on the right course" toward satisfaction of the *himeros* for lamentation, see Flatt 2017: 391–92.

body on its apex, "grieving in their heart" (*ἀχνύμενοι κῆρ*, 23.165), but do not immediately light the blaze. Instead, Achilleus kills and adds to the pyre not only four horses and two dogs but also the twelve Trojan prisoners that he had promised Patroklos, while withholding Hektor's body to feed to the dogs (171–83). Achilleus' human sacrifice and continued disrespect of Hektor's corpse is followed by the initial failure of Patroklos' pyre to catch on fire (192); thus, Achilleus' refusal to give Hektor funeral rites is juxtaposed with a corresponding delay in the completion of Patroklos' funeral, "which he unconsciously does not want."[28] Moreover, each of the men's bodies are preserved (for the time being) since, as the narrator explains, Aphrodite and Apollo keep away from Hektor's corpse both the ravenous dogs and the sun's desiccating light (184–91). It is only after Achilleus has summoned the winds, Boreas and Zephyros, in prayer that the pyre finally starts burning, and then the hero spends all night pouring libations and grieving for Patroklos "like a father mourns over his child when he burns his bones" (218–25).[29] When the fire goes out at dawn, Achilleus arranges for Patroklos' bones to be gathered up and stored in a golden bowl in his tent (236–54), saving and keeping close the last physical vestiges of his companion.

Even after a mound has been raised for Patroklos and his funeral games have been celebrated, Achilleus does not cease from his desirous mourning. At the conclusion of the games in Patroklos' honor, the other Achaians eat again and then "take satisfaction (*ταρπήμεναι*) of sweet sleep" (24.2–3), fulfilling their desires. Achilleus, however, is sleepless and preoccupied with Patroklos (4–11):

> *κλαῖε φίλου ἑτάρου μεμνημένος, οὐδέ μιν ὕπνος*
> *ᾕρει πανδαμάτωρ, ἀλλ᾽ ἐστρέφετ᾽ ἔνθα καὶ ἔνθα,*
> *Πατρόκλου ποθέων ἁδροτῆτά*[30] *τε καὶ μένος ἠΰ,*
> *ἠδ᾽ ὁπόσα τολύπευσε σὺν αὐτῷ καὶ πάθεν ἄλγεα,*
> *ἀνδρῶν τε πτολέμους ἀλεγεινά τε κύματα πείρων·*
> *τῶν μιμνησκόμενος θαλερὸν κατὰ δάκρυον εἶβεν,*
> *ἄλλοτ᾽ ἐπὶ πλευρὰς κατακείμενος, ἄλλοτε δ᾽ αὖτε*
> *ὕπτιος, ἄλλοτε δὲ πρηνής·*

[28] Nagler 1974: 165–66.

[29] This simile links Achilleus in his desirous grieving for Patroklos with Priam in his similar grieving for Hektor (introduced in 22.409–28), and anticipates their shared mourning near the epic's conclusion.

[30] I have chosen to read *ἁδροτῆτα* in place of the metrically impossible *ἀνδροτῆτα*, which appears in the MSS. Bozzone 2015 has convincingly argued that, in the similar formula *γοόωσα λιποῦσ᾽ ἀνδροτῆτα καὶ ἥβην* (*Il.* 16.858 = 22.364), *ἀνδροτῆτα* is an error of early textual transmission, and that *ἁδροτῆτα* was likely the original. Aristophanes and Aristarchus athetized 24.6–9, and Macleod 1982: 85 pronounces their case "strong" because these lines elaborate on line 4, "he was crying as he remembered his close companion" (*κλαῖε φίλου ἑτάρου μεμνημένος*), and because the sense "runs smoothly from line 5 to line 10." I do not consider this elaboration superfluous as it represents a capstone to the already well-established theme of Achilleus' longing for Patroklos. On the authenticity of these lines, see also Clarke 1978: 385–86.

He was crying as he remembered his close companion, and sleep,
which conquers all, did not take him, but he tossed and turned,
longing for (*potheōn*) Patroklos' vigor and fair force,
and all the things he endured with him and the pains he suffered,
while attempting wars of men and troublesome waves;
continually recalling these things, he shed a blooming tear,
lying first on his side, then on his back,
then prone on his chest...

Here, once more, Homer thematizes Achilleus' unresolved *pothē* for Patroklos, which denies him peace and keeps him weeping and restless.[31] As we learn next, instead of sleeping he enacts a grim routine, which he appears to continue for twelve days (cf. 31): at night, he wanders along the beach, then at dawn binds Hektor's body behind his chariot and drags him three times around Patroklos' burial mound, finally leaving the corpse stretched out face downwards in the dust (11–18). The narrator summarizes Achilleus' iterative action using the aggressive verb *meneainō*: "thus he disgraced brilliant Hektor, raging" (*μενεαίνων*, 22). Yet again, Achilleus' continued longing for Patroklos is bound up with his unrelenting aggression against Hektor, and his spatial conjoining of these two objects of desire marks their libidinal association.

What is keeping Achilleus from resolving his desire for Patroklos, from taking satisfaction of lamentation? While Freud, in his seminal essay "Mourning and Melancholia" (1916), identified the subject's gradual detachment of libido from the lost love object as the psychological process constituting mourning,[32] other psychoanalytic theorists have argued that the internalization of libidinal attachment that Freud associated primarily with "melancholia" is a fundamental aspect of all mourning. Rather than leaving the lost object behind us, we bring it within us, where it becomes a part of our inner world. Melanie Klein considers the establishment of the lost person in the subject's ego as a "good" object to be key to the completion of mourning. This "idealization" of the beloved gives the mourner a sense of reassurance and security, during which "recreative processes can set in and hope return."[33] Ultimately, the desiring subject both preserves the lost object and achieves a harmonious inner world, rehabilitating a mind that has been injured by the painful loss.[34]

Yet, according to Klein, hostility toward the lost object can impede successful mourning. She (1994 [1940]: 105) writes, "when hatred against the lost loved person wells up in the mourner, his belief in him breaks down and the process of

[31] See also Austin 2020: 13 and 2021: 106–8 on the contrast between the satiety of the army and Achilleus' insatiety.

[32] Freud 1957 [1916]: 244–45, 256–57. [33] Klein 1994 [1940]: 110.

[34] Klein 1994 [1940]: 103–6, 112–14. See also Abraham 1988 [1924]: 435–38.

idealization is disturbed." This hatred often manifests in manic "feelings of triumph over the dead person." Thus, aggression toward the lost beloved keeps the mourner's inner world from being repaired.

Klein's model helps to illuminate Achilleus' psychological impasse. As we have seen, Homer figures Achilleus' triumphant mutilation of Hektor's body as a hostile expression of his libidinal attachment to Patroklos, and insistently connects Achilleus' aggression with the persistence of his mourning. The poet appears to be showing how the hero's ongoing abuse of Hektor as a "bad" object prevents him from achieving mental peace, from successfully idealizing Patroklos and, ultimately, internalizing him as a "good" object.[35] Achilleus' aggression against Hektor must be neutralized, or at least controlled, for the completion of his mourning over Patroklos.

This completion is, in turn, necessary for a gratifying conclusion to the *Iliad*'s narrative. Achilleus' longing for Patroklos and aggessive desire for revenge against Hektor have motivated the second arc of the main plot, and must be resolved for the epic to end and for the audience's narrative desire to be satisfied. Moreover, the poet's focus on Achilleus' psychology in Book 23 has reinvested the audience in these driving desires. The vivid depiction of Achilleus' grieving invites both our empathy and pity, although his disrespect of Hektor's corpse may diminish our sympathy for the hero, particularly as we remember the pain that it has caused for the Trojans. Indeed, by the beginning of Book 24, having been confronted with the unsatisfied desires of both Achilleus and the Trojans, we are doubly wanting.

Approaching the End

Homer confirms the problem presented by Achilleus' enduring aggressive desire through reintroduction of the divine perspective. In a sudden change of scene to Mt. Olympos, the narrator describes the "blessed gods" as a collective pitying Hektor and repeatedly urging Hermes to steal his corpse from Achilleus, but then clarifies that this prospect did not please Hera, Poseidon, and Athene due to their hatred of the Trojans (24.23–28). Through the gods' universal sympathy for Hektor, the poet indicates that Achilleus' continuing violence requires remediation, even as the divine disagreement regarding appropriate action once again

[35] Cf. Nagler 1974: 180, who writes, "Achilles wants to be one with Patroclus beyond the grave, but whether he knows it or not this cannot be achieved as long as he nurses his personal hatred. For in *this* death (as opposed to the famous picture at *Od.* 11.543–64) personality must be transcended; one cannot enter that state while still clinging to the petty categories and relationships that pertain to the individual during his life. The story of Achilles and Patroclus is an allegory of any human relationship; its fulfilment must be based on spiritual, not corporeal union, its endurance on what is whole and eternal rather than separate and subject to decay." Also compare with Shay 1994: 115–19, who argues that restoring honor to the enemy (especially after disrespecting the dead adversary) is essential to recovering from combat post-traumatic stress disorder.

reflects the unresolved conflict between Greeks and Trojans in the mortal sphere. The reference to the anti-Trojan faction among the gods also reminds the audience of Hera's and Athene's roles in supporting Achilleus' unbounded aggression during the second arc of the epic's main plot.

Indeed, as this scene develops, the gods—and especially Zeus—are positioned for a final time as key determinants of the *Iliad*'s narrative. When Apollo delivers a blistering critique of Achilleus' treatment of Hektor[36] and the gods' inaction, and Hera in turn objects to Apollo bestowing "the same honor" on a mortal and the child of a goddess, Zeus finally intervenes with a compromise that honors Hektor some but Achilleus more: he will send Thetis to her son with orders to release Hektor's body to Priam in exchange for ransom (24.32–76). Once again, the gods communally decide the direction of plot through a dialectical process in which Zeus serves as the ultimate judge. Zeus's pronouncement, which requires Achilleus to mitigate his aggression and allows the Trojans to reclaim Hektor, creates the conditions for the satisfaction of both Achilleus' and the Trojans' yearning for lamentation, and the corresponding gratification of the audience. The divine king's authoritative establishment of the course of the epic's remainder also arouses the audience's narrative desire to see how the ransoming of Hektor will unfold.[37] This narrative desire works together with our character engagement to keep us enthralled with the *Iliad* until its very end.

The gods' intervention, however, does not detract from the psychological realism of Achilleus' gradual and complex emergence from mourning. According to Freud (1957 [1916]: 255), when the mourner has tested and confirmed the reality of the loved one's death, the ego "is persuaded by the sum of its narcissistic satisfactions in being alive to sever its attachment to the non-existent object." That is, once the mourner is convinced that the loved one is gone, life's pleasures call to the ego, enticing it to rejoin the world of the living. By the time Zeus dispatches Thetis to Achilleus, the hero has thoroughly confirmed the reality of Patroklos' death, having burned his body, gathered his bones, and built his memorial mound.[38] Accordingly, when Thetis finds Achilleus still "groaning thickly" in the midst of companions preparing to sacrifice and roast a large

[36] Apollo declares that Achilleus' mind is not "right" (*ἐναίσιμοι*, 24.40) and compares him to a ravenous lion who has yielded to his "proud passion" (*ἀγήνορι θυμῷ*, 41–43); he also asserts that "one is doubtless going to lose someone closer [than a beloved companion], either a brother from the same womb or a son; but nevertheless, having wept and lamented, he lets him go . . . " (46–48). Both the god's invocation of Achilleus' "proud passion" and his contrast between the hero and another who has lost a male family member echo Aias' earlier critique of Achilleus' refusal to accept the embassy's appeal and rejoin the Greek army, and, as before, indicate that Achilleus is exceeding the bounds of normative masculinity in his aggressive desire.

[37] See also Kozak 2017: 217.

[38] Cf. Segal 1971c: 52–61, who argues that Achilleus' mourning has lessened in intensity by the opening of Book 24, and that when Thetis arrives with Zeus's command to ransom Hektor's body, "he is ready to relinquish the object of his hate, just as he has relinquished to the flames and to Hades the object of his love."

sheep for dinner (24.122–25), the goddess seems to externalize this "pleasure principle," demanding that Achilleus give up his detrimental fixation on the dead. Before conveying Zeus's message, Thetis asks her son the following (128–32):

> *τέκνον ἐμόν, τέο μέχρις ὀδυρόμενος καὶ ἀχεύων*
> *σὴν ἔδεαι κραδίην, μεμνημένος οὔτε τι σίτου*
> *οὔτ' εὐνῆς; ἀγαθὸν δὲ γυναικί περ ἐν φιλότητι*
> *μίσγεσθ'· οὐ γάρ μοι δηρὸν βέῃ, ἀλλά τοι ἤδη*
> *ἄγχι παρέστηκεν θάνατος καὶ μοῖρα κραταιή.*
>
> My child, until when, mourning and grieving,
> will you eat out your heart, remembering neither food
> nor bed at all? But it is a good thing even to mix with a woman
> in sexual union; for you will not live long, but already
> death and hard fate stand by you.

With this opening, Thetis gently chides Achilleus for his incessant, self-destructive mourning, and reminds him of his unsatisfied desires for food and sex, which his longing for Patroklos and aggressive desire for vengeance had pushed aside. Only after these words does she bid him to relinquish Hektor's body for ransom, and Achilleus immediately assents without protest, saying "may it be so" (133–39).[39] As Bonnie Honig (2013: 28) has suggested, building on the work of Henry Staten (1995: 44–46), this scene seems to represent "the *interruption of mourning* by bodily wants and desires, by hunger for food and sex... we get a displacement of pain by pleasure, or of one pain (loss) by another (hunger)." In Thetis' visitation, we appear to see the life instinct pulling Achilleus out of the depths of mourning, preparing him to give up at least the aggressive aspect of his libidinal attachment to Patroklos.

After indicating Achilleus' readiness to release Hektor, the poet turns again to the Trojans to show how Priam's desire to regain Hektor's corpse, in concert with Zeus's will, drives the plot toward its conclusion. Zeus sends Iris to order Priam to ransom Hektor from Achilleus (24.143–88), and Priam immediately starts loading a wagon with the ransom, explaining to Hekabe the divine epiphany while also declaring "dreadfully my drive (*μένος*) and passion (*θυμός*) bid me to go toward the ships into the wide camp of the Achaians" (198–99). Imbricated divine and mortal wishes continue to motivate the epic narrative jointly as Iris here seems to instill in the Trojan king a resolve to act on the desire that he had already

[39] Crotty 1994: 71 remarks that "The very terseness of Achilles' response suggests that he is already predisposed to do what the gods command." Likewise, Austin 2021: 110 concludes that "Achilles' release remains a personal reality, an internal release, which surpasses the results of divine efforts to mitigate his insatiate behavior."

conceived (22.412–20). Priam is now securely established as the desiring subject in a final narrative triangle, with Hektor as the desired object and Achilleus as the rival who, driven by his own desire, has perpetrated and sustains the father's loss.

When Hekabe warns of Achilleus' ruthless violence, Priam declares his determination to reclaim Hektor's body even at the cost of his own life (24.224–27):

> *εἰ δέ μοι αἶσα*
> *τεθνάμεναι παρὰ νηυσὶν Ἀχαιῶν χαλκοχιτώνων,*
> *βούλομαι· αὐτίκα γάρ μεκατακτείνειεν Ἀχιλλεὺς*
> *ἀγκὰς ἑλόντ' ἐμὸν υἱόν, ἐπὴν γόου ἐξ ἔρον εἵην.*

> If it is my fate
> to die beside the ships of the bronze-cuirassed Achaians,
> I am willing (*boulomai*); may Achilleus kill me at once
> after I have taken my son in my arms and put away the lust for lamentation (*eron goou*).

Here the Trojan king asserts the absolute force of his motivating desire, and confirms that only physical reunion with his son will enable him to sate himself with lament[40] and so resolve his longing. Later, the narrator emphasizes again how Priam spares no personal expense to redeem Hektor's corpse, reporting that he did not withhold a precious goblet from the ransom gifts, for "exceedingly he wished in his heart to ransom his dear son" (*περὶ δ' ἤθελε θυμῷ/ λύσασθαι φίλον υἱόν*, 236–37). Priam's powerful desire seems to be representative of the larger Trojan mindset insofar as Iris finds the king at the very center of the mourning royal family, ringed by grieving sons, daughters, and daughters-in-law (160–68). His psychology serves to remind the audience of the unmitigated longing of the Trojans more generally, and to reactivate our own corresponding sympathetic and empathetic desires.

However, it is the melancholic cast of Priam's mourning in particular that makes him psychologically capable of approaching Achilleus with the ransom offer. In his willingness to die by Achilleus' hand and when he smears his head and neck with dung (24.164–65), Priam demonstrates again how he has turned the aggressive libido associated with Hektor's loss inwards against himself rather than outwards against his enemy.[41] Homer thematizes this mental state by figuring the king's journey to Achilleus' tent as a symbolic death, complete with the lamentation of his household "as if he were going to his death" (328), a descent in darkness, and the guidance of the traditional psychopomp Hermes.[42] Priam's

[40] Nagler 1974: 192. See also Purves 2019: 163.

[41] Priam also externally redirects some aggression toward his surviving sons, whom he reviles as "disgraces," "liars," "dancers," and "thieves," and wishes dead instead of Hektor (24.248–62).

[42] Whitman 1958: 217–18; Nagler 1974: 184–85; Redfield 1994: 214.

mourning contrasts with Hekabe's, in that she, instead of internalizing her aggression, has displaced it externally onto Achilleus, whose liver she wishes to eat (212–13).[43] Hekabe cannot imagine putting away her lust for lamentation by holding Hektor in her arms. Instead, she suggests that they "weep apart sitting in the hall" (208–9) and imagines that Hektor's destiny is "to sate (ἆσαι) the swift dogs far apart from his parents" (211). The fact that Priam does *not* share her desire for vengeance allows him to humble himself before Achilleus and move a step closer to resolving his own—and Hekabe's—longing.

Resolutions of Desire

Although Achilleus has started submitting to the pull of life even before Priam arrives,[44] the Trojan king's submissive approach seems to be essential for convincing him to give up his hitherto relentless aggression and so fully emerge from mourning. Priam's posture offers a satisfaction of Achilleus' aggressive desire that both addresses and transcends the hero's fixation on Hektor. Ever since Agamemnon removed Briseis, Achilleus had been expecting a supplication that would restore his status as preeminent warrior. He did not receive that supplication from Agamemnon's embassy in Book 9, nor from Agamemnon himself in Book 19. Priam, however, finally gives Achilleus what he wants, grasping his knees and kissing his hands (24.478), utterly humbling himself and acknowledging the Greek hero's dominance.[45] Priam's kingly status and, especially, identity as Hektor's father make this act even more powerful, as he himself recognizes in his following entreaty of Achilleus: "I dared what no other mortal yet has done, to bring to my mouth the hand of the man who killed my son" (505–6). The Greek hero later confirms that he is impressed by Priam's extraordinary self-abasement when he wonders to the king how he "dared" to come "into the sight of the man who killed many good sons of yours" (520–21). As Kevin Crotty (1994: 71) comments, "there could scarcely be a more extravagant proof of Achilles' victory." He interprets this moment as the fulfillment of Zeus's earlier statement in Book 24 that he would give Achilleus more honor than Hektor (66–76) and Donna Wilson (2002: 127) connects it to Zeus's assertion that he would award

[43] Kozak 2017: 220 observes that Hekabe's cannibalistic rage "mirrors [Achilleus'], over lost love."

[44] Priam finds Achilleus having just finished eating and drinking with his companions Automedon and Alkimos (24.474–76), although the poet avoids here any mention of the satiation of desire. As Kozak 2017: 223 remarks, the hero's repast suggests "that Achilles is already in a different place than the last time the narrative aligned with him.... Something has changed."

[45] See also Taplin 1992: 270, who writes that this action "satisfies the condition that Achilleus missed at 9.387," where he demands that Agamemnon pay him back the "heart-grieving outrage" (θυμαλγέα λώβην). Cf. Purves 2019: 164–75 on the complex meaning of Priam's reaching gesture, and the ways in which it also serves to identify the two men with one another and even evoke a father–son relationship.

Achilleus *kudos* (24.110). Additionally, it can be construed as the final bestowal of the honor that Achilleus desired and Zeus promised in Book 1 when the hero first came into conflict with Agamemnon and the Achaian army.

Furthermore, by bringing gifts of ransom to Achilleus, Priam corrects Agamemnon's earlier failure to follow the reconciliation paradigm of Book 1 in his efforts to appease the angry hero. In that paradigm, Chryses is mollified by the return of his daughter Chryseis, while his divine champion Apollo is propitiated with a sacrificial hecatomb. Though Agamemnon offers Briseis' return and compensatory gifts to Achilleus in Book 9, he does not actually send them, and only reconciles with the hero when he produces the woman and gifts in Book 19. Odysseus asserts that the public bestowal of Agamemnon's gifts will cause Achilleus to "be melted in your mind" (φρεσὶ σῇσιν ἰανθῇς, 19.174), yet at this point Achilleus' aggressive desire is already redirected toward Hektor, and so these gifts do not satisfy him. Now, finally, Priam comes bearing ransom in accordance with Zeus's plan for him "to bring gifts to Achilleus that will melt his heart" (δῶρα δ' Ἀχιλλῆϊ φερέμεν, τά κε θυμὸν ἰήνῃ, 24.119). This formulaic line is repeated four times, by Zeus, Iris, and Priam himself (119 = 147 = 176 = 196), marking the importance of these gifts as a vehicle for undoing Achilleus' aggression and indicating how this episode repeats the epic's paradigmatic reconciliation. As Wilson (2002: 129) has explained, this ransom, like Priam's supplication, represents the honor (*timē*) that Achilleus has won by killing Hektor.[46] It is a substitute for Hektor's corpse that allows Achilleus to maintain his symbolic dominance while letting go of his detrimental psychological and physical attachment to his enemy. Achilleus later affirms that he has released Hektor's body because Priam has given him "not unseemly ransom" (594).

While Priam's supplication and ransom gifts are essential for mitigating Achilleus' aggression, Homer presents the Trojan king's speech of entreaty as most significant in enabling the hero to resolve his mourning. In this speech (24.486–506), Priam calls upon Achilleus to remember his father Peleus, growing old without his son's protection in Phthia, and so to pity him too, bereft of many sons and particularly Hektor, and reduced to the abject position of supplicating his children's killer. Although Priam does not immediately seem to inspire Achilleus' pity, the narrator reports that he "roused up in him a yearning for lamentation of his father" (τῷ δ' ἄρα πατρὸς ὑφ' ἵμερον ὦρσε γόοιο, 507). The Greek hero gently pushes the old king away, and the two men together "recall" (μνησαμένω) their losses and "cry" (κλαῖ'; κλαῖεν); Priam laments for Hektor, while Achilleus laments in alternation for his father and Patroklos (508–12). Eventually, the narrator relates that the Greek hero "had taken satisfaction of lamentation" (γόοιο τετάρπετο) and that the "yearning (ἵμερος) went away from

[46] See also Zanker 1994: 116 and Staten 1995: 30.

his diaphragm and limbs" (513–14): Achilleus' (acute) mourning is over. Emily Austin (2020: 14–16) observes that here for the first time Achilleus' yearning for lamentation has a specified object—his father. But what does Peleus have to do with Patroklos, and why does Priam's mention of him cause Achilleus to satisfy at last his impulse to lament?

Once again, Melanie Klein's work on the psychology of mourning can provide a possible answer to these questions.[47] Klein (1994 [1940]: 113) argues that each person's inner world

> consists of innumerable objects taken into the ego, corresponding partly to the multitude of varying aspects, good and bad, in which the parents (and other people) appeared in the child's unconscious mind throughout various stages of his development... all these objects are in the inner world in an infinitely complex relation both with each other and with the self.[48]

According to Klein, when a person experiences loss, this carefully constructed and balanced inner world is destroyed. For her, the work of mourning is not only to internalize the lost person as a "good" object but also to rebuild this inner world, reinstating "all his loved *internal* objects which he feels that he has lost. He is therefore *recovering* what he had already attained in childhood."[49] As Klein's words indicate, the parents are the primary and most important objects internalized within the ego, and therefore successful mourning restores the parents as "good" inner objects.[50]

Priam's reminder of Peleus appears to help Achilleus process and overcome the disruption to his inner world occasioned by Patroklos' loss. In Achilleus' case, it is not both of his parents, but rather his father only who is an integral part of this inner world and whose internal presence as a "good" object seems to have been disturbed. Achilleus' mother, Thetis, is ever present for the hero in the *Iliad*, appearing whenever he is suffering, and watching over his interests carefully; in Book 24, Zeus remarks that it would be impossible to steal Hektor's body from Achilleus since "his mother always attends him, day and night alike" (24.72–73).[51] Because Achilleus has never separated from his mother, she is not internalized as an object in his inner world. On the other hand, when he came to Troy, Achilleus

[47] Cf. Austin 2020: 18–19, who offers two other potential answers, though she herself seems unconvinced: (1) weeping for the father is part of the normal human life cycle, and thus helps Achilleus process "the unexpected loss of his comrade"; (2) insofar as yearning for lamentation reflects a longing to recover a life shared with the lost person, lamenting a *living* father carries a potential for satisfaction that lamenting a *dead* friend does not.

[48] Klein describes the assembly of these internalized objects as the "super-ego."

[49] Klein 1994 [1940]: 113 (her italics).

[50] Klein's theory that the mourning subject must reinstate his parents in order to restore his inner world represents her major innovation on Freud's and Abraham's understanding of mourning, as she herself observes (Klein 1994 [1940]: 113–14).

[51] MacCary 1982, especially pp. 78, 81, 126.

left behind his aged father Peleus in Phthia. Achilleus' positive identification with his father is absolutely central to who he is, as his frequent naming by patronymic makes clear, starting in the first line of the *Iliad*, where he is called "the son of Peleus, Achilleus" (*Πηληϊάδεω Ἀχιλῆος*). During the embassy of Book 9, both Odysseus and Phoinix invoke Peleus in order to convince Achilleus to rejoin the Greek community, but Achilleus asserts that he will return to Phthia, where Peleus will find a wife for him and where he will enjoy the possessions amassed by his father (9.393–400).

Yet the loss of Patroklos throws Achilleus' inner relationship with his father into crisis. In his first speech to Thetis after learning of Patroklos' death, Achilleus draws attention to the fact that Hektor stripped from Patroklos the armor that the gods gave to Peleus, and then he wishes that Peleus had never married Thetis (18.82–87). In his lament speech of Book 19, he connects Patroklos' death with the prospective death of his father (19.321–22, 334–35) and also with Peleus' grief in his absence, as he awaits news of his son's death (336–37).[52] Patroklos' shade also mentions Peleus (23.89–90) and, as we have seen, Achilleus dedicates a lock of hair to Patroklos that Peleus had promised to dedicate to the river Spercheios on Achilleus' safe return (23.144–49). When Priam invokes Peleus, he appears to enable Achilleus to properly grieve his now permanent separation from his beloved father and to restore him as a "good" object in his ego, reconstituting his shattered inner world.[53] At the same time, in this final episode of lamentation, Achilleus seems to release his remaining anger—which was unstuck by Priam's supplication and ransom gifts—and positively internalize Patroklos within his ego, achieving peace at last.[54]

Homer indicates this successful completion of mourning not only with the satisfaction of Achilleus' yearning for lamentation but also with his following gentleness toward Priam. After Achilleus is done with lament, he raises Priam from his suppliant position and "pities his grey head and grey chin" (24.515–16). Achilleus' aggression—a defining feature of his mourning—has suddenly dissipated. Moreover, his act of kindness and sympathetic feeling recall the concern for his fellows that defined Patroklos. These traits were particularly manifested in Patroklos' profound sympathy for the Achaian army's suffering, which motivated his entrance into battle. Indeed, Menelaos says of Patroklos that "he was known to

[52] See also Austin 2021: 24–25, who observes the "total loss" that Achilleus articulates in this moment.

[53] Cf. Alden 2000: 251–53, 287–89, who recognizes the prime significance of the father–son relationship in the *Iliad*, and argues that Priam's supplication of Achilleus is successful because it represents "the claim of the true father" at the top of the "ascending scale of affection" motif in the *Iliad*.

[54] Thus, Klein 1994 [1940]: 109 writes, "Through tears, which in the unconscious mind are equated with excrement, the mourner not only expresses his feelings and thus eases tension, but also expels his "bad" feelings and his "bad" objects, and this adds to the relief obtained through crying." Klein further explains how through crying, "persecution decreases and the pining for the lost loved object is experienced in full force. To put it in other words: hatred has receded and love is freed" (110).

all to be sweet while he was alive" (17.671–72).[55] Achilleus' change of behavior appears to confirm that he has successfully internalized Patroklos as a "good" object; in his treatment of Priam, Achilleus seems to be identifying with Patroklos' characteristic compassion.

Achilleus' verbal repudiation of lamentation also signifies the end of his mourning. He tells Priam (24.522–24),

> ἀλλ' ἄγε δὴ κατ' ἄρ' ἕζευ ἐπὶ θρόνου, ἄλγεα δ' ἔμπης
> ἐν θυμῷ κατακεῖσθαι ἐάσομεν ἀχνύμενοί περ·
> οὐ γάρ τις πρῆξις πέλεται κρυεροῖο γόοιο·
>
> But come now, sit down upon a chair,
> and let us allow the pains to lie at rest in our hearts, although we grieve;
> for there is no point in chilly lamentation…

Achilleus acknowledges that both men's longings for their lost loved ones will never be satisfied (they still "grieve") but also indicates that he has internalized both his desire and its object. He is done with mourning and so lamentation has outlived its "point" for him.[56] The second hemistich of line 523 repeats exactly the formula with which Achilleus' dismissed his aggressive desire toward Agamemnon (18.112 = 19.65), ending their conflict and the first arc of the epic's main plot. Here it indicates to the audience the resolution of Achilleus' second set of triangular desires as he calmly receives Priam.[57]

Furthermore, Achilleus' speech to the Trojan king may represent a transformation of Patroklos' loss into the realm of the symbolic, with language replacing the lost object.[58] Achilleus' discussion of the inevitable evil allotted by Zeus to mortals, as evidenced by both Peleus' and Priam's misfortunes (24.525–48), constitutes a religious or philosophical reflection on grief as a shared human

[55] For Patroklos' kindness, see also *Il.* 23.280–81 and Taplin 1992: 192. Cf. Shay 1994: 44–49, who argues that gentleness is a common feature of soldiers whose loss is felt particularly strongly by comrades-in-arms; Patroklos' characterization thus helps to establish the conditions for Achilleus' extreme mourning and revenge.

[56] Cf. Austin 2021: 109: "Achilles' understanding of lament's futility to restore the dead to life points to the cycle which he has been enmeshed in. He emerges from *pothê*-driven insatiety, not because that insatiety has been satisfied, but because it has been let go."

[57] Despite his new attitude, Achilleus remains aware of the fragility of his mental rehabilitation. He warns Priam not to push him to return Hektor's body immediately, recognizing the danger of his aggressive desire erupting again as Priam reclaims Hektor (24.560–70, 584–86). After this admonition, the narrator reports, "thus he spoke, and the old man was afraid and obeyed his command," repeating the line from Book 1 that had described Chryses' response to Agamemnon's threatening dismissal when he sought to ransom his daughter (24.571 = 1.33). This echo of Chryses' and Agamemnon's conflict—rather than their reconciliation—indicates how the resolution of this final triangle of desire could go sour if both participants do not act with the utmost delicacy. See also Rabel 1997: 202.

[58] See Abraham and Torok 1994 [1972]: 126–28, who argue that "introjection" of the lost object is actually its expression in words; language—which constitutes a communal, social relationship—fills the empty space left by the object. Introjection thus represents "the successful replacement of the object's presence with the self's cognizance of its absence."

experience. As Crotty (1994: 77) has recognized, it represents something new, a cognitive response to loss. It is different from the mourner's inarticulate vocalizations or even from lament speeches, which are full of emotion, personal, and specific, which "hypercathect" the relationship with the lost object.[59] Here, and later with his mythological *exemplum* of Niobe (24.602–17), Achilleus generalizes loss through speech instead of dwelling on Patroklos.

With this acknowledgment of commonality between himself and his enemy Priam,[60] Achilleus continues the erosion of the distinction between their desiring subjectivities that had begun when they united in shared mourning (24.509–12).[61] The merging of Achilleus' and Priam's minds and experiences resolves the audience's conflict of empathy, which was created in Book 22 with the narrative foregrounding of the Trojans' grief. No longer must we choose or vacillate between empathetic alignment with Achilleus or the Trojans; rather, we can comfortably identify with both parties at once. Moreover, Achilleus' acceptance of Priam's supplication and subsequent consolation of the grieving father make him a wholly sympathetic character once again, after his alienating violence. Now, too, we can maintain dual allegiances, taking pleasure in his triumph and in the end of his mourning, even as we continue to wish sympathetically for a corresponding conclusion to the Trojans' grief.

Homer emphasizes the final resolution of Achilleus' desires and gratifies the audience by completing this episode's reprise of the paradigmatic reconciliation scene in Book 1.[62] The Greek hero accepts the ransom gifts in exchange for Hektor's body (24.579), formally putting to rest his aggressive desire, and later agrees to a cessation of hostilities with the Trojans for eleven days (656–70), as Apollo in Book 1 was propitiated by the sacrificial hecatomb and ended his destructive plague. Once Hektor's corpse has been prepared for the journey home, Achilleus and Priam share a meal together, as the priest Chryses and the Achaians shared the sacrificial feast in Book 1, and the preparation of the meat in each case is described with the same formulaic language (24.623–24~1.465–66). In both scenes, the participants "put aside their lust (*eron*) for drink and food" (πόσιος καὶ ἐδητύος ἐξ ἔρον ἕντο, 24.628 = 1.469), in a resolution of physical desire

[59] Freud 1957 [1916]: 245 writes that during the mourning process, "the existence of the lost object is psychically prolonged. Each single one of the memories and expectations in which the libido is bound to the object is brought up and hypercathected, and detachment of the libido is accomplished in respect of it."

[60] On this commonality, see also Crotty 1994: 80–88 and Muellner 1996: 174.

[61] On their "shared experience" in this moment of grieving, see also Nagler 1974: 189. See further Macleod 1982: 26 for other narrative indications of the parallelism of their grief; Redfield 1994: 215 for the way that the murderer–suppliant simile (24.480–83) confuses Achilleus and Priam with one another; and Seaford 1994: 10 for their shared participation in "death ritual."

[62] See also Rabel 1997: 200, who observes how "Achilleus gives up his wrath in a passage marked by repetition of the four type-scenes that brought an end to the wrath of Apollo"; and Crotty 1994: 87–88, who draws a connection between the *philotēs* of Achilleus and Priam in this scene and the "reconciliatory friendship" of Chryses and the Achaians.

with further-reaching psychological resonance. After their meal, Achilleus and Priam "took (pleasurable) satisfaction" (τάρπησαν) in beholding one another (24.633), as Apollo similarly "was taking pleasure" (τέρπετ') in the Achaians' singing of a paean after their feast (1.474).[63] In Book 24, Priam also suggests to Achilleus that they "take satisfaction" (ταρπώμεθα) in sleep (24.636), again using language that marks this scene as a pleasurable consummation of desire.[64] Accordingly, when they have concluded their agreement of the burial truce, Priam and Achilleus go to bed (673–76), just as the Achaians took their rest after their celebration in the paradigmatic reconciliation scene (1.475–76). Significantly, the epic's last mention of Achilleus features him sleeping beside Briseis, finally reunited with his concubine (24.675–76). Together with his desires for lamentation and revenge, Achilleus' desires for food, sex, and sleep all appear to be satisfied as he makes his narrative exit.[65]

Besides putting to rest Achilleus' driving desires, this culminating episode resolves the *Iliad*'s narrative on an even more profound level. It symbolically corrects, or reverses, Agamemnon's original refusal to return Chryseis to her father, which first initiated triangular aggression and set the epic's plot in motion. As scholars have recognized, Priam's supplication of Achilleus recalls in many respects Chryses' entreaty of Agamemnon, with which the *Iliad*'s main narrative began;[66] however, while Agamemnon rejected Chryses' offer of ransom, Achilleus accepts the ransom gifts and returns the child.[67] In this final triangle of desire, longing for lost loved ones is remediated, even if it cannot be satisfied, and violent escalation is avoided.

Nevertheless, the audience, invested in both Achilleus' and the Trojans' psychologies, cannot be entirely satisfied until the Trojans' lust for lamentation is also sated, their mourning completed. Priam had indicated that his desire to lament was still unfulfilled when he resisted Achilleus' attempt to make him end his mourning prematurely, before he had recovered his son's remains and given him funeral rites (24.553–55). In a sign of this irresolution, Hermes does not let the Trojan king take satisfaction of sleep, but rather wakes him up in the middle of the night and shepherds him, with Hektor's corpse, back to Troy (682–94). On his way to the city, Priam resumes his lamentation (696), and he is soon joined

[63] Rabel 1997: 205. See also Austin 2021: 111–12, who interprets the satisfaction of Achilleus and Priam in feasting and mutual gazing as a further indication that "Achilles is newly released from insatiety." Cf. Edwards 1980: 21–22 on how both scenes diverge from the typical pattern of after-dinner conversation.

[64] See also Taplin 1992: 277–78, who writes, "After satisfying sorrow and hunger, there should be sleep," and observes how Priam's call for sleep helps Achilleus emerge from a mourning state that had been defined by (*inter alia*) sleeplessness or poor sleep.

[65] Cf. Taplin 1992: 80, who interprets this moment as Achilleus' assertion of "life in the teeth of imminent death."

[66] Macleod 1982: 33–34 catalogues the resemblances.

[67] Murnaghan 1997: 38 and Wilson 2002: 128, 132. Indeed, Whitman 1958: 259–60 has shown how all of Book 24 represents a large-scale reversal of Book 1 on both thematic and formal levels.

outside the walls by all the Trojan men and women, who feel "uncontrollable sorrow" (708). Finally, Andromache and Hekabe are able to reunite with Hektor's body, throwing themselves upon the wagon and touching his head (711–12), just as Achilleus had held the head of Patroklos during his funeral procession (23.136). Now, with Hektor's corpse at hand, there is a communal indulgence in lamentation that threatens to be ceaseless; the narrator reports that the sun would have set on the Trojans' mourning, if Priam had not intervened to bring Hektor's body into the house for the prothesis, promising, "then you will sate yourself with weeping" (ἄσεσθε κλαυθμοῖο, 24.713–17).[68]

Priam's action initiates Hektor's formal funeral rites (24.719–804), which end the Trojans' mourning and gratify the audience more perfectly.[69] Hektor is laid out and professional mourners sing dirges (*thrēnoi*); then Andromache, Hekabe, and Helen each deliver personal lament speeches (*gooi*), which are followed by group antiphonal refrains. Indeed, Helen's closing lament is answered by the groaning of the "boundless community" (δῆμος ἀπείρων, 776), which perhaps extends beyond the Trojan citizenry to include the external audience too, mourning in empathetic identification with the bereaved Trojans. Finally, the Trojan people gather wood, build the funeral pyre, and burn Hektor's body. Homer describes the following dawn with a formula that has only appeared once before in the *Iliad* to mark the breaking of day after the paradigmatic reconciliation at Chryse (24.788 = 1.477). This repeated line connects both moments as restorative resolutions. The Trojans ritually snuff out the pyre and shed a final tear while gathering Hektor's bones, then they lay his remains in a golden box, and cover them with a memorial mound. Having thus acknowledged Hektor's death and satisfied their desire for lamentation, they enjoy a funeral feast that concludes the epic narrative.

Audience (Dis)satisfaction

The *Iliad*'s ending resolves Achilleus' triangular desires and the main plot that they motivated, but leaves the epic's Trojan War superplot distinctly unresolved. The war is not over, and the completion of Hektor's funeral also means the end of the truce negotiated by Achilleus and Priam. Starting in Book 4, as we have seen, Homer features in his epic multiple authoritative prophecies of Troy's fall that arouse the audience's narrative desire to find out exactly how and when this

[68] Thus the mourning of the Trojan community over Hektor's body once again echoes in antiphonal responsion the mourning of the Achaian community over Patroklos' body, which similarly would have persisted through sunset but for Achilleus' parallel intervention (23.153–55).

[69] Flatt 2017: 393–95 identifies the formal lament speeches during Hektor's funeral as the basis for the audience's ultimate gratification in their "commemoration of Hector's outstanding heroism" and prevision of Troy's fall.

traditional eventuality will come about. In this respect, the poem's conclusion leaves us wanting.

Indeed, Homer magnifies our narrative desire for the remainder of the Trojan War story in the *Iliad*'s final books with frequent prediction and foreshadowing of events that postdate Hektor's funeral. Achilleus' own imminent death becomes an abiding theme of the main plot's second arc; Hektor, as he dies, even prophesies the precise contours of Achilleus' doom—how Paris and Apollo will kill him near the Skaian Gates (22.359–60). Both Priam and Andromache foresee the fall of Troy and the cruel fates of themselves and their family (22.59–76, 24.727–38). The unexpected appearance of the beautiful Kassandra as the first Trojan to perceive and announce Priam's return with Hektor's body (24.699–706), seems meant, as Oliver Taplin (1992: 280–81) has argued, to evoke her future concubinage to Agamemnon, and indeed the enslavement of all the Trojan women after the city is sacked.[70]

Book 24 also brings our attention to the unfinished superplot by thematizing Paris' and Helen's key and continuing roles in the Trojan War story. Here the poet finally explains that Hera and Athene hate the Trojans because of the insult Paris delivered to the goddesses when he "praised her who offered him grievous lustfulness" (τὴν δ' ᾔνησ' ἥ οἱ πόρε μαχλοσύνην ἀλεγεινήν, 24.25–30),[71] that is, when he judged most beautiful their rival Aphrodite and was rewarded with destructive sexual desire for Helen, the wife of another man. Paris is mentioned again as one of the sons whom Priam verbally abuses as cheating, dancing, good-for-nothings (248–62); while Hektor, protector of Troy, is dead, Paris survives, reminding the audience not only of his instigation of the war as subject of desire but also of his destiny to become Achilleus' killer.[72] Helen too reappears at the epic's close as the last to lament over Hektor. In her speech, she wishes that she had died before marrying Paris (763–64), sending off the audience with a final reminder of her devastating union with the Trojan prince, which is implicitly linked to Hektor's death—and other losses to come. While Paris and Helen remain safe and sound together, united by transgressive desire, the war will go on.

With these references to the larger Trojan War story, Homer keeps us unsatisfied, hungry for more epic. At the same time, he demonstrates his mastery of the whole Trojan War tradition—he knows what has happened and will happen beyond the bounds of the *Iliad*. Thus, he entices us with the promise of more

[70] See also Kozak 2017: 26, who notes how Kassandra is a key figure more generally in the story of Troy's fall, first predicting it to deaf ears, then being raped during the sack by Aias of Oileos, and finally given to Agamemnon. She writes, "Kassandra here acts like a sting at the end of a Marvel movie, looking forward to the next film in a series of interconnected stories."

[71] Aristarchus athetized these lines. For discussion and defense of their authenticity, see Macleod 1982: 88 and Richardson 1993: 276–78.

[72] However, in the *Iliad*'s culminating scene between Achilleus and Priam, which is designed to provide a large measure of narrative closure, Paris' survival is suppressed. Priam recalls only the deaths of many of his fifty sons, most especially Hektor (24.493–501).

story, if he should choose to relate it. In this way, the poet ensures that when he takes up the lyre again, he has an audience eager for his next song.

What is more, with the *Iliad*'s conclusion, Homer has also guaranteed a rapt audience for a *re-performance* of his epic. Through the echoes and reversals of Book 1 in Book 24, the poet points us backwards to the poem's beginning. Even as the epic's ending gratifies our sympathetic and empathetic desires, and satisfies our narrative desire to comprehend the curing of Achilleus' wrath and the resolution of both his mourning and that of the Trojans, it also reminds us where the story started. And, unless we have perfect memories, this provokes our desire to experience the narrative again, to relearn how precisely the plot unfolds to its denouement, and so to come to know and understand better the *Iliad*'s intricate story and characters in all of their detail and richness. This is the desire that motivates scholars of Homer,[73] and that has motivated this book.

[73] So Kozak 2017: 234 writes of herself, "And at the end, I am left with a nagging curiosity of how we all got to the end. So then, because I am an addict, I start once more at the beginning." I share her feeling.

Bibliography

Abraham, Karl. 1988 [1924]. "A Short Study of the Development of the Libido, Viewed in the Light of Mental Disorders." In *Selected Papers on Psychoanalysis*, translated by Douglas Bryan and Alix Strachey, with introduction by Ernest Jones, 418–502. London.

Abraham, Nicolas and Maria Torok. 1994 [1972]. "Mourning *or* Melancholia: Introjection *versus* Incorporation." In *The Shell and the Kernel: Renewals of Psychoanalysis*, Vol. 1, edited, translated, with introduction by Nicholas T. Rand, 125–38. Chicago; London.

Acadia, Lilith. 2021. "Queer Theory." Oxford Research Encyclopedia of Literature. Published online. https://doi.org/10.1093/acrefore/9780190201098.013.1003.

Adkins, A. W. H. 1963. "'Friendship' and 'Self-Sufficiency' in Homer and Aristotle." *Classical Quarterly* N. S. 13: 30–45.

Alden, Maureen. 2000. *Homer Beside Himself: Para-Narratives in the* Iliad. Oxford.

Alexiou, Margaret. 1974. *The Ritual Lament in Greek Tradition*. Cambridge.

Allan, William and Douglas Cairns. 2011. "Conflict and Community in the *Iliad*." In *Competition in the Ancient World*, edited by Nick Fisher and Hans van Wees, 113–46. Swansea.

Allen-Hornblower, Emily. 2015. "Revisiting the Apostrophes to Patroclus in Iliad 16." In *Donum natalicium digitaliter confectum Gregorio Nagy septuagenario a discipulis collegis familiaribus oblatum: A Virtual Birthday Gift Presented to Gregory Nagy on Turning Seventy by his Students, Colleagues and Friends*. Washington, DC. http://chs.harvard.edu/CHS/article/display/4702.

Altieri, Charles. 2003. *The Particulars of Rapture: An Aesthetics of the Affects*. Ithaca.

Arend, Walter. 1933. *Die Typischen Scenen Bei Homer*. Berlin.

Arieti, James A. 1985. "Achilles' Guilt." *The Classical Journal* 8 (3): 193–203.

Arthur, Marylin B. 1981. "The Divided World of *Iliad* VI." In *Reflections of Women in Antiquity*, edited by Helene P. Foley, 19–44. New York.

Auerbach, Erich. 2003 [1953]. *Mimesis: The Representation of Reality in Western Literature*. Fiftieth anniversary edn., translated by Willard R. Trask, with a new introduction by Edward W. Said. Princeton.

Austin, Emily P. 2015. "Grief as *ποθή*: Understanding the Anger of Achilles." *New England Classical Journal* 42 (3): 147–163.

Austin, Emily P. 2020. "Achilles' Desire for Lament: Variations on a Theme." *Classical World* 114 (1): 1–23.

Austin, Emily P. 2021. *Grief and the Hero: The Futility of Longing in the* Iliad. Ann Arbor.

Austin, Norman. 1994. *Helen of Troy and Her Shameless Phantom*. Ithaca.

Bakker, Egbert J. 2009. "Homer, Odysseus, and the Narratology of Performance." In *Narratology and Interpretation: The Content of Narrative form in Ancient Literature*, edited by Jonas Grethlein and Antonios Rengakos, 117–36. New York; Berlin.

Bakker, Egbert J. 2013. *The Meaning of Meat and the Structure of the* Odyssey. Cambridge.

Barker, Pat. 2018. *The Silence of the Girls*. New York.

Barrett, D. S. 1981. "The Friendship of Achilles and Patroclus." *Classical Bulletin* 57: 87–93.

Barthes, Roland. 1966. "Introduction à l'analyse structurale des récits." *Communications* 8 (1): 1–27.

Barthes, Roland. 1974. *S/Z*, translated by Richard Miller. First American edn. New York.

Bassett, Samuel Eliot. 1938. *The Poetry of Homer*. Berkeley.

Bassi, Karen. 1997. "Orality, Masculinity, and the Greek Epic." *Arethusa* 30 (3): 315–40.

Beck, Deborah. 2005. *Homeric Conversation*. Hellenic Studies Series 14. Cambridge, MA.

Beck, Deborah. 2012. *Speech Presentation in Homeric Epic*. Austin.

Beekes, Robert. 2010. *Etymological Dictionary of Greek*. Leiden.

Bell, Matthew. 2014. *Melancholia: The Western Malady*. Cambridge.

Benveniste, Emile. 1973. *Indo-European Language and Society*, translated by Elizabeth Palmer. London.

Bergren, Ann. 2008. "Helen's Web: Time and Tableau in the *Iliad*." In *Weaving Truth: Essays on Language and the Female in Greek Thought*, 43–55. Washington, DC; Cambridge, MA.

Bersani, Leo. 1995. *Homos*. Cambridge, MA.

Beye, Charles R. 1974. "Male and Female in the Homeric Poems." *Ramus* 3: 87–101.

Block, Elizabeth. 1982. "The Narrator Speaks: Apostrophe in Homer and Vergil." *Transactions of the American Philological Association* 112: 7–22.

Blondell, Ruby. 2010. "'Bitch That I Am': Self-Blame and Self-Assertion in the *Iliad*." *Transactions of the American Philological Association* 140 (1): 1–32.

Blondell, Ruby. 2013. *Helen of Troy: Beauty, Myth, Devastation*. Oxford.

Blondell, Ruby. 2018. "Helen and the Divine Defense: Homer, Gorgias, Euripides." *Classical Philology* 113: 113–33.

Boedeker, Deborah Dickmann. 1974. *Aphrodite's Entry into Greek Epic*. Mnemosyne, Bibliotheca Classica Batava: Supplementum v. 32. Leiden.

Boll, Franz. 1917. "Zur homerischen Presbeia." *Zeitschrift für die deutsch-österreichischen Gymnasien* 68: 1–6.

Boll, Franz. 1919–20. "Noch einmal zur homerischen Presbeia." *Zeitschrift für die deutsch-österreichischen Gymnasien* 69: 414–416.

Bonnet, Corinne. 2017. "Le dieux en assemblée." In *Les dieux d'Homère: polythéisme et poésie en Grèce ancienne*. Kernos, Supplément 31, edited by Gabriella Pironti and Corinne Bonnet, 87–112. Liège.

Bortolussi, Marisa and Peter Dixon. 2003. *Psychonarratology: Foundations for the Empirical Study of Literary Response*. Cambridge.

Bouvier, David. 2017. "Le choix d'Aphrodite et les causes de la guerre." In *Les dieux d'Homère: polythéisme et poésie en Grèce ancienne*. Kernos, Supplément 31, edited by Gabriella Pironti and Corinne Bonnet, 177–202. Liège.

Bowie, A. M. ed. 2019. *Homer Iliad Book III*. Cambridge Greek and Latin Classics. Cambridge.

Bowra, C. M. 1930. *Tradition and Design in the* Iliad. Oxford.

Bozzone, Chiara. 2015. "The Death of Achilles and the Meaning and Antiquity of Formulas in Homer." *Paper delivered at the 146th Annual Meeting of the Society for Classical Studies*. New Orleans.

Brewer, W. F. and E. H. Lichtenstein. 1982. "Stories are to Entertain: A Structural-Affect Theory of Stories." *Journal of Pragmatics* 6: 473–86.

Brillet-Dubois, P. 2011. "An Erotic Aristeia: The Homeric Hymn to Aphrodite and its Relation to the Iliadic Tradition." In *The Homeric Hymns: Interpetative Essays*, edited by A. Faulkner, 105–32. Oxford.

Brooks, Peter. 1984. *Reading for the Plot: Design and Intention in Narrative*. Cambridge, MA.

Brügger, Claude. 2018. *Homer's Iliad: The Basel Commentary. Book XVI*, edited by Anton Bierl and Joachim Latacz; English edn. translated by Benjamin W. Millis and Sara Strack, and edited by S. Douglas Olson. Boston; Berlin.

Burgess, J. S. 2001. *The Tradition of the Trojan War in Homer and the Epic Cycle*. Baltimore.

Butler, Judith. 2004. *Precarious Life: The Powers of Mourning and Violence*. London.
Cairns, Douglas L. 2001. "Affronts and Quarrels in the *Iliad*." In *Oxford Readings in Homer's* Iliad, edited by D. L. Cairns, 203–19. Oxford.
Calame, Claude. 1999. *The Poetics of Eros in Ancient Greece*. Princeton.
Calhoun, G. M. 1937. "Homer's Gods—Prolegomena." *Transactions of the American Philological Association* 68: 11–25.
Caracciolo, Marco. 2016. *Strange Narrators in Contemporary Fiction: Explorations in Readers' Engagement with Characters*. Lincoln.
Carson, Anne. 1998. *Eros the Bittersweet*. 1st Dalkey Archive edn. Normal.
Caserio, Robert L., Lee Edelman, Judith Halberstam, José Estaban Muñoz, and Jim Dean. 2006. "The Antisocial Thesis in Queer Theory." *Publications of the Modern Language Association* 121 (3): 819–28.
Chantraine, Pierre. 2009. *Dictionnaire étymologique de la langue grecque: Histoire de mots*. Nouvelle édition. Paris.
Chodorow, Nancy J. 2015. "From the Glory of Hera to the Wrath of Achilles: Narratives of Second-Wave Masculinity and Beyond." *Studies in Gender and Sexuality* 16 (4): 261–70.
Christensen, Joel P. 2019. "Human cognition and narrative closure: The *Odyssey*'s open-end." In *The Routledge Handbook of Classics and Cognitive Theory*, edited by Peter Meineck, William Michael Short, and Jennifer Devereaux, 139–55. London.
Clader, Linda L. 1976. *Helen: The Evolution from Divine to Heroic in Greek Epic Tradition*. Leiden.
Clarke, W. M. 1978. "Achilles and Patroclus in Love." *Hermes* 106 (3): 381–96.
Cohen, Cathy. 1997. "Punks, Bulldaggers, and Welfare Queens: The Radical Potential of Queer Politics?" *GLQ: A Journal of Lesbian and Gay Studies* 3 (4): 437–465.
Collins, Leslie. 1988. *Studies in Characterization in the Iliad*. Frankfurt am Main.
Coplan, Amy. 2004. "Empathic Engagement with Narrative Fictions." *The Journal of Aesthetics and Art Criticism* 62 (2): 141–52.
Coray, Marina. 2016. *Homer's Iliad: The Basel Commentary. Book XIX*, edited by Anton Bierl and Joachim Latacz; English edn. translated by Benjamin W. Millis and Sara Strack, and edited by Douglas S. Olson. Boston; Berlin.
Crotty, Kevin. 1994. *The Poetics of Supplication: Homer's* Iliad *and* Odyssey. Ithaca.
Currie, Bruno. 2016. *Homer's Allusive Art*. Oxford.
D'Angour, Armand. 2013. "Love's Battlefield: Rethinking Sappho Fragment 31." In Erôs *in Ancient Greece*, edited by Ed Sanders, Chiara Thumiger, Chris Carey, and Nick J. Lowe, 59–72. Oxford.
Davidson, James. 2007. *The Greeks and Greek Love: A Radical Reappraisal of Homosexuality in Ancient Greece*. London.
Davison, J. A. 1965. "Thucydides, Homer, and the 'Achaean Wall.'" *Greek, Roman and Byzantine Studies* 6: 5–28.
Dean-Jones, Lesley. 1991. "The Cultural Construct of the Female Body in Classical Greek Science." In *Women's History and Ancient History*, edited by Sarah B. Pomeroy, 111–37. Chapel Hill.
Deleuze, Gilles and Félix Guattari. 1983. *Anti-Oedipus: Capitalism and Schizophrenia*. Minneapolis.
Devereux. 1978. "Achilles' 'Suicide' in the *Iliad*." *Helios* 6: 3–15.
Dickson, Keith. 1990. "A Typology of Mediation in Homer." *Oral Tradition* 5 (1): 37–71.
Dickson, Keith. 1992. "Kalchas and Nestor: Two Narrative Strategies in 'Iliad' 1." *Arethusa* 25 (3): 327–358.

Dodds, E. R. 1951. *The Greeks and the Irrational.* Berkeley.

Doherty, Lillian Eileen. 1995. *Siren Songs: Gender, Audiences, and Narrators in the* Odyssey. Ann Arbor.

Donlan, Walter. 1993. "Duelling with Gifts in the *Iliad*: As the Audience Saw It." *Colby Quarterly* 29 (3): 155–72.

DuBois, Page. 1982. *Centaurs and Amazons: Women and the Pre-History of the Great Chain of Being.* Ann Arbor.

Duckworth, George E. 1933. *Foreshadowing and Suspense in the Epics of Homer, Apollonius, and Vergil.* Princeton.

Dué, Casey. 2002. *Homeric Variations on a Lament by Briseis.* Lanham.

Eagleton, Terry. 2003. *Sweet Violence: The* Idea *of the Tragic.* Malden; Oxford.

Ebbott, Mary. 1999. "The Wrath of Helen: Self-Blame and Nemesis in the *Iliad*." In *Nine Essays on Homer*, edited by Miriam Carlisle and Olga Levaniouk, 3–20. Lanham.

Edelman, Lee. 2004. *No Future: Queer Theory and the Death Drive.* Durham; London.

Edwards, Mark W. 1980. "Convention and Individuality in Iliad 1." *Harvard Studies in Classical Philology* 84: 1–28.

Edwards, Mark W. 1987. *Homer: Poet of the* Iliad. Baltimore.

Edwards, Mark W. 1991. *The Iliad: A Commentary. Volume V: books 17–20*, edited by G. S. Kirk. Cambridge.

Elmer, David F. 2005. "Helen *Epigrammatopoios*." *Classical Antiquity* 24 (1): 1–39.

Elmer, David F. 2013. *The Poetics of Consent: Collective Decision Making and the* Iliad. Baltimore.

Elmer, David F. 2020. "The *Odyssey* and the Desires of Traditional Narrative." In *Zbornik radova međunarodnog znanstvenog skupa "Natales grate numeras?"*, edited by D. Sorić, L. Mijić, and A. Bartulović, 3–22. Zadar.

Eng, David L. 2000. "Melancholia in the Late Twentieth Century." *Signs* 25 (4): 1275–81.

Eng, David L. with Judith Halberstam and José Estaban-Munos. 2005. "Introduction: What's Queer about Queer Studies Now?" *Social Text* 23 (3–4, 84–85): 1–17.

Erbse, Hartmut. 1969–1988. *Scholia Graeca in Homeri Iliadem (scholia vetera).* Berlin.

Fantuzzi, Marco. 2012. *Achilles in Love: Intertextual Studies.* Oxford.

Felson, Nancy and Laura Slatkin. 2004. "Gender and Homeric Epic." In *The Cambridge Companion to Homer*, edited by Robert Fowler, 91–114. Cambridge.

Felson-Rubin, Nancy. 1994. *Regarding Penelope: From Character to Poetics.* Princeton.

Fenik, Bernard. 1968. *Typical Battle Scenes in the Iliad.* Hermes 21. Wiesbaden.

Finley, M. I. 1955. "Marriage, Sale and Gift in the Homeric World." *Revue Internationale des Droits de l'Antiquité* iii. Vol. 2: 167–94.

Flatt, Tyler. 2017. "Narrative Desire and the Limits of Lament in Homer." *The Classical Journal* 112 (4): 385–404.

Foley, Helene. 1978. "'Reverse Similes' and Sex roles in the *Odyssey*." *Arethusa* 11 (1/2): 7–26.

Forsyth, Neil. 1979. "The Allurement Scene: A Typical Pattern in Greek Oral Epic." *California Studies in Classical Antiquity* 12: 107–20.

Franco, Cristiana. 2014. *Shameless: The Canine and the Feminine in Ancient Greece*, translated by Matthew Fox. Berkeley.

Freud, Sigmund. 1957 [1916]. "Mourning and Melancholia." In *The Standard Edition of the Complete Psychological Works of Sigmund Freud.* Vol. XIV (1914–1916), translated and edited by James Strachey, 243–58. London.

Freud, Sigmund. 1960 [1923]. *The Ego and the Id*, translated by Joan Riviere, revised and edited by James Strachey. New York.

Friedman, Rachel. 2001. "Divine Dissension and the Narrative of the Iliad." *Helios* 28 (2): 99–118.
Friedrich, Paul and James Redfield. 1978. "Speech as a Personality Symbol: The Case of Achilles." *Language* 54: 263–88.
Frontisi-Ducroux, F. 1986. *La cithare d'Achille: Essai sur la poétique de l'*Iliade. Biblioteca di Quaderni Urbinati di Cultura Classica 1. Rome.
Gaca, Kathy L. 2008. "Reinterpreting the Homeric Simile of Iliad 16.7–11: The Girl and Her Mother In Ancient Greek Warfare." *American Journal of Philology* 129 (2): 145–71.
Genette, Gérard. 1980. *Narrative Discourse: An Essay in Method*, translated by Jane E. Lewin. Ithaca.
Gerrig, Richard. 1993. *Experiencing Narrative Worlds: On the Psychological Activities of Reading*. New Haven.
Girard, René. 1965. *Deceit, Desire, and the Novel: Self and Other in Literary Structure*. Baltimore.
Glotz, Gustave. 1904. *La solidarité de la famille dans le droit criminel en Grèce*. Paris.
Gould, John P. 1973. "Hiketeia." *Journal of Hellenic Studies* 93: 74–103.
Graver, Margaret. 1995. "Dog-Helen and Homeric Insult." *Classical Antiquity* 14 (1): 41–61.
Graziosi, Barbara and Johannes Haubold. 2003. "Homeric Masculinity: *HNOPEH* and *AΓHNOPIH*." *Journal of Hellenic Studies* 123: 60–76.
Graziosi, Barbara and Johannes Haubold. eds. 2010. *Homer Iliad: Book VI*. Cambridge Greek and Latin Classics. Cambridge.
Grethlein, Jonas. 2005. "Eine Anthropologie des essens: Der Essensstreit in der 'Ilias' und die Erntemetapher in Il. 19.221–224." *Hermes* 133: 257–279.
Grethlein, Jonas. 2006. *Das Geschichtsbild der Iliad: Eine Untersuchung aus phänomenologischer und narratologischer Perspektive. Hypomnemata, Bd. 163.* Göttingen.
Griffin, Jasper. 1980. *Homer on Life and Death*. Oxford.
Griffin, Jasper. 1986. "Homeric Words and Speakers." *Journal of Hellenic Studies* 106: 36–57.
Griffin, Jasper. ed. 1995. *Homer Iliad IX*. Oxford.
Grube, G. M. A. 1951. "The Gods of Homer." *Phoenix* 5 (3/4): 62–78.
Hainsworth, Bryan. 1993. *The Iliad: A Commentary. Volume III: books 9–12*, edited by G. S. Kirk. Cambridge.
Halperin, David M. 1990. *One Hundred Years of Homosexuality: And Other Essays on Greek Love*. New York; London.
Halperin, David M. 1995. *Saint Foucault: Toward a Gay Hagiography*. Oxford.
Halperin, David M., John J. Winkler, and Froma I. Zeitlin. eds. 1990. *Before Sexuality: The Construction of Erotic Experience in the Ancient World*. Princeton.
Hauser, Emily. 2017. *For the Most Beautiful*. New York; London.
Heiden, Bruce. 1996. "The Three Movements of the *Iliad*." *Greek, Roman and Byzantine Studies* 37: 5–22.
Heiden, Bruce. 2008. *Homer's Cosmic Fabrication*. Oxford.
Holland, Gary. 1993. "The Name of Achilles: A Revised Etymology." *Glotta* 71: 17–27.
Holmberg, Ingrid. 2014. "Sex in Ancient Greek and Roman Epic." In *A Companion to Greek and Roman Sexualities*, edited by Thomas K. Hubbard, 321–41. Chichester.
Homer, Sean. 2005. *Jacques Lacan*. Routledge Critical Thinkers. New York; London.
Honig, Bonnie. 2013. *Antigone Interrupted*. Cambridge.
Hooker, James. 1987. "Homeric *Φίλος*." *Glotta* 65: 44–65.

Hubbard, Thomas K. 2013. "Peer Homosexuality." In *A Companion to Greek and Roman Sexualities*, edited by Thomas K. Hubbard, 132–53. Chichester.

Jamison, Stephanie W. 1994. "Draupadí on the Walls of Troy: 'Iliad' 3 from an Indic Perspective." *Classical Antiquity* 13 (1): 5–16.

Janko, Richard. 1992. *The* Iliad: *A Commentary, Volume IV: books 13–16*, edited by G. S. Kirk. Cambridge.

Jong, Irene J. F. de. 1985. "Iliad 1.366-392: A Mirror Story." *Arethusa* 18 (1): 5–22.

Jong, Irene J. F. de. 1987a. *Narrators and Focalizers: The Presentation of the Story in the* Iliad. Amsterdam.

Jong, Irene J. F. de. 1987b. "Silent Characters in the *Iliad*." In *Homer: Beyond Oral Poetry*, edited by J. M. Bremer, I. J. F. de Jong, and J. Kalff, 105–21. Amsterdam.

Jong, Irene J. F. de. 2009. "Metalepsis in Ancient Greek Literature." In *Narratology and Interpretation*, edited by Jonas Grethlein and Antonios Rengakos, 87–115. Berlin.

Jong, Irene J. F. de. ed. 2012. *Homer Iliad Book XXII*. Cambridge Greek and Latin Classics. Cambridge.

Jose, Paul E. and William F. Brewer. 1984. "Development of Story Liking: Character Identification, Suspense, and Outcome Resolution." *Developmental Psychology* 20 (5): 911–24.

Kakridis, Johannes Th. 1949. *Homeric Researches*. Lund.

Kakridis, Johannes Th. 1971. *Homer Revisited*. Lund.

Keen, Suzanne. 2007. *Empathy and the Novel*. Oxford.

Kelly, Adrian. 2007. *A Referential Commentary and Lexicon to* Iliad *VIII*. Oxford.

Kelly, Adrian. 2008. "The Babylonian Captivity of Homer: The Case of the Dios Apate." *Rheinisches Museum* 151: 259–304.

Kennedy, G. A. 1986. "Helen's Web Unraveled." *Arethusa* 19: 5–14.

Kim, Jinyo. 2000. *The Pity of Achilles: Oral Style and the Unity of the Iliad*. Lanham.

King, Katherine Callen. 1987. *Achilles: Paradigms of the War Hero from Homer to the Middle Ages*. Berkeley.

Kirk, G. S. 1985. *The Iliad: A Commentary. Volume I: books 1–4*, edited by G. S. Kirk. Cambridge.

Kirk, G. S. 1990. *The Iliad: A Commentary. Volume II: books 5–8*, edited by G. S. Kirk. Cambridge.

Klein, Melanie. 1994 [1940]. "Mourning and Its Relation to Manic-Depressive States." In *Essential Papers on Object Loss*, edited by Rita V. Frankiel, 95–122. New York; London.

Knox, Ronald and Joseph Russo. 1989. "Agamemnon's Test: 'Iliad' 2.73–75." *Classical Antiquity* 8 (2): 351–58.

Konstan, David. 1997. *Friendship in the Classical World*. Cambridge.

Konstan, David. 2013. "Between Appetite and Emotion, or Why Can't Animals Have *Erôs*?" In Erôs *in Ancient Greece*, edited by Ed Sanders, Chiara Thumiger, Chris Carey, and Nick J. Lowe, 13–26. Oxford.

Kozak, Lynn. 2017. *Experiencing Hektor: Character in the* Iliad. New York; London.

Krieter-Spiro, Martha. 2015. *Homer's Iliad: The Basel Commentary Book III*, edited by Anton Bierl and Joachim Latacz; English edn. translated by Benjamin W. Millis and Sara Strack, and edited by S. Douglas Olson. Boston; Berlin.

Krieter-Spiro, Martha. 2018. *Homer's Iliad: The Basel Commentary Book XIV*, edited by Anton Bierl and Joachim Latacz; English edn. translated by Benjamin W. Millis and Sara Strack, and edited by S. Douglas Olson. Boston; Berlin.

Krischer, Tilman. 1971. *Formale Konventionen der homerischen Epik*. Zetemata 56. Munich.

Kullmann, Wolfgang. 1955. "Ein vorhomerisches Motiv im Iliasproömium." *Philologus* 99: 167–92.

Kurke, Leslie. 2013. "Imagining Chorality: Wonder, Plato's Puppets, and Moving Statues." In *Performance and Culture in Plato's* Laws, edited by Anastasia-Erasmia Peponi, 123–70. Cambridge.

Lacan, Jacques. 2006 [1958]. "The Signification of the Phallus." In *Écrits: The First Complete Edition in English*, translated by Bruce Fink, 575–84. New York.

Lacan, Jacques. 2017 [1958]. "XXI. The 'Still Waters Run Deep' Dreams." In *Formations of the Unconscious: The Seminar of Jacques Lacan Book V*, edited by Jacques-Alain Miller, translated by Russell Grigg, 350–65. Malden; Cambridge.

Lacey, W. K. 1966. "Homeric *Eδνα* and Penelope's *Κύριος*." *Journal of Hellenic Studies* 86: 55–68.

Lagache, Daniel. 1993. "The work of mourning: ethnology and psychoanalysis [1938]." In *The Work of Daniel Lagache. Selected Papers 1938–1964*, translated by Elisabeth Holder, 15–29. London.

Lang, Mabel. 1983. "Reverberation and Mythology in the Iliad." In *Approaches to Homer*, edited by Carl A. Rubino and Cynthia Shelmerdine, 140–64. Austin.

Latacz, Joachim. 1966. *Zum Wortfeld "Freude" in der Sprache Homers*. Heidelberg.

Latacz, Joachim. 2015. "The Structure of the Iliad." In *Homer's Iliad, The Basel Commentary: Prolegomena*, edited by Anton Bierl and Joachim Latacz; English edn. translated by Benjamin W. Millis and Sara Strack, and edited by S. Douglas Olson, 151–63. Boston; Berlin.

Lateiner, Donald. 1995. *Sardonic Smile: Nonverbal Behavior in Homeric Epic*. Ann Arbor.

Leaf, Walter. ed. 1971. *The Iliad*. 2nd edn. Amsterdam.

Leavitt, Jonathan D. and Nicholas J. S. Christenfeld. 2011. "Story Spoilers Don't Spoil Stories." *Psychological Science* 22 (9): 1152–54.

Lemon, Lee T. and Marion J. Reis. 1965. *Russian Formalist Criticism; Four Essays*. Regents Critics Series. Lincoln.

Lendle, O. 1968. "Paris, Helena und Aphrodite: Zur Interpretation des 3. Gesanges des Ilias." *Antike und Abendland* 14: 63–71.

Lesser, Rachel H. 2015. "Listening for the Plot: The Role of Desire in the *Iliad*'s Narrative." PhD diss. University of California, Berkeley.

Lesser, Rachel H. 2019. "Female Ethics and Epic Rivalry: Helen in the *Iliad* and Penelope in the *Odyssey*." *American Journal of Philology* 140 (2): 189–226.

Lesser, Rachel H. 2021. "Sappho's Mythic Models for Female Homoeroticism." *Arethusa* 54 (2): 121–61.

Lévi-Strauss, Claude. 1969. *The Elementary Structures of Kinship*, revised, edited, and translated by James Harle Bell, John Richard Von Sturmer, and Rodney Needham. Boston.

Liebert, Rana Saadi. 2017. *Tragic Pleasure from Homer to Plato*. Cambridge.

Lloyd, Michael. 2004. "The Politeness of Achilles: Off-Record Conversation Strategies in Homer and the Meaning of 'Kertomia.'" *Journal of Hellenic Studies* 124: 75–89.

Lohmann, Dieter. 1970. *Die Komposition der Reden in der Ilias*. Berlin.

Lohmann, Dieter. 1988. *Die Andromache-Szenen der Ilias*. Zürich.

Lord, Albert Bates. 2000 [1960]. *The Singer of Tales*. 2nd edn. Harvard Studies in Comparative Literature 24. Cambridge, MA.

Louden, Bruce. 2006. *The Iliad: Structure, Myth, and Meaning*. Baltimore.

Lowenstam, Steven. 1993. *The Scepter and the Spear: Studies on Forms of Repetition in the Homeric Poems*. Lanham.

Luca, Roberto. 2001. *Eros & Epos. Il lessico d'amore nei poemi omerici*. Bassano del Grappa.

Lynn-George, Michael. 1988. Epos: *Word, Narrative and the* Iliad. Language, Discourse, Society. Basingstoke.

Lyons, Deborah J. 2012. *Dangerous Gifts: Gender and Exchange in Ancient Greece*. Austin.

MacCary, W. Thomas. 1982. *Childlike Achilles: Ontogeny and Phylogeny in the* Iliad. New York.

Mackie, Hilary. 1996. *Talking Trojan: Speech and Community in the* Iliad. Lanham.

Macleod, C. W. ed. 1982. *Homer Iliad Book XXIV*. Cambridge Greek and Latin Classics. Cambridge.

Marks, Jim. 2016. "Herding Cats: Zeus, The Other Gods, and the Plot of the *Iliad*." In *The Gods of Greek Hexameter Poetry*, edited by James J. Clauss, Martine Cuypers, and Ahuvia Kahane, 60–75. Stuttgart.

Martin, Richard P. 1989. *The Language of Heroes: Speech and Performance in the* Iliad. Ithaca.

Martin, Richard P. 2003. "Keens from the Absent Chorus: 'Troy to Ulster.'" *Western Folklore* 62 (1/2): 119–142.

Mauritsch, P. 1992. *Sexualität im frühen Griechenland. Untersuchungen zu Norm und Abweichung in den homerischen Epen*. Alltag und Kulture im Altertum 1. Vienna.

Mayer, Adrienne. 2014. *The Amazons: Lives and Legends of Warrior Women Across the Ancient World*. Princeton.

Meyer, Leonard. 1956. *Emotion and Meaning in Music*. Chicago.

Minchin, Elizabeth. 2007. *Homeric Voices: Discourse, Memory, Gender*. Oxford.

Minchin, Elizabeth. 2010. "From Gentle Teasing to Heavy Sarcasm: Instances of Rhetorical Irony in Homer's 'Iliad.'" *Hermes* 138 (4): 323–43.

Minchin, Elizabeth. 2019. "The cognition of deception: falsehoods in Homer's *Odyssey* and their audiences." In *The Routledge Handbook of Classics and Cognitive Theory*, edited by Peter Meineck, William Michael Short, and Jennifer Devereaux, 109–21. London.

Monro, David B. and Thomas W. Allen. 1920. *Homeri Opera*. 3rd edn. Oxford.

Monsacré, Hélène. 1984. *Les larmes d'Achille: Le héros, la femme et la suffrance dans la poésie d'Homère*. Paris.

Montanari, Franco. 2017. "The failed embassy: Achilles in the *Iliad*." In *The Winnowing Oar—New Perspectives in Homeric Studies*, edited by Christos Tsagalis and Andreas Markantonatos, 43–56. Boston; Berlin.

Morrison, James V. 1991. "The Function and Context of Homeric Prayers: A Narrative Perspective." *Hermes* 119: 145–57.

Morrison, James V. 1992. *Homeric Misdirection: False Predictions in the Iliad*. Ann Arbor.

Mueller, Martin. 1984. *The Iliad*. London.

Muellner, Leonard Charles. 1976. *The Meaning of Homeric εὔχομαι Through its Formulas*. Innsbruck.

Muellner, Leonard Charles. 1996. *The Anger of Achilles: Mênis in Greek Epic*. Ithaca.

Müller, Heinz Martin. 1980. *Erotische Motive in Der Griechischen Dichtung Bis Auf Euripides*. Hamburg.

Muñoz, José Estaban. 2019. *Cruising Utopia: The Then and There of Queer Futurity*. 10th anniversary edn. New York.

Murnaghan, Sheila. 1997. "Equal Honor and Future Glory: The Plan of Zeus in the *Iliad*." In *Classical Closure: Reading the End in Greek and Latin Literature*, edited by Deborah H. Roberts, Francis M. Dunn, and Don Fowler, 23–42. Princeton.

Murnaghan, Sheila. 1999. "The Poetics of Loss in Greek Epic." In *Epic Traditions in the Contemporary World*, edited by M. Beissinger, J. Tylus, and S. Wofford, 203–20. Berkeley.

Myers, Tobias. 2019. *Homer's Divine Audience: the* Iliad*'s Reception on Mount Olympus.* Oxford.

Nagler, Michael N. 1974. *Spontaneity and Tradition: A Study in the Oral Art of Homer.* Berkeley.

Nagy, Gregory. 1979. *The Best of the Achaeans: Concepts of the Hero in Archaic Greek Poetry.* Baltimore.

Naiden, F. S. 2006. *Ancient Supplication.* New York.

Nimis, Stephen. 1987. *Narrative Semiotics in the Epic Tradition: The Simile.* Bloomington.

O'Brien, Joan V. 1993. *The Transformation of Hera: A Study of Ritual, Hero, and the Goddess in the* Iliad. Lanham.

Ormand, Kirk. 2014. *The Hesiodic* Catalogue of Women *and Archaic Greece.* Cambridge.

Owen, E. T. 1946. *The Story of the Iliad.* Toronto.

Parry, Adam. 1972. "Language and Characterization in Homer." *Harvard Studies in Classical Philology* 76: 1–22.

Pavlock, Barbara. 1990. *Eros, Imitation, and the Epic Tradition.* Ithaca; London.

Penrose, Walter Duvall, Jr., 2016. *Postcolonial Amazons: Female Masculinity and Courage in Ancient Greek and Sanskrit Literature.* Oxford.

Peponi, Anastasia-Erasmia. 2012. *Frontiers of Pleasure: Models of Aesthetic Response in Archaic and Classical Greek Thought.* New York.

Peradotto, John. 1974. "Verisimilitude, Narrative Analysis, and Bricolage." *Texas Studies in Literature and Language* 15 (5): 803–32.

Perysinakis, I. N. 1991. "Penelope's *EEΔNA* Again." *Classical Quarterly* 41 (2): 297–302.

Phelan, James. 2004. *Living to Tell about It: A Rhetoric and Ethics of Character Narration.* Ithaca.

Pironti, Gabriella. 2007. *Entre ciel et guerre: figures d'Aphrodite en Grèce ancienne.* Liège.

Pironti, Gabriella. 2017. "De l'éros au récit : Zeus et son épouse." In *Les dieux d'Homère: polythéisme et poésie en Grèce ancienne.* Kernos, Supplément 31, edited by Gabriella Pironti and Corinne Bonnet, 63–83. Liège.

Pomeroy, Sarah B., Stanley M. Burstein, Walter Donlan, and Jennifer Tolbert Edwards. eds. 1999. *Ancient Greece: a Political, Social, and Cultural History.* New York.

Postlethwaite, N. 1985. "The Duel of Paris and Menelaos and the Teichoskopia in *Iliad* 3." *Antichthon* 19: 1–6.

Pucci, Pietro. 1987. *Odysseus Polytropos: Intertexual Readings in the* Odyssey *and the* Iliad. Ithaca.

Pucci, Pietro. 1993. "Antiphonal Lament Between Achilles and Briseis." *Colby Quarterly* 29: 253–72.

Pucci, Pietro. 1998 [1979]. "The Song of the Sirens." In *The Song of the Sirens: Essays on Homer,* 1–9. Lanham.

Pucci, Pietro. 2018. *The Iliad—The Poem of Zeus.* Trends in Classics—Supplementary Volumes. Volume 66. Boston; Berlin.

Pulleyn, Simon. ed. 2000. *Homer: Iliad I.* Oxford.

Purves, Alex C. 2006. "Falling into Time in Homer's Iliad." *Classical Antiquity* 25 (1): 179–209.

Purves, Alex C. 2010. *Space and Time in Ancient Greek Narrative.* Cambridge.

Purves, Alex C. 2019. *Homer and the Poetics of Gesture.* Oxford.

Rabel, Robert J. 1988. "Chryses and the Opening of the Iliad." *American Journal of Philology* 109 (4): 473–81.

Rabel, Robert J. 1997. *Plot and Point of View in the* Iliad. Ann Arbor.

Ransom, Christopher. 2011. "Aspects of Effeminacy and Masculinity in the *Iliad*." *Antichthon* 45: 35–57.

Ready, Jonathan. 2011. *Character, Narrator, and Simile in the* Iliad. Cambridge.

Reckford, Kenneth J. 1964. "Helen in the *Iliad*." *Greek, Roman and Byzantine Studies* 5: 5–20.

Redfield, James M. 1979. "The Proem of the Iliad: Homer's Art." *Classical Philology* 74 (2): 95–110.

Redfield, James M. 1994. *Nature and Culture in the* Iliad: *The Tragedy of Hector*. Expanded edn. Durham.

Reece, Steve. 1993. *The Stranger's Welcome: Oral Theory and the Aesthetics of the Homeric Hospitality Scene*. Ann Arbor.

Reichel, Michael. 2002. "Zur sprachlichen und inhaltlichen Deutung eines umstrittenen Iliasverses (II, 356 = 590)." In *Epea pteroenta: Beiträge zur Homerforschung: Feschrift für Wolfgang Kullmann zum 75. Geburtstag*, edited by Michael Reichel and Antonios Rengakos, 163–72. Stuttgart.

Reinhardt, Karl. 1961. *Die Ilias Und Ihr Dichter*. Göttingen.

Reinhardt, Karl. 1997 [1938]. "The Judgement of Paris." In *Homer: German Scholarship in Translation*, edited by G. M. Wright and P. V. Jones, 170–91. Oxford. (Reproduced from *Tradition und Geist*, Göttingen, 1960, 16–36. Originally published as *Das Parisurteil*, Frankfurt, 1938.)

Richardson, Nicholas. 1993. *The Iliad: A Commentary Volume VI: books 21–24*, edited by G. S. Kirk. Cambridge.

Richardson, Scott Douglas. 1990. *The Homeric Narrator*. Nashville.

Robbins, E. 1990. "Achilles to Thetis: Iliad 1.365–412." *Échos Du Monde Classique* 9: 1–15.

Robinson, David B. 1990. "Homeric *φίλος*: love of life and limbs, and friendship with one's *θυμός*." In *'Owls to Athens': Essays on Classical Subjects Presented to Sir Kenneth Dover*, edited by E. M. Craik, 97–108. Oxford.

Roisman, Hanna M. 2006. "Helen in the *Iliad*: *Causa Belli* and Victim of War: From Silent Weaver to Public Speaker." *American Journal of Philology* 127 (1): 1–36.

Rosner, J. 1976. "The Speech of Phoenix: *Iliad* 9:434–605." *Phoenix* 30: 314–27.

Rubin, Gayle. 2011. *Deviations: A Gayle Rubin Reader*. Durham.

Russo, Joseph. 2012. "Re-Thinking Homeric Psychology: Snell, Dodds and Their Critics." *Quaderni Urbinati di Cultura Classic*, N. S. 101 (2): 11–28.

Russo, Joseph and Bennett Simon. 1968. "Homeric Psychology and the Oral Epic Tradition." *Journal of the History of Ideas* 29 (4): 483–98.

Rutherford, R. B. 2001. "From the *Iliad* to the *Odyssey*." In *Oxford Readings in Homer's* Iliad, edited by Douglas L. Cairns, 117–46. Oxford.

Rutherford, R. B. ed. 2019. *Homer Iliad Book XVIII*. Cambridge Greek and Latin Classics. Cambridge.

Sanders, Ed, Chiara Thumiger, Chris Carey, and Nick J. Lowe. eds. 2013. Erôs *in Ancient Greece*. Oxford.

Schadewaldt, Wolfgang. 1944. *Von Homers Welt und Werk*. Stuttgart.

Schadewaldt, Wolfgang. 1966 [1938]. *Iliasstudien*. 3rd edn. Darmstadt.

Schadewaldt, Wolfgang. 1975. *Der Aufbau Der Ilias*. Frankfurt.

Schein, Seth. 1984. *The Mortal Hero: An Introduction to Homer's* Iliad. Berkeley.

Schönberger, Otto. 1960. "Zu Ilias 3, 146–180." *Gymnasium* 67: 197–201.

Schwartz, Martin. 1982. "The Indo-European Vocabulary of Exchange, Hospitality, and Intimacy." *Proceedings of the Eighth Annual Meeting of the Berkeley Linguistics Society* 188–204.

Scodel, Ruth. 1982. "The Autobiography of Phoenix: *Iliad* 9.444–95." *American Journal of Philology* 103: 214–23.

Scodel, Ruth. 2002. *Listening to Homer: Tradition, Narrative, and Audience*. Ann Arbor.

Scodel, Ruth. 2008. *Epic Facework: Self-presentation and Social Interaction in Homer*. Swansea.

Scodel, Ruth. 2012. "ἦ and Theory of Mind in the *Iliad*." In *Homer, gedeutet durch ein grosses Lexikon*, edited by Michael Meier-Brügger, 319–34. Berlin.

Scodel, Ruth. 2017. "Homeric fate, Homeric poetics." In *The Winnowing Oar: New Perspectives in Homeric Studies; Studies in Honor of Antonios Rengakos*, edited by Christos Tsagalis and Andreas Markantonatos, 75–94. Boston; Berlin.

Scully, Stephen P. 1984. "The Language of Achilles: The *ΟΧΘΗΣΑΣ* Formulas." *Transactions of the America Philological Association* 114: 11–27.

Scully, Stephen P. 1986. "Studies of Narrative and Speech in the *Iliad*." *Arethusa* 19 (2): 135–153.

Seaford, Richard. 1994. *Reciprocity and Ritual: Homer and Tragedy in the Developing City-State*. Oxford.

Sedgwick, Eve Kosofsky. 1992. *Between Men: English Literature and Male Homosocial Desire*. New York.

Segal, Charles. 1968. "The Embassy and the Duals of *Iliad* 9.182–98." *Greek, Roman and Byzantine Studies* 9: 101–114.

Segal, Charles. 1971a. "Andromache's *Anagnorisis*" *Harvard Studies in Classical Philology* 75: 33–57.

Segal, Charles. 1971b. "Nestor and the Honor of Achilles (Iliad 1.247–84)." *Studi Micenei Ed Egeo-Anatolici* 13: 90–105.

Segal, Charles. 1971c. *The Theme of the Mutilation of the Corpse in the Iliad*. Mnemosyne, Supplements, Volume 17. Leiden.

Shay, Jonathan. 1994. *Achilles in Vietnam: Combat Trauma and the Undoing of Character*. New York.

Sheppard, John Tresidder. 1922. *The Pattern of the Iliad*. London.

Silk, Michael. 2007. "Pindar's Poetry and Poetry: A Commentary on *Olympian* 12." In *Pindar's Poetry, Patrons, and Festivals: From Archaic Greece to the Roman Empire*, edited by Simon Hornblower and Catherine Morgan, 177–97. Oxford.

Sinos, Dale S. 1980. *Achilles, Patroklos and the Meaning of* Philos. Innsbruck.

Sissa, G. 2008. *Sex and Sensuality in the Ancient World*, translated by George Staunton. New Haven.

Slatkin, Laura M. 1991. *The Power of Thetis: Allusion and Interpretation in the Iliad*. Berkeley.

Smith, Murray. 1995. *Engaging Characters: Fiction, Emotion, and the Cinema*. Oxford.

Snell, Bruno. 1953. *The Discovery of the Mind: The Greek Origins of European Thought*. Cambridge.

Snell, Bruno. ed. 1955–2010. *Lexikon des frühgriechischen Epos*. Göttingen.

Snodgrass, Anthony M. 1974. "An Historical Homeric Society." *Journal of Hellenic Studies* 94: 114–25.

Stanley, Keith. 1993. *The Shield of Homer*. Princeton.

Staten, Henry. 1995. *Eros in Mourning: Homer to Lacan*. Baltimore.

Sullivan, Nikki. 2003. *A Critical Introduction to Queer Theory*. New York.

Suzuki, Mihoko. 1989. *Metamorphoses of Helen: Authority, Difference, and the Epic*. Ithaca.

Taillardat, J. 1982. "*ΦΙΛΟΤΕΣ, ΠΙΣΤΙΣ* et FOEDUS." *Revue des études grecques* 95: 1–14.

Tanner, Tony. 1979. *Adultery in the Novel: Contract and Transgression*. Baltimore.

Taplin, Oliver. 1990. "Agamemnon's Role in the *Iliad*." In *Characterization and Individuality in Greek Literature*, edited by Christopher Pelling, 60–82. Oxford.

Taplin, Oliver. 1992. *Homeric Soundings: The Shaping of the* Iliad. Oxford.

Taplin, Oliver. 2001. "The Shield of Achilles within the *Iliad*." In *Oxford Readings in Homer's* Iliad, edited by Douglas L. Cairns, 342–64. Oxford.

Telò, Mario. 2020. *Archive Feelings: A Theory of Greek Tragedy*. Columbus.

Thornton, Agathe. 1984. *Homer's Iliad: its Composition and the Motif of Supplication*. Göttingen.

Todorov, Tzvetan. 1977. *The Poetics of Prose*. Ithaca.

Tsagalis, Christos. 2004. *Epic Grief: Personal Laments in Homer's* Iliad. Berlin.

Vermeule, Blakey. 2010. *Why Do We Care About Literary Characters?* Baltimore.

Vermeule, Emily. 1979. *Aspects of Death in Early Greek Art and Poetry*. Berkeley.

Vernant, Jean-Pierre. 1989. *L'individu, la mort, l'amour: soi-meme et l'autre en Grèce ancienne*. Paris.

Wade-Gery, H. T. 1952. *The Poet of the* Iliad. Cambridge.

Walsh, Thomas R. 2005. *Fighting Words and Feuding Words*. Lanham.

Warwick, Celsiana. 2019a. "The Maternal Warrior: Gender and *Kleos* in the *Iliad*." *American Journal of Philology* 140 (1): 1–28.

Warwick, Celsiana. 2019b. "We Two Alone: Conjugal Bonds and Homoerotic Subtext in the *Iliad*." *Helios* 46 (2): 115–139.

Wees, Hans van. 1988. "Kings in Combat: Battles and Heroes in the *Iliad*." *Classical Quarterly* 38 (1): 1–24.

Wees, Hans van. 1992. *Status Warriors: War, Violence and Society in Homer and History*. Amsterdam.

Wees, Hans van. 1998. "A Brief History of Tears: Gender Differentiation in Archaic Greece." In *When Men Were Men: Masculinity, Power, and Identity in Classical Greece*, edited by Lin Foxhall and John Salmon, 10–53. London.

Weil, Simone. 1956 [1939]. *The Iliad, or The Poem of Force*, translated by Mary McCarthy. Wallingford.

Weiss, Michael. 1998. "Erotica: On the Prehistory of Greek Desire." *Harvard Studies in Classical Philology* 98: 31–61.

West, Martin L. 1975. *Immortal Helen*. London.

West, Martin L. ed. and trans. 2003. *Greek Epic Fragments*. Loeb Classical Library. Cambridge, MA.

West, Martin L. 2011. *The Making of the* Iliad: *Disquisition & Analytical Commentary*. Oxford.

Whitman, Cedric Hubbell. 1958. *Homer and the Heroic Tradition*. Cambridge, MA.

Wilamowitz, Ulrich. 1916. *Die Ilias und Homer*. Berlin.

Willcock, M. M. 1964. "Mythological Paradeigma in the *Iliad*." *Classical Quarterly* 14: 141–154.

Willcock, M. M. 1978. *The Iliad of Homer Books I–XII*. London.

Wilson, Donna F. 2002. *Ransom, Revenge, and Heroic Identity in the* Iliad. Cambridge.

Wilson, Emily. 2021. "Slaves and Sex in the *Odyssey*." In *Slavery and Sexuality in Classical Antiquity*, edited by Deborah Kamen and C. W. Marshall, 15–39. Madison.

Winkler, John J. 1985. *Auctor & Actor: A Narratological Reading of Apuleius's Golden Ass*. Berkeley.

Wöhrle, Georg. 2002. "Sexuelle Aggression als Motiv in den homerischen Epen." In *Epea pteroenta: Beiträge zur Homerforschung: Feschrift für Wolfgang Kullmann zum 75. Geburtstag*, edited by Michael Reichel and Antonios Rengakos, 231–38. Stuttgart.

Worman, Nancy. 1997. "The Body as Argument: Helen in Four Greek Texts." *Classical Antiquity* 16 (1): 151–203.
Worman, Nancy. 2001. "This Voice Which Is Not One: Helen's Verbal Guises in Homeric Epic." In *Making Silence Speak*, edited by André Lardinois and Laura McClure, 19–37. Princeton.
Worman, Nancy. 2002. *The Cast of Character: Style in Greek Literature*. Austin.
Yasumura, Noriko. 2011. *Challenges to the Power of Zeus in Early Greek Poetry*. London.
Zanker, Graham. 1994. *The Heart of Achilles: Characterization and Personal Ethics in the* Iliad. Ann Arbor.
Zunshine, Lisa. 2006. *Why We Read Fiction: Theory of Mind and the Novel*. Columbus.

Index

For the benefit of digital users, indexed terms that span two pages (e.g., 52–53) may, on occasion, appear on only one of those pages.